FRAUD AND MISCONDUCT IN BIOMEDICAL RESEARCH

FRAUD AND MISCONDUCT IN BIOMEDICAL RESEARCH

Fourth Edition

Edited by

Frank Wells

Michael Farthing

The ROYAL
SOCIETY *of*
MEDICINE
PRESS *Limited*

© 2008 Royal Society of Medicine Ltd

Published by the Royal Society of Medicine Press Ltd
1 Wimpole Street, London W1G 0AE, UK
Tel: +44 (0)20 7290 2921
Fax: +44 (0)20 7290 2929
E-mail: publishing@rsmpress.co.uk

British Library Cataloguing in Publication Data
A catalogue record for this book is available from the British Library

ISBN: 978-1-85315-786-8

Distribution in Europe and Rest of the World:
Marston Book Services Ltd
PO Box 269
Abingdon
Oxon OX14 4YN, UK
Tel: +44 (0)1235 465500
Fax: +44 (0)1235 465555
Email: direct.order@marston.co.uk

Distribution in USA and Canada:
Royal Society of Medicine Press Ltd
c/o BookMasters Inc
30 Amberwood Parkway
Ashland, OH 44805, USA
Tel: +1 800 247 6553/ +1 800 266 5564
Fax: +1 410 281 6883
Email: order@bookmasters.com

Distribution in Australia and New Zealand:
Elsevier Australia
30–52 Smidmore Street
Marrickville NSW 2204, Australia
Tel: +61 2 9517 8999
Fax: +61 2 9517 2249
Email: service@elsevier.com.au

Typeset by Phoenix Photosetting, Chatham, Kent
Printed in Great Britain by Belmont Press, Northampton

Contents

Contributors

Jane Barrett FFPM LLM
Director and Medical Advisor, MedicoLegal Investigations Ltd, Cambridge, UK

Pierre-Henri Bertoy
Associate Director, Inspectorate and Companies Department, Afssaps, Paris, France

Nicky Dodsworth DCRR MRQA MICR
Senior Director, Global Quality Assurance, Premier Research Group Ltd, Bracknell, UK

Helena van den Dungen PhD
Clinical Quality Assurance, Global Head Country Management, Novartis Pharma AG, Basel, Switzerland

Stephen Evans MSc FRCP(Edin)
Professor of Pharmacoepidemiology, London School of Hygiene and Tropical Medicine, London, UK

Michael JG Farthing DSc(Med) MD FRCP FMedSci
Vice-Chancellor and Professor of Medicine, University of Sussex, Brighton, UK

Erick Gaussens PhD
Senior Consultant, Product Life, Paris, France

C Kristina Gunsalus JD
Special Counsel and Adjunct Professor, College of Law, Medicine and Business, University of Illinois at Urbana-Champaign, Urbana, USA

Michael R Hamrell PhD
President, MORIAH Consultants, Yorba Linda, USA

Jean-Marc Husson MD PhD ACCAH(Paris) FFPM
Specialist in Pharmaceutical Medicine, Switzerland; Co-Director of European Diploma in Pharmaceutical Medicine Eudipharm, Lyon, France

Sabine Kleinert MD MRCP
Senior Executive Editor, *The Lancet*, London, UK

Ana Marusic
Editor in Chief, *Croatian Medical Journal*, Zagreb, Croatia

Drummond Rennie MD FRCP MACP
Adjunct Professor of Medicine, University of California, San Francisco, USA; Deputy Editor, *Journal of the American Medical Association*

Povl Riis Professor of Medicine MD DMSci DMhc FRCP (London)
Editorial Board Member, *Journal of the American Medical Association*; Chairman of EU Stakeholder Boards for Brain Research; Member of the Metabolic Syndrome

John Saunders MA MD FRCP FRSA
Honorary Professor, University of Wales Swansea, UK; Chairman, Committee for Ethical Issues in Medicine, Royal College of Physicians of London, London, UK; former chairman, Multi Research Ethics Committee (MREC) for Wales & Gwent LREC, UK

Richard Smith MD
Chief Executive of UnitedHealth Europe; member of the board of the Public Library of Science; Visiting Professor at the London School of Hygiene and Tropical Medicine; former editor of the *BMJ* and Chief Executive of the BMJ Publishing Group, London, UK

Nicholas H Steneck PhD
Director, Research Ethics and Integrity Program, Michigan Institute for Clinical and Health Research and Professor Emeritus of History, University of Michigan, Ann Arbor, USA; Consultant, Office of Research Integrity, Rockville, USA

Elizabeth Wager MA
Publications Consultant, Sideview, Princes Risborough, UK

Frank Wells FRCP FRCPE FFPM
Retired Pharmaceutical Physician, Ipswich, UK

Preface

It is with some regret that a fourth edition of this book still has relevance today. We and our contributors have worked hard in different ways since the publication of the third edition to promote the responsible conduct of research, but sadly research fraud and other forms of research misconduct are still alive and well, and may even be on the increase. In the last 5 years, there has been a series of high-profile cases of research misconduct that have made the national press in the USA, Europe and Asia. Some of the elite journals, such as *Nature* and *Science*, have had to retract a number of fraudulent papers by individuals who were considered to have been leaders in their fields.

Formerly, the major detected culprits of research misconduct have emanated from the USA and Europe, but in the last few years, there have been several major cases from Asia, notably Korea, China and Japan. Research misconduct is thus a truly global phenomenon. The Korean stem-cell fraud case, perpetrated by Hwang and colleagues, reverberated across the world. It brought disgrace to previously revered scientists, embarrassed the leading scientific journals that had published the work, and made scientific collaborators in other continents wary of future partnerships with investigators in whom they could not be fully confident.

In this new edition, we have taken a slightly different approach to that adopted previously. We have structured this book as a 'standard text', whereas previous editions have been more a compendium of essays. We want this book not only to provide an up-to-date account of research misconduct worldwide, but also to be a useful reference source for those responsible for teaching research and publication ethics, as well as a guide for those involved in detecting and investigating allegations of misconduct in institutions undertaking research. Thus we believe that the book will have a broad appeal: from new research students to established investigators involved in research supervision and instilling good practice, and from academic and commercial sponsors, monitors and auditors to academic leaders and research administrators, who are ultimately responsible for ensuring the highest standards of conduct in research-intensive organizations.

We have assembled a first-class team of contributors from all corners of the world to bring their special expertise to this topic. Some have contributed to previous editions of the book, while others are new. We start at the beginning, with definitions and descriptions of the ethical principles underpinning the conduct of research, moving on to an update on the state-of-play of research misconduct in different regions of the world. We then look at the available preventive strategies that are employed to try to minimize the occurrence of research misconduct.

In this edition, we have placed a greater emphasis on methods of detecting research misconduct. While the 'whistleblower' remains an essential element of any detection strategy, we emphasize the role of the auditor and we explore the role of evolving statistical and electronic approaches to detect dishonest numerical and digital manipulation.

Finally, we provide more detailed accounts of the approach to investigating allegations of research misconduct and how national advisory bodies can contribute to the process. The need to ensure that these processes are robust and can survive in a litigatory sophisticated world is becoming increasingly evident. Lawyers are now commonly involved, and will not waste any opportunity to find flaws in the investigative process as part of a defence strategy.

These are challenging times for research-intensive institutions. The competition for research funding has never been greater and the need for leading researchers to keep ahead of the game has never been more evident. The pressures to produce, the need to climb the promotional ladder and the drive to commercialize new discoveries may all be factors that encourage investigators to allow standards to slip. We hope that this book offers some answers to the 'whys and wherefores' of research misconduct and goes some way to providing some solutions.

Michael Farthing, Frank Wells

SECTION 1

SETTING THE SCENE

1 The concept of scientific dishonesty: Ethics, value systems, and research

Povl Riis

Introduction

I have been interested in the problem of scientific dishonesty ever since the classic cases occurred in the USA and elsewhere from the mid-1980s onwards, and later with my involvement in the formation of the Danish Central Committee (undertaken before we had ever had a recent major case in the country). Here, however, I want to take a much broader look at the whole question, in particular trying to put it into the broader context of biomedical ethics. The publication of a fourth edition of this book creates the possibility of adding further perspectives and a broader scope of the topic, while still preserving its fundamental ethical and existential base.

The three concepts in my subtitle appear all the time in today's publications. Research is, of course, a well-known term; ethics has acquired linguistic citizenship in medicine in the last 30–50 years, but value systems are a 'johnny-come-lately' in our vocabulary. Nevertheless, the meaning of each term is often considered self-evident, and all of them are often used with a variety of different connotations. Any discussion of these key concepts in the context of scientific dishonesty needs, then, to start with definitions.

Definitions

Research

Research is defined here as an original endeavour comprising:[1]

- an idea leading to the first ('original') attempt to link two masses of knowledge (already existing or arising out of known previous research) with the aim of detecting causal relationships and not merely coincidences
- the transfer of the idea to one or more precise questions, characterized by the existence of potential answers
- a bias-controlling methodology intending to link the question(s) to potential answers (*methodology* is defined as the art of planning, technically carrying through,

interpreting, and publishing scientific research) – good scientific methodology not only reduces the number of 'honest mistakes' within a project, but also makes the research more transparent; hence, it has a preventive effect on the prevalence of scientific dishonesty.

Value systems

Value systems cover all the measures of the non-material qualities of human life. Examples with a special relevance for scientific dishonesty are truth, reliability, responsibility, justice, and freedom. Values may be subgrouped into *common values* in a society (including those forming the basis of laws) and *individual values*, reflecting value diversity. The latter term is synonymous with *value pluralism* – on the one hand, a welcome part of citizens' freedom; on the other, a potential cause of difficulty (e.g. for committees monitoring research ethics or scientific honesty and being faced with value judgements intending to reflect a 'social consensus').

If, for instance, a scientific project aiming at evaluating the reliability and risks of preimplantation diagnostic procedures in fertilized human eggs is sent to a research ethics committee, both lay and scientific members might reflect social diversity and not social consensus. Some members might find the method promising, compared with villus biopsy or amniocentesis, because infertile couples could be helped more effectively. Others might find the perspectives frightening because these represent a discrimination against people with malformations or other congenital handicaps.

When values themselves comprise spectra – such as freedom, justice, and truth – the value universe becomes even wider, and so cut-off points have to be introduced on the value scales. Such cut-off points are called *norms*, a typical example being the term 'freedom', defined as the sum of the individual citizen's personal options. In a democratic society, another fundamental value, 'justice', needs the application of a norm on the freedom scale: personal freedom has to be limited at a point where any extension would reduce the freedom of other citizens. (In other words, this is a normative cut-off point.)

Ethics

As a term loaded with awe, ethics is often not defined at all – or is done so merely etymologically from its Greek derivation, *ethos*, meaning habits. However, again, to use the term in a serious context, we have to provide a contemporary definition. Here, ethics is defined as:

• The collection of fundamental values, attitudes, and norms considered by most of the population as essential for personal life, life with one another, and life in relation to a society's institutions. Some of these values vis-à-vis biomedical research and national health services are equality, the 'good Samaritan' duty, justice, truth, responsibility, professional competence, and freedom.
• The relation between ethics and the law is bimodal. Ethics, with its fundamental values, forms the basis of legislation. Nevertheless, it also comprises values that are

not controlled by the law, but are still decisive elements in societal and personal life.

Value universes of biomedical research

Until recently, science had an elite status. Scientists were considered more honest than ordinary citizens, and hence an idea was current that research dishonesty did not occur outside fiction (as in 'Dr Jekyll and Mr Hyde'). Today, however, we know better, and so can deal with this aspect in theoretical terms. The value universes of biomedical research concern two main subgroups:

- those related to society in general – the *external universe*
- those related to the research community itself – the *internal universe*.

The former is concerned with the safety and trust of patients (not only patients in general, but also trial patients in particular, as well as healthy volunteers).

Thus, the first aspect is the ethics of the research so far as the safety of and respect for the citizens acting as subjects are concerned. The evaluation rests primarily with research ethics committees, but the necessary premises also depend on the honesty of the researchers – and hence on knowing the risks to the participants, the potential benefits of the expected results, and an up-to-date survey of the literature.

The second aspect of the honesty/dishonesty concept is how scientists recruit their trial subjects: do they fairly present all the undisputed facts to potential participants?

Thirdly, are the results interpreted totally independently of any sponsors of the research? If the results are untrue for any reason, clinicians may be misled in their treatment, even to the extent that the criminal law becomes involved should patients' health or even lives have been endangered. In this way, the societal value universe comes into close and serious contact with research activities.

Within the internal universe, scientists' curricula vitae form the most important basis for decisions on grants, academic appointments or promotions, travel to conferences, etc. Here, with the volume of scientific publications as the currency of the research market, any counterfeiting will have the same negative effects as in the monetary sphere. Values such as truth, justice, and responsibility are all at stake. The result may be that honest investigators sometimes lose out, because they have to spend much time on the project. Conversely, the fraudster can recruit patients faster; can work sloppily in the laboratory; or, most seriously, can fabricate the results or be a sleeping partner in several projects, but still an author in all the publications, thereby collecting much of the currency (here represented by authorship and coauthorship).

To sum up, the value spectrum of research has an external part orientated towards society, and an internal part orientated towards the research community itself. Courts and laws control the former (with problems arising from the research community's lack of transparency). Independent bodies with experience in research must control the latter, but at the same time must work as society's 'open eye'. In addition, these bodies must extend their interests into the grey zone between dishonesty and good scientific practice.

Why do scientists transgress?

The motives behind scientists' transgressions of the prevalent norms for our value universes are partly *universal* – in other words, similar to those behind legal and non-scientific moral transgressions – and partly *special* to the competitive research community. The latter aim at changing the ratio between original ideas and the necessary time and effort spent on methodology to obtain more publications for the curriculum vitae without any effort or insecurity. In a neighbouring area, there is neither frank dishonesty nor good scientific practice. Instead, there are numerous 'me too' projects, lacking any originality, good methodological planning, or the risk that the research will be fruitless (because the project ends not with an answer 'yes' or 'no', but with a 'sorry, no answer').

All this is also true for non-legitimate authorship – for instance, the practice (often considered as a right by heads of departments) of adding names to a paper. Again, such behaviour is only partly dishonest, although it is not in accordance with good scientific practice. Nevertheless, both 'me too' projects and gift authorship contribute to the still prevalent attitude in too many research units that 'We know best about the good traditions in science, and no outsiders should try to teach us anything new or different.' In other words, both of these phenomena in the grey zone are moral pollutants at a time when honest scientists and editors are trying to clean up the temple of science.

The other motive encountered in scientific dishonesty is the attempt to reduce the standing of competitors by accusing them of irregularities in their research (a euphemism for dishonesty). This is done either by a direct accusation to a national committee or, more often, by a campaign of rumour-mongering. The motive is often masked as a profound interest in the purity of science, and, even when the accused has been cleared after a thorough investigation, it often achieves its purpose through the psychological burden placed on the accused, the loss of productive time, and the lingering doubts (reflecting the old saying 'There's no smoke without fire'). This kind of whistle-blowing has a different motive from that of the 'ideal whistleblower', who is usually a junior 'hands-on' member of the same department as the accused and is concerned about apparent irregularities. Competitive, false whistleblowing, conversely, takes place between research scientists equally highly placed in the research hierarchy.

What is the driving force for fraud?

The driving force that unites the motives into active dishonesty varies from a criminal element to more cautious attempts to buy valid currency on the black market (more publications on the curriculum vitae). For obvious reasons, we know very little about these intentions, because sanctions are often taken in proved cases without scientists disclosing their motives. Such a policy of 'admit as little as possible' is well known from ordinary courts of law, but it is a source of wonder how often intelligent people can embark on dishonest research, given that they ought to 'know better'. My qualified bet is that they know very well about the consequences of such behaviour, but think that they are too smart to get detected.[1]

Scientific dishonesty in relation to its nature, prevalence, and consequences

The four classic examples of fraudulent behaviour are fabrication, falsification, plagiarism, and theft. All represent transgression of laws and fundamental values known to the transgressor, and so are closely related to the crimes found in a country's penal code. Hence, it is justifiable to speak of a general intention to deceive, whether or not the transgression is admitted when the facts come to light. The consequences of such serious scientific dishonesty are most serious in clinical research dealing with life-threatening diseases, as, for instance, in an example of treating disseminated breast cancer with bone marrow transplantation. An obvious parallel is set by the so-called alternative treatments marketed for serious disease without scientific evidence and directly addressing laypeople. Here, however, there has been no professional authorization of the alternative methods, and hence a mixture of individual conceit and protective group insufficiency leads to a general blamelessness.

The next example of dishonest behaviour among scientists deals primarily with the way in which research results are evaluated and interpreted, and falls into the subgroup of biomedical ethics labelled 'publication ethics'. Data archaeology and 'cleansing' of results for outliers – in other words, results that, if included, would seriously lower r-values and increase p-values – occur when scientists work with their raw data. Data massage, or archaeology, means that scientists apply enough statistical tests until one of them produces a sufficiently low p-value, without mentioning this multiple hypothesis testing in the subsequent publication. Such dishonest use of statistics is cognate with the exploitation of mass significance – for example, using a 0.05 level of significance and applying 20 significance tests on related data from the same group of subjects, not realizing or forgetting that, by chance, at least one of them will show a $p < 0.05$. If done by an experienced scientist, such a practice will be fraudulent; if done by a tyro, then it can be an honest mistake, caused by a lack of methodological insight.

Another dishonest practice occurs in preparing the manuscript. The authors leave out references that point to previous original research, thereby indicating a spurious personal priority, even if this is not overtly claimed.

A case from 2002 illustrates this, in the perspective of a change in the Danish legally based system, which originally dealt only with biomedical research, to a system dealing with all research sectors. The case is principally important because it was the reason for a change in the government's attitude to the law, weakening the previous strong independence of the Danish Board of Scientific Dishonesty. The case arose following the publication of a book by Bjørn Lomborg, a Danish political scientist, on carbon dioxide and changes in global climate.[2] In a complaint to the Board of Scientific Dishonesty, three people accused Lomborg of combining a scientific format for the publication with a very selective choice of references against the influence on climate of carbon dioxide from man-made sources. The Board did not find signs of fraud, but still concluded that the content and conclusions were not in accordance with good scientific standards.[3] Lomborg complained to the Ministry of Science, Technology and Development, which directed the Board to reopen the case, but fortunately they refused to do so, with reference to their formal freedom and independence. Consequently, the case is still 'suspended', at a time when the global scientific and political consensus is very much in favour of the influence of carbon dioxide on the global climate.

These types of scientific dishonesty are probably common, but are often undisclosed. They can distort results that are important for patients, and thereby have a societal perspective, but most cases are relevant only for the internal universe – that is, they affect competition between scientists.

Gross slovenliness may affect both active data collection and the publication process. Examples include not searching the global literature, not testing batches of reagents, not ensuring accuracy of numerical analyses, and not reading proofs of papers properly. Again, in a young, inexperienced scientist, such slovenliness might be accepted as venial – honest, but immature and non-professional (although this would not apply to any adviser). For an experienced scientist, however, such behaviour must be characterized as dishonest. It is often related to non-legitimate authorship, as when a senior scientist, often the boss, is a coauthor of a paper reporting work that is then shown to have been fraudulent. Here, the boss cannot be excused on the basis of not having participated directly in the dishonesty.

Spurious authorship is the inflationary technique mentioned above. It may occur through a chief's supposed prerogative for coauthorship on all the publications coming from the department, or (at the opposite end of the institutional hierarchy) senior scientists may exclude the names of young, legitimate researchers from an article. Often this occurs after the juniors have left the department, with their seniors thinking of them as mere 'water-carriers' despite their important contributions. The same dishonest attitude is shown with authorships as exchangeable currency – for instance, gift authorship, ghost authorship, or barter authorship. Sometimes, these take the form of production collectives ('I will make you a coauthor if you do the same for me, given that we are not rivals').

Until formal regulations were introduced,[4] duplicate publication was frequent, with publication of the same data in two or more different journals, without any cross-reference to the other and without informing the editors. Other examples of inflating curricula vitae are the 'salami technique' (in which data are cut into thin slices and published separately), or the reverse, the 'Imalas technique', in which one, two, or more cases are added to an already published series without any statement that most of these have been described elsewhere. (Little is added, save another publication for the curriculum vitae.)

All these examples of dishonest publication ethics overstep the values of truth and justice within the internal universe. Very rarely do they have an additional societal perspective, or result in a lower public trust in the scientist. The prevalence of such transgressions is unknown, but one study in a national context showed that it was high.[5] The preventive measures detailed below are probably insufficient to eliminate or even reduce the number of non-legitimate authorships. Instead, several other, and more difficult, measures are being introduced, including a demand that authors specify their contribution in detail, with the ultimate decision on who is an author resting with the editor.[6]

The last subgroup of scientific dishonesty is more a matter of etiquette. An example is when a scientist presents the common work of a group to which he or she is a co-worker, but mentions only his or her own name and none of the co-workers in slides and talks. Clearly, such practices are an internal matter for the research group, but they are still important, because the resulting personal antagonisms waste much time and other research resources.

Common to almost all the disclosed cases of scientific dishonesty (irrespective of their position on the scale of seriousness) are the two excuses also heard in courtrooms: 'I thought that everybody did it' and 'I didn't know'. Both have to be rejected in coming to a verdict – the first because it presupposes a judicial relativism influenced by the number of transgressions, the second because ignorance of the law is no excuse.

Good scientific practice

Experience from national control systems has shown how important it is to create a new category between full-blown scientific dishonesty and full respect for all the relevant ethical values (i.e. *good scientific practice*: GSP). In this grey zone are the transgressions that cannot be classified as scientific dishonesty but are not GSP. Hence, these are referred to as practices 'not in accordance with GSP', where GSP represents the national consensus by scientific societies, research councils, independent scientific editors, and the like.[7] In courses for young scientists, this intermediate category can be used to produce examples close to everyday research work. As a result, examples need not be drawn from the full-blown cases of criminal scientific dishonesty, which readily lose their effect because the commonest reaction is: 'I could never become involved in such a scenario.'

New biomedical research methods

The increasing scope of research methods in biomedicine (e.g. stem cell techniques and nanoscience/nanomedicine) creates new ethical perspectives concerning consent and security, for instance related to risks to human participants and to ecology.

Although the basic ethical principles of existing national and international codes also cover these areas, the present lack of knowledge about risks might lead in the direction of too optimistic (or even dishonest) ways of informing potential trial participants about the risk:benefit ratios in trials. Ethical questions related to nanoscience/nanomedicine have been thoroughly covered in a recent EU Opinion publication.[8]

Globalization of research ethics

The increasing research collaboration between developing and developed countries creates a number of new ethical challenges related to social and cultural issues, benefits, risks, genuine consent, standards of care, ethical reviews or research projects, and what happens when the research is over. A number of national and international reports have dealt with the ethical problems related to the topic, but have not directly dealt with fraud and other forms of dishonesty. Still, the imbalance of power between scientists, local co-workers, and participating citizens, and differences and conflicts related to benefits, mean that committee members and editors must be more alert in the prevention or detection of dishonesty such as the 'rubber-stamping' of research protocols by non-independent committee members.[9,10]

Social transfer of values

Values ought to underlie academic education, and not be part of any formal curriculum that is first met in the classroom. In other words, the values behind GSP have deep roots and can be reinforced during scientific training only by being made visible in everyday life. Hence, there are several steps in attaining GSP:

1. The first step is the visibility and priority given to fundamental human values (truth, reliability, justice, and freedom) in children's upbringing. In other words, honest scientific behaviour is not an ethical subspecialty of a profession, but the projection of general ethical constituents onto a professional universe.
2. The second step is the visibility of general values within the research society and an accompanying respect for them during daily activity in research institutes and departments. Probably the strongest influence is personal example, and full correspondence between spoken principles and everyday practice. If the head of the department espouses the right views on authorship, but consistently twists them to expect being a coauthor of all of the department's publications, then junior researchers find themselves working with double standards.
3. The third step is to set up obligatory courses in GSP for all young scientists and would-be specialists. These will catalyse the development of widespread GSP, including the time-consuming change of the traditions of spurious authorship, so that there is a better correlation between scientific productivity and the number of papers in a curriculum vitae.
4. The fourth step is for the controlling body to publish selected cases from the full spectrum of scientific dishonesty in an annual report. And, if any word gets out of a possible case before there has been adjudication, then openness is the keyword. This should not be in the form of details or premature conclusions, but a confirmation that the case does exist, with the promise that direct information will be supplied once it has been concluded.

Value conservation and the control of scientific dishonesty

For countries that have had no formally established bodies responsible for managing scientific dishonesty – and even for countries with unofficial mechanisms for examining allegations – it may be valuable to consider the different models and procedures.

The most common set-up is institutional, usually established unprepared and ad hoc if an allegation arises in a university or another scientific institution. The initial way of tackling such problems is often an official denial, or at least deep silence. If the case cannot remain in the dark in the long run, then the institution sometimes reacts fiercely with sanctions to show its high moral standards, despite the earlier downgrading of the case. Moreover, inter-institutional distributions of power between involved scientists and the leadership may represent a strong bias against justice. Historically, one may apply Montesquieu's triad, demanding that the three components – the leg-islature, the judiciary, and the executive – be kept independent of one another. Here, on the contrary, they are mixed to an unacceptable degree.

The alternative to the institutional set-up is the national, or regional, committee. This may be established in two principal ways – either on a legal basis or created by research councils, academies, and scientific societies in common. Further, its remit may be restricted to biomedical research or be extended to cover all kinds, such as the humanities, social sciences, and physical and engineering sciences. If such a body deals only with inquiries and investigations, but not with sanctions (which are left to the institutions), at least part of the triad is split into its individual components. If further definitions of scientific dishonesty (or, more importantly, of GSP) are promulgated widely, then another step has been taken to secure a high degree of fairness for both the accused and the whistleblower.

Such a structure may, for instance, have the following levels of action when a case is raised:[11]

1. Suspicion arises locally via a whistleblower or the independent committee's own channels (e.g. through the media).
2. The committee decides whether the case should be considered.
3. The involved parties are informed and asked for their comments, in accordance with judicial principles.
4. If the committee decides on an investigation, then an independent specialist group is formed once both parties have accepted the suggested membership.
5. The ad hoc investigative group's report is open for comment from all the parties, and then is evaluated by the committee. Does the case point to scientific dishonesty, to non-accordance with GSP, or to an empty suspicion?
6. The conclusion is forwarded to the parties and the institution. The latter decides on sanctions if scientific dishonesty has been substantiated, and reports back to the committee so that any dispute between the sanctions taken by different institutions can be minimized.

It may seem strange that scientific dishonesty and fraudulent behaviour within bio-medicine have attracted so much attention, whereas very little has been written about ethical transgressions in other scientific disciplines – especially in those where the motives for dishonesty (such as strong competition) would make such behaviour just as feasible as in biomedicine. Nevertheless, few countries have extended their national control system to include all scientific sectors.[12] Given the increasing number of trans-disciplinary studies involving medicine and, for instance, the humanities and often qualitative research disciplines, such an extension should be important not only in an overall scientific perspective but for biomedical research as well.

That even global interest in preventing and controlling scientific fraud and other kinds of dishonesty has not prevented severe cases is illustrated by the South Korean case in stem cell research,[13] the Norwegian case in drug research and oncology,[14,15] and the Croatian case in gynaecology.[16]

Finally, the preventive value of an independent national or regional committee(s) should be emphasized. Publicity about individual cases has a 'vaccination effect' on the research community, but this is enhanced if national and international developments are commented on in a national committee's annual report.[17] The didactic use of concrete cases is easier if it is based on experiences of a national overview rather than on sporadic anecdotes through the media. As I have already mentioned, the cases included in courses for young scientists have a much stronger impact when they originate in concrete – even anonymized – cases from a contemporary spectrum, collected out there in real life.

Conclusions

The field of scientific dishonesty has developed from individual, often serious, cases 30–40 years ago to a stage where the multitude of different transgressions seems to form a basis for a more systematic analysis of motives and methods. The traditional epidemiological figures – true incidences and prevalences – remain unknown, and are probably not even ascertainable. As the criminological literature shows, individual transgressions can be counted only if disclosed, and the same is true for deviant scientists with a relapsing tendency to act dishonestly in science. Nevertheless, data from the national control systems seem to show that serious cases of fraud and its societal effects are relatively rare.[18]

Instead, the spectrum is dominated by cases with internal consequences for the research community – spurious authorship and lack of planning with well-defined shares for each member of a project group – and cases with both internal and external (i.e. societal) consequences due to dishonest methodology – such as data massage, removal of outliers, and the inflation of originality and personal priorities. The number of significant cases reported worldwide that have been managed by institutions or transferred to the law courts has been too small to indicate that these mechanisms should be widely applied. Instead, such cases have indicated the need to establish independent systems – national or regional – that are based on principles long developed and tested in ordinary judicial systems. The important first step in creating these is to bring editors of national journals and members of research councils, scientific academies, associations, universities, and scientific societies together, to devise a system that will protect both the accused and the whistleblower against unfair procedures. The aim is to make such values the basis for GSP that is both visible and respected.

It is here, with such values – far away from applied statistics, techniques of randomization, methods for polymerase chain reactions, and the like – that the important societal perspective of scientific dishonesty is to be found. Non-material values such as truth, justice, freedom, responsibility, and many others represent the essential grid that makes the greater society and the scientific one cohere – and to form the necessary trust and reliability to enable citizens to work together, or to depend on each other's information and results. In other words, if a society unofficially accepts that speed limits can be ignored, that tax evasion is a kind of Olympic sport, and that fraudulent receipt of social security is venial, then young scientists will meet the demands of GSP less prepared and less able to be influenced. In these circumstances, the only alternative is to thrust an ungrateful task onto official bodies such as a National Committee or Boards on Scientific Dishonesty.

References

1. Riis P. Sociology and psychology within the scope of scientific dishonesty. *Sci Eng Ethics* 2000; **6**: 35–9.
2. Lomborg B. *The Sceptical Environmentalist: Measuring the Real State of the World.* Cambridge: Cambridge University Press, 2001.
3. Danish Boards on Scientific Dishonesty. *Annual Report 2005.* Copenhagen: Directorate of Science and Innovation, 2006.
4. International Committee of Medical Journal Editors. Acceptable secondary publication. In: *Uniform Requirements for Manuscripts Submitted to Biomedical Journals: Writing and Editing for Biomedical Publication*, Section III.D.3. www.icmje.org (updated October 2007).
5. Danish National Committees on Scientific Dishonesty. *Annual Reports 1993–1997.* Copenhagen: The Research Councils, 1993–1997.
6. Riis P, Andersen D. Scientific authorship. In *Annual Report 1996.* Copenhagen: The Research Councils, 1996: 31–5.
7. Andersen D. Guidelines for good scientific practice. In: *Annual Report 1997.* Copenhagen: The Research Councils, 1997: 15–18.
8. European Group on Ethics (EGE). *Opinion on the Ethical Aspects of Nanomedicine.* Brussels: European Commission, 2007.
9. Working Party of Nuffield Council of Bioethics. *The Ethics of Research Related to Health Care in Developing Countries.* London: Nuffield Foundation, 2002.
10. Marshall PA. *Ethical Challenges in Study Design and Informed Consent for Health Research in Resource-Poor Settings.* Geneva: UNICEF/UNDP/World Bank/WHO Special Programme on Research and Training on Tropical Diseases, 2007. www.who.int/tdr/publications/publications/seb_topic5.htm.
11. Andersen D, Attrup L, Axelsen N, Riis P. *Scientific Dishonesty and Good Scientific Practice.* Copenhagen: Danish Medical Research Council, 1992.
12. Danish Ministry of Science. Instruction: Committees on Scientific Dishonesty. Supplement to Law No. 676 of 19 August 1997.
13. Philips M. Should coauthors share liability? *Science* 2002; **298**: 1554.
14. Werkö L. Utredning av forskningsfusk: myndigheternas ansvar. *Läkartidningen* 2006; **103**: 2563–5.
15. Ulfendahl M, Rydqvist B. Sverige behover ny instans som utreder forskningsfusk. *Läkartidningen* 2006; **103**: 3261–2.
16. Chalmers I. Role of systematic reviews detecting plagiarism: case of Asim Kurjak. *BMJ* 2006; **333**: 594–6.
17. Danish National Committee on Scientific Dishonesty. Guidelines for agreements at the initiation of research projects, on the rights and duties in the storage and use of research data, and guidelines concerning authorship. *Dan Med Bull* 1999; **46**: 60–7.
18. Andersen D. Cases during the Committee's first five years. In: *Annual Report 1997.* Copenhagen: The Research Councils, 1997: 9–14.

2 Ethical issues in the publication process

Richard Smith

Introduction

Sometimes, editors of scientific journals will encounter major cases of fabrication, falsification, or plagiarism, but much more often they will have to deal with a host of 'minor' ethical issues. Although I describe these issues as 'minor', it may well be that their cumulative effect is more damaging to the scientific record than that of 'major' misconduct. For example, there is a large body of evidence that pharmaceutical companies are very likely to get the results they want from the clinical trials that they sponsor.[1] In addition, positive results are likely to be published more than once, whereas negative results may not be published at all.[2] The result is that doctors and patients may think that drugs are much more effective – and safer – than they actually are, leading to poor prescribing and medical care.

This chapter describes many of the ethical issues that arise in the publication process, but once editors are sensitized to ethical issues, they will discover that they arise almost every day and come in many forms. The chapter cannot be comprehensive, and I have chosen to provide major rather than complete references. There are books, including one written by me, for those who want to read more.[3,4]

Patient consent for case reports

Case reports used to be the staple diet of medical journals, and interestingly they are becoming popular again – illustrating how scientific journals are prone to fashionable trends just like other human creations. Until perhaps 15 years ago, nobody worried about patients consenting to publication of reports about their cases. Medical journals were assumed to be read only by doctors, and just as a hundred doctors might discuss a case in a meeting without the patient consenting, so cases could be discussed in journals. The most that journals would do would be to put a black band across the eyes of pictures of the faces of patients – a means of guarding anonymity that is wholly ineffective.

As editor of the *BMJ*, I became painfully aware in the early 1990s that our systems were inadequate when a patient rang me in great distress to describe how she was contemplating killing herself after the *BMJ* had published pictures of pathological specimens that came from her. (I am deliberately being inexact, as I do not have her consent to tell this story.) It had never occurred to any of us that the specimens could be identified as coming from a particular patient. But we should have stopped to think. Case reports are published because they are unusual in some way. Most readers may not be able to identify the patient, but there is every chance that the patient themselves, their friends and relatives, and members of the medical team that looked after them will be able to identify the patient. Medical journals are no longer read only by doctors. They are available on the World Wide Web and searchable through Google, for example. It is not possible to guarantee anonymity. The old advice from bodies such as the International Committee of Medical Journal Editors (ICMJE) that authors and editors should try to ensure anonymity was no longer adequate. It became essential to get consent from patients.

A case before Britain's General Medical Council (GMC) added to the impetus for change. In 1995, three doctors appeared before the council charged with serious professional misconduct because they had published a report on a patient without, it was claimed, gaining adequate consent from the patient.[5,6] The report, published in the *British Journal of Psychiatry* in 1993, concerned three patients with bulimia nervosa who had bled themselves.[7] The paper came from Aberdeen, and the local newspaper picked up the story. It published only details that were in the case report (which included, for instance, 'Ms C is a 26-year-old preregistration doctor'), but a friend of one of the patients was able to identify her from the newspaper report. The patient made a complaint to the GMC, saying that, although she had consented to the use of her case for teaching and research, she had not consented to its publication in a journal. The doctors were found not guilty, but the GMC changed its advice – emphasizing the need to gain consent. This case showed that the consent should not be general, but specific – with the patient being able to read what will be published and understand how extensively available the report will be.

The *BMJ* thus moved to a policy of always requiring written consent, using a standard form that made clear that the *BMJ* was available to all on the Web. But – as is so common with complex ethical issues – we began to think that we had gone too far.[8] We regularly published 'fillers' that were brief stories about patients. Often, they were stories from years ago and it was impossible to gain consent. Should we never publish such stories – even though they were popular with readers and often carried a useful lesson? We put this question to our Ethics Committee, which was formed in 1999, and it helped us establish a policy that was a compromise. We then gathered a series of cases, and – with the Ethics Committee – re-evaluated our policy in the light of these cases. The current *BMJ* policy is as follows, and seems to be both ethically acceptable and workable:

1. Publication of any personal information about a patient will normally require the consent of the patient. This will be so even if identifying details are removed.
2. Personal information about a patient will not be published over the patient's refusal, except in the most exceptional circumstance of overriding importance to public health.

3. Publication without the consent of the patient will be permitted if all of the following conditions are met:
   (i)   The patient who is the focus of the article is untraceable without an unduly burdensome effort and it is also impossible or unreasonable to expect consent to be obtained from the patient or the patient's next of kin.
   (ii) The article contains a worthwhile clinical lesson or public health point that could not be as effectively made in any other way. ('Worthwhile' is intended to sit on a spectrum between 'interesting', which is the publication threshold with patient consent, and 'overriding public health importance', which is the publication threshold over patient refusal.)
   (iii) A reasonable person in the patient's position would not be expected to object to the publication of the case. (This requires an assessment of the intrusiveness of the disclosure and the potential that it has for causing the patient, or the patient's family, embarrassment or distress. Particular attention must be paid to differences in cultural and social attitudes. It must not be assumed that what is a matter of indifference in one society will have the same status in another.)
   (iv) The risk of identification of the patient is minimized by measures designed to prevent the identity of the patient being revealed either to others or to the patient themselves. (These measures will include anonymization of the case or the author, or both. Publication without consent of photographs will require particularly scrupulous attention to anonymization.)

This policy involves judgement. It is usual in my experience that judgement is inescapable in these ethical issues. They cannot be reduced to simple rules.

A particular issue that kept arising with the *BMJ*'s policy was that the journal was accused of hypocrisy because it published in its news pages pictures of patients who had not given written consent. We discussed the issue with our Ethics Committee, and reached the following conclusion:

> 'We believe that the *BMJ* would be at a disadvantage among other media if we didn't use such images, and pictures can often tell a story more powerfully than words. But we cannot take responsibility for the consent of people who are shown in pictures that we have obtained from agencies, libraries, other publications, and other commercial sources. We state clearly where pictures have come from, and we assume that they and their photographers have obtained relevant permission from models in any images showing people. Reputable picture agencies and other sources are unlikely to take the legal and financial risk of selling sensitive images without appropriate consent. If we doubt that someone photographed could have given consent – owing to severe mental illness, dementia, or learning disability, for example – we use our discretion and try to avoid images that might allow that person to be identified.' (www.bmj.com/cgi/content/full/330/7497/916.)

Another problem that remains largely unresolved – and may be unresolvable – is that of consent for the publication of family trees. Such trees are of vital importance in genetics, but should every person who appears in a tree give consent? And should they give consent just for their information or for the whole tree? With widely scattered families, gaining consent from every member would clearly be extremely difficult, if not impossible. In addition, in such families, members are generally not aware of each other's medical histories. A further problem is that if a family tree were to be published without their consent, family members could be presented with distressing genetic information that they might prefer not to know.

Then there are the problems of getting consent for publication of reports of patients who are not capable of giving consent. And what about forensic cases, where patients with criminal convictions might refuse publication but where there might be valuable lessons? I have perhaps laboured this particular ethical issue, but the story does illustrate clearly how ethical issues are common in publication and often not amenable to simple rules.

Informed consent for research

At first thought, the issue of getting consent from patients who are included in research might seem simple. Surely patients should always give written consent, and surely journals should always ensure that such consent has been given. But yet again this proves to be a highly complex matter.[9]

Some ethicists have argued that patients should always give written consent – because to be included in an experiment without giving consent is itself a form of abuse, even if it is impossible for the patient to suffer any other physical or psychological harm. Some researchers are very irritated by this position. They point to double standards. If clinicians are uncertain of the best treatment for a patient, as is commonly the case, they can nevertheless recommend a particular treatment and simply ask for the patient's consent to take the treatment. In contrast, researchers with the same uncertainty must obtain written consent not simply for taking the treatment but also for randomization and participation in a trial. Yet, the researcher argues, it is the researchers who are confronting the uncertainty and devising experiments from which it is possible to learn. Why should it be more difficult for them? I see this less as an argument for relaxing standards for researchers but more as an argument for tightening them for clinicians, obliging them to share their uncertainty with patients.

Researchers also argue that it is in some sense unethical to increase the bureaucracy around trials – making them more difficult and expensive to undertake – when there is so much in health care that is not known.

The ethical position that written consent is an absolute requirement is obviously difficult to maintain when we consider research in those who are unconscious, seriously ill, or incompetent to consent. The absolute position would mean that research in these patients would be impossible, which would clearly be against the interest of such patients.

Then what about research that uses only medical records or stored human tissue – perhaps blood? Many argue that there is substantial benefit from such research and no real harm – a utilitarian position. More difficult is the question of waiving consent in order not to undermine the validity of the experiment. If the outcome measure of a trial is subjective and patients know that they are, for example, in a trial of using a specially trained nurse, they may give positive responses to avoid seeming to be rude. Again, if the chance of harm is minimal, should it not be possible to waive consent?

Another difficult issue is around 'audit' versus 'research'. Traditionally audit – which should be part of all clinical practice and is trying to answer the question 'How are we doing with what we know we should be doing?' – does not require ethics committee approval and informed consent, whereas research – trying to find out the best thing to do – does. But are all projects clearly research or audit? The answer is 'no', and Derek Wade, a member of the *BMJ* Ethics Committee, has suggested that whether or not a project requires third-party approval and informed consent should depend not on an arbitrary division but rather on answers to the following questions:[10]

- How much does this deviate from current normal (accepted, local) clinical practice?
- What is the (additional) burden imposed on the patients (or others)?
- What (additional) risks are posed to the patients (or others)?
- What benefit might accrue to the patients (or others)?
- What are the potential benefits to society (future patients)?

Again, simple rules are not possible. Journals and editors have to make decisions on what is acceptable – and many, I suggest, are not well equipped to make such decisions. Few editors have much training in ethics and very few journals have the support of ethicists.

Checking approval from research ethics committees or institutional review boards

Editors might legitimately argue that it is not for them to make judgements on whether research is ethically acceptable: rather, that is the job of research ethics committees or institutional review boards, as they are called in the USA. Many of these committees do include ethicists and patients as well as clinicians, and they have a legitimacy to make judgements that journals lack. Editors might decide that what is good enough for ethics committees is good enough for them. Indeed, it might be presumptuous for editors to overrule ethics committees.

There are, however, several reasons why editors cannot rely entirely on ethics committees. The first reason is that the researchers may not have gained the approval of a committee. This might happen because no committee is available. Some countries do not have such committees, or it might be that there is no committee for the particular kind of research. In Britain, for example, until nearly a decade ago, ethics committees were based only in hospitals, meaning that there was no committee for research in primary care. There were also problems with getting approval for research in the private as opposed to the public sector. Or researchers may not get approval because they do not think that their kind of research needs approval: there is a lack of clarity over exactly which types of research or audit need approval. Or it may simply be that researchers could not be bothered to seek approval, a serious offence.

A second reason why editors cannot rely on ethics committees is that much may have changed with research between when a protocol was approved by an ethics committee and when the research was completed and submitted for publication. Indeed, there is much evidence showing how protocols change.[11] Research that was 'ethical' may have become 'unethical'.

Editors should also review the decisions of ethics committees, because the committees may not be fully competent. Many argue that research that is scientifically unacceptable is automatically unethical because it is consuming resources, including possibly the time of patients, without it being possible to reach a conclusion. Some ethics committees are not competent to reach a decision on the validity of the science. Instead, they may have assumed that the science is competent and have concentrated on issues such as the risk to patients and the quality of consent.

A final reason for editors to review the decisions of ethics committees is to provide a check on the work of the committees. Many, even most, cases are not clear-cut, and it is useful to have a second opinion. Or it may be that the committee is corrupted – overinfluenced perhaps by a dominant chair or clinician. Or they could be wrong.

But what should editors do when they 'overrule' an ethics committee, deciding that a piece of research approved by the committee is ethically unacceptable? They should clearly provide feedback to the researchers and the committee. It might be that, after debate, consensus can be reached. Or it might be that the 'offence' is comparatively minor and that the best response will be to publish the research together with a commentary from the editorial team and possibly responses from the authors and ethics committee.

If, however, editors reach the conclusion that the ethics committee has made an important error, then the editor should report the committee to its parent body – rather in the way that he or she might report an author suspected of misconduct. It is not for the editor to judge whether the committee has misbehaved, but it is the duty of the editor to ensure that there is adequate inquiry into the possible misbehaviour. The editor would then be obliged to act on the findings of the inquiry – for example, going ahead and publishing a paper where the committee is judged to have made the right decision. Great difficulties arise, however, when the editor decides that the inquiry into the ethics committee has been inadequate. I did not have this experience as an editor, but I did several times decide that inquiries into authors where we had asked for an inquiry had not been adequate. Our response then was to go ahead and publish our concerns.

Failure to publish and publishing too much

Iain Chalmers, one of the founders of the Cochrane Collaboration, has famously argued that failure to publish research is misconduct.[12] His argument is that researchers owe it to participants in research and the world at large to publish. If they do not publish, then the world at large does not have access to all research available on a subject – for example, the effectiveness or safety of a treatment – and so may be misled. This is particularly the case if researchers fail to publish negative findings, and evidence shows that it is negative findings that are least likely to be published – leading to a bias in favour of treatments.[13]

By definition, editors can have limited impact on failure to publish – apart from publicly urging researchers to publish. Editors can, however, be part of the problem by having a bias towards publishing positive results. Editors are regularly accused of this 'publication bias', although evidence shows that the problem of failure to publish negative studies lies more with authors than editors. At the *BMJ*, we tried hard to ask not whether results were interesting but rather whether the question being asked was important. If we judged it important and thought that the methods used to answer the study were reliable, then we would publish, regardless of whether the results were negative or positive.

Editors, or rather publishers, may, however, compound the problem of failure to publish by making it very hard for authors to achieve publication of studies. Major journals such as the *Lancet* and the *New England Journal of Medicine* publish less than 10% of the studies they are sent. Authors who have their studies rejected then begin to work their way down the 'food chain' of journals, and conventional wisdom is that it is possible to get almost anything published if the authors are willing to persist and go to the very bottom of the food chain. Authors may, however, give up after a while, tired of a tedious and somewhat arbitrary process. There is an argument that in the days of the Internet it should be much easier to publish – in online journals such as those produced by BioMed Central and the Public Library of Science. Some argue that this is bad, because too much 'poor' research may be published. Counter-arguments are that a great deal of poor-quality research is already published, that peer review is too much of a lottery (see below), and that it is much better to have research published in full – so that it can be critically appraised – rather than simply referred to in the media, as often happens.

One complex problem around publication is whether editors should refuse to publish particular kinds of research – for example, that funded by the tobacco industry. Those who argue against publication say that it gives undeserved respectability to the industry and that the research cannot be trusted because the industry has been shown to distort evidence. The same argument could be applied to research funded by the pharmaceutical industry – which would be a large proportion of the research published in medical journals. The counter-argument is that to deny publication to research funded by the tobacco industry is systematically to distort the scientific record. The *BMJ* decided against a blanket ban, but some leading journals will not publish research funded by the tobacco industry.[14]

The scientific record may also be distorted by researchers publishing studies more than once, and there is a substantial body of evidence showing that around one-fifth of studies may be published more than once.[2] It may be that exactly the same study is published more than once – called 'duplicate publication' by editors – or, more commonly, there is substantial overlap between two studies – 'redundant publication'. A judgement on when the overlap is excessive is obviously subjective, and editors may be much more likely than authors to see redundancy. Editors are, however, on stronger ground when authors fail to declare that their study is close to another – implying deliberate deception.

Editors have long been unhappy about redundant publication, and initially their objection was mainly that their resources were being wasted in reviewing the same studies. Authors were not impressed by this selfish concern, and a much more important reason for resisting redundant publication is that it distorts the scientific record. Because positive rather than negative research is more likely to be published repeatedly, treatments are made to seem more effective and safer than they actually are – deceiving doctors and patients.[15] Sometimes, this deception may be deliberate.

Conflict of interest

One cause of deception is conflict of interest. We now have overwhelming evidence that research funded by sponsors (usually the pharmaceutical industry in the case of medical journals) is much more likely to produce results favourable to the sponsor and its products than research that is funded with public money.[1]

Editors have been arguing since the early 1980s that authors with conflicts of interest – that is, secondary interests that might have influenced their interpretation of their results – should declare them. However, research undertaken at the end of the 1990s showed that journals were disclosing conflicts of interest in only a tiny fraction of studies.[16] Other research has shown that a large proportion of authors (around two-thirds) do have conflicts of interest.[17] In other words, we had evidence by the late 1990s that conflicts of interest had a strong influence on results, were common, and were rarely disclosed. This was a toxic combination, and the argument that concern with conflict of interest was the 'new McCarthyism' or 'political correctness gone mad' was no longer sustainable.[18]

But how should editors respond? The main response has been to ask authors and reviewers to disclose conflicts of interest and then disclose those of authors to readers. Our experience at the *BMJ* in the late 1990s was that authors usually failed to declare conflicts of interest, even though we defined for them what we meant by conflicts of interest and asked them to sign to say whether they had any such conflicts. Authors probably failed to respond because it was the culture not to respond, because they were confident that they had not been influenced by their conflicts, and because they felt that there was something demeaning about confessing to conflicts of interest. We tried to encourage disclosure by sending a much more specific questionnaire, by changing the term 'conflicts of interest' to 'competing interests', and by concentrating on financial conflicts rather than all conflicts.[19] For whatever reason, the number of authors and reviewers declaring conflicts of interest increased dramatically – and such declarations have now become routine in the *BMJ* and other major journals (although not by any means in all journals).

Is disclosure enough? It cannot always be. For example, no journal would agree to having an editorial on a drug written by an employee of the company that made the drug. But where is the point when disclosure is no longer enough? Few, if any, journals have tried to define that point. And should disclosure include not simply that a conflict exists but also the amount of money involved? There is surely a considerable difference between having had lunch bought for you by a drug company and receiving an annual retainer of $300 000 for advising a company and speaking at meetings. Yet readers are not given this information.

And disclosure cannot work for reviewers, because readers rarely know the names of reviewers. Peer review (see below) is usually conducted anonymously. Editors should know the conflicts of reviewers, but they do not share the information with either authors or readers. The *BMJ* introduced open peer review, whereby the authors but not the readers would know the names of reviewers. One of the main consequences of this change was that authors drew attention to conflicts of interest of reviewers that the latter had failed to declare.

If editors do discover that authors or reviewers have failed to declare conflicts of interest, then they should inform the author or reviewer and the readers. When authors or reviewers asked me whether they should declare particular conflicts of interest, I would reply: 'If in doubt, disclose. Little is lost by declaring conflicts of interest, but it is very embarrassing to have to disclose later something that was not declared initially. Editors and readers will suspect deception, and trust will be undermined.'

Editors have been increasingly concerned with the conflicts of interest of authors and reviewers, but – unsurprisingly – have been much less assiduous in managing the conflicts of interest of themselves, their teams, their editorial boards, and their owners.[20] Some journals have explicit policies that forbid editors from owning shares in companies – particularly pharmaceutical companies – whose business may be influenced by material that might be published in the journal. But, generally, journals fail to disclose their own conflicts of interest – and yet these may be considerable. Consider, for example, the case of reprints. If a journal publishes the results of a major clinical trial sponsored by a drug company, then it might sell that company a million dollars worth of reprints – and the profit in such a sale will be perhaps $700 000. Editors, many of whom are under budgetary pressure, know which studies will prompt such sales. This is a major conflict of interest, and yet is rarely disclosed or even discussed.

Peer review

If peer review were a perfect process – deciding with surgical precision whether conclusions were supported by methods and data – then perhaps conflicts of interest would matter less. But, as I have argued elsewhere and as a systematic review has found, peer review is a highly imperfect process.[21,22] It is slow, expensive, a lottery, hopeless at detecting error and fraud, prone to bias, and easily abused. Two decades of research into peer review have produced substantial evidence of its defects but almost no evidence of its benefits. So, ironically, peer review, which is at the heart of the scientific process, is based largely on faith rather than evidence. Yet scientists continue to equate it with democracy as the 'least bad' system available.

What are the ethical implications for editors of the lack of evidence to support peer review? One implication might be that they should be familiar with the evidence that is available (as cardiologists should be aware of the evidence on the interventions they use) and should be transparent about the deficiencies of peer review. However, familiarity with the evidence and transparency are both rare. Another implication might be that editors should search – within studies – for improved methods of peer review. Such searches are also rare. Another implication might be that editors should open up the process – because a transparent flawed process is less bad than a closed flawed process. Yet, despite evidence that open peer review is just as good as – and possibly better than – closed peer review, most editors have kept with a closed process.[23] My iconoclastic view is that peer review should be transformed from a black box to an open scientific discourse. This is not as radical as it sounds, since it would simply bring the dissemination of science back to its origins when scientists would present their findings not in journals but in meetings and have these findings debated on the spot.

Authorship or contributorship?

The publication issue that gives rise to the most disputes is authorship. It matters greatly to both authors and editors, but authors think mainly about credit whereas editors think about accountability. In fact, the two are inseparable.

One problem with authorship is that many people who appear as authors on studies have actually contributed very little, if anything.[24–26] They do not meet the criteria for authorship established by the ICMJE. These criteria amount to taking full intellectual ownership of the study. Indeed, a series of studies have shown that only about half of authors meet the ICMJE criteria and as many as a fifth of authors may have done nothing at all – apart from head the department in which the research was done. Yet there have been a series of cases where research that has proved to be fraudulent has included high-profile authors who then deny any responsibility for misconduct. This infuriates editors, who think that these authors are enjoying the credit but denying the accountability.

A second problem with authorship is that researchers who have done a great deal of work – perhaps gathering or analysing large amounts of data – may be denied authorship because they do not meet the criteria set by the editors. In fact, authors do not seem to know much about the editors' criteria and do not accept them when they do.[27] Authorship seems often to be decided on grounds of power rather than intellectual ownership, with the powerful being included and the powerless excluded.

The fundamental difficulty is that authorship is the wrong concept. Most modern scientific research is a team effort involving people from different intellectual disciplines with different skills. Creating a scientific paper is much more like making a film than writing a novel – which is why Drummond Rennie, Deputy Editor of *JAMA*, and others have argued for contributorship rather than authorship.[28] Researchers do not have to be sorted into authors and non-authors. Instead, they simply describe what they did.

Slowly, very slowly, this idea is being accepted, and I believe it to be much more honest in that people do not have to pretend to accept full intellectual responsibility for a study, but can simply describe what they contributed – and accept both credit and responsibility for that part. But Rennie and others have argued that somebody must take responsibility for the whole – and be described as a 'guarantor'. Their concept of the guarantor was that he or she would review all the data and take full intellectual responsibility, but this is clearly difficult with studies that might include molecular biology, clinical input, and statistical and economic analysis. Another concept – which we adopted at the *BMJ* – was that the guarantor could accept accountability in the way that a minister accepts accountability for a government department or, indeed, an editor accepts accountability for a journal. The accountability is discharged not through checking every fact but through appointing good people and establishing clear policies and systems.

Developing world

The developing world throws up several ethical issues for editors. Perhaps the most important is the simple fact that 90% of morbidity and premature mortality occurs in the developing world but only 10% of health research relates to the developing world. Should editors simply accept this injustice or rail against it? Should they try and influence the research agenda? Should they make it easier for researchers from the developing world to publish in major, international journals? Or should editors of international journals support journals in the developing world?

These major questions are increasingly discussed, but more attention has been paid to the ethics of research conducted in developing countries by researchers from developed countries. One question that has been much debated is whether it can be acceptable to conduct research in the developing world that will primarily benefit patients in the developed world – perhaps because the treatment will be unaffordable in the developing world. Another question is whether it can be acceptable to conduct a trial of a low-cost intervention against placebo in the developing world when an evidence-based but unaffordable treatment is available in the developed world.

Relating to the mass media

It used to be that journals would refuse to publish research that had been trailed in the mass media. Two editors of the *New England Journal of Medicine* – Franz Ingelfinger and Bud Relman – followed this policy very strongly, arguing that it was irresponsible to publicize research that had not been fully peer-reviewed. The policy was criticized by journalists on the grounds that the journals – which often took a year to publish studies – were holding back information that could be important for the health of the public. In fact, these arguments were self-serving, with the editors and the journalists both wanting the 'scoop'. The policy also became increasingly unworkable as more and more journalists attended major medical conferences where new results were presented. Most journals are therefore now much less strict than were Ingelfinger and Relman.

A more modern problem is journals hyping the research that they publish in order to get coverage in the mass media – or even accepting or commissioning work that they know will get coverage. Editors and publishers like coverage in the mass media because it raises the profile of their journals and may bring more submissions, a higher impact factor, and more subscriptions or visits to websites. Indeed, there is much evidence that coverage in the mass media increases visits to websites – and these visits can lead directly to increased income, as most journals charge for full access to papers.

Many public health practitioners believe that it was hunger for publicity that led the *Lancet* to publish its highly controversial study that linked the MMR (measles, mumps, and rubella) vaccine with autism and led to a fall in vaccinations.[29] There is no evidence that this was the case, but it may well be that the press releases put out by many journals tend to overemphasize the importance of findings – if for no other reason than that there is no room for the 'ifs and buts' that are the stuff of science.

Acting on ethical problems

Around 15 years ago, I attended a workshop run by Raanan Gillon, the Editor of the *Journal of Medical Ethics*, to discuss the ethical issues faced by editors. Gillon began by asking the assembled editors what issues they had encountered. Most said that they had not encountered any – but I hope that any reader of this chapter will be convinced that ethical issues are thrown up all the time in the publication process. If editors do not recognize ethical problems, they cannot act on them – and, until recently, most did not. The creation of the Committee on Publication Ethics (COPE) 10 years ago did, however, begin to change the culture. It helped editors recognize ethical issues and made clear that they had a duty to act on them.

Much of this book is concerned with major research misconduct, and editors have a very clear duty to act if they suspect such misconduct. They must, however, resist the temptation to reach judgements and apply punishments. They should not do this for two main reasons. Firstly, serious accusations must be investigated with due process – and editors do not have the means to ensure such process. Secondly, editors do not have the legal legitimacy to make such judgements. The role of editors and journals is to notify the appropriate authority – usually an employer – and ensure that it conducts a proper inquiry and acts on what it finds.

Editors similarly have a duty to act on the ethical issues raised in this chapter, and sometimes this will mean notifying the appropriate authority, as with major misconduct. At other times, however, it will simply mean respectful interaction with the authors. Editors also, I believe, have a duty to establish clear policies and to help authors avoid stumbling into poor ethical practice.

Support and accountability for editors

Few editors have had training in ethics, and most have had little experience of the ethical issues thrown up by publication – not least because most editors of medical journals have been appointed because of their research achievements and have had little training and direct experience of editing journals. Editors thus need support and advice, which is supplied by organizations such as the World Association of Medical Editors, COPE, the European Association of Science Editors, and the Council of Science Editors. Much of this support is, however, general rather than specific, which is why the *BMJ* formed its own Ethics Committee – to give specific advice that could be based on seeing all the relevant papers. The *BMJ* regards its Ethics Committee as a success, and, indeed, I quickly wondered how it was that that we had got through 160 years without one. Few if any other journals have, however, copied the experience.

Much more attention has been paid to managing the independence and accountability of editors. Traditionally, editors have independence, but a whole series of editors have been fired for poor reasons in the past 15 years – and, of course, independence cannot be absolute. It is beyond the scope of this chapter to write much about editorial independence and accountability – except to say that it is far from straightforward to balance the two. The balance seems to lie with the owners establishing the mission of the journal, the editors presenting a strategy to a distinguished board that has independence from the journals, and the editors then being left to make day-to-day decisions. There also needs to be a transparent process for dealing with complaints, but few journals have such a process – even though most minor companies and organizations do. Why should journals be different?

Journals and business ethics

I could not end this chapter without writing something about the business ethics of journals. Most journals publish mostly original research, and most of that research is funded with public money. The traditional business model is for journals to charge for subscriptions to the material they publish, and often these subscriptions are very expensive – even as much as $15 000 for a year's subscription. Most people – including most researchers, doctors, and patients – do not have subscriptions. They thus do not have access to the research – despite it being funded with public money. This business model has caused grief among academics – particularly as publishers have tended to increase the price of subscriptions each year by well above the rate of inflation. Academics have also recognized that most of the value of the research lies in the research itself, which is hard to do, rather than in the publication process. Furthermore, it is academics who edit the journals, conduct the peer review, and buy and read the journals. The value added by publishers is minimal, and yet the copyright for the research studies and the substantial profits made by journals belong to the publishers, not the researchers. Publishers, to put it bluntly, are making substantial profits by ripping off academics and by restricting access to publicly funded research. This, I have argued elsewhere, is 'unethical'.

The arrival of the Internet has provided an alternative. Research can be published on the Internet and made available, 'open access', to all – meaning that it is both free to access and free to publish elsewhere (with attribution), quote, and 'mine' (i.e. to search many studies, possibly using robots). Many organizations are promoting open-access publishing, and are publishing on an open-access basis. An increasing number of research funders, including the US government, are requiring that authors publish the studies that they fund on an open-access basis. As I have argued for more than a decade, open-access publishing will become the normal way of publishing.

Conclusion

This has been a rapid survey of the many ethical issues thrown up in publishing science. It will, I hope, be clear to all readers that the issues are complex and not amenable to simple solutions – but crying out for further thought and debate.

References

1. Lexchin J, Bero LA, Djulbegovic B, Clark O. Pharmaceutical industry sponsorship and research outcome and quality: systematic review. *BMJ* 2003; **326**: 1167–70.

2. Smith R. Publishing too much and nothing: serious problems not just nuisances. In: Smith R. *The Trouble with Medical Journals*. London: RSM Press, 2006: 119–24.

3. Hudson A, McLellan F. *Ethical Issues in Biomedical Publication*. Baltimore: Johns Hopkins University Press, 2000.

4. Smith R. *The Trouble with Medical Journals*. London: RSM Press, 2006.

5. Court C. GMC finds doctors not guilty in consent case. *BMJ* 1995; **311**: 1245–6.

6. Smith R. Publishing information about patients. *BMJ* 1995; **311**: 1240–1.

7. Parkin JR, Eagles JM. Blood-letting in bulimia nervosa. *Br J Psychiatry* 1993; **162**: 246–8.

8. Smith R. Informed consent: edging forwards (and backwards). *BMJ* 1998; **316**: 949–51.

9. Doyal L, Tobias J. *Informed Consent in Medical Research*. London: *BMJ* Books, 2000.

10. Wade DT. Ethics, audit, and research: all shades of grey. *BMJ* 2005; **330**: 468–71.

11. Chan AW, Hróbjartsson A, Haahr MT et al. Empirical evidence for selective reporting of outcomes in randomized trials: comparison of protocols to published articles. *JAMA* 2004; **291**: 2457–65.

12. Chalmers I. Underreporting research is scientific misconduct. *JAMA* 1990; **263**: 1405–8.

13. Dickersin K, Min YI. Publication bias: the problem that won't go away. *Ann N Y Acad Sci* 1993; **703**: 135–46; discussion 146–8.

14. Roberts J, Smith R. Publishing research supported by the tobacco industry. *BMJ* 1996; **312**: 133–4.

15. Tramèr MR, Reynolds DJM, Moore RA, McQuay HJ. Impact of covert duplicate publication on meta-analysis: a case study. *BMJ* 1997; **315**: 635–40.

16. Hussain A, Smith R. Declaring financial competing interests: survey of five general medical journals. *BMJ* 2001; **323**: 263–4.

17. Bekelman JE, Li Y, Gross CP. Scope and impact of financial conflicts of interest in biomedical research. A systematic review. *JAMA* 2003; **289**: 454–65.

18. Rothman KJ. Conflict of interest: the new McCarthyism in science. *JAMA* 1993; **269**: 2782–4.

19. Smith R. Making progress with competing interests. *BMJ* 2002; **325**: 1375–6.

20. Haivas I, Schroter S, Waechter F, Smith R. Editors' declaration of their own conflicts of interest. *CMAJ* 2004; **171**: 475–6.

21. Smith R. Peer review – a flawed process at the heart of science. *J R Soc Med* 2006; **99**: 178–82.

22. Jefferson T, Alderson P, Wager E, Davidoff F. Effects of editorial peer review: a systematic review. *JAMA* 2002; **287**: 2784–6.

23. Smith R. Opening up peer review. *BMJ* 1999; **318**: 4–5.

24. Shapiro DW, Wenger WS, Shapiro MF. The contributions of authors to multi-authored biomedical research papers. *JAMA* 1994; **271**: 438–42.

25. Goodman N. Survey of fulfilment of criteria of authorship in published medical research. *BMJ* 1994; **309**: 1482.
26. Flanagin A, Carey LA, Fontanarosa PB et al. Prevalence of articles with honorary authors and ghost authors in peer-reviewed medical journals. *JAMA* 1998; **280**: 222–4.
27. Bhopal R, Rankin J, McColl E et al. The vexed question of authorship: views of researchers in a British medical faculty. *BMJ* 1997; **314**: 1009.
28. Rennie D, Yank V, Emanuel L. When authorship fails: a proposal to make contributors accountable. *JAMA* 1997; **278**: 579–85.
29. Wakefield AJ, Murch SH, Linnell AAJ et al. Ileal-lymphoid-nodular hyperplasia, non-specific colitis and pervasive developmental disorder in children. *Lancet* 1998; **351**: 637–41.

3 What is research misconduct?

Drummond Rennie and C Kristina Gunsalus

Introduction

The central questions that we address in this chapter are these: Do we need strict definitions for what constitutes research misconduct? And if we do, what should they be? In the USA, the issue was framed by the Commission on Scientific Integrity thus:[1]

> 'How narrow or broad should the federal definition be? Specifically, should it include other misconduct beyond fabrication, falsification, and plagiarism? How should questions about intent and honest differences in interpretation of data be addressed? How should the line be drawn between serious and less-serious offenses?'

A very different view has been presented for the Scandinavian countries:[2]

> 'In the Nordic countries, formal definitions have never been considered critical or even feasible, since dishonesty is regarded as ranging from minor deviations from good scientific practice to obvious misconduct. Scientific dishonesty has therefore been broadly characterized, and the establishment of a verdict relies on sound judgement rather than rigorous definitions.'

The differences between these two positions depend on the experiences, attitudes, and opinions of the groups of scientists, lawyers, administrators, and politicians who formulated them. But these are themselves shaped by the ethos and conditions of the respective countries from which they come. In the 1970s and 1980s, numerous events, widely reported in the media, forced the USA to produce definitions of unacceptable conduct that satisfied lawyers and would withstand the test of litigation. In a small country such as, say, Denmark, where clinical scientists live near each other, personal accountability to an individual scientist's colleagues may matter more and be easier to achieve than in the USA, where research centres may house hundreds of scientists and be separated by thousands of miles. Nevertheless, when a very serious case emerges, as happened in Norway with the revelation of Sudbø's multiple falsifications,[3] attitudes can harden, and institutions face up to what is a universal challenge.[4] Moreover, the nature of good science does not differ from country to country. Science is accessible all over the world, published by international journals that expect the same standards of all researchers. In this chapter, we will examine why we need a definition of research misconduct, what that definition should be, and whether it should apply universally.

Can formal definitions be avoided if good research practices are promoted?

Although, ever since the Ten Commandments, there have been instructional tracts promoting good behaviour that are freely available and universally taught, the prohibited offences continue to be committed. Teaching good practices is essential. But when theft occurs, we demand an official reaction, according to rules that give teeth to investigators, and power to those who adjudicate and sanction.

In its Code of Practice for Research, the fledgling UK Research Integrity Office (UKRIO) declared that 'a strong emphasis on promoting good practice is seen as preferable to a regulatory or statutory model'.[5] It may be preferable – but it is an unrealistic solution. To expect promotion of good practices to solve the problem flies in the face of the extensive and well-documented experience in the USA, where prolonged and energetic efforts, mandated by law, have been made for over 20 years to promote, advertise, and teach good scientific practices.[6] Such efforts are necessary, but by no means sufficient, and in the absence of statutes or official regulations and sanctions for non-adherence, cases of serious research fraud will continue to be grievously mishandled. While essential, mere instruction cannot prevent, or assist in handling, the many egregious acts of misconduct that occur in any extensive human enterprise, including research.

Why do we need a definition?

Scientists, especially those who find it hard to imagine anyone can stoop to falsifying the scientific record, commonly start from the position that 'everyone knows' that such and such an action, when committed during the pursuit of science, is wrong. They may have difficulty understanding the need for standards.[7] We, however, believe firmly that unless we have clear definitions of research misconduct, at the very least we shall always be at cross-purposes when discussing how to prevent it, and how to deal with allegations as they arise. It is a basic tenet that it is unfair to make a researcher liable for conduct that is not already clearly defined as being wrong. In the USA, and increasingly in other countries, findings of research misconduct are being challenged in court, so a robust definition, able to withstand legal assault, is legally required.

The basic fairness inherent in human relations, reaching far beyond legal requirements, mandates that people be able to know the rules of the game in which they are playing and by which they are being judged. It is not fair to punish people through ex post facto pronouncements. This is particularly essential when a career, reputation, and livelihood (or, in some places, life) may be on the line.[7] The consequences to a researcher of an accusation of research misconduct are always very serious, putting the researcher under great psychological pressure, and often straining the researcher's financial resources. For the accused, a finding of misconduct is a catastrophic event. Given that science can operate only in a climate of trust, loss of reputation effectively ends that scientist's career and wrecks his or her life and livelihood. The gravity of the consequences increases the need for a clear definition, lest frivolous accusations from individuals who merely dislike a scientist's behaviour destroy good researchers. As the size of a research enterprise grows, so do the numbers of people involved, the costs, and the size of the rewards. With the increase in the stakes, so grows the importance of getting the research right, and the need to respond effectively when things go wrong.

Acts of misconduct distort the research record, and so waste the time and efforts of others. They may, in the field of medicine, result in faulty and possibly dangerous treatments. They will, if unchecked, unfairly inflate the reputations and positions of those who commit them. They are therefore destructive of science, and often profoundly demoralizing to those in the perpetrator's institution who suspect the truth. To give an example, we once served on a panel as outside members adjudicating a very simple case of misconduct in the laboratory. Through serious administrative bungling, the whole issue had escalated to the point that the institution was split into warring factions, constructive work in some departments had largely ground to a halt, and one professor recorded having attended over 300 meetings on the matter.

As a cumulative consequence of the above, more and more findings of research misconduct are being challenged in court. We do not have the luxury of staying isolated from the legal system. Unless the definition satisfies the law, we shall perpetuate legal confusion, and guarantee injustice for accused, accuser, and society. This definition must satisfy scientists and serve the interests of science itself, as well as the public who pay for, and can benefit from, the research. If such issues are to be resolved fairly and promptly, each institution must have a proactive system already in place that defines the process to be followed after an allegation has been made. If this is not done, the institution's response will always be reactive, hurried, inefficient, at variance with that of other institutions, unfair, biased, and often at odds with the law.

What should our approach to a definition be?

In this chapter, we make the assumption (which we suspect does not hold in most countries) that whatever definition is adopted, there are bodies empowered to give meaning to the definitions and able to investigate, adjudicate, and sanction such behaviours.

The definition should not include actions occurring during the practice of research but that are not peculiar to research and that are already sanctioned by law – for example, murder, blackmail, arson, sexual harassment, and so on. An argument can be made to widen the definition to include all crimes that affect research. For example, malicious sequestration of crucial scientific data or specimens may amount to theft, but, since the law is unlikely to be brought to bear on the perpetrator given the specimens' trivial monetary value, perhaps theft in such circumstances should be included. However, we believe such misbehaviours should best be left to individual research institutions to discipline. Sox and Rennie[8] have described a case of multiple fabrications performed by a single researcher, who, because he used his own falsified research 'data' and publications in further applications for government research grants, is, at the time of writing, serving a prison sentence for defrauding the US government. Here, the university's investigation and adjudication had to do with whether there had been falsification of the research record, and only when that had been proven did the government step in and charge him with the monetary fraud. (See also the Swedish Medical Research Council's comments in Box 3.1.)

BOX 3.1   Extracts from paragraphs 6 and 7 of guidelines for the work of The Swedish Research Council's Expert Group for Investigation of Suspected Research Misconduct[a]

6. ... It cannot be ruled out that dishonesty in research, besides entailing liability for breach of duty or misconduct at work, may also constitute another offence. People who, for example, receive research grants by entering fabricated or distorted data in their applications may presumably, in certain cases, be deemed to have committed fraud. This offence is defined as being committed: 'If a person by deception induces someone to commit or omit to commit some act that involves gain for the accused and loss for the deceived' (*Swedish Penal Code*, Chapter 9, Section 1).

7. **The notion of 'good scientific practice' is given a limited definition in the Expert Group's work**. It would, of course, be an advantage in terms of the rule of law if either the requirements of 'good scientific practice' or the kinds of documents that may be deemed to constitute deviations from such practice could be specified in advance. This is hardly feasible. However, it is paramount that the notion of 'good scientific practice' should not, in this context, be interpreted so broadly that protests may be lodged against new ideas and new methods in research. Deviations from good scientific practice may, for example, consist in fabrication of data; theft or plagiarism of data, hypotheses, or methods without the source being cited; or other distortion of the research process (e.g. incorrect inclusion or exclusion of data, or misleading data analysis that distorts the interpretation).

[a]Adopted by the Research Council's Board on 29 September 2004.

Jerks or crooks?

In science, as in all professions, there are numerous individuals whose behaviour may be rude, insensitive, selfish, arrogant, incommunicative, disruptive, and in numerous ways obnoxious and uncollegial. This does not invalidate their science nor necessarily mean that they are guilty of anything more than being hard to abide, so, as one of us (CKG) has written, 'We have to have a definition that separates the crooks from the jerks.'[9] The latter are the scientists who refuse to share data after publication even if it is a condition of publishing; who refuse to give credit; who continually republish their own data; who fail to mentor and bring forward their juniors, but appropriate from them instead. These are the scientists whose 'little murders', in Jules Feiffer's phrase, sever the delicate threads of trust that hold our community together. The behaviours of jerks do much to poison relations with their fellow researchers, but are usually ones that should be left to their employers, who must have their own standards, to monitor and sanction.

Definition: the importance of uniformity

Physical laws do not change from country to country, and the practice of science and the scientific method must be fundamentally the same throughout the world. Uniform definitions of what constitutes bad scientific behaviour therefore make sense. As an illustration of the problem, one of the authors (DR) is an editor of a large international medical journal, based in the USA, but receiving a high proportion of manuscripts from outside the USA. Scientific journals publish papers depending on their quality, and not on the institution, city, or country of origin. Editors, then, are forced to start with the assumption that scientists everywhere are held to the same standards of accountability.

In the case of multiple falsifications mentioned above,[8] we noted that authors in the USA, who are governed by regulations on research misconduct and are held accountable if allegations are raised against them, are effectively held to a higher standard than those in almost all other countries. The editors also know from published experience that if the same allegations concerned a paper received from the majority of other countries, the matter would not be pursued and the authors not held accountable.[10–15] Such cases, in the absence of clear definitions and of any processes for dealing with allegations, typically remain unresolved for many years. Given the appalling experience of editors dealing with accusations brought in other countries, some have begun to wonder whether the time has come for US journals to accept papers only from countries with effective definitions and processes in place.

In addition, since many institutions lack the expertise, the will, or the money to set up the mechanisms for resolving allegations of research misconduct on their own (and have their validity tested in court), everything is much easier for institutions when there is some central authoritative statement from some respected body that defines behaviour so egregious that it must be sanctioned. So, it all starts with a clear definition.

Conditions and criteria necessary for any workable system

Any definition must, then, be universal in two senses: universal geographically, and universal across all research disciplines and not confined to clinical research. The definition and other rules governing research misconduct must be promulgated by some official and widely accepted body having the legal power to make them stick, and these rules must be published. A definition of what constitutes research misconduct is necessary, but, by itself, is insufficient. We assume that such a definition must be accompanied by a process having the following elements:

- *Notice* to those accused of the charges against them.
- *Opportunity to respond to the charges* and to all evidence used to draw conclusions.
- *Opportunity to have an advocate or representative* accompany all those participating in official proceedings (including those accused, those serving as witnesses, and those bringing allegations).
- *Appropriate powers in those charged with performing investigations* to have access to all relevant evidence and witnesses. An investigation cannot stand if those charged with establishing relevant facts do not have full access to all relevant evidence and witnesses. This may require subpoena power in some settings.
- *Separation of investigation and adjudication* (i.e. those who perform investigations and make findings of fact should be separated from those who judge the totality of the case and impose sanctions).[1,16]
- *Meaningful consequences* for those who violate standards, for institutions that countenance misconduct, and for any form of retaliation against those who, in good faith, raise questions about the propriety of scientific conduct.
- *The opportunity for appeals.* After a proceeding is complete, there must be at least one opportunity to seek review of the procedures and fairness employed in reaching the conclusions.
- *Timeliness.* Justice delayed is justice denied, so it is essential that the times by which each stage of the investigation and adjudication is to be concluded be specified.

Experience in the USA

Before moving on to precise definitions, it is useful, in understanding the need for a definition and a process, to look at what has happened in the USA. In this section, we will discuss *process* as much as *definition*. We do so because having definitions for what is wrong behaviour must surely imply that allegations will be followed by action. Without such a process, defining acts that are wrong is a meaningless exercise.

In view of the sheer size of the scientific enterprise and research output in the USA, it is perhaps not surprising that it was the first country to see scientific misconduct as a national problem, requiring a national response. The gradual evolution of the idea of misconduct specifically relating to scientific research is well illustrated in the USA, and it is worth our while contrasting this history with the very different history in the UK, despite the fact that no one has ever shown differences in the nature or quality of science or the integrity of scientists between the two countries. The long-drawn-out fight over the definition of research misconduct in the USA provides useful lessons to any other country establishing standards. Moreover, the great gulf between lawyers, accustomed to dealing with misconduct of every sort, and scientists, trained to trust, but verify, is well illustrated in the history of the development of regulations governing research misconduct in the USA.

We have summarized the turbulent history in the USA of scientific fraud during the late 1970s to the year 2001.[17,18] In brief, a few individual cases, occurring usually at prestigious research institutions such as Yale and Harvard, were extensively reported in the media. While the public, who by and large paid for the science, got its collective mind around the idea that scientific degrees did not necessarily guarantee rectitude, the world was treated to the spectacle of venerable institutions and scientific societies in states of confusion and denial, making up their own rules as they went along, in the harsh glare of media attention. The institutional responses were patently idiosyncratic, frequently bungled, sometimes illegal, and often unfair.

Members of the US Congress soon became involved, and started holding public hearings, citing their responsibilities to safeguard the public purse. At the hearings, it soon became clear that there was little common ground between the members of the scientific establishment who were brought in to testify, and the legislators, by and large lawyers, who grilled them. The scientific miscreants on display, and the eminent leaders of the learned societies, together managed to make themselves look recalcitrant and science look bad.

The representatives of the scientific establishment, by making self-interested assertions that the problem was vanishingly rare[19] (assertions for which there was never any evidence, and which every new case plainly showed to be false), achieved the seemingly impossible: making the members of Congress appear to be better scientists than those whom they questioned.

It was obvious to members of the US Congress, nearly half of whom are lawyers, immersed in legalistic thinking, that regulation was required. Scientists argued for self-regulation while each new case undermined that argument, proving to the public that in such an emotional issue, when outsiders threaten to intrude, the professions 'circle the wagons' and have to be forced to do the right thing. It became clear that powerful members of Congress, who read the newspapers and understood the public's indignation at discovering that the scientists whom they funded were not always pure, would intervene to force regulation. They would claim the right to reach into all research organizations receiving government money – which effectively meant all such institutions. In the face of this perceived threat, and to assist the two sides in understanding each other as well as the issues as a prelude to drawing up regulations, two large umbrella organizations, the American Association for the Advancement of Science (AAAS) and the American Bar Association (ABA), set up a series of exploratory meetings in the mid-1980s. In 1989, the first regulations were enacted, and a body set up: the Office of Scientific (later Research) Integrity (OSI, ORI).

The definition of misconduct adopted in 1989, under Congressional pressure, was as follows:[17,20]

> 'Fabrication, falsification, plagiarism or other practices that seriously deviate from those that are commonly accepted within the scientific community for proposing, conducting, or reporting research.'

This definition caused problems for many reasons. Everyone agreed that fabrication, falsification, and plagiarism (FFP) were antithetical to good science. But the phrase 'other practices that seriously deviate' was immediately seized upon by the Federation of American Societies for Experimental Biology (FASEB), who argued that this clause could allow penalties to be applied to novel or breakthrough science. The Federation mobilized its members to remove this phrase completely and limit the definition to FFP.[21] As we noted:[17]

'Underlying the objections to the "other practices that seriously deviate ..." clause is the fear that the vague language will result in application of a vague and misty standard of misconduct that cannot be known in advance. It seems fundamentally unfair to stigmatize someone for behavior they had no way of knowing was wrong. Unhappily, consideration of cases shows that some of the most egregious behaviors, abuse of confidentiality, for example, are not covered by the FF&P label. We cannot have a definition that implies that this sort of behavior is not wrong. Moreover, since we cannot possibly imagine every scenario in advance, the definition must ensure that perpetrators of acts that are deceptive and destructive to science are not exonerated. If they are, the public and our legislators, applying the standards of common sense, will rightly deride the outcome as nonsensical.'

Since the ORI, the government office charged with oversight of scientific integrity within biomedicine (the research field controlled by the US Public Health Service) never invoked the 'other practices ...' clause, but the other large scientific grant-awarding government agency, the National Science Foundation (NSF), did, researchers funded by different government agencies effectively came to be covered by different definitions of research misconduct. In addition, ORI announced that it would not take cases of alleged plagiarism if the authors of a work had been coauthors together. ORI's decision was purely administrative, and designed to reduce the number and complexity of their formidable backlog of cases – not least because such cases proved singularly awkward to sort out. By definition, ORI asserted, all such cases fell into the category of 'authorship disputes', and would not be examined for the elements of plagiarism. NSF never instituted such a policy, and continued to examine cases where students or co-workers alleged that their contributions had been appropriated by another without cause or attribution. No system in which some could have their complaints examined while others could not would succeed for long.

Science is a risky enterprise, often requiring much trial and error. No one could possibly undertake scientific experiments if error was construed as misconduct. As Mishkin[22] has pointed out, 'misconduct' in legal parlance means a *wilful* transgression of some definite rule. Its synonyms include 'misdemeanour', 'misdeed', 'misbehaviour', 'delinquency', 'impropriety', 'mismanagement', and 'offence', *but not 'negligence' or 'carelessness'*.

Distinguishing error from misconduct requires making a judgement about intent. While scientists are often cowed by this necessity, citizens routinely make them in other settings, most notably in an established criminal justice system that employs juries.

It is our opinion that this assessment should be made only at the time of adjudication, after the facts of a case of scientific misconduct have been determined: for example, 'words were copied' or 'no primary data have been produced'. This sequential approach has two salutary effects. First, it reduces the potential that the factual determinations will be obscured by other considerations. The danger otherwise is that – as has frequently happened – a panel's sympathy for the accused ('he's too young, too old, meant well', etc.) interferes with a rigorous analysis of events. Second, this approach introduces proportionality into the response – what, if any, consequence should there be, in light of all the relevant circumstances? This factor is important in the final sense of whether the process 'worked' or not – both for participants and for observers.

The scientific dialogue model

Originally, the ORI tried to keep misconduct proceedings in the hands of scientists rather than lawyers. The 'scientific dialogue model' that they advanced soon came under criticism for being unfair and flawed.[17] Changes were made, and the standards for responding to allegations gradually became more structured and legalistic so that results could withstand scrutiny from administrative tribunals. Defendants, faced by the loss of their livelihoods, hired lawyers to insist on their basic right to fundamental fairness and due process. Most fundamental among these rights are the rights to know and to respond to all evidence to be used against an accused. Unfortunately, these rights were all too easy to overlook while collegiality prevailed ('the scientific dialogue'), and where hard issues were not always faced directly or even-handedly.

The early 1990s: the heat increases

Despite these problems, and the heat that they engendered, in February 1993 we concluded on a note of cautious optimism:[17]

> '... practically everything to do with scientific misconduct is changing rapidly: the definition, the procedures, the law and our attitudes ... It will take time to accumulate a body of experience (a case law, as it were) and to get it right. The challenge is to seize the opportunity, to capitalize on the wealth of accumulating information, and to focus on the long-term goals of strengthening science and the society that depends on it.'

Our optimism was premature. In 1994, despite more than 20 years of widely publicized cases of misconduct, more than a dozen congressional hearings, years of regulations as a result of congressional impatience with science (and layers of modifications to them), and, first, an Office of Scientific Integrity and then of Research Integrity, there remained widespread division and dismay. The definition was still hotly debated, as was the process owed an accused scientist, the extent of federal oversight, how to protect whistleblowers, and how to prevent misconduct. At the same time, in the early 1990s, several high-profile cases were decided against government science agencies and their ways of proceeding.[1]

Asserting that the US Federal Government had an interest in professional misconduct involving the use of federal funds in research and which could affect the public health, a government Commission on Research Integrity (the 'Ryan Commission') was set up to examine the issue. Both of us were members. The Commission recommended that the definition of research misconduct (Box 3.2) should be 'based on the premise that research misconduct is a serious violation of the fundamental principle that scientists be truthful and fair in the conduct of research and the dissemination of its results'.[1] The Commission, which we will henceforth in this section call 'we', strongly recommended the development of a common federal definition of research misconduct and other forms of professional misconduct related to research. With its definitions, we put forward examples within the report (Box 3.2).

BOX 3.2   **US Commission on Research Integrity definitions of misconduct[1]**

1. Research misconduct

Research misconduct is significant misbehavior that improperly appropriates the intellectual property or contributions of others, that intentionally impedes the progress of research, or that risks corrupting the scientific record (the record encompasses any documentation or presentation of research, oral or written, unpublished) or compromising the integrity of scientific practices. Such behaviors are unethical and unacceptable in proposing, conducting, or reporting research or in reviewing the proposals or research reports of others.

Examples of research misconduct include but are not limited to the following:

- *Misappropriation*: An investigator or reviewer shall not intentionally or recklessly
  (a) plagiarize, which shall be understood to mean the presentation of the documented words or ideas of another as his or her own, without attribution appropriate for the medium of presentation; or
  (b) make use of any information in breach of any duty of confidentiality associated with the review of any manuscript or grant application.
- *Interference*: An investigator or reviewer shall not intentionally and without authorization take or sequester or materially damage any research-related property of another, including without limitation the apparatus, reagents, biological materials, writings, data, hardware, software, or any other substance or device used or produced in the conduct of research.
- *Misrepresentation*: An investigator or reviewer shall not with intent to deceive, or in reckless disregard for the truth,
  (a) state or present a material or significant falsehood; or
  (b) omit a fact so that what is stated or presented as a whole states or presents a material or significant falsehood.

2. Other forms of professional misconduct

(a) Obstruction of investigations of research misconduct

The Federal Government has an important interest in protecting the integrity of investigations into reported incidents of research misconduct. Accordingly, obstruction of investigations of research misconduct related to federal funding constitutes a form of professional misconduct in that it undermines the interests of the public, the scientific community, and the Federal Government.

Obstruction of investigations of research misconduct consists of intentionally withholding or destroying evidence in violation of a duty to disclose or preserve; falsifying evidence; encouraging, soliciting or giving false testimony; and attempting to intimidate or retaliate against witnesses, potential witnesses, or potential leads to witnesses or evidence before, during, or after the commencement of any formal or informal proceeding.

(b) Noncompliance with research regulations
Responsible conduct in research includes compliance with applicable federal research regulations. Such regulations include (but are not limited to) those governing the use of biohazardous materials and human and animal subjects in research.

Serious noncompliance with such regulations after notice of their existence undermines the interests of the public, the scientific community, and the Federal Government and constitutes another form of professional misconduct.

By defining the central terms used in the definition of misconduct, we obviated the problem endemic in institutional proceedings in which every investigative panel secured a dictionary and defined for itself key elements upon which its findings depended. This common and understandable impulse all too frequently compromised the integrity of individual misconduct proceedings, as the resulting ad hoc definitions did not pass the 'laugh', let alone the 'red-face', test. In addition to providing a fuller internal definition of plagiarism, our proposed definition explicitly addressed other issues upon which faculty review panels repeatedly stumbled. For example, we incorporated misconduct in reviewing papers or grant applications into the definition of offences outside acceptable professional conduct.

We also researched and then recorded the legal reality in the USA that the 'standard of proof' required in civil proceedings is the 'preponderance of the evidence', not the higher standards of 'clear and convincing' or 'beyond a reasonable doubt'. These issues had derailed many an institutional proceeding and prevented them from reaching a finding. Another very important component of our work was the declaration that, while intent should be a necessary requirement for a finding of fabrication or falsification, a finding of carelessness suffices to support a finding of plagiarism.

We broadened the definition beyond the then-prevailing standard of 'fabrication, falsification, and plagiarism' to include other forms of unethical behaviour not then governed by any specific regulations (Box 3.2). Guided by actual cases, we defined research misconduct as (1) misappropriation (including plagiarism), (2) interference (e.g. tampering with someone else's research), and (3) misrepresentation. In addition, we included categories of lesser misconduct that, while not 'scientific misconduct', still warranted response. These included obstruction of misconduct investigations, retaliation against those participating in investigations, and non-compliance with research regulations. We recognized that, although research institutions might make their own rules, the governmental definition had, after 1989, become de facto the one in general use.

Definitions carry little meaning without effective procedures. In our report, we did not merely define bad acts, but laid out the rights and responsibilities of scientists. We recommended that educational programmes on research integrity should be required in institutions receiving federal money. We wanted, first, to ensure that information about good professional conduct be provided as a fundamental element of education; secondly, to make discussion of these matters more common and less threatening; thirdly, to make it possible for the powerless to ask questions; and, finally, to make it harder for the clever sociopath to slide by. We recommended that there be 'funding for scholarship, teaching, and research in science ethics. Such funded research should include an experimental audit of the prevalence of data misrepresentation.' We also recommended that 'professional societies each adopt a code of ethics in research' and initiate 'activities that will further promote the ethical conduct of research and professionalism in science'.[1]

Recognizing that whistleblowers provide an important quality control mechanism in science, and mindful of the numerous examples of abuse of whistleblowers who had brought forward well-founded allegations, we set forth a detailed statement of principles – 'Responsible Whistleblowing: A Whistleblower's Bill of Rights' – in which we spelled out the rights and responsibilities of whistleblowers, of the accused and of their institutions.[1] For further discussion of whistleblowing, see Chapter 15.

Based upon our collective experience, the testimony presented at our meetings, our research, and information presented by commissioned papers, we made a number of recommendations about how misconduct proceedings should be conducted. For example, we advised that investigation and subsequent adjudication should always be separated organizationally; that 'legal, law-enforcement, and scientist-investigator staff participate in each federally conducted investigation and ensure that scientists participate in hearings and appeal procedures'; that 'those conducting investigations have subpoena power over persons and documents'; and that 'authorship or collaborative' disputes (those previously dismissed by the ORI, for administrative reasons) should be addressed by institutions and by federal funding agencies.

While our proposals protected institutional decisions from second-guessing if based on properly conducted procedures, they recognized the built-in conflicts that institutions can face when investigating their own scientists, some of whom might be influential and bring in large amounts of money. We proposed 'widespread, systematic public disclosure of all outcomes of federal research and research-related professional misconduct cases, with detailed, specific statements of their rationale, in view of the strong public interest in the disclosure of information underlying such cases'.[1]

We articulated the elements required for fair process, by articulating the various interests at stake in these proceedings – including those of the accused, whistleblowers, witnesses, and funding agencies. We recommended internal checks and balances throughout, even for the federal agencies providing the funding for research. We suggested approaches for streamlining processes, made numerous recommendations to improve the effective oversight of institutional performance, and broadened the array of sanctions that could be applied against those found guilty of misconduct, and against institutions failing to carry out investigations properly.

The reaction

While the Commission's report was characterized by a disinterested observer, the editor of the *Lancet*, as 'a superb piece of analysis',[23] and many academics pronounced themselves content with the Commission's definition,[24] it met with widespread condemnation by the leaders of the scientific establishment. Although the Commission consisted largely of scientists (as well as ethicists, administrators, and lawyers), the reaction from the scientific elite in the USA was immediate, loud, defensive, dismissive, confused, and self-contradictory. Given that the reaction was in response to a careful report based on the articulated 'fundamental principle that scientists should be truthful and fair in the conduct of research and the dissemination of research results', this reaction seemed at times hysterical. The President of the Federation of American Societies for Experimental Biology (FASEB) wrote to the Secretary for Health and Human Services that the 'Commission's report is so seriously flawed that it is useless as a basis for policy making and should be disavowed … we find the definition to be unworkable, and therefore unacceptable.'[25] He was quoted in the press as calling the report 'an attack on American science'.[23] The same letter objected to what was called an expansion of the definition of plagiarism, even though the Commission had been guided in its definition by the Academy's own report, *Responsible Science*,[6] a report that the latter strongly endorsed.

The leadership of the National Academy of Sciences (NAS) also wrote a letter criticizing the Commission report. While acknowledging that the Commission 'repeatedly states that the primary investigative responsibility rests with the research institutions',[26] it brushed these statements aside in raising the bogeyman of a vast expansion of an intrusive federal bureaucracy if the Commission's recommendations were to be implemented. The NAS nowhere acknowledged that it was the abject failure of many research institutions to respond appropriately to allegations of misconduct that led to the Commission's original formation by Congress. The NAS failed to say that the report called for government agencies to investigate allegations only in certain very limited circumstances: in cases involving more than one institution, or where the institution had not conducted a proper investigation.[27] Nor did it note that the government already has such an oversight role, which would, if anything, be diminished if the Commission's recommendations were followed.

In hindsight, what was most threatening in the Commission Report was the 'Whistleblower's Bill of Rights'.[1] The Commission was accused of failing to 'protect adequately the rights of scientists who are accused of misconduct'. Yet what moved the Commission was not the rights of scientists who were accused, who already had excellent protections, but the plight of accusers who blew the whistle in good faith, and who were later proved right, but who suffered considerable harm, often from the guilty and their institution. The Commission had heard testimony from a great many in this position.

Perhaps the most persistent, peculiar, and revealing criticism of the report, and, indeed, of any proposed regulation, was the continuing allegation that regulation would impede scientific progress because truly original science might easily be labelled misconduct. In hundreds, even thousands of cases, this has never happened.

Finally, some scientists still claimed that, because science is 'self-correcting', no rules were necessary. The corollary of this position is that it does not matter if the record is never put right. In the medical field alone, however, the truth is that much science is never replicated, and this assertion says nothing about the costs – institutional and human – imposed by gross fraud, the loss of morale among co-workers, the anger on the part of the public and politicians, and the outrage of the media.

Our report grew out of the failures of the past, including the failure of the 1989 government definition to stand up to legal challenge and to work effectively when applied to real cases. The vehemence of the reaction to the report, which proposed that scientists should be truthful and fair, and which was crafted to make it work in the real world of research and of lawyers, was telling. So was its widespread misrepresentation. Upon reflection, we conclude that this must stem from the fact that few of the scientists who objected had much experience in dealing with allegations of misconduct. Together, they suggest that scientists continue to feel threatened by the spectre that malicious allegations might be brought against them. Above all, objecting scientists failed to grasp the fact that, in this real world, legal challenges dominate the field, and that, in response to these realities, the Commission introduced precision – which in turn provides protections for those involved in misconduct proceedings, most especially the accused scientist.

The US government-wide regulations of December 2000

During the ensuing five years, cases occurred and were reported in the media, and were summarized in regular reports from the ORI and the NSF. Gradually, as the media, the public, and the profession realized that the system was working in a routine and reasonably efficient manner, the heat died down. Meanwhile, the administration embarked on the lengthy process of making common regulations that would govern all types of research, not just those in biomedicine.

On 6 December 2000, after a two-month public comment period, the Clinton administration issued the new, government-wide regulations defining research misconduct and laying down the rules for investigation and adjudication of allegations of misconduct concerning research done with US federal funds (Box 3.3).[28] Since all important universities and research institutions receive such funds, these regulations have become institutional rules, although institutions are allowed to have their own additional rules if they wish to impose a higher internal standard.

We strongly believe that they should. And we say this because the new definition, confining itself to 'fabrication, falsification, or plagiarism in proposing, performing, or reviewing research, or in reporting research results', leaves out many actions that we find destructive of good science, and which are not covered by other laws. We were both involved in assessing one case in which a junior investigator had sequestered irreplaceable data and materials from her colleagues – an action that would not be judged to be scientific or research misconduct by the new regulations, although common sense would tell us that the investigator's conduct in the performance of research was wrong and damaging to science. We are troubled, then, that by making the definition too narrow, other egregious behaviours might seem to be condoned. It would send the worst possible signal if the academic community were to conclude that such behaviour – by default – was acceptable.

This new definition is again appropriately silent on prolonged non-compliance with other research regulations, such as the unethical treatment of human research subjects

---

BOX 3.3   **Extract from US Federal Policy on Research Misconduct**[a,28]

I. Research[b] misconduct defined

Research misconduct is defined as fabrication, falsification, or plagiarism in pro-posing, performing, or reviewing research, or in reporting research results.

- Fabrication is making up data or results and recording or reporting them.
- Falsification is manipulating research materials, equipment, or processes, or changing or omitting data or results such that the research is not accurately represented in the research record.[c]
- Plagiarism is the appropriation of another person's ideas, processes, results, or words without giving appropriate credit.
- Research misconduct does not include honest error or differences of opinion.

II. Findings of research misconduct

A finding of research misconduct requires that:

- There be a significant departure from accepted practices of the relevant research community; and
- The misconduct be committed intentionally, or knowingly, or recklessly; and
- The allegation be proven by a preponderance of evidence.

[a]No rights, privileges, benefits or obligations are created or abridged by issuance of this policy alone. The creation or abridgment of rights, privileges, benefits or obligations, if any, shall occur only upon implementation of this policy by the Federal agencies.

[b]Research, as used herein, includes all basic, applied, and demonstration research in all fields of science, engineering, and mathematics. This includes, but is not limited to, research in economics, education, linguistics, medicine, psychology, social sciences, statistics, and research involving human subjects or animals.

[c]The research record is the record of data or results that embody the facts resulting from scientific inquiry, and includes, but is not limited to, research proposals, laboratory records, both physical and electronic, progress reports, abstracts, theses, oral presentations, internal reports, and journal articles.

---

or mistreatment of laboratory animals used in research, because there are already regulations governing these problems. And again, the new regulations do not super-sede criminal or other civil laws that have nothing to do with the faithful reporting of good science (e.g. laws on sexual harassment).

The new rules drew extensively from the Commission Report. From the incorpo-ration of interior definitions of critical terms and of states of mind for offences, to articulation of necessary procedural safeguards, the Report provided the rationale. We strongly recommend that anyone interested in the formulation of adequate insti-tutional responses to allegations of research misconduct, read both the Commission Report and the US government regulations of December 2000.

Lessons from the US experience

It took 20 years to achieve a set of widely accepted regulations in the USA. In the hope that examination and understanding of this experience might prevent a great deal of 'reinvention of wheels', we shall summarize here what we believe to be the essential elements. First, however, let us consider the *catalysts*:

- Repeated dramatic incidents resulting in publicity showing that research institutions operated in ignorance, denial, and cover-up; and there was recurrent shaming of institutions in the media (this is the present position in the UK and most other countries).
- A few powerful politicians, highly sceptical of the research establishment's reassurances that all was well, repeatedly exposing how thin these reassurances were, pushing for regulation, and, finally, exasperated by the do-nothing approach of science, forcing regulation tied to the continuance of federal research funds.
- Numerous meetings attended by representatives of science, lawyers, administrators, and legislators.
- The establishment of oversight offices predicated on the assumption that research misconduct was basically a clinical research problem. Followed by a gradual realization that misconduct can occur in every branch of research, from mathematics to the humanities, and that administering its regulations would be much easier if all researchers were governed by the same rules.
- Learning from experiment and hard experience. The 'scientific model' did not work when the unfairness and illegality of the process were exposed (usually by lawyers or journalists). Scientists had to learn that processes for appeal were necessary, and that investigation and adjudication should be separated. Gradually a case law built up, and the process was absorbed into those of administrative law.[16,29,30]
- Greater education all round. Everyone concerned came to realize that it is beneficial to ensure that students – no matter who their mentor is – receive certain baseline information about good practice, and that, because scientists are mortals, it made sense to have processes in place to deal efficiently and routinely with those who strayed.

What factors hold reform back? Professional societies

Constantly retarding the process of reform are several factors. Many distinguished scientists cannot accept that scientific misconduct can occur until it happens near them and they have to deal with it. More generally, it seems to be a human trait to seek power without accountability, so scientific organizations can be expected to oppose almost all regulation, including any amendment to even previously condemned regulations.

As an example, some bullfighters in Spain routinely shave the horns of the bulls that they face – sometimes by as much as five inches – to reduce their risk of injury, as this shaving impairs the weaponry, vision, and balance of the bull. It is well known that this occurs, and it is regarded as wrong. But when the Spanish government proposed a system of examinations to detect irregularities, the bullfighters went on strike, saying that they should be trusted to regulate themselves.[31] This example illustrates a general issue, and merely points out that professional societies cannot be relied upon to remedy the problem – indeed, they and their prominent representatives have often made it worse. They rarely have the backbone to take effective actions to discipline their members. Indeed, even if they wish to, they lack the legal power to do so. In the case of science, there are so many such societies in so many disciplines that it makes little sense to approach the problem of research misconduct in this way.

We would all like our professions to behave in a way that, to most of us, would define professionalism – that is, to regulate themselves effectively. But our experience with scientific misconduct in the USA shows us that, as with bullfighters in Spain, there must be some higher body to force regulation upon researchers. We can expect that nothing much will happen in countries without effective systems in place, and change will occur only when the pain and shame of bad publicity becomes unbearable. Professional societies and large research institutions react defensively when this subject is raised, circling the wagons, and obfuscating the issue. They will go to great lengths to prevent outside government intervention, maintaining that there is no problem; that they have the problem well in hand; that the problem must be left in their hands, as others do not understand it; that the motives of outsiders are malicious and, no matter how constructive, constitute an 'attack on science'; and that research misconduct is too ineffable a construct to be pinned down in words by bureaucrats. Finally, they tend to assert that a model that focuses entirely on education and prevention, but is toothless when it comes to regulating actual misconduct, will make the problem go away, thus satisfying the press, the public, the politicians, and their fellow professionals. If left to professional societies, effective governance of research misconduct is unlikely to occur.

The UK

The Committee on Publication Ethics (COPE)

Editors are the first to see complete reports of investigations, and they put their journals' reputations behind what they publish. They are often the first people to be contacted when questions arise about the honesty of articles, and the ones expected to deal with the problem. Perhaps that is why those who have pushed for effective regulation in the UK are largely medical editors such as Richard Smith and Fiona Godlee of the *BMJ*, and Richard Horton of the *Lancet* (all prominent founder-members of the Committee on Publication Ethics, COPE), as well as the editors of this book, Michael Farthing and Frank Wells.[32] COPE is an extraordinarily effective organization, and has earned worldwide respect for the forthright way in which its members have tried to face up to the many ethical problems editors encounter. Its very success, however, has drawn attention to its limitations. It is largely an organization of clinical editors; and it has no power to mandate any definition of misconduct, secure evidence, or investigate, adjudicate and sanction serious misconduct. Various definitions of misconduct put forward by COPE are shown in Box 3.4.[33]

BOX 3.4   **Extracts from the Committee on Publication Ethics (COPE) guidelines on good publication practice**[33]

Study design and ethical approval – definition

Good research should be well justified, well planned, appropriately designed, and ethically approved. To conduct research to a lower standard may constitute misconduct.

Data analysis – definition

Data should be appropriately analysed, but inappropriate analysis does not necessarily amount to misconduct. Fabrication and falsification of data do constitute misconduct.

Authorship – definition

There is no universally agreed definition of authorship, although attempts have been made. As a minimum, authors should take responsibility for a particular section of the study.

Plagiarism – definition

Plagiarism ranges from the unreferenced use of others' published and unpublished ideas, including research grant applications, to submission under 'new' authorship of a complete paper, sometimes in a different language. It may occur at any stage of planning, research, writing, or publication; it applies to print and electronic versions.

Dealing with misconduct –principles

1. The general principle confirming misconduct is the intention to cause others to regard as true that which is not true.
2. The examination of misconduct must therefore focus, not only on the particular act or omission, but also on the intention of the researcher, author, editor, reviewer, or publisher involved.
3. Deception may be by intention, by reckless disregard of possible consequences, or by negligence. It is implicit, therefore, that 'best practice' requires complete honesty, with full disclosure.
4. Codes of practice may raise awareness, but can never be exhaustive.

The Joint Consensus Conference of 1999 Statement

In October 1999, 10 years after the USA had formally adopted regulations, a groundbreaking meeting was held in Edinburgh to debate the issue. In the words of its Consensus Statement:

> 'Patients benefit not only from good quality care but also from good scientific research. We all expect high standards of scientific and medical research practice. The integrity, probity, skill and trustworthiness of scientific and medical researchers are essential if public confidence is to be assured. In the design and execution of biomedical and healthcare research, public

participation is essential. The Joint Consensus Conference on Misconduct in Biomedical Research was convened in order to debate, address and offer guidance on key questions because "every single case [of fraud and misconduct] reduces public confidence, abuses the use of public and charitable funds, and causes insult and frustration to the vast majority of careful, honest workers".'[34]

To understand the difficulties in deciding on a workable definition of research misconduct, it is useful to look at the one proposed in Edinburgh:

> 'Behaviour by a researcher, intentional or not, that falls short of good ethical and scientific standards.
>
> No definition can or should attempt to be exhaustive. It should allow for change. The definition should not be read as being restricted to fabrication, falsification of data and plagiarism. It is intended to cover the whole range of research misconduct.'

This definition was doomed from the start. While it was an important evolutionary step for the UK, it fails as a definition in almost every respect. It is not universal, since it was developed in a closed meeting, where the principal interest was in clinical research, so the broad base and lengthy discussion necessary for useful consensus were never achieved. It was not official, having no mandate and no legal powers to make its recommendations happen.

Moreover, it is not specific, nor does it provide clear guidance on the meaning of its critical terms. Indeed, it is so vague, non-specific, and all-encompassing that it is unworkable. What are 'good ethical standards'? In which field? In what circumstances? By whose judgement? There are whole areas of research – for example, research on stem cells, or on aborted fetuses – where ethical scientists hold strongly divergent opinions about 'good' standards. Worst of all, the definition includes unintentional behaviour that falls short of good scientific standards. If this sort of thing is misconduct, how could anyone ever dare to attempt science? In addition, the statement that the definition 'is intended to cover the whole range of research misconduct' is circular.

As to 'clear and fair process', although the specifics of handling accusations of misconduct are essential ingredients of any successful system, the Consensus Report says little or nothing specific about procedures, so most of the elements necessary for a useful system are undefined or absent. The US experience illustrates that getting the process right matters as much as having the right definition. In fact, one could posit that the low-key acceptance of the US Government definition of 2000 is rooted as much in the growing comfort that proceedings – if never pleasant – are not unfair or biased by design. Much can be learned from the US experience with process, both by those with institutional responsibilities and by those who are caught in a specific situation.[16,29,30]

The UK Medical Research Council and the Wellcome Trust

The US Congress had shown that a fail-safe way to attract everyone's attention and trump professional obfuscation is to link professional and institutional compliance to funding. All institutions receiving government money had to adopt the government definition and process of investigation and adjudication as conditions of funding. While free to set up additional requirements and standards for their own researchers, few research institutions went to the trouble of devising extra rules, so the government regulations for research conducted with government money effectively became the universal regulations.

This seems to have been the approach of the powerful funders of research in the UK – the Medical Research Council (MRC) and the Wellcome Trust – who have used their financial clout to dictate institutional policy. The MRC published standards in 1997 (Box 3.5) and the Wellcome Trust, the largest research funder in the UK, published its Statement on the Handling of Allegations of Research Misconduct in 2002 (modifying it in 2005) (Box 3.6). It is clear that both borrowed heavily from the definition developed in the USA.

The UK Research Integrity Office (UKRIO) and other countries

In 2006, the UK began setting up a body, the UK Research Integrity Office (UKRIO), to try to address the issue of research misconduct.[5] We, and others, have recommended a move like this for many years.[18,35] Despite the strenuous efforts of clinical editors there, the UK is nearly two decades behind the USA and Scandinavia in introducing this sort of initiative.[2] The lessons repeatedly being played out across the globe, for example in the falsifications associated with some stem cell research in South Korea, are that countries without robust systems governing research misconduct already in place doom their entire research community to confusion and loss of credibility when incidents occur.

BOX 3.5   **Extract from UK MRC Policy and Procedure for Inquiring into Allegations of Scientific Misconduct**[a,b]

Annex, Item 2.11: Scientific misconduct or misconduct means fabrication, falsification, plagiarism or deception in proposing, carrying out or reporting results of research and deliberate, dangerous or negligent deviations from accepted practice in carrying out research. It includes failure to follow established protocols if this failure results in unreasonable risk or harm to humans, other vertebrates or the environment and facilitating of misconduct of research by collusion in, or concealment of, such action by others.

It does not include honest error or honest differences in the design, execution, interpretation or judgment in evaluating research methods or results or misconduct (including gross misconduct) unrelated to the research process.

[a]Statement by the Medical Research Council, London, 1997.
[b]Under Item 1.2 ('Scope'), it is made clear that these policies and procedures apply only to those working for the MRC at the time of the allegations.

BOX 3.6 **Extract from Wellcome Trust definition of research misconduct (2002, modified 2005)**[a]

1.1 'Research misconduct' is defined by the Trust as:

> The fabrication, falsification, plagiarism or deception in proposing, carrying out or reporting results of research or deliberate, dangerous or negligent deviations from accepted practices in carrying out research. It includes failure to follow established protocols if this failure results in unreasonable risk or harm to humans, other vertebrates or the environment and facilitating of misconduct in research by collusion in, or concealment of, such actions by others. It also includes intentional, unauthorised use, disclosure or removal of, or damage to, research-related property of another, including apparatus, materials, writings, data, hardware or software or any other substances or devices used in or produced by the conduct of research.

1.2 It does not include honest error or honest differences in the design, execution, interpretation or judgement in evaluating research methods or results or misconduct unrelated to the research process. Similarly it does not include poor research unless this encompasses the intention to deceive.[b]

[a]In formulating these guidelines, the Trust has drawn on the Medical Research Council's Ethics Series, in particular *Good Research Practice* (December 2000) and *Policy and Procedure for Inquiring into Allegations of Scientific Misconduct* (December 1997) and the General Medical Council's *Good Practice in Medical Research* (2002). It has also been informed by the *Joint Consensus Conference on Misconduct in Biomedical Research*, Royal College of Physicians of Edinburgh (January 2000) and the Biotechnology and Biological Sciences Research Council's 'Statement on Safeguarding Good Scientific Practice'.
[b]Based on the definitions given in the MRC's *Policy and Procedure for Inquiring into Allegations of Scientific Misconduct* (December 1997) and the GMC's report *Good Practice in Medical Research* (2002).

Conclusions

In this chapter, using the long and extensively documented US experience, we have argued for a clear and universal definition of research misconduct. We have described how definition and process are interwoven, and that the political fights that have occurred are the inevitable battles that take place when a profession asserts that it can govern itself while at the same time demonstrating to the public, who pay the bills, that it is unable to do so. The US definition of research misconduct is truncated and flawed. It is our opinion that when the scientific societies narrowed the definition to include only fabrication, falsification, and plagiarism (FFP), they made a serious mistake. That being said, the US definition, together with a clear process that has been tested in the courts, allows routine, prompt, and fair handling of cases and the assurance that bad actors will be held accountable.

As cases of bad scientific behaviour are reported from every country where the research enterprise goes forward, it should be no surprise that institutions and countries are scurrying around to try to invent definitions for themselves. A good start would be for them to conduct a careful examination of the experience of others, such as the USA, and to look at their definitions. In particular, we believe that it would be useful to emulate the definitions recommended in the report of the Commission on Research Integrity.[1] Every country that sets up its own definition has to ask itself how the physical laws of science and scientific practice should differ across national boundaries – and if they do not, why universal definitions should not apply.

References

1. Commission on Research Integrity. *Integrity and Misconduct in Research: Report of the Commission on Research Integrity*. Washington, DC: US Department of Health and Human Services, Public Health Service, 1995.
2. Nylenna M, Andersen, D, Dahlquist G et al. Handling of scientific dishonesty in the Nordic countries. National Committees on Scientific Dishonesty in the Nordic Countries. *Lancet* 1999; **354**: 57–61.
3. Sudbø Case: Norwegian Institute of Public Health Warning, 23 January 2006.
4. Hallen A. *Responsible Research*. Research Council of Norway, 2006.
5. The UK Panel for Research Integrity in Health and Biomedical Sciences (UKRIO). *Code of Practice for Research*. London: The UK Research Integrity Office, 2008.
6. National Academy of Sciences, National Academy of Engineering, and Institute of Medicine. *Responsible Science: Ensuring the Integrity of the Research Process*. Volumes 1 and 2. Washington, DC: National Academy Press, 1992/93.
7. Gunsalus CK. Rethinking unscientific attitudes about scientific misconduct. *Chron High Educ*, March 28, 1997, B4.
8. Sox HC, Rennie D. Research misconduct, retraction, and cleansing the medical literature: lessons from the Poehlman case. *Ann Intern Med* 2006; **144**: 609–13.
9. Gunsalus CK. Paper presented at Symposium on Integrity and Misconduct in Science, held at the Annual Meeting of the American Association for the Advancement of Science, Chicago, IL, 6 February 1992.
10. Smith J, Godlee F. Investigating allegations of scientific misconduct. *BMJ* 2005; **331**: 245–6.
11. White C. Suspected research fraud: difficulties of getting at the truth. *BMJ* 2005; **331**: 281–8.
12. Smith R. Investigating the previous studies of a fraudulent author. *BMJ* 2005; **331**: 288–91.
13. White C. Three journals raise doubts on validity of Canadian studies. *BMJ* 2004; **328**: 67.
14. Chalmers I. Role of systematic reviews in detecting plagiarism: case of Asim Kurjak. *BMJ* 2006; **333**: 594–6.
15. Kmietowicz Z. University drops case against Croatian academic accused of plagiarism. *BMJ* 2007; **335**: 1014.
16. Gunsalus CK. Institutional structure to ensure research integrity. *Acad Med* 1993; **68**(9 Suppl): S33–8.

17. Rennie D, Gunsalus CK. Scientific misconduct. New definition, procedures, and office – perhaps a new leaf. *JAMA* 1993; **269**: 915–17.

18. Rennie D. An American perspective on research integrity. *BMJ* 1998; **316**: 1726–8.

19. United States Congress. House Committee on Science and Technology. Subcommittee on Investigations and Oversight. *Fraud in Biomedical Research. Hearings Before the Subcommittee on Investigations and Oversight of the Committee on Science and Technology, U.S. House of Representatives, Ninety-seventh Congress, First Session, March 31, April 1, 1981.* Washington, DC: US Government Printing Office, 1981.

20. US Department of Health and Human Services, Public Health Service. Responsibilities of awardee and applicant institutions for dealing with and reporting possible misconduct in science: final rule. *Fed Regist* 1989; **54**: 32446–51.

21. Schachman HK. What is misconduct in science? *Science* 1993; **261**: 148–9.

22. Mishkin B. The investigation of scientific misconduct: some observations and suggestions. *New Biol* 1991; **3**: 8213.

23. Goodman B. Scientists are split over finding of Research Integrity Commission. *Scientist* 1996: **1**.

24. Kaiser J. Commission proposes new definition of misconduct. *Science* 1995; **269**: 1811.

25. Bradshaw RA. Letter to Secretary of Health and Human Services, Donna Shalala, 4 January 1996. Bethesda: Federation of American Societies for Experimental Biology, 1996.

26. Alberts B, Council of the National Academy of Sciences. Letter from the Council of the National Academy of Sciences to William Raub, Science Advisor, Department of Health and Human Services, 15 March, 1996. Washington DC: National Academy of Sciences, 1996.

27. Ryan KJ. Scientific misconduct in perspective: the need to improve accountability. *Chron High Educ* 1997; B: 1.

28. Office of Science and Technology Policy, Executive Office of the President. Federal Policy on Research Misconduct. *Fed Regist* 2000; **65**: 76260–4.

29. Gunsalus CK, Preventing the need for whistleblowing: practical advice for university administrators. *Sci Eng Ethics* 1998; **4**: 51–64.

30. Gunsalus CK. How to blow the whistle and still have a career afterwards. *Sci Eng Ethics* 1998; **4**: 75–94.

31. Selsky A. Threatened walkout by Spain's matadors leaves bewilderment. *Houston Chronicle* Saturday 1 March, 1997: 26.

32. Farthing M. *The Birth of the Committee on Publication Ethics.* London: BMJ Books, 1998.

33. Committee on Publication Ethics (COPE). Guidelines on good publication practice. *J Postgrad Med* 2000; **46**: 217–21.

34. Chantler C, Chantler S. Deception: difficulties and initiatives. *BMJ* 1998; **316**: 1731–2.

35. Farthing M, Horton R, Smith R. UK's failure to act on research misconduct. *Lancet* 2000; **356**: 2030.

SECTION 2

THE HISTORICAL ASPECTS OF RESEARCH MISCONDUCT

4 An interpretive history of research misconduct policy in the USA and Canada

Nicholas H Steneck

Introduction

US policy makers have been grappling with research misconduct for nearly 30 years, and Canadian policy makers for about 20. The problems each have faced along the way – episodes of major violations of accepted research practices, public criticism of lax government oversight, researchers' objections to government intervention – have been much the same. The similarities notwithstanding, the two countries have taken different approaches to finding solutions and setting policy.

This summary of events in the USA and Canada both describes and critiques. The opening sections cover four major periods in US policy development: (1) pre-policy (1981–85); (2) policy development (1985–93); (3) policy refinement (1993–2000); and (4) policy implementation (2000 onwards). The dates are approximate and the periods merge into one another. The next section covers events in Canada leading up to and following the 1994 *Tri-Council Policy Statement: Integrity in Research and Scholarship*. The final section compares the US and Canadian experiences, with the goal of suggesting ways to make research misconduct policy more effective.

Pre-policy period (1981–85)

US efforts to develop research misconduct policy can be traced to reports of a number of prominent cases in the late 1970s. In response in August 1981, Senator Albert Gore Jr opened hearings on *Fraud in Biomedical Research* and in so doing began the US debate on the significance and proper response to research misconduct.[1]

During the hearings and through most of the subsequent history of research misconduct policy, two key questions have dominated most discussions:

1. How common is research misconduct?
2. Can researchers effectively monitor their own behaviour?

Researchers and the agencies that fund them argued at the 1981 hearing that misconduct is rare and kept under control through self-regulation. Critics of the research establishment felt otherwise, arguing that the few reported cases were merely the tip of a much larger iceberg.

The differences of opinion that emerged in 1981 and that persist to this day are not surprising. By 1980, regulations regarding the use of animal (1960s) and human (1970s) subjects in experiments had already been adopted. The prospect of yet more government regulation was not welcomed by a community that valued its independence. Likewise, by the 1980s, critics had reason to question the integrity of research, beginning with its role in the Cold War and the environmental problems of the 1960s, and including major ethical breaches, such as the infamous Tuskegee experiments. More was at stake in the debate over research misconduct than the few cases that were widely discussed in the press and popular books, such as *Betrayers of the Truth*.[2]

While the divisions may not be surprising, the approach taken to policy making is. Centuries ago, the commitment to rigorous, evidence-based reasoning became the main, identifying characteristic of the disciplines the shaped the growth and professionalization of research. However, when asked for advice about how to respond to misconduct, researchers repeatedly relied on opinion and personal experience rather than evidence. Throughout the long history of the debate over research misconduct, well-meaning 'experts' have tirelessly argued that 'research misconduct is rare', without questioning whether this view has any grounding in evidence.

The evidence available in the early 1980s for judging the prevalence of research misconduct was admittedly mixed. Some early surveys reported alarmingly high rates of misconduct: 32% in one case.[3] However, these surveys did not control for duplicate reporting, did not provide clear definitions, and generally had low response rates. Their conclusions about prevalence, therefore, could reasonably be dismissed. However, the fact that many researchers (50% in the Tangney study) said that they did not report suspected misconduct should have at least cast doubt on whether the few confirmed cases could be relied on to estimate prevalence.[3] But the curiosity and scepticism that is supposed to motivate researchers did not extend to their own behaviour. They did, however, take other steps to respond to research misconduct.

In response to the growing number of reported cases, research institutions slowly developed policies that defined unacceptable behaviour as well as procedures for responding to suspected misconduct. A few professional societies, such as the Association of American Colleges and the Association of American Universities, issued reports on ways to respond.[4,5] A few universities, such as the University of Michigan, took steps to plan for investigations and to promote integrity before any misconduct was reported.[6] More often, institutional policies were developed after the fact.

Overall, these efforts did not achieve the level of accountability that a few prominent members of Congress, such as Representative John Dingell of Michigan, were seeking. After one attempt at legislation, vetoed by President Ronald Reagan in 1984, Congress passed the Health Research Extension Act of 1985. This Act required the Secretary of Health and Human Services (HHS) to develop procedures for investigating research misconduct and to require research institutions (1) to provide assurance that they had adopted 'an administrative process to review reports of scientific fraud in connection with biomedical and or behavioral research at or sponsored by' them and (2) to report 'to the Secretary any investigation of alleged scientific fraud which appears substantial'.[7] With the passage of this Act, the period of active research misconduct policy development in the USA commenced.

Policy development (1985–93)

Under the US system of government, the Legislative Branch (Congress, made up of the House and Senate) sets broad legislative agendas and passes laws, which the Executive Branch (the Office of the President and its subordinate departments and independent agencies) then implements and enforces. (The third branch of government, the Judiciary, interprets laws and intervenes in disagreements between the Legislative and Executive Branches.) The Health Research Extension Act of 1985 established the end points that Congress was seeking, but left the details to the relevant departments and agencies. As is so often the case in making key public policy decisions, working out the details proved to be the difficult part of the job. The difficulties in this case stemmed from several different sources.

First, the problems resolving old cases and the appearance of several new cases in 1987 placed pressure on HHS, the specific focus of the Health Research Extension Act, to respond quickly. The most troublesome old case was that of Harvard researcher, John Darsee, which was used by National Institutes of Health (NIH) researchers Walter Stewart and Ned Feder to challenge the ability of science to police itself.[8] Delay and controversy over the publication of Stewart and Feder's analysis assured continued Congressional interest in a quick resolution. So did two new cases that were reported and widely discussed in 1987. One involved Nobel laureate David Baltimore and became widely known as the 'Baltimore case', even though Theresa Imanishi-Kari was the person accused of misconduct.[9,10] The second was that of AIDS researcher Robert Gallo, in which some of the actions Gallo took in claiming credit for the discovery of the AIDS virus were directly challenged.[11,12]

Second, the prospect of more government regulation mobilized a new force that policy makers had to contend with: anti-regulation members of the research community, who closely monitored every development with an eye toward limiting government authority. Congress wanted assurance that researchers suspected of fraud did not continue to receive public funding until the charges were resolved; researchers urged the presumption of innocence and complete confidentiality until any charges were proven. One small skirmish in the battle over regulation was fought over a system (ALERT) that the NIH initiated in 1981 to enable programme officers to check agency records for suspected misconduct before issuing awards. The system was broadened in 1987 to include all HHS research, but was greatly limited in the early 1990s after considerable objection from the research community.[13]

Finally, the most difficult problem that the USA has faced in developing a comprehensive research misconduct policy is the complexity for funding and regulating research. Immediately after the Second World War, policy makers considered unifying US science policy under a central science organization with significant public representation. However, under the guiding hand of the wartime science advisor Vannevar Bush, the USA ultimately adopted a decentralized system that spread research funding across more than a dozen federal agencies and left many key decisions about priorities and funding in the hands of scientists. Developing a system that protects the public's investment in research from unprofessional research practices within this decentralized research establishment has not been an easy task.

As the target of the 1985 legislation, HHS responded quickly. Three years before Congress acted, the Assistant Secretary of Health (ASH) had directed the NIH 'to coordinate the development of policies and procedures for dealing with research misconduct and related activities'. The year after the 1985 Health Revitalization Act was passed, the NIH issued policies and procedures for dealing with 'possible misconduct', in the process establishing a basic framework for addressing research misconduct that has been followed ever since.[14] The key elements of this framework include:

- a basic definition organized around – but in the early policies not limited to – fabrication, falsification, and plagiarism (FFP)
- authority based on the right of government to intervene in activities that it conducts, regulates, or, most importantly, *funds*
- dependence on research institutions to take primary responsibility for responding to reports of misconduct and promoting integrity in research
- a phased approach to investigation and adjudication that protects the rights and privacy of both the accused and the accuser.

With this framework, which stressed the importance of 'high ethical standards in research' and the need 'to investigate and resolve promptly and fairly all instances of alleged or apparent misconduct', HHS policy makers hoped that they had developed an appropriate response to Congressional concerns.

However, one key issue in the 1986 NIH report left the door open to further Congressional prodding – the issue of administrative responsibility. The NIH proposed to assign responsibility for implementing its policy to 'Misconduct Policy Officers' (MPR), stressing that this designation 'need not entail creation or change in title of a position provided the functions described in this issuance can be appropriately discharged'.[14] It further proposed that all responsibilities should be assigned to the Deputy Director for Extramural Research and Training, and expected research institutions to delegate authority to an existing institutional official. Congress, however, had other ideas. In 1988, Representatives Dingell and Henry Waxman circulated drafts of a bill that would have required HHS to establish a new office to handle all aspects of research misconduct and perhaps even do investigations.[13] Before Congress could act, Assistant Secretary for Health James Mason took the lead, establishing two new offices: the Office of Scientific Integrity (OSI) in the NIH and the Office of Scientific Integrity Review (OSIR) in the Public Health Service (PHS)*.[15] In so doing, the PHS established the precedent for assigning misconduct and integrity issues to separate offices.

---

*The PHS currently includes the Agency for Healthcare Research and Quality, the Agency for Toxic Substances and Disease Registry, the Centers for Disease Control and Prevention, the Food and Drug Administration, the Health Resources and Services Administration, the Indian Health Service, the NIH, and the Substance Abuse and Mental Health Services Administration, and the offices of the Regional Health Administrators.

HHS policy decisions had no necessary bearing on other agencies, and most of the latter chose to continue to deal with misconduct largely on an ad hoc basis. The one exception to this rule was the National Science Foundation (NSF), which adopted a similar definition and principles but opted for a different model for administrative responsibility. Instead of establishing a new office to deal with misconduct investigations, the NSF turned to its Inspector General, an independent, oversight office that is part of the federal Inspector General system established in 1978.[16] These decisions were announced in a notice of proposed rule making in February 1987 and issued as final regulations in July of the same year.[17]

In many ways, the difference between the approaches taken by HHS and the NSF mattered little to researchers. Both offices used FFP as the main component of their definition. Both separated inquiries (initial appraisal of the general merit of an accusation) from investigations (the detailed review of evidence). Both also provided for independent adjudication, although this is more difficult to accomplish in HHS, since investigation and adjudication are under one authority (the Secretary of HHS). Both placed the primary responsibility for investigations and reporting on research institutions. There was, however, one important difference that over time has had significant implications.

In turning to its Inspector General, the NSF placed responsibility for responding to misconduct in an office that was experienced at doing investigations. It brought scientists and others into this office to take on the new work, but did not establish a new office. In contrast, as a matter of principle, HHS turned directly to scientists for leadership in its new investigative office, OSI. The assumption behind this approach was that the self-policing that Congress was seeking would run more smoothly if scientists were seen as working directly with other scientists in resolving cases.[18] At the time, this assumption promised to allay the fears about regulatory burdens held by some members of the research community. In retrospect, it turned out to be an unwise assumption. With Congress constantly looking over its shoulder, the OSI struggled to deal with its two most prominent investigations: the Imanishi-Kari and Gallo cases. In the end, the findings of misconduct announced in both cases were eventually thrown out on appeal.

Policy definition (1993–2000)

The turmoil caused by the Imanishi-Kari and Gallo cases led to many calls for reform. Typical headlines from the early 1990s read: 'Report to Congress hits several Universities and NIH for handling of misconduct cases', 'U.S. called lax in policing medical research', 'Scientist accused of faking data calls the scandal a "witch hunt" ', and 'NIH fraud procedures under attack'.[19-22] Two complaints above all others lay behind these attacks: first, the fairness of the investigative process and, second, the definition of misconduct.

The first complaint about fairness had some grounding in fact. During the early years of policy formation, policy makers and administrators were simultaneously developing and applying the rules. This was particularly true for universities, which often did not take misconduct seriously until forced to do so by their first case.[23] With government now monitoring their investigations, they needed clear rules and reliable contacts, which were sometimes slow in coming. To make government operations more efficient, in 1993 HHS decided to combine the functions of OSI and OSIR in a single office, thereby establishing the Office of Research Integrity (ORI).[24] With this change, ORI became, and still is, the only office in the US government specifically and solely charged with promoting integrity and responding to allegations of research misconduct. Every other 'misconduct office' (and there are now nearly 20) combines its misconduct activities with other duties.

Complaints about the definition of misconduct were not as easily resolved, and in some respects came to dominate policy discussions. The main point of contention was the 'serious deviation from accepted practices' clause in the federal definitions. Critics feared that including this clause would draw the government into cases that were simply normal scientific disagreements, thereby restricting scientific or academic freedom.[25] In practice, the clause was never used as the sole justification for opening an investigation of misconduct, but the threat of undefined government action was sufficient to prompt a great deal of discussion and two major committee investigations: one by the National Academies of Science[26] and the other by a special committee set up by HHS and Congress.[27]

The 'serious deviation' clause was first used in government policy in 1986 by the PHS:[14]

> '"Misconduct" is defined as (1) serious deviation, such as fabrication, falsification, or plagiarism, from accepted practices in carrying out research or in reporting the results of research; or (2) material failure to comply with federal requirements ...'

Fabrication, falsification, and plagiarism are included in this definition as examples of the behaviours that the PHS would respond to, and not a limit on government action. Had this definition been retained, it would have allowed government and research institutions to look broadly at any practice that was significantly at odds with responsible research practices in the interest of protecting the public's investment in research. From the standpoint of maximum public accountability, this approach makes a great deal of sense. From the perspective of researchers worried about undue government regulation, it does not. For the next 14 years, influential researchers and professional societies undertook a well-orchestrated effort to narrow significantly the scope of the government definition.

The first step in narrowing the definition was taken within a year. The new NSF policy, published in 1987, moved fabrication, falsification, and plagiarism from the 'such as' clause and gave them independent status:[17]

> '"Misconduct" means (1) fabrication, falsification, plagiarism, or other serious deviation from accepted practices in proposing, carrying out, or reporting results from research; ...'

Although not intended by the NSF when crafting its definition, with this change, 'research misconduct' quickly became more or less synonymous with FFP in the USA, with 'serious deviations' being relegated to a catch-all category that the government could use when needed.

It was the 'use-when-needed' feature that upset a few prominent members of the research community, being based primarily on anecdotal evidence and exaggerated predictions. The lack of evidence notwithstanding, the issue was taken up, debated at length, and specifically addressed in two crucial reports. The first, the 1992 National Academies report, *Responsible Science*, recommended that:[26]

> '... federal agencies should review their definitions of misconduct in science to remove ambiguous categories such as "other serious deviations from accepted research practices".'

The second, the 1995 Ryan Commission report, recommended changing FFP to MIM (misappropriation, interference, and misrepresentation), prefaced by the explanation that:[27]

> 'Research misconduct is significant misbehavior that improperly appropriates the intellectual property or contributions of others, that intentionally impeded the progress of research, or that risks corrupting the scientific record or compromising the integrity of scientific practices.'

Neither recommendation was immediately adopted. The NSF Inspector General strongly rejected the notion that the 'serious deviations' clause was unnecessary or had been misused.[28] The PHS debated the merits of the clause, made a number of changes to its definition, and then eventually gave way to pressure and removed it.

The final step in undermining the broad approach to misconduct policy implicit in the 'serious deviations' clause came in 2000. Shortly after the Ryan Commission report was published, the White House Office of Science and Technology Policy (OSTP) established a working group to develop a government-wide research misconduct policy. After three years of deliberation, the working group published a draft (May 1999) and then a final *Federal Research Misconduct Policy* (December 2000). The new policy completely reversed the role of the 'significant deviations' clause. In the original policy, government proposed to respond to all '*significant deviations ... from accepted practices*', including, but not limited to, FFP. Under the new policy, government action was limited not only to FFP but to FFP that represented 'a *significant departure from accepted practices* of the relevant research community' (italics added).[29] Those who fought hard for these changes over the years felt that the limitations were necessary to protect the freedom and independence of researchers. Whether the changes did anything to protect the integrity of research or the public's investment in research is doubtful, as will be argued in the closing section of this chapter.

Apart from bringing the definition debate to a close, the 2000 OSTP policy clearly reaffirmed the long-standing position by government that research institutions and not the federal government 'bear primary responsibility for prevention and detection of research misconduct and for the inquiry, investigation, and adjudication of research misconduct alleged to have occurred in association with their own institution'.[29] The central importance of research institutions had been expressed in all major policy documents, beginning with the 1986 NIH Interim Policy. But, through the 1990s, both the NSF and ORI retained independent authority to pursue cases if they felt that research institutions could not or would not conduct proper investigations. As the new OSTP policy was taking shape, the PHS rethought this position and eventually limited the ORI's authority to oversight rather than independent investigations. The change had little impact on the work of the ORI's renamed Division of Investigative Oversight, which still carefully reviews the evidence and findings in all cases that fall under its jurisdiction (PHS-funded research).[30] The NSF did not change and still has the authority to conduct its own investigations.

Recent policy developments (2000 onwards)

To ensure that uniformity would be quickly brought to US research misconduct policy, the OSTP gave federal agencies one year to comply, a deadline that turned out to be unrealistic. The federal rules for policy making are complex, requiring advanced notification, comment periods, response to comments, and more. The NSF implemented its new policy in April 2002, coming close to the one-year deadline.[31] The Environmental Protection Agency[32] and the Department of Labor[33] adopted misconduct policies in 2003, the Department of Defense[34] and the National Aeronautics and Space Administration[35] in 2004, and the Department of Veterans Affairs[36] and the HHS[37] in 2005. Other research funding agencies have adopted or are still preparing to adopt misconduct policies.

The most important impact of the 2000 OSTP policy was the impetus that it provided for action. Prior to 2000, most government agencies that fund research did not have formal research misconduct policies; most now do. The OSTP policy has also brought more uniformity to US policy. Agencies are obligated to adopt the new, narrower definition, thereby uniformly restricting federal interest to FFP. They all to one extent or another rely on research institutions to carry out investigations. And they all require some reporting, which, in principle, should make it easier to track the amount and types of misconduct that take place in the USA. However, in a number of significant ways, there is still considerable diversity in US policy, as well as some serious omissions and shortcomings.

The primary way diversity enters US policy is through the different approaches that agencies have taken to implementing the 2000 OSTP policy. Some agencies, such as HHS and the NSF, clearly delegate authority to one office, which has primary responsibility for receiving and responding to allegations. These agencies have clear policies and procedures, and are actively engaged in promoting awareness of the importance of integrity in research. There are some significant differences in the way in which these offices operate. For example, the ORI's investigative oversight is limited to FFP; the NSF Inspector General can, as part of its authority, expand investigations of suspected improper research behaviour to include fraud and waste. The ORI publishes the names of individuals found to have committed misconduct; the NSF does not, unless the person is debarred. The NSF can conduct its own investigations if it feels that a research institution is not doing a proper job; the ORI cannot. Apart from these differences, these two offices follow the definitions and framework set out in the OSTP policy in a way that is easily accessed and followed.

Other agencies have diffused their research misconduct authority throughout their organization, making it more difficult to know how to report and/or to track the record of these agencies in responding to research misconduct. For example, the Department of Energy (DOE), which funds biomedical and behaviour research, relies primarily on its contracting officers and a research misconduct clause inserted into all contracts to implement the 2000 OSTP policy. Allegations that come directly to the DOE are referred to the head of the relevant 'DOE Element' (major division), who is directed to consult first with the DOE Inspector General office. The DOE Inspector General can choose to carry out an investigation. If it does not, the case is referred to the contracting officer, who directs the institution to conduct an inquiry consistent with the research misconduct language inserted in the contract. The institution must report to the contracting officer, but further tracking and reporting is not specified.

This diffused or decentralized approach to implementation, which has been followed by other agencies, has significantly limited the effectiveness of the 2000 OSTP policy. It is difficult to locate most of the agency policies that have been adopted. Once located, it is often a challenge to know how they are implemented and who is responsible for implementation. The DOE Office of Science, which seems to be the lead 'element' in the DOE for misconduct policy, has no information on the DOE policy on or directly linked to its home page. The only way to find the DOE policy is to do a search for 'research misconduct'. The DOE Inspector General has not issued any reports on research misconduct since the DOE policy was implemented. Such shortcomings and the lack of information on the government's overall response to research misconduct are, unfortunately, the rule and not exceptions. The clarity and uniformity that the OSTP was presumably attempting to bring to government policy has not emerged, and the OSTP has done little to follow up on its initial effort.

Diversity and ambiguities arise even in agencies that have centralized authority. The 2005 HHS misconduct policy applies to all PHS operating divisions, including the Food and Drug Administration (FDA). However, the FDA has independent authority under Title 21 to investigate clinical research misconduct, as set out in *Guidance for Industry and Clinical Investigators: The Use of Clinical Holds Following Clinical Investigator Misconduct*. Under this guidance document, researchers can be penalized for improper record keeping, failure to follow protocols, and other deviations from the FDA's complex research rules. This and other FDA policy statements do not mention the OSTP definition. 'FFP' in FDA regulations usually stands for 'fresh frozen plasma' and has nothing to do with the OSTP definition of research misconduct!

The independent authority of the FDA to define and deal with clinical research misconduct raises one further shortcoming in US research misconduct policy, namely its relative neglect of privately funded research. The FDA is authorized to review privately funded research that is used in applications for new drug and medical device approval. Other research does not come under the OSTP misconduct regulation unless it is publicly funded, even if government uses the research to make policy decisions that impact upon the public. The sensitivity of the US government to private interests was manifest in a recent case in which the DOE Office of Science attempted to withhold public release of a misconduct investigation report, arguing that the report was the property of the institution that conducted the investigation and not the DOE, which had funded the research.[38]

Research misconduct policy in Canada

In contrast to the government-driven approach followed in the USA, Canada has relied more on research institutions to lead the way in developing research misconduct policy. Canada has also placed more emphasis on identifying broad principles to guide researchers on responsible conduct and less on the precise definition of research misconduct for investigation purposes. These differences are due in part to governmental differences. The three Research Councils (Tri-Councils) that administer Canada's federal government investment in academic research do not have a 'mandate to be regulators or quasi-judicial bodies'.[39] (Congress has specifically given US funding agencies this authority.) But Canadian policy makers also at first had the luxury of developing their policies before any major scandals broke and the advantage of lessons learned from the US experience. The luxury of no major cases, unfortunately, did not last very long.

By the late 1980s, when government policy makers in the USA were drafting their first regulations, Canadian universities began to discuss ways to promote integrity in research and the steps that should be taken if researchers failed to live up to high standards for integrity. The deliberative process they were going through is reflected in *A Code of Research Ethics* adopted at Queen's University, Kingston, Ontario, in October 1987. The University had already adopted policies that provided guidance for the use of human subjects, animals, and computers in research. This new policy was designed to formalize the general principles ('good sense, trust, collegiality, and justice') that were essential not only for these policies but for all university research. The scope of the proposed Code was therefore broad and did not provide detail on what should be done if researchers failed to live up to the high standards set for integrity. When disputes arose, administrators were simply encouraged to resolve them through 'reasonable discussion among those involved'. If this did not work, the dispute was then to be referred up through the University's administrative ranks and handled like any other staff grievance.[40]

The reliance on research institutions and established governance mechanisms is readily apparent in the policy adopted by the University of Toronto three years later, and since revised. Following the emphasis on basic principles, members of the University community were reminded that they were expected to maintain 'the highest standards of ethical conduct in every aspect of research'. Four principles were then highlighted as especially important for integrity in research: (1) the accurate presentation and interpretation of experimental data; (2) acknowledgement of the work of others; (3) maintaining confidentiality; (4) the appropriate use and allocation of money or other resources. If someone failed to adhere to these standards, the situation was handled the way in which any other question about staff behaviour would be handled:[41]

> 'Allegations of misconduct will be taken seriously by the University following the established practices and procedures of the University and all inquiries and proceedings will be conducted expeditiously.'

No description of the investigative process was needed, because this process was set out in other University policies.

Not everyone was comfortable with this principle-based, institutional approach to research misconduct policy. In January 1992, the Canadian Association of University Teachers (CAUT), perhaps fearing too little due process and aware of its own role in influencing policy through collective bargaining agreements, urged universities to adopt 'negotiated procedures for dealing with allegations of fraud or other research misconduct'. CAUT wanted procedures based on a clear definition of research misconduct, which they suggested might be limited to FFP and failure to comply with regulations. They also wanted universities to include the main elements of due process in their policies, starting with 'the right to a full, fair and impartial hearing, with complete access from the onset of any investigation to all charges and the evidence for them'. Finally, CAUT was concerned that good-faith whistleblowers be protected and that any injured parties 'receive justice'.[42]

The move toward more formal policies that included clearer definitions and provisions for due process took a small step forward in January 1994 when the three Canadian research councils issued the *Tri-Council Policy Statement: Integrity in Research and Scholarship*.[43] This document retained the principle-oriented approach adopted in earlier university policies, summarized under five basic responsibilities (paraphrased here): (1) giving due credit; (2) obtaining permission to use others' work; (3) 'using scholarly and scientific rigour' in all work; (4) following proper authorship practices; (5) disclosing conflicts of interest. It also confirmed that the primary responsibility for maintaining integrity in Canadian research rested with research institutions.[44] The subsequent Framework for Tri-Council Review of Institutional Policies Dealing with Integrity in Research (1996) provided specific guidance on how institutions should receive, investigate, and adjudicate allegations of misconduct. And institutions were now required to report the results of investigations to the appropriate research council, which could impose additional sanctions if there were reasons to do so.[45]

As an effort to develop an agency policy that applied broadly across Canadian research institutions, the *Tri-Council Policy Statement* and *Framework* lacked an important ingredient – a clear definition of research misconduct. The *Statement* was intentionally written from a positive perspective, with the Councils noting that they expected '... the highest standards of research and scholarship' and would regard '... any action that is inconsistent with integrity as misconduct'.[44] As a goal, 'highest standards' are admirable. As a practical standard for raising allegations, they are not. The *Framework* required universities to adopt 'a general statement of research integrity principles and description of what constitutes misconduct', but gave no recommendations for a definition. Whether they should have done more to provide guidance has remained an issue for discussion to the present day.

Shortly after the Tri-Council Policy was announced, news broke of a major case of research misconduct involving Canadian researcher Roger Poisson at St Luc Hospital in Montreal. St Luc Hospital was one of 483 institutions participating in the US-funded National Surgical Adjuvant Breast and Bowel Project. Poisson was one of the most successful recruiters for this project, accounting for an unreasonably high 19% of the women enrolled.[46] His success, unfortunately, was based on fraudulent practices, which were first noticed by a data manager in June 1990. As a US-funded project, the misconduct was investigated by the study coordinator at the University of Pittsburgh,

Bernard Fisher, and by the ORI, which issued a finding of research misconduct in April 1993. Inexplicably, the published finding escaped public attention until reported in the *Chicago Tribune* on 13 March 1994 by science reporter John Crewdson.[47] Crewdson allegedly 'scooped' CBC's *Fifth Estate*, which aired its programme on the episode a week later.[48] With the public notice of the Poisson case, Canadian policy makers finally found themselves working in the same charged atmosphere of public oversight that had emerged in the USA a decade earlier.

With the increased public attention and urging from the Tri-Councils, Canadian universities devoted more attention to investigations and policy development. However, without more central guidance, no clear patterns emerged. McGill University (1995) included falsification, plagiarism, conflict of interest, and misuse of research funds under 'The Duty of Honesty and Integrity', but did not specify whether these violations or failures to live up to the duties set out in other parts of the policy constituted misconduct. McGill also chose to rely on existing disciplinary procedures and did not establish new procedures for investigating misconduct.[49] Saint Mary's University (1995) outlined separate procedures for investigations, and also provided a detailed definition of 'scholarly misconduct'. The latter included FFP, taking unfair advantage of privileged access to information, not allowing the University to get due profit from intellectual property, and failure to comply with regulations and reveal conflicts of interest.[50] Lakehead University (1995) also established a separate investigative process, and added other provisions to its definition of misconduct, including violations of proper authorship practices, duplicate publication, and the 'deliberate destruction of one's own research data in order to avoid the detection of wrongdoing' or tampering with someone else's data.[51] Many of the Canadian policies also retained the broad 'code of conduct' format adopted in the first policies, thus leaving open the door to even wider interpretations of research misconduct.

In the years following the adoption of the Tri-Council Policy, there have been calls for a more unified Canadian policy. To explore whether Canada should move in this direction, the Health Canada-appointed Canadian Research Integrity Committee (CRIC) convened a workshop in Ottawa in January 2007 to assess the strengths and weaknesses of the current system and to make recommendations on next steps. The workshop highlighted the tensions that exist in Canada and in many other countries.[39] 'There was some consensus that Canada needs to do better in establishing consistent approaches to addressing research misconduct and promoting research integrity across the country.' But reluctance to establish a national office or to develop clearer national standards was also very much in evidence. In the end, the delegates referred the matter back to the CRIC for further deliberation, a decision one commentator characterized as: 'Deny, deny, deny. Sweep it under the carpet.'[52] Such criticism notwithstanding, Health Canada concluded that at the January 2007 Research Integrity Workshop, 'agreement was reached on the requirement for national approaches to address research misconduct and promote research integrity'.[53] Efforts to develop these approaches are currently under way.[54]

Analysis and conclusions

Once spurred to action, US and Canadian research funding agencies and research institutions over time succeeded in developing systems for responding to cases of major research misconduct. Canadians still rely primarily on research institutions to set standards and carry out investigations, with minimum government oversight. The federal government is more involved in setting policy and tracking cases in the USA, through the common federal definition, federal offices, and more detailed reporting requirements, but accepts the basic premise that the primary responsibility for responding to and investigating misconduct lies with research institutions. Under both systems, major and some minor cases of misconduct have been investigated, the accused parties found guilty or cleared of charges, and fraudulent research withdrawn or corrected. In a few cases, some taxpayers' money has also been recovered.

Are these developments sufficient to declare research misconduct policy development a success in the USA and Canada? The answer to this question depends on how 'success' is measured.

The practical goal of US and Canadian efforts has been to develop a system for responding to cases of misconduct. Research misconduct undermines public trust and puts public funding for research at risk. The US approach to misconduct has probably been more successful in meeting this goal, although there are still significant weaknesses in the US system. In federal agencies where the responsibility for misconduct is assigned to offices with other duties and conflicting responsibilities, there is no guarantee that allegations will be taken seriously and vigorously pursued. As authority is further dispersed, as it is in the Canadian system, the incentives for pursuing cases can decline further. Based on these tendencies and events in the USA and Canada, the historical evidence suggests that clear, central authority improves the effectiveness of a nation's ability to respond to major cases of research misconduct.

Apart from individual cases, research misconduct policies presumably have the secondary goal of reducing the amount of misconduct and promoting integrity in research more generally. This goal has not been as successfully achieved in either the USA or Canada. Studies of research behaviour suggest that 1 in every 100–1000 researchers engages in practices that seriously deviate from professionally accepted standards.[55] Based on these numbers, US agencies should be investigating about 1000 cases a year or higher, and Canadian agencies about 100. The fact that they are not suggests that many cases of significant research misconduct go unreported and undetected each year.[55] Such cases undoubtedly waste public funding and undermine the validity of the research record, although their impact has yet to be measured.

The practices that fall under definitions of 'research misconduct' are not the only misbehaviours in research that waste funds, undermine the validity of the research record, or endanger public health and welfare. Studies of research behaviour suggest that researchers engage in other 'questionable practices', such as including undeserving authors on papers (honorary authorship) or failing to list individuals who made major contributions to the paper (ghost authorship); publishing the same work more than once without proper acknowledgement (duplicate publication); using improper study design or statistical analyses; misrepresenting research in abstracts; or providing inaccurate or incomplete information about research design to mislead or slow the work of competing researchers. While seemingly less significant in terms of immediate impact, these often widely engaged-in practices (10%, 20%, or higher) probably waste far more public funds and distort the research record more than the few cases of research misconduct (narrowly defined) that now are the focus of public policy making and attract so much public attention.[56]

Major cases of misconduct cannot, of course, be ignored. Governments and research institutions must take them seriously and have mechanisms in place to respond to them. However, making individual cases of misconduct the focus of misconduct policy and allowing these cases to drive public policy making, as has happened in both the USA and Canada, is not good policy and does not properly protect the public's investment in research.

Public funding for research is based on the premise that it is useful and serves public needs. Research misconduct policy should therefore focus on those behaviours that most compromise the usefulness of publicly supported research. To move in this direction, governments and research institutions must devote more attention to problem assessment. What behaviours compromise the integrity of research? What impacts do these behaviours have, measured in terms of wasted research funds, lost investigator time, misguided policy decisions (e.g. misguided treatment recommendations), and lost lives? As significant problems are identified, researchers and research institutions must endeavour to improve self-regulation. If they do not, increased government regulation becomes a necessity.

The US effort to promote integrity in research lost its way in the debate over definitions, narrowing its attention over time to a smaller and smaller range of activities. Canadian efforts maintained a broader focus, but have not engaged the problem of effectiveness. The fact that both countries have recognized their responsibility to set high standards for integrity in research is important and deserves recognition. The fact that neither has achieved an effective system for promoting these standards means that there is still more work to do.

References

1. United States Congress. House Committee on Science and Technology. Subcommittee on Investigations and Oversight. *Fraud in Biomedical Research. Hearings Before the Subcommittee on Investigations and Oversight of the Committee on Science and Technology, U.S. House of Representatives, Ninety-seventh Congress, First Session, March 31, April 1, 1981.* Washington, DC: US Government Printing Office, 1981.
2. Broad WJ, Wade N. *Betrayers of the Truth: Fraud and Deceit in the Halls of Science.* New York: Simon and Schuster, 1982.
3. Tangney JP. Fraud will out – or will not? *New Sci* 1987; **115**(6 August): 62–3.
4. Association of American Medical Colleges. *The Maintenance of High Ethical Standards in the Conduct of Research.* Washington, DC: Association of American Medical Colleges, 1982.

5. Association of American Universities. *Report of the Association of American Universities Committee on the Integrity of Research*. Washington, DC: American Association of Universities, 1983.

6. The University of Michigan Joint Task Force on Integrity of Scholarship. *Maintaining the Integrity of Scholarship*. Ann Arbor, MI: University of Michigan, 1984.

7. United States Congress. Health Research Extension Act of 1985.

8. Stewart WW, Feder N. The integrity of the scientific literature. *Nature* 1987; **325**: 207–14.

9. Gavaghan H. Fraud investigation probes the Baltimore affair. *New Sci* 1988; **118**(21 April): 26.

10. Kevles DJ. *The Baltimore Case: A Trial of Politics, Science, and Character*. New York: Norton, 1998.

11. Joyce C. Inquiry deepens on conduct of American AIDS expert, Robert Gallo. *New Sci* 1990; **125**(3 March): 20.

12. Crewdson J. *Science Fictions: A Scientific Mystery, a Massive Cover-up, and the Dark Legacy of Robert Gallo*. New York: Little, Brown, 2002.

13. Gold BD. Congressional activities regarding misconduct and integrity in science. In: National Academy of Sciences, National Academy of Engineering, and Institute of Medicine. *Responsible Science: Ensuring the Integrity of the Research Process*. Washington, DC: National Academy Press, 1993; **2**: 90–115.

14. National Institutes of Health. Special Issue: Policies and Procedures for Dealing with Possible Misconduct in Science. *NIH Guide Grants Contracts* 1986; **15**(11): 1–37.

15. Health and Human Services. Statement of organizations, functions, and delegations of authority. *Fed Regist* 1989; **54**: 11080–1.

16. Inspector General Act of 1978. Title 5, Appendix. Washington, DC: US Government Printing Office, 1978.

17. National Science Foundation. Misconduct in Science and Engineering Research: Final Regulations. *Fed Regist* 1987; **52**: 24466–70.

18. Hallum JV, Hadley SW. OSI: why, what, and how. *ASM News* 1990; **56**: 647–51.

19. Cordes C. Report to Congress hits several universities and NIH for handling of misconduct cases. *Chron High Educ* 1990; **37**(12 September): A22, A25.

20. Leary WE. U.S. called lax in policing medical research. *New York Times* 9 September 1990. query.nytimes.com/gst/fullpage.html?res=9COCE4D91331F93AA3575 ACOA966958260.

21. Anonymous. Scientist accused of faking data calls the scandal a 'witch hunt'. *New York Times* 17 May 1991; Sec A: 16.

22. Gladwell M. NIH fraud procedures under attack. *Washington Post* 2 August 1991; Sec A: 23.

23. Steneck NH. Fostering responsible conduct in science and engineering research: current university policy and actions. In: National Academy of Sciences, National Academy of Engineering, and Institute of Medicine. *Responsible Science: Ensuring the Integrity of the Research Process*, Volume 2. Washington, DC: National Academy Press, 1993: 3–25.

24. Office of Research Integrity, 45 USC 2896. ori.hhs.gov/policies/regulations_statory.shtml.

25. Schachman HK. What is misconduct in science? *Science* 1993; **261**: 148–9, 183.

26. National Academy of Sciences, National Academy of Engineering, and Institute of Medicine. *Responsible Science: Ensuring the Integrity of the Research Process*. Volumes 1 and 2. Washington, DC: National Academy Press, 1992/93.

27. Commission on Research Integrity. *Integrity and Misconduct in Research: Report of the Commission on Research Integrity*. Washington, DC: US Department of Health and Human Services, Public Health Services, 1995.

28. National Science Foundation. Office of Inspector General. *Semiannual Report to the Congress*. Washington, DC: National Science Foundation, 1992.

29. Office of Science and Technology Policy, Executive Office of the President. Federal Policy on Research Misconduct. *Fed Regist* 2000; **65**: 76260–4.

30. Office of Public Health and Science. Statement of Organization, Functions, and Delegations of Authority. *Fed Regist* 2000; **65**: 30600–1.

31. National Science Foundation. Research misconduct. 45 CFR 689. Washington DC: US Government Printing Office, 2002.

32. Environmental Protection Agency. Policy and Procedures for Addressing Research Misconduct. 2003. www.epa.gov/brownfields/pg/pg0904_5.htm.

33. Department of Labor. Research Misconduct, Statement of Policy. *Fed Regist* 2003; **68**: 53862–6.

34. Department of Defense. Research Integrity and Misconduct. 2004. www.dtic.mil/whs/directives/corres/pdf/321007p.pdf.

35. National Aeronautics and Space Administration. Investigation of Research Misconduct. 14 CFR 1275. Washington, DC: US Government Printing Office, 2004.

36. Department of Veterans Affairs. Research Misconduct. *VHA Handbook* 2005; (1058.2): T1–28.

37. Department of Health and Human Services. Public Health Service Policies on Research Misconduct. *Fed Regist* 2005; **70**: 28370–400.

38. Schwartz WM, Senior FOIA Official. Decision and Order of the Department of Energy. Appeal. Eugenie Reich. Washington, DC: Department of Energy, 2007.

39. Canadian Research Integrity Committee. *Research Integrity: Towards a Canadian Approach*. Ottawa: Health Canada, 2007.

40. Queen's University, Kingston, Ontario. *A Code of Research Ethics*. 1987. www.queensu.ca/secretariat/senate/policies/resethic.html.

41. University of Toronto. *Policy on Ethical Conduct in Research*. University of Toronto, 1991.

42. Canadian Association of University Teachers. *CAUT Policy Statement on Fraud and Other Misconduct in Academic Research*. January 1992 (revised March 1993).

43. Friesen H. Many controls now in place to catch scientific misconduct. *The Gazette* 26 March 1994: Sec B6.

44. Canadian Institutes of Health Research, Natural Sciences and Engineering Research Council, Social Sciences and Humanities Research Council. *Tri-Council Policy Statement: Integrity in Research and Scholarship*. 1994. www.nserc.gc.ca/professors_e.asp?nav=profnav&lbi=p9.

45. Canadian Institutes of Health Research, Natural Sciences and Engineering Research Council, Social Sciences and Humanities Research Council. *Framework for Tri-Council Review of Institutional Policies Dealing with Integrity in Research*. 24 June 1996. www.nserc.ca/institution/framework_e.htm.

46. Angell M, Kassirer JP. Setting the record straight in the breast-cancer trials. *N Engl J Med* 1994; **330**: 1448–50.

47. Crewdson J. Fraud in breast cancer study: doctor lied on data for decade. *Chicago Tribune* 13 March 1994; Sec A1.

48. Boone M. *Fifth Estate* scooped on breast-cancer story; but different material and emphasis on drug study make show worth the watch. *The Gazette* 15 March 1994; Sec B6.

49. McGill University. McGill University Policy on Research Ethics. 1995 [cited 2008 January]; http://www.mcgill.ca/researchoffice/policies/sponsored/policies/ethics/.

50. Saint Mary's University. *Policy Statement on Integrity in Research and Scholarship and Procedures for Reporting and Investigating Scholarly Misconduct*. 1995. www.stmarys. ca/academic/fgsr/documents/Misconduct.pdf.

51. Lakehead University. *Guidelines and Policy for the Ethical Conduct of Research and Procedures for Investigating Misconduct*. 1995. policies.lakeheadu.ca/policy.php?pid=102.

52. Kondro W. Call for arm's-length national research integrity agency. *CMAJ* 2007; **176**: 749-50.

53. Health Canada. *Summary of Discussion, Science Advisory Board Meeting, March 28–29, 2007*. Health Canada, 2007.

54. Gillis A. Crossing the line: academic misconduct is a reality, but what's less certain is how often it occurs and what's the best way to combat it. *University Affairs* 2008. www.universityaffairs.ca/issues/2008/january/_print/crossing_line.html.

55. Titus SL, Wells JA, Rhoades LJ. Repairing research integrity. *Nature* 2008; **453**: 980–2.

56. Steneck NH. Fostering integrity in research: definitions, current knowledge, and future directions. *Sci Eng Ethics* 2006; **12**: 53–74.

5 Historical aspects of research misconduct: Europe

Frank Wells

Introduction

In an overview and guide to the literature of misconduct and fraud in scientific research, published in 1995 by the British Library, Grayson wrote: 'the notion that scientists might deliberately violate ethical norms of conduct for personal gain or gratification is deeply abhorrent to many people despite the fact that such violations in other areas of life might be viewed much more tolerantly.'[1] That abhorrence of subject or sponsor exploitation probably accounts for such behaviour not being common, and still largely holds good today; but human nature being what it is, such exploitation will always be with us, although hopefully to a diminishing extent.

Attitudes towards research have always been ambivalent, and have swung between extremes; before scientific methodology was able to be proved, research projects were considered to be sorcery and quackery. Then came an uncritical acceptance or even reverence for science, particularly biomedical science or research; now there is a far more critical approach to research reports and results, not least because of greater public education through various aspects of the media, especially the newspapers and television.

In the three previous editions of this book, Stephen Lock gave succinct accounts of the history of fraud and misconduct in biomedical research throughout the world.[2-4] However, because of a lack of any written accounts of this occurring elsewhere, circumstantially he concentrated on the USA and, to a lesser extent, the UK. I commend these earlier historical accounts, but will describe in detail one case to which Lock alluded. He cited the Malcolm Pearce case as the high-profile episode that made it obvious that, in the UK, just as elsewhere, fraud affected research in hospitals and laboratories as well as in general practice,[4] although he referred to GP research fraud as perceived by the medical *Prominenten* as being a squalid affair confined to poorly qualified and practising GPs (which, actually, was not true, although Lock's assessment of the perception was probably correct – many cases with which I had already dealt were among highly qualified and experienced doctors). Richard Smith has also referred to the Pearce case in an article published as recently as 2006 as 'Britain's highest profile case'.[5] Although I was involved in investigating this case, I have never previously written about it myself, but I am going to do so now as I can shed a different light on some aspects of it.

The Pearce case

As Smith described, Pearce, who was an honorary consultant and senior lecturer in the Department of Obstetrics and Gynaecology at St George's Hospital Medical School and an assistant editor on the *British Journal of Obstetrics and Gynaecology*, published two papers in one issue of the journal. There was nothing necessarily irregular in that, although having two articles from the same author in one edition of a distinguished journal was unusual. However, the Editor-in-Chief of the journal was Professor Geoffrey Chamberlain, and he was also head of the department at St George's where Malcolm Pearce worked. One of the papers was a case report of the embryo of an ectopic pregnancy being reimplanted and leading to a baby being born – something that had never before been done, although it has since.[6] It was an anaesthetist, reading this article in theatre soon after it appeared, and with the corroboration of the senior theatre technician, who first suspected that this patient did not exist, as there were no records of such an event ever happening. Just to make sure, the theatre technician checked with other colleagues that this had never happened. The anaesthetist reported her suspicions to the Dean of the Medical School, Sir William Asscher, with whom I had myself been a medical student at the London Hospital Medical College. He called me, and we held a brief discussion, following which the Dean set up a committee of enquiry to investigate fully the anaesthetist's allegation. This meticulous investigation, conducted on the lines recommended by the Royal College of Physicians, not only confirmed that the patient had not existed but also revealed that the second paper published in the journal – on a trial of treating recurrent miscarriage in nearly 200 women with polycystic ovary syndrome[7] – had never taken place. Furthermore, Pearce had invented the name of the pharmaceutical company that he purported to have sponsored this study. His motive, therefore, could not possibly have been greed, but was almost undoubtedly vanity – he wanted to be the first person to have described a successful outcome to the relocation of an ectopic pregnancy. But he also demonstrated a phenomenon that I have seen time and time again – that of multiple episodes of fraud committed by the same person. This has led me firmly to believe and to advocate that once a person has committed fraud, he is likely to do so again, and should therefore never, ever, be used as a research investigator again. And, *en passant*, I have yet to meet a female research fraudster. All of my 26 cases are men.

Geoffrey Chamberlain came out of this episode rather badly; he was a coauthor of the ectopic pregnancy paper, in which he could not possibly have had any involvement as the case did not exist. So he resigned as editor of the journal, resigned his presidency of the Royal College of Obstetricians and Gynaecologists, and retired from the department at St George's where he was professor. He was guilty of nothing more than accepting gift authorship and a considerable error of judgement, but he was not himself guilty of research misconduct.

Malcolm Pearce was duly found guilty and dismissed from his post. The facts were reported to the General Medical Council (GMC), whose Professional Conduct

Committee found him guilty of serious professional misconduct and erased his name from the Medical Register. Strangely, Pearce never admitted his guilt, and some years later when I met one of his relatives at a meeting, at which I had been lecturing on fraud and misconduct in medical research and had mentioned this case, he told me that the family remained deeply disturbed by Pearce's refusal to come to terms with what had happened to him.

Classic cases of misconduct: the UK

In the first edition of this book, it was acknowledged that it would be difficult to give an accurate account of the history of medical research misconduct before the last quarter of the then current century, and this still holds good. Little was written. In Europe, however, there were a few notorious episodes before then that were well documented, including the existence of 'philosophicall robbery' or plagiarism, described as long ago as 1664 by Robert Boyle, whose works were frequently plagiarized and pirated.[8] In the field of psychology, after many years of controversy, it had been shown beyond a reasonable doubt that Sir Cyril Burt committed fraud in his comparison of monozygotic twins.[9] And, in the history of scientific fraud, one should recall 1913 and the discovery of a human skull next to an ape's jaw with a canine tooth worn down like a human's. The general community of British paleoanthropologists came to accept the idea that the fossil remains belonged to a single creature that had had a human cranium and an ape's jaw. But 40 years later, Piltdown 'man' was exposed as a forgery. The skull was modern and the teeth on the ape's jaw had been filed down.

Returning to the beginning of the last quarter-century, one of the first reported European cases of research misconduct occurred in 1975 with the clinical trial data falsification by Dr J P Sedgwick of High Wycombe. He forged the signatures of seven other doctors participating in the same multicentre drug trial, and submitted results showing that the active drug was having a uniform and consistent effect that was significantly different from the test results submitted by doctors based in other centres. The pharmaceutical company reported Sedgwick to the GMC, and, at the end of the disciplinary hearing, his name was duly removed from the Medical Register.[10]

Misconduct in Europe

Elsewhere in Europe, no other specific cases were published for over a decade, and even in the UK the next published case was not until 1988, when Dr U Siddiqui, a consultant psychiatrist in Durham, was found guilty of fabricating clinical trial results, including inventing at least one non-existent patient, and was also erased from the Medical Register.[11] However, across the North Sea, first in Denmark and then in Norway and Finland, the biomedical fraternity were taking an active part in establishing committees on scientific dishonesty. The detailed procedures conducted by such committees were described in detail in the third edition of this book.[12–14] Essentially, having all inspired the confidence of the stakeholders in various aspects of biomedical research, these committees receive complaints of suspected research misconduct, which they then assess to determine whether or not there is a prima facie case to answer. If there is, then the employer of the person who has committed fraud or misconduct is notified accordingly so as to take appropriate action.

National bodies on scientific integrity

In the period since the publication of the third edition of this book, there have been some positive changes in the prevention, detection, investigation, and prosecution of research misconduct in Europe – but not many. Chief of these has been the establishment of national bodies in the UK, Norway, Germany, the Netherlands, and elsewhere to advise on these aspects of research misconduct, even though these bodies have no statutory powers. A UK Panel for Research Integrity in Health and Biomedical Sciences (UKRIO), announced in April 2006, has so far had a profile that is so low that seemingly very few workers in the field know of its existence. Nevertheless, it is supposed to provide the focus for promotion of good practice in research in health and biomedical sciences, and aims to 'embed a culture of good conduct into the research system'. It has a website (www.ukrio.org.uk/), and the intention is to reinforce a zero-tolerance approach to misconduct in all its forms. That, of course, is commendable, but the panel was only established initially for three years, and after two-thirds of its planned initial existence, there is little to show for its activities. It operates independently of government, sponsors, industry, and universities, and takes no responsibility for dealing with allegations of research misconduct, leaving it to the employer or research sponsor to take appropriate action.

By contrast, the track record of the Danish Committees on Scientific Dishonesty, which have been producing Annual Reports since 1995, is impressive. Starting originally with just the Committee for Health and Medical Science, there are now three Committees on Scientific Dishonesty in Denmark, the other two being the Committee for Social Science and the Humanities, and the Committee for Natural Science, Agricultural and Veterinary Science and Technical Science. They, too, have a website (www.fist.dk/site/english/councils-commissions-committees/the-danish-committees-on-scientific-dishonesty). As well as giving a detailed summary of every one of the cases dealt with during the previous year, all maintaining the anonymity of the complainant and that of the alleged miscreant, every Annual Report includes a monograph on an important related topic by a distinguished worker in the field. For example, in the 2004 report, Professor Phillipe Grandjean of the Department of Environmental Medicine at the University of Southern Denmark wrote authoritatively on public and private research culture and its importance for the occurrence of dishonesty.[15] In this article, he pointed out the effects of conflicts of interest, which are so often ignored, and the associated risk of dishonesty, and concluded that preventing research misconduct is linked to promoting responsible research in its widest sense; no doubt should be allowed to be raised as to the reliability of research, and there must be no slackening of the rigorous requirements made of research quality. This, Grandjean postulated, should apply whether the research is private or public and regardless of who is paying.

During 2004, the Danish Committee for Health and Medical Science (USF) considered and finalized their opinion on seven cases. Typical of these was a case dealing with fabrication of data in two clinical drug trials in which the pharmaceutical company whose product was under investigation informed the Danish drug licensing authority that data with which it had been provided by the suspect triallist were not based on actual clinical observations. The licensing authority asked the USF to take a position on whether the triallist had acted in a scientifically dishonest fashion, and (not surprisingly) found that the defendant had been guilty of scientific dishonesty. With that ruling, the university employer of the triallist was able to take forthright disciplinary action without delay.

I have described the Danish situation in some detail because it remains outstanding in its practicality and surely is a model that should be studied closely by other European countries with the objective of establishing a similar system, appropriate for the country in question. Certainly, the other Nordic countries have followed suit, and, as already mentioned, Germany and the Netherlands have adopted appropriate mechanisms for dealing with research misconduct. It is to be hoped that their existence and that of UKRIO are successful in helping to raise awareness of the need to minimize the incidence of research misconduct and fraud both in their own countries and in Europe as a whole.

Recent cases: Europe

A recent high-profile event, which precipitated the setting up of the Norwegian national committee to handle cases of dishonesty in research, was the Jon Sudbø case.[16] Sudbø, who was a consultant at the Norwegian Radium Hospital in Oslo, fabricated data for 900 patients in a study on the use of non-steroidal anti-inflammatory drugs in relation to the development of oral cancer. The study was published in October 2005 in the *Lancet*,[17] which retracted the article as soon as the fabrication came to light.[18] Sudbø also 'fundamentally mishandled' data for a 2001 article in the *New England Journal of Medicine (NEJM)*[19] and a 2005 article in the *Journal of Clinical Oncology*,[20] subsequently retracted.[21] The Norwegian hospital swiftly appointed an investigative committee, headed by the director of clinical epidemiology at the Karolinska Institute in Stockholm, Sweden. It appeared that Sudbø sought accolades and 'professional pride'. He achieved this, as scientists in the field had hailed the April 2001 *NEJM* article as an important step toward preventing oral cancer. This article particularly received attention because it identified a simple means for identifying people at high risk for mouth cancer. Sudbø concluded the article by recommending that leukoplakia displaying a particular characteristic be treated 'as true carcinomas' and he showed a picture of a second leukoplakia sample when, in fact, it was simply a magnification of an earlier picture.

But it was the 2005 *Lancet* paper that tipped researchers off to the fabrications. The study supposedly drew data from patients listed in the Cohort of Norway (CONOR), an epidemiological database. However, when one of the CONOR collaborators read it, she immediately became suspicious because CONOR did not exist for the time period when data collection supposedly took place. She contacted the Radium Hospital with the information, which then set the fraud investigation in motion.

Writing about this case, Arvid Hallén, Director General of the Research Council of Norway, commented: 'Research is by nature truth-seeking. Reliability is therefore a fundamental prerequisite for all research. Research has such an impact on our lives that it is of the utmost importance that there is a relationship of trust between research and society. The recent case of research fraud uncovered at the Norwegian Radium Hospital in Oslo is therefore a very serious matter.'[22] The case shook the Norwegian scientific community.

Another case, this time from Holland, is also of interest. A Dutch neurologist, Dr H J Gelmers, was found guilty of committing serious scientific fraud between 1989 and 1993 after he falsified reports for medical research and concealed earnings from the tax authorities. As part of the Second European Stroke Prevention Study, for the German pharmaceutical company Boehringer Ingelheim, he made 438 false case record forms.[23] The study was investigating whether dipyridamole reduced the chances of patients having a second stroke. However, reports included patients who had never participated, and patient visits were reported that had not taken place. None of the patients later interviewed by the forensic investigators had been informed of the research by Gelmers, and nor were their GPs. Compounding all this, most of the €272 000 earned from the research was not disclosed to the tax authorities. Gelmers was fined a sum equivalent to his unpaid tax, with a conditional prison sentence of 180 days if he failed to pay the fine, and, separately, he was suspended from practising medicine for a year by the Dutch equivalent of the UK GMC.

This particular case went on much longer than it should have done; the pharmaceutical company had begun to have doubts about the accuracy of the data in 1992, because the research observations of this doctor appeared too perfect, with too few side effects compared with the known side-effect profile of this particular drug. An external investigation concluded that protocols were not being followed, and the company removed Gelmers' data from the research and informed the inspectorate of the Dutch licensing authority. However, from that moment on, both Gelmers and the director of patient care at the hospital where he worked refused to cooperate with the authority. This went on for years, during which time the Dutch Association of Neurologists also launched an investigation, and it was not until 1999 that the public prosecution service became involved.

The court that heard this case said that it could not get away from the impression that both the accused and others attempted to cover up the established facts in order to prevent or limit as far as possible the damage to the accused and the profession in general. The court regarded this behaviour as extremely reprehensible, and commented that Gelmers had been solely interested in his own honour and glory. Trust in medical science and medical ethics, the court stated, had been seriously damaged.

Recent cases: the UK – no research ethics committee approval

Cases considered recently by the UK GMC Fitness to Practise Panel have been many and varied. I will, in summary, cite five of them. Further details of these and all the other cases considered and concluded by the GMC can be referenced on the GMC website (www.gmc-uk.org/concerns/hearings_and_decisions/ftp).

Case 1

The first case was that of a junior doctor in training studying for an MSc in palliative care at King's College London. As part of his MSc coursework, he submitted a research study project entitled 'Short periods of hospice stay and anxiety in the bereaved: a cross sectional study at six months following bereavement'. This research project involved the collection of data through questionnaires to be completed by the bereaved at a hospice in Surrey, and in his dissertation he stated, 'Following local ethical approval, it was agreed that this [the hospice] would be a suitable environment to introduce the questionnaire.' However, one of the staff at the hospice who happened also to be on the local research ethics committee (LREC), and who read the dissertation, knew that the LREC had never received an application with the above title. The LREC administrator confirmed this, and it transpired that the investigator had not received any ethical approval from anywhere for this study. Furthermore, it also transpired that he had not even obtained approval for the project to be conducted at the hospice. This was therefore referred to the King's College Examinations Misconduct Committee, which found that the case against him had been proved, and in due course these matters were referred to the GMC.

The Fitness to Practise Panel, meeting in July 2007, concluded that the above statement in his research project was misleading, was intended to mislead, and was inappropriate and dishonest. It ruled that his behaviour brought the profession into disrepute and that his fitness to practise was impaired because of his misconduct. However, the Panel, noting his contrition and the support and references he had received from his senior colleagues, decided not to suspend his registration as a medical practitioner, but felt that it was necessary and proportionate to impose conditions on his registration for a period of 12 months. These conditions were largely related to the conduct of research and to the appointment of a mentor. The Panel will reconsider his case in July 2008.

Case 2

The second case involved a consultant ophthalmologist who, although his involvement in a research project was flawed, was also found guilty of bringing the profession into disrepute on a number of different fronts. Concerning the research irregularity, he conducted two separate but connecting trials without the approval of a research ethics committee or the consent of patients. The other instances included failure to tell a patient about a lens problem reported by the manufacturer and confirming to a colleague that there had been no problem with the lenses, when there had; failing to attend a Boots clinic by purporting to be ill when in fact he was not; and making exaggerated claims in a brochure, which led the Advertising Standards Authority to find the claims to be in breach of the Committee of Advertising Practice (CAP) Code. He was suspended for a year and then allowed back on the Medical Register, but only with conditions regarding his surgical activities.

Case 3

The third case involved an academic consultant endocrinologist, Dr Richard Wilson, who, some years previously, had agreed to be the chief investigator for a clinical trial to assess the safety and efficacy of voglibose compared with placebo and glibenclamide. For the reasons below, he had been found guilty in 2002 by the Professional Conduct Committee of the GMC of serious professional misconduct for what he did (or did not do) in this trial, and his registration as a medical practitioner was made conditional for a period of three years. The Fitness to Practise Panel reconsidered his case in 2005, and again in October 2006.

Dr Wilson had fallen short in the conduct of this study in a number of different ways: he had failed to carry out any, or perform any adequate, physical examinations during the first visit of the patients recruited to the trial; he did not conduct adequate examinations of joints as specifically required by the protocol; he completed many of the Clinical Report Forms incorrectly, making up much of the data, indicating that he had carried out examinations when he had not; and he permitted seven patients to participate in the study when he knew that they should have been excluded. The clinical trial monitor had become increasingly concerned about a number of aspects of the conduct of the trial, largely because Dr Wilson was never there when he had arranged to be, but he had been fiercely defended by his research nurse, who was a very experienced outpatient sister, dedicated to working with Dr Wilson.

Eventually, however, it was the research nurse who blew the whistle; she had become deeply concerned that she had been allowed to get out of her depth in virtually running the study, never having been trained in research methodology. She realized that she had been expected to withdraw original medication from some patients and place them on placebo without Dr Wilson's involvement, and that she had had to obtain informed consent from patients participating in the study because Dr Wilson failed to do so. All this had been too much, and so she went to the professor who headed the department of endocrinology with all her concerns. These were backed up by both the clinical trial monitor and the quality assurance professional from the company, who had conducted a 'for cause' audit. The professor instituted a committee of inquiry, and eventually the case was referred to the GMC, as indicated above.

The effects of Dr Wilson's conditional registration were unexpected, as he resigned from the department in which he had been working for some years and then left clinical practice completely; the Fitness to Practise Panel meeting in 2005 therefore had to vary the conditions of his continued registration to include a clause requiring him to fulfil certain retraining needs. One year later, these had not been met, and the Panel therefore determined that his case should be reviewed again two years later. Other conditions applied, including an embargo on his conducting any research.

Case 4

The fourth case was that of another junior doctor who plagiarized two assignments while undertaking a Medical Science Course at Keele University. The first assignment contained several passages that were copied directly from published papers, which he failed to attribute to their authors. The second assignment was a more serious case, because he had on this occasion plagiarized the work of another student. Furthermore, he denied this second act of plagiarism throughout a university investigation and the university panel hearing that followed, so that a fellow student had to appear before a university panel, and only at the very end of the hearing did he admit that he had plagiarized. His defence was that this was something that happened all the time. His registration was suspended for a period of nine months, during which he became contrite.

Case 5

The fifth case involved a doctor who, one year previously, had had his name suspended from the Medical Register for a period of 12 months. This was because he had included the names of Professor A, Dr B, and Dr C or agreed to their names being included in articles as coauthors, knowing that they were not coauthors, on a total of 86 occasions between 1998 and 2003. Not surprisingly, when the 12 months were up, the Fitness to Practise Panel expected to see the doctor and to have received evidence of his trying to redeem himself and to keep up to date while he was off the Medical Register. However, in July 2007, despite being advised that he should attend the hearing of the Panel or provide considerable evidence of his attempts to have his name restored, he did not attend, and in effect told the Panel that he did not know what they were talking about. The Panel concluded that he had no insight into the seriousness of his situation and had not engaged in a meaningful way with the GMC, and they struck him off the Medical Register.

These five cases demonstrate how seriously research misconduct, including failing to seek research ethics committee approval, plagiarism, fabrication of data, and gift authorship, is continued to be considered in the UK by the GMC. They exemplify what has happened in the UK ever since the Sedgwick case in 1975, although all of them took several years to reach the GMC after the misdemeanours were first suspected. It is to be hoped that the existence of the UKRIO will both act as a further deterrent to the committing of research misconduct and enable cases that still occur to be dealt with much more expeditiously. Meanwhile, elsewhere in Europe, other than the cases cited and the establishment of bodies dedicated to maintaining research integrity or investigating scientific dishonesty, it is frankly difficult to relate what has happened in this field, as so little has been reported or documented. Nevertheless, it is highly likely that the incidence of fraud and research misconduct elsewhere in Europe is no less than it is in the Nordic countries and the UK.

Registration of clinical trials

Another aspect of research misconduct, on which Sir Iain Chalmers has both spoken and written authoritatively, is under-reporting of research, given that this can lead to seriously misleading recommendations for clinical practice and for new research. Chalmers' analysis of a survey of unpublished controlled trials, published in 1989,[24] led in the following year to his presenting a paper at the First Congress on Peer Review in Biomedical Publishing entitled 'Underreporting research is scientific misconduct'. This analysis, and the presentation that followed, were largely based on academic studies. However, 10 years previously, Elina Hemminki had shown that biased under-publication of studies funded by industry might be a particular cause for concern.[25] The registration of clinical trials is a relevant issue in this regard. If all clinical trials were to be registered before they began, there would be an index of studies from which results would ultimately be expected, be they positive, inconclusive, or negative. There would then be a degree of honesty reflected in the publication of such results – or indeed in the recognition that editors might have decided not to publish a whole sequence of negative results on the grounds that they would not make interesting reading – as well as in the availability of results for meta-analysis. In 1998, the Association of the British Pharmaceutical Industry (ABPI) adopted a very encouraging policy in this regard, led by Glaxo Wellcome and Schering Health Care, and strongly advocated by the Ethics Committee of the Faculty of Pharmaceutical Medicine. This was to lead the world in registering clinical trials.[26] Sadly, this policy was poorly supported and, when Glaxo Wellcome merged with Smith Kline Beecham in 2000 to become GlaxoSmithKline, the policy was dropped.

Since then, things have moved very slowly, but hopefully in the right direction; in 2002, Tonks, writing in the *BMJ*, advocated a clinical trials register for Europe,[27] and a 2004 editorial, again in the *BMJ*, commented: 'Last month GlaxoSmithKline announced that it would publish summaries of all its clinical trials of a new product once it had been launched. The decision followed news of a lawsuit alleging that the company had concealed the results of paroxetine because they might have spoiled marketing plans. GSK said it had been considering the move for some months.'[28] One year later, in January 2005, the industry announced a global commitment to clinical trial registration and publication – similar to the ABPI declaration of 1998 – but it remains to be seen whether this will be upheld.[29]

Publication issues

Nevertheless, in the publishing world, two organizations stand out. They are the Committee on Publication Ethics (COPE), referred to in detail elsewhere in this book, and the International Committee of Medical Journal Editors (ICMJE), which has made real progress by insisting that, as a prerequisite for consideration for publication as from 1 July 2005, all clinical trials other than phase I studies must be registered in a public trials registry prior to when the first subject was enrolled.[30] In early 2006, there were only two registries accepted by the ICMJE: ClinicalTrials.gov (www.clinicaltrials.gov) (a service of the US National Institutes of Health) and the International Standardised Randomised Clinical Trial Numbering scheme (isrctn.org). There has been a subsequent explosion of growth in the number of registries that have opened. One that is fundamental for Europe, because it registers and gives a unique number to all clinical trials throughout the continent, is the European Clinical Trials Database, EudraCT (eudract.emea.europa.eu). The World Health Organization (WHO) has also developed an International Clinical Trials Registry Platform, ICTRP (www.who.int/ictrp/en), through which all WHO registries will be accessible. It is planned that this will be an internationally accepted centralized repository for clinical trial information (registries and results) and be fully functional by 2008.[31]

The ethical review process

Research ethics committees have an important role to play, as Saunders emphasizes in Chapter 8. The training of research ethics committee members is viewed as essential in Denmark, Estonia, Sweden, and the UK, but a survey conducted in 2006 by the European Forum for Good Clinical Practice (EFGCP) throughout the European Union, plus Norway and Switzerland, revealed that these were the only four countries that required research ethics committee members to undergo any form of training for their duties.[32] A workshop held in Vienna in March 2007, attended by representatives of 22 countries within the European Union, addressed this situation, and hopefully the responsibility of research ethics committees to take appropriate action whenever research misconduct is brought to their notice will be fulfilled in the future.

Fraud and misconduct policies

Meanwhile there is clear evidence in the UK that research fraud and misconduct policies are being adopted by NHS Trusts throughout the country, and over 50 such Trusts have taken these policies on board. They apply to all the NHS units that are the responsibility of the Trust, and a typical example states that the purpose of the policy is to set out clearly what constitutes research misconduct and fraud and the process to be followed when research fraud or misconduct is suspected or identified. The policy typically also states that it has been developed using guidelines published in 2004 and 2005 by the Department of Health.[33,34] Thus, there are definitions of what constitutes fraud and misconduct; a clear statement of the responsibilities of the Trust Executive Director and any other involved members of staff when any allegation of research misconduct or fraud is made; and guidance on the path to be taken in reporting suspected research misconduct or fraud, including conducting an investigation (with outside help if necessary), and on the outcomes of that investigation, including reporting researchers to ethics committees and to their professional bodies. Finally, such policies are typically required to be reviewed on a two-year basis, and the fact that they were in place in most NHS Trusts by December 2007 is a major step forward, at least in the UK, in raising awareness of the possibility of research misconduct and of having the wherewithal to deal with it without delay.

An independent pharmaceutical consultant and medical lawyer has commented on an important role for pharmacists, particularly hospital pharmacists, in dealing with fraud and misconduct: they often work in a pivotal position to witness and report such events. For example, they may interact with the study sponsor, and may also be delegated responsibilities by the investigator or the investigator's institution for maintaining records of the delivery, use by each research subject, and return to the sponsor of any unused investigational medicinal products.[35] Where effective standard operating procedures (SOPs) to deal with research fraud or misconduct are not available, or where existing SOPs remain inadequate or are misapplied or abused, the

Public Interest Disclosure Act 1998 (PIDA) in the UK protects employees acting as whistleblowers from victimization should they raise genuine concerns about a category of malpractice specified in the Act. The initial disclosure, whether or not it is correct or confidential, should normally be made to a manager, a director, or the employer within the whistleblower's own workplace to resolve any problems within that organization. For a hospital pharmacist, disclosure may be directly to the sponsoring department. It goes without saying that any disclosure of alleged malpractice must be made in good faith.[36]

Conclusions

History has a habit of repeating itself, and none of the cases that have appeared, worldwide, during the past few years have demonstrated any differences from all the cases described earlier, except, of course, in the details. Human nature is flawed, and the temptation to cheat, fabricate, falsify, or plagiarize, coupled with degrees of arrogance and greed, will indeed always remain with us. That temptation will, from time to time, fail to be resisted. My hope is that the biomedical world will securely have in place mechanisms that will minimize the occurrence of research misconduct and that, when it does occur, will deal with it responsibly and expeditiously. The evidence, demonstrated at the first World Conference on Research Integrity, held in Lisbon in September 2007,[37] is that the will is there.

References

1. Grayson L. *Scientific Deception*. London: The British Library, 1995: vii.
2. Lock SP. Research misconduct 1974–1990: a resume of recent events. In: Lock SP, Wells FO, Farthing MGF, eds. *Fraud and Misconduct in Medical Research*, 1st edn. London: BMJ Books, 1993: 5–24.
3. Lock SP. Research misconduct 1974–1990: a resume of recent events. In: Lock SP, Wells FO, Farthing MGF, eds. *Fraud and Misconduct in Medical Research*, 2nd edn. London: BMJ Books, 1996: 14–39.
4. Lock SP. Research misconduct 1974–1990: an imperfect history. In: Lock SP, Wells FO, Farthing MGF, eds. *Fraud and Misconduct in Biomedical Research*, 3rd edn. London: BMJ Books, 2001: 51–63.
5. Smith R. Research misconduct: the poisoning of the well. *J R Soc Med* 2006; **99**: 232–7.
6. Pearce JM, Manyonda IT, Chamberlain GVP. Term delivery after intrauterine relocation of an ectopic pregnancy. *Br J Obstet Gynaecol* 1994; **101**: 716–17.
7. Pearce JM, Hamid RI. Randomised controlled trial of the use of chorionic gonadotrophin in recurrent miscarriage associated with polycystic ovaries. *Br J Obstet Gynaecol* 1994; **101**: 685–8.
8. Hunter M. *Robert Boyle Reconsidered*. Cambridge: Cambridge University Press, 1994: 215–16.
9. Tucker WH. Reconsidering Burt: beyond a reasonable doubt. *J Hist Behav Sci* 1997; **33**: 145–62.

10. Anonymous. Erasures from register. *BMJ* 1975; **ii**: 392.

11. Anonymous. GMC Professional Conduct Committee. *BMJ* 1988; **296**: 306.

12. Brydensholt HH. The Danish Committees on Scientific Dishonesty. In: Lock SP, Wells FO, Farthing MGF, eds. *Fraud and Misconduct in Biomedical Research*, 3rd edn. London: BMJ Books, 2001: 126–30.

13. Launis V. Scientific fraud and misconduct in Finland. In: Lock SP, Wells FO, Farthing MGF, eds. *Fraud and Misconduct in Biomedical Research*, 3rd edn. London: BMJ Books, 2001: 131–3.

14. Nylenna M. Experiences of fraud and misconduct in healthcare research in Norway. In: Lock SP, Wells FO, Farthing MGF, eds. *Fraud and Misconduct in Biomedical Research*, 3rd edn. London: BMJ Books, 2001: 134–9.

15. Grandjean P. Public and private research culture and its importance for the occurrence of dishonesty. In: *Annual Report of the Danish Committees on Scientific Dishonesty*. Copenhagen: The Research Councils, November 2005: 9–12.

16. Vastag B. Cancer fraud case stuns research community. *J Natl Cancer Inst* 2006; **98**: 374–6.

17. Sudbø J, Lee JJ, Lippman SM et al. Non-steroidal anti-inflammatory drugs and the risks of oral cancer: a nested case–control study. *Lancet* 2005; **366**: 1359–66.

18. Horton R. Retraction [of Ref 17]. *Lancet* 2006; **367**: 382.

19. Sudbø J. Human papillomavirus infection as a risk factor for squamous-cell carcinoma of the head and neck. *N Engl J Med* 2001; **345**: 376–7.

20. Sudbø J, Samuelsson R, Risberg B et al. Risk markers of oral cancer in clinically normal mucosa as an aid in smoking cessation counselling. *J Clin Oncol* 2005; **23**: 1927–33.

21. Anonymous. Retraction [of Ref 20]. *J Clin Oncol* 2006; **24**: 5621.

22. Hallen A. *Responsible Research*. Oslo: The Research Council of Norway, 2006.

23. Sheldon T. Dutch neurologist found guilty of fraud. *BMJ* 2002; **325**: 734.

24. Hetherington J, Dickersin K, Chalmers I, Meinert CL. Retrospective and prospective identification of unpublished controlled trials: lessons from a survey of obstetricians and paediatricians. *Paediatrics* 1989; **84**: 374–80.

25. Hemminki E. Study of information submitted by drug companies to licensing authorities. *BMJ* 1980; **280**: 833–6.

26. Wells F, Lunnon MW. First Report of the Ethics Sub-Group. Society of Pharmaceutical Medicine. *Int J Pharm Med* 2000; **14**: 58–64.

27. Tonks A. A clinical trials register for Europe. *BMJ* 2002; **325**: 1314–15.

28. Herxheimer A. Open access to industry's clinically relevant data. *BMJ* 2004; **329**: 64–5.

29. Chalmers I. From optimism to disillusion about commitment to transparency in the medico-industrial complex. *J R Soc Med* 2006; **99**: 337–41.

30. International Committee of Medical Journal Editors. *Uniform Requirements for Manuscripts Submitted to Biomedical Journals: Writing and Editing for Biomedical Publication*. www.icmje.org (updated October 2007).

31. O'Halloran H. Transparency in disclosure of clinical trial information. *J Eur Med Writers Assoc* 2006; **15**: 15–17.

32. EFGCP Ethics Working Party Subgroup on Ethics Committees Reviewing Investigational Medicinal Products within the European Union. The procedure for the ethical review of protocols for clinical research projects in the European Union. *Int J Pharm Med* 2007; **21**: 1–113.

33. NHS R&D Forum. *Good Practice Guidance – Research Misconduct and Fraud*. London: Department of Health, July 2004.

34. Department of Health. *Research Governance Framework for Health and Social Care*, 2nd edn. London: Department of Health, April 2005.

35. Ankier SI. Fraud and misconduct in research. *Hosp Pharmacist* 2002; **9**: 214.

36. Ankier SI. Blowing the whistle. *Health Manage* 2002; **6**: 17–18.

37. Steneck N, Mayer T. Summary of the first International Conference on Research Integrity, Lisbon, 16–19 September 2007. European Science Foundation: *Science Policy Briefing* 2007; **30**: 6.

SECTION 3

THE PREVENTION OF RESEARCH MISCONDUCT

6 The promotion of good publication practice

Elizabeth Wager

Introduction

Although peer-reviewed journals have existed for over 200 years,[1] guidance for authors about expected standards of publication behaviour are surprisingly rare, and the best-known ones have been developed relatively recently. A survey of over 200 well-established biomedical journals with online instructions in English found, for example, that 41% gave no guidance about authorship criteria.[2]

Formal training in publication ethics, as part of research training, also appears to be the exception rather than the rule in UK medical colleges and universities, although this is harder to quantify. Within the pharmaceutical industry, although the conduct of clinical trials is carefully regulated to the internationally agreed standards of Good Clinical Practice (GCP), the production of publications has no such widely accepted framework. Similarly, whereas personnel who run clinical trials must be trained in GCP, training in responsible publication practices is much less widespread.

ICMJE Uniform Requirements

The best-known guidelines covering many aspects of publication practice are the statements of the International Committee of Medical Journal Editors (ICMJE – also known informally as the 'Vancouver Group' after the site of their first meeting). These statements form the so-called Uniform Requirements for Manuscripts Submitted to Biomedical Journals (or URM).[3] This document, first issued in 1979, was originally designed simply to standardize formats for submissions to avoid retyping papers if they were rejected by one journal and submitted to another.[4] Ed Huth, who has chronicled the development of the URM, notes that 'In its early years, the controversies surrounding the URM involved surprisingly heated arguments on reference formats ... and on other style issues. By the middle 1980s, however, the ICMJE had clearly started to shift its focus to consideration of important ethical issues facing authors and editors, including listing people as authors when the work was done only by others, duplicate publication, and scientific fraud.' The second edition of the URM, published in 1982, included a statement on duplicate publication. By 1988, statements on authorship criteria were added. The 1994 version introduced the term 'redundant publication'. The most recent version of the URM (issued in 2003) includes advice about authorship, editorship, conflicts of interest, obligation to publish negative studies, overlapping publications, privacy, and confidentiality.

Up to 1997, the ICMJE maintained a list of journals that endorsed the URM, and this exceeded 500 titles. The list is no longer maintained, so it is not possible to know exactly how many journals currently follow the URM. However, two surveys of journal instructions to authors suggest that the ICMJE remains influential. Altman found that 43% of a sample of 167 high-impact medical journals referred to the ICMJE guidelines in their instructions to authors in 2003.[5] In a similar survey of 234 journals, I found that 51% of those that included guidance about authorship in their instructions in 2006 referred to the URM.[2] However, both surveys also found that, although many journals claim to endorse the URM, a surprising proportion (57% in the 2003 Altman survey and 35% in my 2006 survey) cited an outdated version. If journal editors (and journal staff responsible for preparing instructions to authors) are unaware of the latest version of the URM, it seems safe to assume that an even larger proportion of clinicians and researchers are unfamiliar with them.

Research from the UK, India, the Netherlands, and France has shown that a considerable proportion of researchers are either ignorant of, or disagree with, the ICMJE authorship criteria.[6–9] However, the ICMJE URM have, undoubtedly, influenced guidance on publication practices provided by many individual journals. The URM are also widely cited in pharmaceutical company publication policies, especially in relation to determining authorship.

Individual journal instructions to authors/contributors

Despite the general lack of ethical guidance in the instructions issued by many journals,[10] there are some notable exceptions that provide helpful advice and promote good practice. Journals with extensive and thoughtful guidance covering research and publication misconduct include (but are not limited to) the *BMJ*,[11] *Lancet*,[12] *JAMA*,[13] *Obstetrics & Gynecology*,[14] and *Annals of Emergency Medicine*.[15]

While such efforts to educate potential authors about publication ethics are laudable, there is little or no evidence that they have any effect. Journal editors continue to complain that authors fail to comply with their instructions.[16] While failure to follow instructions about article length, reference style, and typescript layout are clearly visible, and relatively easily remedied, failure to follow requirements about multiple submissions, redundant publications, or authorship is often impossible to detect.

Good Publication Practice for pharmaceutical companies

Although the ICMJE Uniform Requirements provide helpful guidance about many aspects of publication ethics that are applicable to all publications, until recently they gave virtually no specific guidance about publications developed by drug companies. One area of considerable concern was the role of professional medical writers in preparing documents and how this should be disclosed. Following a three-way meeting between journal editors, academic investigators, and drug company employees organized by the Council of Biology Editors in 1998, a set of guidelines was developed to fill the gaps left by the URM.[17] Their aim was to encourage responsible practice within the pharmaceutical industry. The title 'Good publication practice for pharmaceutical companies' was chosen to emphasize the fact that publication is the final stage of research and to suggest parallels with the well-established frameworks for Good Clinical Practice and Good Laboratory Practice.

Unfortunately, at about the same time, the Committee on Publication Ethics (COPE) also developed a set of guidelines for journal editors and called these Good Publication Practice, so it is important to distinguish the pharmaceutical industry guidelines (GPP-pc) from the COPE guidelines (COPE-GPP).

GPP-pc was developed by an informal group of drug company employees who worked on publications, although it had its origins in the three-way meeting. Participants in the original meeting (editors and researchers) were given a chance to comment on the text, and it was also circulated among several major pharmaceutical companies. The final version was published in 2003.[17] The GPP-pc guidelines cover relations between investigators and commercial research sponsors, and set out the role of professional writers and how they should interact with named authors. They encourage disclosure not only of research funding but also of writing assistance, with the aim of eradicating the practice of 'ghostwriting' when medical writers are not acknowledged. They reiterate the ICMJE guidance on redundant and premature publication.

Perhaps the most challenging aspect of GPP-pc is that it calls upon pharmaceutical companies to endeavour to publish the results of all their clinical trials. In the late 1990s, when the guidelines were being developed, the pharmaceutical industry was largely opposed to proposals for trial registration, which were designed to reduce the problem of publication bias. Many companies viewed trial results as commercial property and believed that funding the study gave them the right to decide whether and how to publish it. This position had been repeatedly challenged, and failure to publish had even been suggested to be a form of research misconduct.[18,19] However, it was not until 2005 that trial registration became widely accepted by the industry, following the announcement by the ICMJE in 2004 that members of the committee would no longer consider trials for publication unless they had been registered.[20,21]

Growing calls for prospective trial registration also coincided with a lawsuit in the USA in which GlaxoSmithKline was accused of failing to publish the results of all its studies.[22,23] Several companies, including GlaxoSmithKline, have since made public commitments to publish all clinical trials of marketed products, and this position has also been promoted by industry associations.[24]

When GPP-pc was being developed, over 70 companies were asked if they would publicly endorse the guidelines. At the time of publication, just nine drug companies agreed to be listed, although employees from several other companies had been involved in developing the guidelines. Communication agencies, which develop a large proportion of industry-sponsored publications, were more willing to endorse the guidelines, despite the fact that they were never approached directly. This suggests that the requirement to publish findings from all clinical trials may have prevented many drug companies from endorsing the guidelines (this provision, obviously, did not apply to the agencies, since they do not sponsor research). Another factor that probably reduced the number of companies that endorsed the guidelines was the fact that the US industry association, Pharmaceutical Research and Manufacturers of America (PhRMA), published a similar, but less demanding, set of guidelines in 2002.[25] The PhRMA principles drew heavily on the GPP-pc document (which had been circulated to many companies before it was finally published), but the requirement to publish results of all trials was notably watered down, requiring companies only to 'commit to timely communication of meaningful results of controlled clinical trials of marketed products' and specifically excluding 'exploratory studies' from this requirement. (Interestingly, the 2002 document also stated, 'sponsors do not commit ... to make the designs of clinical trial protocols available publicly at inception, as in a clinical trials registry', but the PhRMA position on trial registration was reversed in 2005.[24])

The small number of companies publicly supporting GPP-pc could be taken as a sign of failure and lack of influence. Yet the GPP-pc guidelines are cited in the publication policies of several major companies, and appear to have influenced the development of the PhRMA principles. They were also strongly endorsed in a House of Commons Select Committee report on the UK pharmaceutical industry produced in 2005.[26] The GPP-pc guidelines therefore appear to have had some indirect influence, and may have encouraged pharmaceutical companies to develop publication policies that encouraged responsible practice. Some journals (notably the *BMJ* and those published by BioMed Central) include links to the GPP-pc website in their instructions to authors and require that publications from the pharmaceutical industry should follow the guidelines.

Guidelines for medical writers

Since the GPP-pc guidelines, which were the first to mention medical writers, were produced, a more detailed code of conduct and two position statements on the role of professional writers have been published. The first statement came from the American Medical Writers Association (AMWA), but it gave little detailed advice about good practice.[27] A more detailed code of conduct was published by the European Medical Writers Association (EMWA) in 2005.[28] This gives detailed recommendations about when writers qualify for authorship of papers and how they, and their funding source, should be acknowledged when they are not listed as authors. Most recently, the International Society of Medical Publication Professionals (ISMPP) has issued a position statement on the role of medical writers.[29] These three documents are aimed at individual writers (rather than entire pharmaceutical companies) and promote responsible practices in developing publications. In particular, they seek to prevent ghost authorship (when deserving authors are not acknowledged) and guest authorship (when individuals who have made little or no contribution to a publication are listed). They also seek to prevent companies from preparing documents (e.g. review articles or editorials) and then seeking suitable 'authors' prepared to put their names on them despite having had nothing to do with their development.

Statements from editors' organizations

While the ICMJE statements are probably most widely known and referred to, two other organizations of journal editors have produced policy statements and guidelines on various aspects of publication misconduct. The Council of Science Editors (CSE, formerly called the Council of Biology Editors) has produced a white paper on promoting integrity in scientific journal publications and a discussion paper on authorship.[30,31] The World Association of Medical Editors (WAME) has also issued policy statements on authorship, trial registration, ghostwriting, and conflicts of interest. WAME has also produced recommendations on publication ethics policies for medical journals that cover several of the previous topics plus plagiarism and study ethics.[32] Although no formal surveys have been published, these guidelines appear to be less often cited in journal instructions than those of the ICMJE, so it is hard to assess their influence.

COPE has produced a code of conduct for editors,[33] which it promotes among its members (currently around 2000 journals). The European Association of Science Editors (EASE) publishes a handbook for editors that includes sections on good refereeing practice and the ethics of scientific publication.[34]

Journal peer-review practices

Some editorial practices may prevent certain types of publication misconduct. Requiring that all trials be registered, and including a registration number on every publication, are aimed to reduce non-publication, and should improve the detection of redundant publication.[35] The initiative from the ICMJE of refusing to publish trials unless they have been registered has acted as a major spur for registration.[20,21,36] However, it is too early to measure the effects of widespread adoption of such requirements, since they were only introduced in a small number of journals in 2005, although increasing numbers of journals are following the example set by the ICMJE and are now demanding registration numbers.

Trial registration may also help to reduce selective or misleading reporting, since reported results can be compared with the original register entry, which should show when outcomes have been omitted or misrepresented (e.g. if secondary end points are presented as if they were the primary outcome). Selective reporting has been shown to be widespread.[37] In a series of 102 trials approved by a Danish research ethics committee, Chan et al found that 50% of efficacy end points and 65% of safety end points were incompletely reported.[38] In a similar study, Chan et al found that, in 40% of trials approved by the Canadian Institutes of Health Research, the primary outcomes were different from those stated in the protocols.[39] Such misconduct is difficult for journals to detect, but may be prevented by trial registration or reviewing the trial protocol alongside the report of the findings.

Institutional guidelines

Many academic institutions have guidelines on research conduct, and these sometimes include publication issues. These often refer to other guidelines, such as the

ICMJE authorship criteria, but, given the research suggesting that many academics are unaware of these criteria, or choose to ignore them, the influence and enforcement of such institutional policies may be limited. Boyd et al interviewed academics at two US institutions and found that less than half of them were able to state their conflict of interest policy.[40] In an earlier survey, Cho et al found considerable variation in institutions' conflict of interest policies and lack of specificity about the type of relationships that were prohibited.[41]

Preventing plagiarism

Plagiarism is receiving increasing attention among academics and journal editors. The rapid growth of material available on the Internet, combined with near-universal access to computers, greatly facilitates plagiarism by 'copying and pasting', and this is now recognized as a serious problem at many academic institutions. However, the standards promoted by universities may differ from those demanded by medical journals. For example, in a case presented to the *BMJ* Ethics Committee, the journal editor contacted an author's institution with clear evidence of plagiarism (in an article submitted to the journal), but the author was not found guilty of misconduct because the university did not judge the degree of plagiarism to be sufficiently serious to warrant disciplinary action.

Many academic institutions are now using plagiarism detection software to reduce cheating by students. Systems that permit students to 'check' their work before submission may help to educate students in correct referencing and in avoiding plagiarism. The University of Newcastle, New South Wales, Australia, introduced a policy of using 'Turnitin' to check student work in 2003, and a subsequent survey of academic staff showed that 84% considered that the use of this software deterred students from plagiarizing.[42] However, most institutions recognize that software alone cannot promote good practice, but recommend an integrated approach to communicate and enforce policies among both students and staff.[43] Many universities have created special resources for this, such as websites about plagiarism.[44]

Punishment as a deterrent

As with other types of misdemeanour, the punishment of offenders may act as a deterrent. Reporting cases of publication misconduct, and any sanctions applied, may also raise awareness and improve practice. However, anecdotal evidence suggests that many journals are reluctant to instigate investigations and may also be reluctant to publicize cases, partly through fears of legal action. Cases presented to COPE and the *BMJ* Ethics Committee have also revealed that academic institutions may be unwilling to investigate cases of publication misconduct, perhaps because of concerns about the resulting bad publicity or perhaps because they lack the policies and mechanisms to organize this properly.

A range of sanctions are available when journal editors receive evidence of misconduct (see Chapters 2 and 10). To be effective as a deterrent, such punishment should be applied consistently. However, virtually no guidance is available to editors, and journal practices appear to vary widely. Cooperation between journal editors to agree punishments appropriate for the various types and severities of publication misconduct is needed, and might usefully be addressed by one or more of the editors' organizations such as COPE, CSE, EASE, or WAME.

Conclusions

There have been several initiatives to promote good practice and deter publication misconduct. Mostly these have taken the form of written guidelines published in journals or on websites. Of these, the ICMJE guidelines are the most widely quoted in journal instructions for authors; however, they are by no means universally known or accepted by researchers. Some academic institutions cover aspects of publication ethics, such as authorship policies and definitions of plagiarism, in their initial training for new researchers.

Since the prevalence of publication misconduct has never been accurately assessed, it is impossible to judge whether initiatives designed to promote good practice have been effective. Drawing analogies from studies of clinical behaviour and decision making, it seems likely that written information alone may not have a marked effect on behaviour but that guidelines should form the basis for a multimodal approach to promoting good practice. Universities that have adopted a firm and coherent policy on student plagiarism (backed up by training for both students and staff), together with a consistent and fair approach to disciplining offenders, have reported improvements in behaviour. Similar approaches to all aspects of publication misconduct should be piloted.

Journal editors, academic institutions, research sponsors, and commercial organizations involved in medical research should work together to agree, promote, and enforce universal standards for responsible publication. A combination of providing clear guidelines, training researchers in the responsibilities of authors and reviewers, and applying consistent sanctions and disciplinary actions after properly managed investigations may reduce misconduct. However, at present, guidelines are fragmented, few institutions provide training for researchers on publication ethics, journals and academic institutions are often unwilling to investigate cases of alleged misconduct, and, even when cases are properly investigated, disciplinary actions or sanctions against offenders are not applied consistently.

References

1. Kronick DA. Peer review in 18th century scientific journalism. *JAMA* 1990; **263**: 1321–2.
2. Wager E. Do medical journals provide clear and consistent guidelines on authorship? *MedGenMed* 2007; **9**: 16.
3. International Committee of Medical Journal Editors. *Uniform Requirements for Manuscripts Submitted to Biomedical Journals: Writing and Editing for Biomedical Publication*, Section III.D.3. www.icmje.org.

4. Huth EJ, Case K. The URM: twenty-five years old. *Science Editor* 2004; **27**: 17–21.

5. Altman DG. Endorsement of the CONSORT statement by high impact medical journals: survey of instructions for authors. *BMJ* 2005; **330**: 1056–7.

6. Bhopal R, Rankin J, McColl E et al. The vexed question of authorship: views of researchers in a British medical faculty. *BMJ* 1997; **314**: 1009–12.

7. Dhaliwal U, Singh N, Bhatia A. Awareness of authorship criteria and conflict: survey in a medical institution in India. *MedGenMed* 2006; **8**: 52.

8. Hoen WP, Walvoort HC, Overbeke AJ. What are the factors determining authorship and the order of the authors' names? A study among authors of the *Nederlands Tijdschrift voor Geneeskunde* (*Dutch Journal of Medicine*). *JAMA* 1998; **280**: 217–18.

9. Pignatelli B, Maisonneuve H, Chapuis F. Authorship ignorance: views of researchers in French clinical settings. *J Med Ethics* 2005; **31**: 578-81.

10. Schriger DL, Arora S, Altman DG. The content of medical journal instructions for authors. *Ann Emerg Med* 2006; **48**: 743–9.

11. *BMJ*. Editorial Policies. resources.bmj.com/bmj/authors/editorial-policies.

12. *Lancet*. Information for Authors. www.thelancet.com/authors/lancet/authorinfo.

13. *JAMA*. Editorial Policies. jama.ama-assn.org/misc/editpolicy.dtl

14. The American College of Obstetricians and Gynecologists. *A Guide to Writing for Obstetrics & Gynecology*, 4th edn, 2005. www.greenjournal.org/misc/WritersGuide.pdf.

15. Callaham ML. Journal policy on ethics in scientific publication. *Ann Emerg Med* 2003; **41**: 82–9.

16. Pitkin RM. The rewards of reading instructions from journal editors. *N Engl J Med* 1998; **339**: 1006.

17. Wager E, Field EA, Grossman L. Good publication practice for pharmaceutical companies. *Curr Med Res Opin* 2003; **19**: 149–54.

18. Simes RJ. Publication bias: the case for an international registry of clinical trials. *J Clin Oncol* 1986; **4**: 1529-41.

19. Chalmers I. Underreporting research is scientific misconduct. *JAMA* 1990; **263**: 1405–8.

20. De Angelis C, Drazen JM, Frizelle FA et al. Clinical trial registration: a statement from the International Committee of Medical Journal Editors. *Lancet* 2004; **364**: 911–12.

21. De Angelis C, Drazen JM, Frizelle FA et al. Is this clinical trial fully registered? A statement from the International Committee of Medical Journal Editors. *Lancet* 2005; **365**: 1827–9.

22. Drug company to make its trial results public. *BMJ* 2004; **329**: 366.

23. Dyer O. GlaxoSmithKline to set up comprehensive online clinical trials register. *BMJ* 2004; **329**: 590.

24. IFPMA, EFPIA, JPMA, PhRMA. *Joint Position on the Disclosure of Clinical Trial Information via Clinical Trial Registries and Databases*. www.ifpma.org.

25. Pharmaceutical Research and Manufacturers of America (PhRMA). *Principles on Conduct of Clinical Trials and Communication of Clinical Trial Results*. www.phrma.org.

26. House of Commons Health Committee Report. *Influence of the Pharmaceutical Industry* (HC 42-1, 5 April 2005). www.parliament.uk/parliamentary_committees/ health_committee.cfm.

27. Hamilton CW, Royer MG. AMWA position statement on the contributions of medical writers to scientific publications. *AMWA J* 2003; **18**: 13–15.

28. Jacobs A, Wager E. EMWA guidelines on the role of medical writers in developing peer-reviewed publications. *Curr Med Res Opin* 2005; **21**: 317–21.

29. Norris R, Bowman A, Fagan JM et al. International Society for Medical Publication Professionals (ISMPP) position statement: the role of the professional medical writer. *Curr Med Res Opin* 2007; **23**: 1837–40.

30. Council of Science Editors. *CSE's White Paper on Promoting Integrity in Scientific Journal Publications*. Reston, VA: CSE, 2006. www.councilscienceeditors.org/ editorial_policies/white_paper.cfm.

31. Council of Science Editors. *Who's the Author? Problems with Biomedical Authorship, and Some Possible Solutions*. www.councilscienceeditors.org/publications/v23n4p111-119.pdf.

32. World Association of Medical Editors. *WAME Recommendations on Publication Ethics Policies for Medical Journals*. wame.org/resources/policies.

33. Committee on Publication Ethics. *A Code of Conduct for Editors of Biomedical Journals*. www.publicationethics.org.uk/guidelines.

34. Maisonneuve H, Enckell PH, Polderman AKS et al. *European Association of Science Editors: Science Editors' Handbook*. Woking, Surrey: EASE, 2003.

35. Sim I, Chan A-W, Gülmezoglu AM et al. Clinical trial registration: transparency is the watchword. *Lancet* 2006; **367**: 1631–3.

36. Zarin DA, Tse T, Ide NC. Trial registration at ClinicalTrials.gov between May and October 2005. *N Engl J Med* 2005; **335**: 2779–87.

37. Chan A-W, Altman DG. Identifying outcome reporting bias in randomised trials on PubMed: review of publications and survey of authors. *BMJ* 2005; **330**: 753.

38. Chan A-W, Hrobjartsson A, Haahr MT et al. Empirical evidence for selective reporting of outcomes in randomized trials. *JAMA* 2004; **291**: 2457–65.

39. Chan A-W, Krleža-Jeric K, Schmid I, Altman DG. Outcome reporting bias in randomized trials funded by the Canadian Institutes of Health Research. *CMAJ* 2004; **171**: 735–40.

40. Boyd EA, Cho MK, Bero LA. Financial conflict-of-interest policies in clinical research: issues for clinical investigators. *Acad Med* 2003; **78**: 769–74.

41. Cho MK, Shohara S, Schissel A, Rennie D. Policies on faculty conflicts of interest at US universities. *JAMA* 2000; **284**: 2203–8.

42. Ryan S, Eckersley C. *Academic Integrity and Use of Turnitin*. www.newcastle.edu.au/ services/teaching-learning.

43. Carroll J, Appleton J. *Plagiarism: A Good Practice Guide*. www.jiscpas.ac.uk/ documents/brookes.pdf.

44. *Plagiarism – University of Leeds Guide*. www.lts.leeds.ac.uk/plagiarism/index.php.

7 Monitoring medical research: Better to prevent than to cure?

Helena van den Dungen

Why and how to monitor the quality and safety of medical research data

The Declaration of Helsinki[1] states that 'medical progress is based on research which ultimately must rest in part on experimentation involving human subjects'. It is of the utmost importance, therefore, that the data derived from medical research are not only carefully collected and do not endanger patient safety during their collection, but are also verifiable and of high quality. Human subjects should not be unnecessarily endangered through their participation in medical research without care being taken to achieve the explicit aim of obtaining usable data. Likewise, medical research involving humans must conform to generally accepted scientific standards (similarly reflected in the Declaration). If data derived from medical research are eventually to be used to make medical and scientific decisions, with the goal of helping and curing future patients, the fact that they are untrue or untrustworthy may have far-reaching effects and may even endanger patients. Clearly, when medical research data are not to be trusted, accurate decision making for future patient care is not possible. Therefore, it is essential to ensure that the data used for medical decision making (e.g. the approval of marketing authorizations for new drugs) are valid. In fact, this should really be a tripartite effort: on the part of the industry developing new drugs; on the part of scientists involved in the generation of information on the product and investigators who conduct the preclinical and clinical trials; and on the part of governments, with their regulatory authorities and ethics committees that are ultimately responsible for the safety and well-being of the public and patients. Optimally, these three parties should cooperate as much as possible. None of these parties can do this by themselves, but their goal is the same, namely safe and effective medicines available to the patients who need them.

All three parties have, of course, their own processes that can be put into use to ensure that this goal is reached. The pharmaceutical industry uses its internal standards, quality control processes, and especially its auditing processes. Investigators and scientists have their professional training and medical–ethical standards. The authorities have, over time, implemented regulations, guidelines, and evaluation processes for medical research to fulfil their responsibility to protect the public.

Increase in regulation

The second half of the twentieth century saw an acceleration in the growth of regulations surrounding the granting of marketing authorizations. More, and more stringent, regulations and ethical standards have been implemented in most global markets. At the same time, and maybe as a consequence of this, reflecting the tightening of regulation of the clinical trial environment, the principles of Good Clinical Practice (GCP) have been introduced to ensure quality and safety. Most of the time, this tightening of regulations has followed the path of incidences, unwanted situations, errors, and (in many cases) scientific sloppiness, misconduct, and fraud, because the authorities felt the need for increased control.

Incidents that contributed to the awareness for the need of regulations in this area included the occurrence of fatal allergic reactions to penicillin, the indiscriminate administration of streptomycin leading to irreversible deafness, and the use of chloramphenicol causing aplastic anaemia in 1 out of 20 000 cases. Eventually, the ethylene glycol disaster led to the 1938 Federal Food and Drug and Cosmetic Act[2,3] being passed by the US Congress to authorize factory inspections and requiring new drugs to be proved safe before marketing in the USA. Until the Second World War, new drugs were developed without methodological studies. In the 1950s and 1960s, the first clinical trials were initiated (British, French, and Austrian groups were among the first), but there were no formal legal requirements. This really changed after multiple cases became evident of humans being harmed from participation in clinical trials, as was made clear in the immediate post-war years, when humans had been used in a highly unethical manner and in wholly unacceptable situations, sometimes merely to satisfy the unhealthy curiosity of so-called scientists. Also, in a number of cases, the use of insufficiently tested drugs led to critical problems. The most widely known case is that of thalidomide.[2] This was developed as a new sleeping pill for use in the first trimester of pregnancy. This drug was found to cause severe fetal abnormalities, which only became evident after it had already been sold in 46 countries, affecting thousands of children.

Over the last few decades, the regulatory mechanisms to deal with these problems have become ever more detailed. Presently, the network of regulations is virtually global, and similar in various markets. In addition, exchange of information and best practices between regulators is accepted on a global level. Regulations fall into a number of different categories:

- requirements for the content of the dossier for application of a marketing authorization for medicinal products, i.e. scientific and quality information on the product, safety and efficacy information collected, type and number of preclinical and clinical trials, and their outcome as the basis of safety and efficacy information (*GCP and pharmacovigilance requirements*)[4,5]
- requirements for production of medicinal products (*GMP requirements*)
- requirements for the essential safety tests to be performed on the products (*GLP requirements*)
- requirements for transport (*GDP requirements*).

Quality of data

There are several stages in the clinical trial and marketing authorization processes where systems to assess the quality of medical research data have been implemented: competent authorities have installed an assessment process with assessors and inspection processes with inspectors; and they have now installed processes for the notification of clinical trials. Approval processes have been established for research ethics committees whose responsibility is to review all clinical protocols. Pharmaceutical companies have established clinical monitoring and auditing of their trial sites, systems and data; and editors of scientific journals have installed processes to avoid duplication or omission of data in their journals.[6] All of these monitoring processes are working towards the objective of ensuring that collected data can be trusted.

Monitoring by the regulatory authorities

During the last two decades, regulators worldwide have put into operation monitoring systems to evaluate and ensure compliance with these regulations, by installing extensive assessment procedures (evaluation of supporting documentation), as well as inspections (monitoring of compliance with respect to the practical aspects of the conduct of clinical trials and verification of the processes and data reported). These inspections are usually directed at GCP, pharmacovigilance, and ethics. They may be conducted at all of the sites involved in all stages of the conduct of the trial: sponsor, investigator, contract research organization (CRO), specialized departments, manufacturer, pharmacy, and legal offices, as well as ethics committees or institutional review boards.

Inspections and inspectors can only function when there is an appropriate legal framework that can be used as the standard against which to inspect. Legal standards are their only basis, and guide where and what to inspect, and when and by whom to prevent arbitrary or even despotic behaviour. Thus, when regulations became more stringent and explicit, this enabled the inspectorates, more effectively, to implement inspections and inspect regulated areas of clinical research. The activities of the regulatory authorities with respect to inspections of clinical trials became more and more visible. So, too, did some of the negative results, such as suspension and even withdrawal of medicines from the market.

Pharmacovigilance inspections

Ideally, any situations where, on the grounds of inadequate efficacy or safety, products should be suspended or withdrawn should be avoided, as these products have already resulted in harm to patients and created public distrust in the medical profession and pharmaceutical industry. However, it is implicit in the standard process of drug development that such problems are frequently only detected after a large population of patients has been exposed to the drug. At present, owing to increasing drug development costs (resulting in high medicine costs and hence high health-care costs), there is very considerable pressure (not only from the industry, but also from patient groups as well as authorities themselves) towards faster drug development processes. That is why more and more emphasis is being put on the need for the implementation of a proactive, effective pharmacovigilance system by the marketing authorization holder. In addition, pharmacovigilance monitoring by the licensing authorities has been strengthened by the introduction of additional guidance and regulations, such as the new Volume 9A of the rules governing medicinal products in the European Union (EU), EudraLex (ec.europa.eu/enterprise/pharmaceuticals/eudralex/homev9.htm).[4] As a result of these pressures, there has been an enormous increase in pharmacovigilance inspection activities.

Investigator site inspections

The more traditional approach to monitoring by the regulatory authorities is the inspection of investigator sites. The most common form that this has taken until now is the preapproval inspection of trial sites of studies that are considered pivotal for the application dossier. As it is, however, virtually impossible to inspect all trials, let alone all trial sites, two selections have to be made as part of the assessment (whether an inspection is needed or not; and, if 'yes', then which site should be inspected). Trials may be selected for inspection on the basis of a number of trigger factors, such as innovative approach, new chemical entities, and important indications or unusual outcomes. The choice of trial sites selected for inspection can be made on the basis of high inclusion rates or possibly as a result of anomalies detected during the assessment process. The inspectorate is then requested to give input and subsequently to conduct the inspection and report. It is important to note that the inspection report is part of the entire application assessment process, and is (usually) not the only conclusive factor in this decision-making process.

Sponsor inspections

Inspection of sponsor companies has also been conducted for many years. Some regulatory authorities have implemented these inspections as separate activities, whereas others have evaluated the compliance of the sponsor with the responsibilities attributed to them and their activities from the perspective of the investigator sites. The assessment of the activities of the sponsor and their fulfilment of the regulatory expectations are as seen at the investigator site, without a physical inspection actually being conducted at the sponsor site. Responsibilities of research ethics committees may be conducted similarly, as detailed below.

Sometimes, these inspections are called 'sponsor-monitoring inspections', as they often focus strongly on the monitoring activities that have been put in place at the investigator sites. As these activities are an essential part of the quality control of the sponsor in the trial, these inspections give a good perspective on the quality systems as a whole that the sponsor uses to ensure oversight of the trial.

Partly related to these types of inspections are the inspections at CROs that have been contracted by the sponsor to perform part or whole of the trial, including, for example, analytical and monitoring activities. These are completely the responsibility of the sponsor, and inspection findings are accordingly attributed to the sponsor.

Inspections by ethics committees and institutional review boards

The approval of clinical trials (and the continuing review once the trial has started) by research ethics committees (RECs) is a pivotal step in the protection of the patients. Inspections by RECs do not (yet) occur in all countries. Notably in the USA and in a number of European countries (e.g. Italy, Spain, the Netherlands and the UK), they take a prominent place. In some countries, the regulations follow closely the GCP requirements for the functioning of RECs; in other countries (the USA, the Netherlands, the UK, and Italy), additional regulations explicitly directed at REC function have been introduced.

Inspections of RECs can occur in different formats. During an inspection of a clinical trial as part of a sponsor or investigator inspection, the REC approval process is always scrutinized. During these inspections, the documentation on the REC approval can be evaluated and checked for timeliness, completeness, and adequacy. REC membership and potential conflict-of-interest situations may also be part of this type of monitoring. In fact, this is similar to what sponsors should have been evaluating during their activities to ensure patient safety and patient protection in their clinical trials.

Inspections of the RECs themselves may also form a part of the monitoring of patient safety and protection by the regulatory authorities. During such inspections, the rules of operation, approval processes, and internal REC documentation may be checked by the inspectors.

Other inspection types

In a category by themselves are the independent investigators conducting clinical trials without the support of the pharmaceutical industry. These are sometimes referred to as academic trials or non-commercial trials, and have their special aspects. According to GCP, these investigators carry the responsibilities of the sponsor as well as of the investigator. They require also a special category of inspection, paying due regard to factors that must be guarded against.

Inspection findings

It is unusual for a regulatory inspection to be without reportable findings. The inspectors look at the trial and the quality systems that have been implemented from outside the system of the trial or sponsor. This has the advantage of being able to identify habits and non-compliance situations that have not otherwise been detected by the participants in the clinical research. It is also inherent to an inspection to report only on the deviations and non-compliance situations. Seldom will an inspection report list all the things that went right; the standard perspective is that the regulations should have been followed.

Inspection findings are reported by the regulatory authorities on their websites, during training sessions held for the industry, in their annual reports, or during industry meetings and conferences.

One thing is clear from these publications: inspection findings are overall similar between inspectorates globally and the findings apply to all aspects of the clinical trials.

Nevertheless, from inspection to inspection and from site to site, the severity and occurrence of findings differ, but, on a global and annual level, all aspects of the trial may be cited in the list of findings. After so many years of regulations and increasing attention to the implementation of quality control into clinical trials, this is undoubtedly disappointing. However, the increase in complexity of clinical research, as well as the increase in quality of, and experience with, inspection techniques, and the higher expectations that follow, all contribute to this.

It is interesting to note the historical differences in the approach to the orientation of inspections between the US Food and Drug Administration (FDA) and the EU inspectors. Traditionally, the FDA inspections lean heavily on verification of individual trial data, whereas in the EU overall, an important focus has been put on the evaluation of the quality systems in place and only secondarily on verification of the data. However, now, in both the USA and the EU, inspectors address both aspects more or less equally.

The most frequently reported inspection findings relate to investigator or sponsor oversight of the clinical trial protocol as a root cause for a number of inspection findings, such as informed consent problems, poor documentation of source data, protocol deviations and under-reporting of adverse events. In many cases, part of the problem is overhasty start-up of the clinical trial at the site and poor training of the investigator and their team, as well as site selection being based on the importance of the investigator for the indicated area of the clinical trial rather than the investigator's clinical trial skills.

These root causes may lead from minor aberrations to critical problems. The critical problems may eventually lead to misconduct and fraud, with various face-saving activities being revealed, together with concealment of errors, amendment of missing documentation and analyses, antedating or postdating of records, or outright invention of data.

Fraud and misconduct

Despite the frequency and seriousness of inspection findings, most data resulting from the conduct of a clinical trial can be relied upon, or verified, even if they are not 100% compliant with GCP. Nevertheless, among the many data sets that are compliant, there are some that are not, for a variety of reasons. Some of the untrustworthy medical research data have simply been collected in a careless manner that has not conformed to generally accepted scientific standards. Some medical research has been conducted badly – in fact has been 'misconducted'. In other cases, it has been proven that data have been knowingly fabricated for financial gain or with the aim of acquiring prestige. All these situations are discovered during inspections. Sometimes, the inspectors are led there by a whistleblower. In some cases, the application dossier gives rise to suspicions, and inspections are carried out to verify the suspicion. In other cases, a routine inspection may discover such irregularities. In addition, there are frequently rumours that raise concerns that identified cases are far outnumbered by those that are undiscovered or covered up. It is only with great difficulty that this unease can be alleviated through regulatory monitoring and inspections. However, it is essential that such concerns *are* addressed, as the implications are enormous. Trial subjects may clearly have been placed at risk in such a trial; and future trial subjects, as well as future patients or consumers, may be at risk if irregularities are not detected and dealt with. For licensing authorities, the reliability of submitted and/or published data is undermined, as is their ability to protect and promote the public health. Moreover, the public's trust in health care, in the pharmaceutical industry, and in the medical profession is thereby undermined.

Additionally, the monetary costs that are incurred when clinical research data cannot be trusted may be very considerable: loss of study data, possible need for re-generation of data, delay in submitting data for registration, and delayed availability of the drug will be a great burden for the company involved. Inspections and the corrective actions that follow are themselves expensive.

Size of the problem

It is extremely difficult to determine how great the problem of untrustworthy data is. The same applies to the risk of faulty judgements on safety and efficacy of treatments. Indeed, how does one calculate the frequency of fraudulent medical research?

Firstly, the definitions used to describe the phenomena of untrue or untrustworthy or unverifiable data differ. Secondly, the total volume of medical research is vast, and its boundaries are not clearly outlined. The total body of scientific medical research, clinical and preclinical, including innovative research, as well as late development clinical trials and post-marketing pharmaceutical research, has to be considered if the frequency of the incidence of misconduct is to be estimated. Trying to decide when misconduct is most prevalent is also difficult, as there is no clear transition from one type of clinical research to another. Furthermore, despite the relevant regulations, not all clinical research projects are registered in voluntary web-based databases or in databases required by the regulatory authorities.

The total occurrence of fraudulent medical research in any cross-section of the total volume of medical research is likewise difficult, if not impossible, to gauge. The percentage that one is likely to come up with depends on the position one has, which area of expertise one applies, and with whom one talks. Interestingly – and many inventories have been made on this topic – in all scientific groups, there are a number of people who have active knowledge of fraud in their direct environment.

Neither percentage nor frequency can be used as a mathematical term to assess the impact of fraudulent data on the progress of science and medical development. The most extreme view is to argue that perhaps no scientific or medical research is completely free of fraud or misconduct in some form. However, less extreme and more realistic is the view that, in the scientific community, there is less and less acceptance of 'mistakes', and issues such as perceived fraud and misconduct are more likely to be notified to the responsible management and to the authorities for them to be scrutinized and dealt with appropriately. Such episodes are now more likely to be made public than previously, and the result of this is that there is a perception that more and more fraud-like activities have occurred. This perception does nothing to instil trust in clinical research.

Resources

In order for a true fraud monitoring system to function, adequate financial resources must be available. It follows that if there is a certain frequency of suspected fraud, it must be possible to maintain sufficient resources. When resources are limited, however, it may be necessary to prioritize when and where a full evaluation should be performed.

Even when they are well resourced, not all clinical trials and all trial sites can be subjected to inspection. Moreover, as the responsibility for the quality and safety of clinical research data is shared between all parties, there might be some resistance to the thought that a full evaluation might be needed. This must be approached in a balanced manner, and it would be helpful to be able to design a risk-based strategy. This approach is increasingly becoming accepted, as it is at the core of auditing by the industry as an inspection strategy. However, predicting the risks that a given data set might be corrupted is very difficult. Also, for such an approach, it is necessary to have an idea about the size of the problem. How should we go about this? How can the public be reassured that, on the whole, the data used upon which medical decisions are based are valid? Is this in fact true? Should a system be developed that is better suited to detect fraud and misconduct? Or is what is already in place in the way of safeguards (inspections, assessors, auditors, and clinical monitors) in medical research and clinical trials sufficient? What other approach is there? Certainly, all parties involved in the conduct of clinical trials should accept that this must be a combined responsibility.

Is it necessary to have an assessment of the frequency with which fraud and misconduct occur to address the problem of how to monitor or audit the problem? This is probably not the case – as even one fraud case is one too many. Every fraud case will have some impact on the available scientific and medical data set that should eventually contribute to the cure of patients. If the data set is untrustworthy, this will delay the development of new cures, and may even endanger the public through the promotion of unsafe treatments and therapies.

It is important to find a way to ensure that the data sets used are of high quality, so that medical decisions can be made safely and with confidence. To know which data are good and which are bad, it is necessary to find a way of monitoring the quality of the research and the derived data. This is admittedly a difficult question, as most fraud cases come to light long after decision making has taken place.

An inspector or an auditor in a pharmaceutical company undoubtedly encounters a higher percentage of fraud than does any other profession. But all professions, increasingly frequently, actively look for irregularities rather than merely working from the presumption of verification. This will possibly further enhance the perception of the frequency of fraud and misconduct.

A complicating factor is that more and more electronic systems are used for the capture and management of medical research data. This brings with it, however, the possibility of verifying through electronic audit trails the actual collection of the data (at what time and by whom) and the way in which these have been handled (changes): see Chapter 12. Also, meta-analysis of collected data and trend analysis are commonly used to select data sets that may need further scrutiny, including inspection or audit.

Additionally, enhanced statistical techniques (see Chapter 11) and signal detection are put in place by pharmaceutical companies, as well as by the regulatory authorities.

The focus of monitoring has therefore dramatically changed from being merely a percentage of verification to a selection of specific sites or areas in a risk-based strategy that uses all the available techniques and information. The results of such activities are more and more openly discussed, reported, and published. Both the availability of new techniques and the risk-based approach contribute to the perception that occurrences of fraud and misconduct occur more and more frequently. They also provide the potential to go back to old trials and evaluate their quality and trustworthiness. Caution should be exercised in doing this, however, as it might open a veritable Pandora's box, further undermining trust in medical research as a whole.

Cure

When fraud is detected, it is usually too late – too late to protect subjects who participated in the research, and sometimes too late to protect patients subjected to treatment based on false data. Moreover, such practices may cause a delay in the progress of medical development and result in unnecessary suffering for patients who do not get potential new treatments. An additional effect is loss of public confidence in the medical and pharmaceutical professions.

Merely putting into place more controls and monitoring to deal with the problem of untrustworthy/unverifiable data that are directed to the cure of a situation that has already gone badly is almost undoubtedly the wrong approach, and is definitely costly. Surely, prevention is better than cure?

Prevention

How much better it would be to develop ways in which to prevent the occurrences of fraud and misconduct as much as possible. Human nature being what it is, there will nevertheless always be some diehard cases of fraudsters who cannot be kept from misbehaving. However, personal experience shows that this only arises in a small number of cases. In many of the cases that I have seen personally during the course of my professional life, the culprits have often been gradually seduced or become embroiled through circumstances and temptation to the point where it would have been difficult to extricate themselves. Face-saving, personal vanity, importance, and pressure to perform from outside are often the cause.

For this majority, there are a number of areas for improvement: training of all personnel at both the sponsor and investigator sites; proper start-up of clinical research projects and trials, ensuring that quality of data is of equal importance as the speed of collection and completion of the trial; ensuring the suitability of the protocol to the trial setting; and the careful placing of trials. Tight oversight by the sponsor (for the trial) and by the principal investigator (at the trial site), which has been cited as the most frequent critical inspection finding, will also certainly contribute to the prevention of fraud and misconduct. This is, after all, only the normal and expected responsibility of the sponsor and the investigator according to GCP. The creation of awareness that detection tools are in place will also probably help to deter the not-so-serious fraudsters and keep them on the right track.

For the real innate fraudsters, who are in fact criminally inclined, active detection will still be the only solution. The attitude should be to aim at detection as early as possible, using all monitoring tools available to the industry, the professional environment, and the regulatory authorities. As more and more advanced tools become available, the percentage of detection should hopefully be an additional threat to suppress the inclination to commit misconduct or fraud.

There is a need for proactive cooperation between industry, investigators and scientists, and the regulatory authorities. When all efforts in this field are combined, problems of misconduct and fraud in clinical research will hopefully eventually be reduced to a minimum. It is in everybody's interests that this be achieved.

References

1. World Medical Association. Declaration of Helsinki, as amended by the 48th WMA General Assembly Somerset West, Republic of South Africa, October 1996.
2. US Food and Drug Administration. *The Story of the Laws Behind the Labels: Part II 1938 Federal Food, Drug, and Cosmetic Act*. Rockville: US Food and Drug Administration, 1981. www.cfsan.fda.gov/~lrd/histor1a.html.
3. US Food and Drug Administration. *Milestones in US Food and Drug Law History*. Rockville: US Food and Drug Administration, 1999. www.fda.gov/opacom/backgrounders/miles.html.
4. European Commission: Enterprise and Industry: Pharmaceuticals. *EudraLex: The rules governing medicinal products in the European Union*. Vol 9, *Pharmacovigilance guidelines*. Brussels: European Commission, 2004. ec.europa.eu/enterprise/pharmaceuticals/eudralex/vol9_en.htm.
5. Therapeutic Goods Administration. *Note for guidance on good clinical practice (CPMP/ICH/135/95)*. Symonston: Therapeutic Goods Administration, 2000. www.tga.gov.au/docs/pdf/euguide/ich/ich13595.pdf.
6. Farthing M. Research Misconduct: an Editor's View. In Lock S, Wells F, Farthing M, eds. *Fraud and Misconduct in Medical Research*, 3rd edn. London: BMJ books, 2001.

8 The role of research ethics committees

John Saunders

Introduction

The term 'research' refers to a class of activity designed to develop or contribute to generalizable knowledge.[1] The regulation of research involves many steps, and none of these should be free of ethical consideration. It is the role of the research ethics committee (REC) to focus on the ethical acceptability of a project, with the primary purpose of protecting the potential research participant and concerned communities, as described in the UK Department of Health (DH) Governance Arrangements for RECs (paragraph 2.3).[2] In the specific context of the clinical trial, it must safeguard the rights, safety, and well-being of all trial subjects, as indicated in the International Conference on Harmonisation (ICH) Guideline for Good Clinical Practice (paragraph 3.1.1).[3] Nevertheless, it should be emphasized that a research study does not become ethical just because it has been approved by the REC. Nothing that the REC approves can release the doctor from his or her prime ethical obligation to the patient's interests. That includes, of course, qualities of honesty and probity in the conduct of research.

It should be noted that RECs may also be referred to as institutional review boards (IRBs) or independent ethics committees (IECs).

Guidelines and codes of practice

It is generally agreed that, in accordance with the Royal College of Physicians (RCP) Guidelines on the Practice of Ethics Committees (paragraph 2.9):[4]

1. Research investigations on human beings, their health information, or their tissues should conform to codes such as those of the World Medical Association Declaration of Helsinki[5] and of the World Health Organization (WHO) and its associated bodies.
2. Investigators should not be the sole judges of whether their research does so conform.

The independence of the committee is emphasized in the Declaration of Helsinki (paragraph 13).[5] An ethics committee:

'must be independent of the investigator, the sponsor or any other kind of undue influence'.

The Declaration goes further, however, in stating that:

> 'The committee has the right to monitor ongoing trials. The researcher has the obligation to provide monitoring information to the committee for review, information regarding funding, sponsors, institutional affiliations, other potential conflicts of interest and incentives for subjects.'

The Declaration is referred to in the EC Clinical Trials Directive,[6] and therefore has legal status in member states of the European Union. In the UK, for example, the 1996 version of the Declaration (not actually the current version) is referred to in the Medicines for Human Use (Clinical Trials) Regulations 2004, which are laid down in UK law.

While the EC Directive refers to clinical trials of investigational medicinal products, its recommendations may be applied to all varieties of health research. There seems no good reason not to include also research involving human participants external to health-care settings. Much psychological research, for example, is pursued in academic units or even in military or industrial settings. RECs may be better regulated, better known, and with a longer history in health care, but recent years have seen the development of other types of ethics committees. In the UK, for example, most universities have some form of ethical scrutiny or are in the process of developing a system to review research on human volunteers outside the remit of the National Health Service (NHS).[7] In considering the role of ethics committees in the prevention of fraud or misconduct, those committees outside the NHS may have a similar part to play. Fraud and misconduct may be equally prevalent in settings external to health care.

Notwithstanding the Helsinki Declaration and the EC Clinical Trials Directive, it should be noted that the role of the REC shows considerable national variation. This has been well documented in Europe, but less so in other parts of the world. In France, for example, epidemiological studies are not considered research studies, while in Austria, ethical review of medical research on humans that does not involve drugs, medical devices, or the application of a new medical method is mandatory only in university settings.[8] Similarly, the independence of REC members is mainly based on the expectation of self-declaration of any conflict of interest. This may be voluntary (e.g. in the Czech Republic) or subject to law (e.g. in Finland). Appointing authorities may be government agencies, universities, hospitals, or research institutes, through nominations by professional bodies and sundry health authorities, with variation not only between but also within different countries (these processes vary between and within England, Wales, and Scotland in the UK, for example). Such variations among RECs in Europe may be studied elsewhere.[8–10]

Developments outside Europe, North America, and Australasia are patchy, especially in poorer countries. The Network of Ethics in Biomedical Research in Africa, which was funded by the European Commission under its Science and Society programme, is providing useful information about the RECs in the 15 participating countries. As global networks assume greater importance, the international practices of

RECs cannot be ignored. Their ability to go beyond their primary role of participant protection will vary according to their prescribed responsibilities, appointing authorities, legal status, structure, membership, operating procedures, training, competence, workload, and accreditation.

Differing roles of RECs

Most literature examining RECs comes from wealthier countries. Poorer countries often have much less well-developed RECs, but the role of the REC may be greater in prevention and policing of abuse. For example, in 2001, the WHO Regional Committee for Africa expressed concern that some health-related studies undertaken in the Region were not subjected to any form of ethics review. A programme, called Networking for Ethics on Biomedical Research in Africa (NEBRA), has now been created to understand ethical issues arising in individual African countries, and to identify people already involved in reviewing ethics of research and identify their needs. Funded by a European Union grant, this initiative involves 15 countries with European partners, including the UK Medical Research Council (MRC), the French National Institute of Health and Medical Research (INSERM), the WHO, and the University Eberhard Karls, Tübingen, Germany. In India, there is a Central Ethics Committee on Human Research (CECHR) of the Indian Council of Medical Research, which has developed ethical guidelines for biomedical research on human subjects and is now planning to audit the functioning of institutional ethics. Some sponsors use independent ethics committees for multicentre clinical trials conducted by private practitioners. With the costs of clinical trials between 40% and 60% lower in India than in developed countries, India is a magnet for such research, and unethical trials have been detected. Accusations of research abuse arose in India in 2005 for example.[11] In South America, one study showed considerable deficiencies in the operation of RECs,[12] and problems in the operation of committees are likely to be widespread internationally. In multinational studies, there may be debate over standards of review between countries and the effectiveness of protection against abuse.

In the UK, where the network of RECs is well developed, there remains continuing debate about the scope of their work. In particular, there is continuing concern over the differentiation of research activity from that of audit or service development. The obligation to submit research to ethical review by the REC is universally acknowledged, but there is currently no structure by which audit studies or those designed to develop the service in some new way can be reviewed. One consequence is a temptation to classify a study as an audit in order to avoid the regulatory framework of research, including research ethics review. Avoiding ethical review is a form of misconduct, and the fact that a project may constitute audit does not necessarily mean that it is not also research. It is easy to state that research is about finding out what you ought to be doing and audit about finding out whether you are doing what you ought to be doing. But projects often do not fall into different classes of activity by such a simple 'either/or' test. As an example, the UK's Confidential Inquiries into Maternal and Perioperative Deaths led to new knowledge that can be generalized and therefore can be considered as research. The 'Confidential Inquiries' are also highly effective audits of the services, and are essential for service development. Advice from the REC, or its chair, on whether a particular study should be submitted to the REC should be part of the remit of any research ethics service. This difficulty also highlights the need for regulatory structures that will examine studies that do fall outside the definitions of 'research'. Clinical ethics committees,[13] where they exist, may be equipped to take on such a role; otherwise, it should be part of clinical governance structures.

Fraud and misconduct

Research that is fraudulent cannot establish a valid conclusion. As such, fraudulent research offends against the dignity,[2] rights, safety or well-being[3] of the participant. Similarly, misconduct, even if not invalidating a conclusion, is unethical by definition. At its worst, research misconduct involves serious abuse of participants: the abuses historically familiar in the Tuskegee Study, American radiation experiments,[14] and the cases described in Pappworth's seminal study[15] and elsewhere in this book. It was gross misconduct, or concern about its possibility, that led to the establishment of RECs in many countries. From this perspective, the prevention of fraud and misconduct is a central concern of the REC, not a secondary function. Just like the policeman on the street, whose chief value may be in preventing crime rather than catching criminals, the REC's significant role lies in prevention rather than the more dramatic one of detection of abuse.

Article 6 of the EC Clinical Trials Directive sets out how the REC should fulfil its responsibilities (Box 8.1).[6] Although, as noted, these do not apply with legal force to studies other than clinical trials of investigational medicinal products or, indeed, apply at all outside the European Union, they provide a useful guide to the REC's duties in all types of research.

Scientific review

RECs are not primarily scientific review committees. In many jurisdictions, the REC may also be remote from the institution in which the proposed research is to take place. Nor are RECs best placed to assess the value of the research in its wider context: how important is the research question and, hence, how ethically valid is it to carry out this work – always remembering the opportunity cost of doing one thing rather than another. These shortcomings need to be stated. RECs are charged with ensuring the scientific worth of the protocol in the EC Directive, and many national jurisdictions specify this role. Whether this role can be fulfilled depends on the competencies of the REC's members or the acceptability of fulfilling this role by delegation. A protocol in neonatology or genetics or psychiatry may involve a scientific knowledge beyond the expertise of any member of the committee – even a committee with a paediatrician, geneticist, or psychiatrist member. Even with a single expert member from the relevant specialty, the REC can hardly match the expertise of the research team. Fulfilling the demands of scientific review may therefore mean either sending the protocol out for external review to a specialist in the field or, alternatively, formally delegating this aspect of the REC's role to a scientific review committee. The time demands of the

---

BOX 8.1   **EC Clinical Trials Directive, Article 6, paragraph 3[6]**

In preparing its opinion, the Ethics Committee shall consider in particular:

(a) the relevance of the clinical trial and the clinical trial design

(b) whether the evaluation of the anticipated benefits and risks as required under Article 3(2)(a) is satisfactory and whether the conclusions are justified

(c) the protocol

(d) the suitability of the investigator and supporting staff

(e) the investigator's brochure

(f) the quality of the facilities

(g) the adequacy and completeness of the written information to be given and the procedure to be followed for the purpose of obtaining informed consent and the justification for the research in persons incapable of giving informed consent as regards the specific restrictions laid down in Article 3

(h) provision for indemnity or compensation in the event of death or injury attributable to a clinical trial

(i) any insurance or indemnity to cover the liability of the investigator or sponsor

(j) the amounts, and, where appropriate, the arrangements for rewarding or compensating investigators and trial subjects and the relevant aspects of any agreement between the sponsor and the site

(k) the arrangements for recruitment of subjects

EC Directive and the reasonable expectation of the research community for prompt review make external review an unattractive option. In the UK, the task of scientific review has been explicitly removed from the REC (see paragraph 9.9 of the DH Governance Arrangements[2]), and the responsibility for the quality of the science has become the responsibility of the sponsor (see paragraphs 2.3.1 and 2.3.2 of the DH Research Governance Framework[16]). Nevertheless, even when this responsibility is fulfilled by delegation, the REC should, in the words of the Governance Arrangements (paragraphs 9.12 and 9.13),[2] 'be adequately reassured about ... the scientific design and conduct of the study'.

Even if the scientific design is sound, the study may still be unnecessary. A systematic review of previous research may reveal that the proposal merely repeats what has already been established. It is a form of scientific misconduct to proceed with a clinical study in such a situation. Again, as with scientific review, the assessment and validity of a preceding systematic review is likely to be beyond the expertise of many RECs. The best solution may be delegation to a more competent scientific review committee, as envisaged in the UK by the Research Governance Framework[16] and as described in the RCP Guidelines (paragraph 10.32):[4]

'Research which duplicates other work unnecessarily or which is not of sufficient quality to contribute something useful to existing knowledge is in itself
unethical ... All proposals for health and social care research must be subjected to review by experts in the relevant fields able to offer independent
advice on its quality. Arrangements for peer review must be commensurate
with the scale of the research.'

Even if it is not the function of the REC itself to systematically review previous scientific
work, it must therefore ensure that such a review has taken place and that it has been
carried out competently. If it has any misgivings about this, the REC may require an
external opinion as to the adequacy of review. If it is dissatisfied with the adequacy of
the scientific review of the study itself, it should require resubmission.

Suitability of investigators

How can the REC assess the suitability of the investigator? Inquiry into qualifications,
previous research experience, and consideration of previous submissions to the REC
may help. It may also be thought that an investigator who cannot give an adequate
explanation of a proposal to the REC can hardly expect the protocol to be approved.
However, pronouncing on the suitability of the qualifications of a practitioner on the
strength of a protocol submitted for ethical review has obvious dangers. Refusal of a
protocol on such grounds may be construed as defamatory and may be extremely damaging to the investigator or others involved. It is the ethics of the protocol that is under
consideration, and the suitability of the investigator and facilities are usually beyond
the REC's competencies. These, too, are functions for research governance structures.
Where such structures are rudimentary, the REC should at least make enquiry – and
often it is the act of enquiry itself that may expose the risks or inadequacies that make
misconduct or fraud more likely. Of course, the situation may sometimes be obvious:
the lack of certified competencies in, or equipment for, resuscitation in the event of
cardiopulmonary collapse might be a case in point.

One established reason for fraud and misconduct is the need to publish significant
numbers of papers in order to make progress in one's career or to earn fees for one's
department. The temptation, as noted elsewhere in this book, to falsify results becomes
greater when time to carry out the project is limited by the number of projects being
undertaken in a department. For that reason, enquiry should be made of other current research activities. An investigator should be asked about the number of projects
currently planned or under way in his/her department and the capacity to complete
them satisfactorily. Details should be explored as to their complexity and the resources
that they demand, rather than merely their number. Other conflicts of interest should
be actively explored, with an examination of detail that goes beyond simple declaration. Such conflicts are common. Academic–industrial relationships that are too close
are likely to reduce the openness of communication and to tempt investigators to prioritize financial and research activity over patient interest.

The investigator should always be interviewed by the committee. The advantages
of this are enormous. Personal contact enables ambivalent responses to enquiry to be

tested on the spot rather than ignored; contradictions can be sensitively and respectfully explored; misunderstandings can be immediately resolved. If the REC's workload is thought to be too great to adopt this method of working, then the solution is to amend its workload. Without the ability to interview the investigator, the quality of review suffers.

Financial issues

As suggested in paragraph (j) of the EC Directive, the REC should always examine financial aspects of any study. Money is the root of much malpractice in medicine, including much research fraud. Rewards from pharmaceutical research in particular are tempting. Departments and/or individuals lose out where inadequate numbers are recruited to trials or where dropout rates are too high. Money is the most tangible motivating factor for many people. Excessive payments may induce investigators to engage in malpractice of all sorts, encouraging participants to take excessive risks or falsify results.

This responsibility is set out in the ICH Guideline for Good Clinical Practice,[3] which advises (paragraph 3.1.2) that the REC:

'should obtain ... information about payments and compensation available to subjects'.

According to paragraph 3.1.8 of the Guideline, the REC:

'should review both the amount and method of payment to subjects to assure that neither presents problems of coercion or undue influence on the trial subjects. Payments to a subject should be pro-rated and not wholly contingent on completion of the trial by the subject.'

Paragraph 3.1.9 suggests that the REC:

'should ensure that information regarding payment to subjects, including the methods, amounts, and schedule of payment to trial subjects, is set forth in the written informed consent form and any other written information to be provided to subjects. The way payment will be prorated should be specified.'

Paragraph 4.8.10 includes the following advice:

'Both the informed consent discussion and the written informed consent form and any other written information to be provided to subjects should include explanations of the following: ... The anticipated prorated payment, if any, to the subject for participating in the trial.'

Per capita payments to the investigator are widely used in recruitment to clinical trials, and such payments relate work done to reward. There is an inevitable conflict of interest between the reward and the temptation to investigators to recruit inappropriate patients to studies or to retain them improperly when recruited. These temptations may be stronger in trials with competitive recruitment of participants. This places a burden on the REC to ensure that recruitment targets can be defended as being realistic.

In the UK, the RCP has recommended that:[4]

'rates of payment should reflect work actually carried out, with personnel costs reflecting normal rates for the professional involved where payments to individuals are made. Estimates of the time required for trial activities should be justified and RECs should review estimates. Sometimes such payments are additional to the investigators' regular incomes and can result either in overwork or in displacing other more pressing clinical activity. Payments should always be made into a Trust or practice account and never into a personal investigator's bank account. Patient information leaflets should make patients aware when Trusts or practices or doctors and other health professionals who recruit patients into trials are being paid for the work undertaken, as well as for the facilities required to enable the work to be done. Participants have a right to see further details regarding these payments if they so wish.'

Registration and publication of research projects

Registration of clinical trials and publication of all research are two further areas where RECs can help discourage fraud and misconduct. Trial registration should be a condition of REC approval. Firstly, registration ensures that the scientific community knows that a trial is taking place or has taken place. Questions may then be asked: disclosure of any activity is always likely to reduce fraud and deceit. Secondly, unless those conducting systematic reviews are able to identify all trials that have been commenced on a particular subject, the inevitable result will be a measure of publication bias. There is a need to be aware of negative data in particular. Results of unpublished studies differ systematically from those that are published. Even when published, negative studies take longer to appear in print.[17] Registration of such studies does at least enable their identification, even if they have not achieved publication. Given the number of trial registers, there is a need for an international collaboration either to establish a single register or link those that already exist. The establishment of an internationally unique trial numbering scheme known as the ISRCTN (International Standard Randomised Controlled Trial Number) is an encouraging first step.[18] For similar reasons, all clinical studies should be published if at all possible. Of course, the study may fail for all sorts of reasons without any suggestion of impropriety: the recruitment numbers that were reasonably anticipated may not be realized, key investigators may move away, or other scientific advances may make the study irrelevant. However, it is unacceptable in principle that an investigator should agree to conditions that may prohibit or impair the possibility of publication, although some delay may sometimes be acceptable. This applies whether the sponsor of the research is a pharmaceutical company, a government department, or any other agency. Investigators should agree a publication policy in advance, and RECs should be aware of what this is.

In its recent guidelines (paragraph 2.58),[4] the RCP has commented on the need for methodological studies to assure the integrity of research:

> 'Methodological studies have found important discrepancies between the protocols and publications of randomised trials. These finding have undermined the credibility of clinical research.[19] RECs are not able to ensure that a trial has been carried out without unacknowledged protocol deviations, such as changes in definitions of outcomes. Even while maintaining the confidentiality of the protocol, accredited external reviewers should be able to examine files without explicit permission from applicants and therefore without the bias introduced by a permission seeking process. Whether construed as audit or methodological research, the importance of assuring the integrity of medical research protects both study participants and future patients.'

One protection for research may therefore be research on research.

Recruitment of research ethics committee members

In most countries, RECs consist of volunteers. Members carry out their duties as part of their role as citizens, not because they are paid. While this has benefits, it also has the drawback that there has been a reluctance to enforce standards. Methods of working have sometimes been sloppy. One unpublished survey (1999) of RECs in the UK pointed out that some committees were completing ethical review in only five minutes and that, despite standard feedback sheets, members felt justified in stating from the outset that research was 'OK' or 'crap'. The earlier (1992) and now dated review of UK RECs by Neuberger[20] noted that 'during the course of my visits, fourteen members fell asleep at meetings'.

It is surely essential that a system of quality review, ideally with formal accreditation, be part of the structure of research ethics review in all countries. Revised information sheets need to be checked. Questions asked should receive full answers, and glib assertions by clinicians must be challenged. This is especially true when the research participant is vulnerable: for example, invasive investigations on children should always be challenged, to ensure that they really do constitute a responsible professional view of what is normal care and are not purely for research. Members should be prepared for meetings and their performance should be assessed. When a meeting is short or an agenda is too long, it is too easy for members to try to read the papers in the meeting itself. Without good standards of performance, misconduct or abuse of research participants is more likely.

In considering fraud and malpractice in research, the main role of the REC is one of prevention. However, RECs may be the recipients of allegations about research malpractice. The investigation of alleged fraud or misconduct is not the role of the REC. If the committee considers that the allegations ought to be investigated, it should ensure that an appropriate body is involved. In the UK, there are now clear pathways, as described elsewhere in this book, with formal guidance in addition from the Medical Research Council.[21]

References

1. Council for International Organizations of Medical Sciences. Preamble. In: *International Ethical Guidelines for Biomedical Research Involving Human Subjects*. Geneva: CIOMS, 2002: 19.

2. Department of Health. *Governance Arrangements for Research Ethics Committees*. London: DH, 2001.

3. International Conference on Harmonisation of Technical Requirements for Registration of Pharmaceuticals for Human Use. *ICH Harmonised Tripartite Guideline for Good Clinical Practice*. Geneva: ICH, 1996.

4. Royal College of Physicians. *Guidelines on the Practice of Ethics Committees in Medical Research with Human Participants*, 4th edn. London: RCP, 2007.

5. *World Medical Association Declaration of Helsinki: Ethical Principles for Medical Research Involving Human Subjects*. 2000. www.wma.net/e/policy/b3.htm.

6. EC Directive: Commission Directive 91/507/EEC of 19 July 1991 modifying the Annex to Council Directive 75/318/EEC of 20 May 1975 on the approximation of the laws, regulations and administrative provisions of the Member States relating to the implementation of good clinical practice in the conduct of clinical trials on medicinal products for human use.

7. Tinker A, Coomber V. University research ethics committees – a summary of research into their role, remit and conduct. *Res Ethics Rev* 2005; **1**: 5–11.

8. European Forum for Good Clinical Practice Ethics Working Party Subgroup on Ethics Committees Reviewing Investigational Medicinal Products within the European Union. The procedure for the ethical review of protocols for clinical research projects in the European Union. *Int J Pharm Med* 2007; **21**: 1–113.

9. Riis P. Steering Committee on Bioethics. Working Party on Biomedical Research. *Ethical Review of Biomedical Research in Europe: Suggestions for Best National Practices*. Strasbourg: Council of Europe, 1998.

10. Megone C, Mason SA, Allmark PJ et al. The structure, composition and operation of European research ethics committees. In: Mason SU, Megone C, eds. *European Neonatal Research: Consent, Ethics Committees and Law*. Aldershot: Ashgate, 2002: 23–42.

11. Mudur G. Indian researchers accused of violating ethical guidelines. *BMJ* 2005; **330**: 60.

12. Hyder A, Wali S, Khan A et al. Ethical review of health research: a perspective from developing country researchers. *J Med Ethics* 2004; **30**: 68–72.

13. Royal College of Physicians. *Ethics in Practice: Report of a Working Party*. London: RCP, 2005.

14. Faden RR, Lederer SE, Moreno JD. US medical researchers, the Nuremberg Doctors Trial and the Nuremberg Code. A review of findings of the Advisory Committee on Human Radiation Experiments. *JAMA* 1996; **276**: 1667–71.

15. Pappworth MH. *Human Guinea Pigs. Experimentation in Man*. London: Routledge & Kegan Paul, 1967.

16. Department of Health. *Research Governance Framework for Health and Social Care*, 2nd edn. London: DH, 2005.

17. Hopewell S, Clarke M, Stewart L, Tierney J. Time to publication for results of clinical trials (Cochrane Methodology Review). *The Cochrane Library*. Chichester: Wiley, 2004: Issue 1.

18. Evans T, Gülmezoglu M, Pang T. Registering clinical trials: a role for WHO. *Lancet* 2004; **363**: 1413–14.

19. Chan A-W, Upshur R, Singh JA et al. Waiving confidentiality for the greater good. *BMJ* 2006; **332**: 1086–9.

20. Neuberger J. *Ethics and Healthcare. The Role of Research Ethics Committees in the United Kingdom*. London: Kings Fund Institute, 1992.

21. Medical Research Council. *Policy and Procedure for Inquiring into Allegations of Scientific Misconduct*. London: MRC, 1997.

SECTION 4

APPROACHES TO THE DETECTION OF RESEARCH MISCONDUCT

9 The role of the whistleblower

Sabine Kleinert

Introduction

Almost every case of research misconduct that comes to light is exposed by some form of whistleblowing, yet only recently has this particular part in the process gained more serious attention. In its International Code of Medical Ethics, the World Medical Association has made it clear that whistleblowing in the widest sense, and in appropriate circumstances, is part of the general duty of every physician by stating that 'A physician shall deal honestly with patients and colleagues, and report to the appropriate authorities those physicians who practice unethically or incompetently or who engage in fraud or deception.'[1]

The status of whistleblowing

When are whistles blown? In everyday life, we use whistles to interrupt foul play in sport, to draw immediate attention and summon help, to call disobedient dogs to order, and to apprehend criminals. In the research context, to 'blow the whistle' is often the last resort of long-standing unease, initial denial, and deep internal searching and questioning for the right approach after a strongly perceived discrepancy of ethical standards. Yet, to blow the whistle still has bad connotations and has led to calls for renaming individuals who do so as 'complainants', a term the US Office of Research Integrity (ORI) uses, but which still has the overtone of a quarrelsome difficult individual. Whatever the terminology, whistleblowers are still all too often seen as disaffected, vexatious, and vindictive colleagues, who step outside the team and transgress the prevailing professional code of silence and cover-up, and who have set out deliberately to damage the reputation of an institution.

Malicious whistleblowing does exist, but there is very little evidence to suggest that it is more than just a tiny proportion of all such cases. Academic medicine and science has long maintained that it can keep its own house in order. Rosamund Rhodes and James Strain[2] argue that academic medicine has failed to respond consistently, effectively, and appropriately to unethical behaviour. Furthermore, rather than seeing whistleblowers as important allies to uphold ethical standards and reputation, institutions continue to regard them as enemies, and punishment, either overt or covert, is a common experience for whistleblowers.

In one of the few systematic studies of experiences of whistleblowers,[3] researchers from the Research Triangle Institute contacted whistleblowers of closed cases that had been brought to the attention of the US-based ORI, and asked about their experience of the consequences of their actions by questionnaire. Of 68 people who regarded themselves as eligible and responded (a 72% response rate), 8 reported that they had been fired and 8 that their position had not been renewed; 19 reported denial of career progression; 29 experienced pressure to drop the allegation; and 27 were subject to counter-allegations. Whistleblowers were more likely to suffer serious consequences if they worked in basic science rather than clinical departments, if they were more junior, and if they reported their suspicions to deans or heads of departments rather than colleagues; 52% reported an impact on their mental health and 34% said that it affected their financial situation. The majority of these experiences happened while the cases were still under consideration, but it is important to remember that the resolution of cases can take many months (and even many years in some instances). As these cases of research misconduct had gone as far as a national oversight body, and the ORI only considers serious research misconduct (intentional fabrication, falsification, or plagiarism), these reports are likely to represent only the tip of an iceberg, and the true incidence of serious repercussions for whistleblowers is likely to be much higher, especially in institutions where due process is wanting. These data are over 10 years old.

So, have things changed? More recent evidence from selected, publicized high-profile cases suggests that the answer is 'no, not very much'. What exactly happens to a whistleblower depends on the type of whistleblower, who is the initial recipient of the information, the relationship of all involved players, and the degree of oversight and protection available in a country.[4] Whistleblowers are most often colleagues or subordinates within a department or an institution, but can also be external, for example from a collaborating institution or an independent colleague in the field. Whistleblowers can be researchers involved in a particular study themselves, who report on unethical practices demanded from them by their institution, or by funders, superiors, or coauthors. Reviewers, editors, and readers can act as external independent whistleblowers when a research paper is submitted or published. Similarly, funders can act as whistleblowers, especially in the often murky and largely uncontrolled area of grant applications, or when required audits reveal lapses in integrity. Independent whistleblowers, such as editors, have the advantage of not being directly involved in a particular department or institution, and are unlikely to suffer personal consequences, but often have little or no real power to demand an investigation. A special situation arises when public media either take the role of whistleblowers or become the conduit for whistleblowers, usually as a last resort. Examples of each of these scenarios illustrate different aspects that need attention.

The postgraduates who used the media to blow the whistle

One of the most common scenarios is the junior laboratory worker who is first bewildered, then shocked, and ultimately often ruined by discoveries that his or her supervisor has engaged in serious research misconduct. A recent example that shook Australian academic medicine is the Bruce Hall affair at the University of New South Wales (UNSW).[5] Bruce Hall, a Professor of Medicine at UNSW, and an internationally well-regarded scientist in immunology, was dramatically and publicly exposed on the Australian live-broadcast radio programme *The Science Show* by two postgraduates from his laboratory. Transcripts of this programme are available on the Australian Broadcasting Commission website, and make fascinating reading.[6] They raised allegations of scientific misconduct, including fabrication, fraud, and misrepresentation in a grant application, and serious deficiencies in workplace relationships and procedures. These complaints were first brought to the attention of the UNSW over a period of 6 months, with a completely unsatisfactory response. One of the reasons why this affair ended up in the media is the provision in the New South Wales whistleblower protection legislation that if there has been no determination within 6 months after a complaint has been lodged, the complainant is free to go to the media. Shortly after that show, the UNSW released the results of two internal inquiries, which were unable to come to a conclusion. Finally, an external inquiry, the Brennan Inquiry, was instigated under the chair of Sir Gerard Brennan, previous Chief Justice of the Australian High Court. When the Brennan Inquiry submitted its final report to the UNSW seven months later, the university's Council initially resolved not to release the findings, but shortly afterwards conceded to a limited release only. The conclusions of the Brennan Inquiry were that Bruce Hall had seriously deviated from practices commonly accepted for reporting research and that he had stated a material and significant falsehood with reckless disregard for the truth and with deliberate intent to deceive.

However, this is not where the Hall affair stops. The UNSW's then Vice Chancellor, Rory Hume, took it upon himself to interpret and judge these findings differently, and ruled that there was no serious scientific misconduct, rather just errors of judgement. Further wrangling in this affair eventually led to Rory Hume's resignation in April 2004 and to a statement by the UNSW Council in June 2004 that it adopted the report of the external independent inquiry into the Hall matter, affirmed its view that the findings constitute the most expert statement available on the issue, and, 'given the lapse of time and considerations of natural justice and cost, resolved that no further disciplinary action be taken by the university'.[7] What happened to the whistleblowers? In a follow-up programme on *The Science Show* on 3 September 2005,[8] Clara He, one of the four postgraduate doctors who raised the allegations, said that, 'given my experience ... I would never, ever do it again, even though I firmly believe I'm doing the right thing.' She explained how she was told by the hospital to relocate to a place with no research facility, and how she was struggling to rebuild her life.

This, admittedly extreme, case shows how institutional failure will eventually lead to local and national soul searching, and, hopefully, the lessons learned will lead to improvements of procedures. The Australian National Health and Medical Research Council (NHMRC), the Australian Research Council, and Universities Australia (formerly known as the Australian Vice Chancellors' Committee) have devised the Australian Code for the Responsible Conduct of Research, which was released in its final version in 2007 after two rounds of public consultation.[9,10] It includes a section on how to manage breaches of the Code and allegations of research misconduct, and stresses transparency and a climate of open exchanges of ideas. Compliance with the Code is a prerequisite for receipt of NHMRC funding. This is progress indeed – but instead of being hailed as heroes who instigated this progress, the whistleblowers are the forgotten victims.

The technician who succeeded despite whistleblowing

One of the most astonishing major research misconduct cases in recent years – that of Eric Poehlman, who ended up having to serve a one-year sentence in a US federal prison – had a very different outcome for the whistleblower than the previous case. As presented in the *New York Times*, Walter DeNino joined Eric Poehlman's laboratory at the University of Vermont, USA, in 2000, as a paid technician after having received several awards for research completed under Poehlman's supervision while in training.[11] He regarded Poehlman as his trusted mentor, and was happy to gain further experience in Poehlman's research field. Eventually, so he hoped, further publications with Poehlman might strengthen his candidacy for medical school. However, after one study yielded some unexpected results, Poehlman had taken electronic files home and returned them to DeNino the following week, explaining that he had corrected some erroneous entries. Miraculously, the results suddenly fitted the prior hypothesis.

DeNino started to become suspicious, and looked closely at data from his original files and patients' records. He found reversed data points in a supposed longitudinal study, figures for measurements that had never been taken, and patients who did not seem to exist. When he asked a previous postdoctoral fellow, who no longer worked in Poehlman's laboratory, for advice, DeNino learnt that there had been previous concerns, which were just brushed off or suppressed by threats. On confrontation, Poehlman was dismissive, with implausible explanations. When DeNino approached another faculty member, he was warned that 'no matter how you proceed, everyone loses ... your career will be ruined because no one is going to protect you.'[11] Finally, after a further deterioration of trust and relationship, DeNino lodged a formal written complaint with the counsel of the university. DeNino's advantage was that the university was determined to conduct an exemplary investigation.

Two days after the formal accusation, Richard Galbraith, programme director of the university's General Clinical Research Center, led the campus police chief to Poehlman's office to impound any evidence. Nevertheless, the investigation took several years, DeNino had to take legal representation, and Poehlman attempted to undermine his credibility – a time that was certainly not an easy one for a young technician. In 2006, Poehlman was sentenced to 1 year and 1 day in prison, the first such sentence for research misconduct in the USA. Walter DeNino is currently a medical student at the University of Vermont.

The independent whistleblower who read a published paper

Another recent high-profile and well-publicized misconduct case shows that an independent whistleblower is probably in the best position to emerge unscathed. The John Sudbø case unravelled after a diligent and knowledgeable reader, Camilla Stoltenberg, who heads the Division of Epidemiology at the Norwegian Institute for Public Health and happens to be the Norwegian Prime Minister's sister, realized that statements made in the paper published by the Norwegian researcher in the *Lancet*[12] about using a particular Norwegian database could not be true, as this database had not yet opened at the time the study was purportedly conducted. Stoltenberg contacted the Radium Hospital in Oslo, where Sudbø worked, with the information. An external independent investigation was instigated promptly by the hospital and conducted under the lead of Swedish epidemiologist Anders Ekbom. In its final report 6 months later,[13] it concluded that 'the bulk of Jon Sudbø's scientific publications are invalid due to the fabrication and manipulation of the underlying data material.'

This case again prompted much discussion, which centred this time less around procedures following the discovered misconduct (as these seemed to have been almost exemplary) but more around possible prevention and the role of co-authors and colleagues in the department, who could have acted as whistleblowers at an earlier stage. Sudbø resigned the day after the report was released, and was subsequently stripped of his medical degree.[14] The actual whistleblower in this case – and perhaps the term 'whistleblower' is least justified in this context, where Stoltenberg in fact only raised legitimate questions – continues to enjoy high regard. It may have helped that Stoltenberg was the Prime Minister's sister. What certainly did help were both her independence and high standing and the swift and fair conduct at the Radium Hospital.

The researcher who wanted to check the data that were going to be published under his name

A different type of whistleblowing – and one that can be arguably most damaging and disheartening, despite the relative seniority of those involved – is when a researcher is involved in the actual research as one of the principal investigators and the university is unsupportive in the case of unreasonable outside pressures (usually by a commercial funding source). In 2002, Aubrey Blumsohn, a senior lecturer in metabolic bone disease at Sheffield University, UK, signed an institutional research agreement with Procter & Gamble Pharmaceuticals (P&G) for US$250 000, together with Richard Eastell, then Dean for Research at Sheffield, to be used in the context of a study investigating the effectiveness of risedronate (Actonel) on bone mineral density in postmenopausal women.[15,16] As is often the case, the company analysed and summarized data from the trial, with Blumsohn and Eastell as authors on abstracts to be presented at a meeting of the American Society of Bone and Mineral Research in Minneapolis in the autumn of 2003.[17] When Blumsohn demanded access to data and to the randomization codes of the trial of this drug to verify the results and the claims made, the company repeatedly refused over many months, but eventually allowed Blumsohn to look at the analysis in the company's offices. It was then that he spotted that 40% of patient data were missing in a graph. He was concerned that the company was omitting data that would have an unfavourable effect on the end result. Concerns raised with Eastell were met with pleas that the university has to consider its good relationship with companies such as P&G, as they are a good source of income. In the past, Eastell had allowed research to be published under his name when in fact only the company had analysed data. Statements, required by some journals, that all authors had access to the data had been made. From his experience, Blumsohn doubted that this could have been the case, as P&G responded to a formal data request by him that 'it is not standard practice of P&G to allow unlimited access to raw data from clinical trials to individual investigators, as these data are proprietary.'

Over a period of almost 2 years, Blumsohn tried to raise his concerns with a number of officials at Sheffield University, including the Dean, but the University never initiated an investigation. He saw no other way but to involve the press. In September 2005, Blumsohn was suspended from Sheffield University after cooperating with an investigation by the *Times Higher Education Supplement* in which an account of the story was first published.[18] He was subsequently offered £145 000 if he agreed to leave Sheffield University as compensation for loss of employment and for 'injury of feelings'. Blumsohn rejected the offer. When this twist was to be published in a further article in the *Times Higher Education Supplement*,[19] Sheffield tried to prevent it by issuing an injunction. In an official statement, Sheffield said:[19]

> 'the university had entered into formal "without prejudice" discussions with Dr Blumsohn's British Medical Association representative. These discussions were at Dr Blumsohn's request and had been undertaken in good faith by the university. The university would like to stress that these negotiations are the result of complex matters that have been ongoing between the university and Dr Blumsohn involving a number of different issues, and these negotiations have not occurred as a result of Dr Blumsohn having concerns about the pharmaceutical company that had been recently reported in the press.'

Blumsohn later accepted an undisclosed settlement offered by the university. He writes a blog entitled *Scientific misconduct: about all manner of corporate pharmaceutical scientific misconduct. If you're not outraged, you're not paying attention.*[20]

Blumsohn's case is very similar to the widely publicized case of Nancy Olivieri, who, after many years of fighting against the University of Toronto's lack of support, was vindicated in a far-reaching report in 2001.[21] When cases remain unsatisfactory and unresolved for such a long time, some people become – arguably understandably so – obsessed by the cause and may come across as 'difficult, disappointed people gone wrong'. Rather than the people involved, what clearly is wrong in such cases is the lack of institutional due process and the lack of national professional oversight.

Whistleblower legislation in selected countries

These examples have shown that – at least in cases of whistleblowing that are made public – the experiences are largely still not happy, and certainly not easy, ones.

Whether cases that do not hit the public eye are mainly those that have been resolved quickly and to everyone's satisfaction or whether, in a majority, the whistleblower has been successfully intimidated remains unknown. Research on the prevalence, role, and outcome of whistleblowing in the context of biomedical research is woefully lacking. Some results of one of the largest ongoing national studies of whistleblowing in the public sector, *Whistling While They Work: Enhancing the Theory and Practice of Internal Witness Management in Public Sector Organisations*, a study by the Australian Research Council Linkage Project,[22] has been released in draft form. In this study, data from 7663 respondents from 118 public agencies in the Commonwealth, New South Wales, Queensland, and Western Australian Governments were analysed. Of the respondents, 71.4% had directly observed at least one of a wide range of examples of wrongdoing in their institution, but only 28% formally reported the wrongdoing. Interestingly, there was little evidence to support a view of whistleblowers as disgruntled and embittered employees. This confirms findings from an earlier small study, where only seven people (3% of the interviewed whistleblowers) cited resentment of management as a reason.[23] In the Australian study, the main reason given for not reporting was that nothing would be done about it, and that the management of their agency would not protect them from reprisals.[22]

So, what legislation is there to protect whistleblowers? Over the past 10 years or so, many countries have introduced better and more detailed legal protection for whistleblowers, although there are important differences in approach and emphasis. These legislations cover whistleblowing in general, including corporate life and hospital settings. In many ways, whistleblowers in research settings are benefiting from experiences of business wrongdoing and corruption scandals such as Enron, and from lessons learned after serious failings in hospital and medical care, such as the Bristol and Shipman affairs in the UK.[24,25] In both the Bristol affair, in which cardiac surgeons tried to cover up their skill deficits and children died unnecessarily, and the case of the British general practitioner Harold Shipman, who murdered his trusting elderly patients, whistleblowers' warnings had initially fallen on deaf ears. In the Bristol affair, the whistleblower Stephen Bolsin, who was the anaesthetist in many of these surgical cases, eventually resettled in Australia, where he is now actively involved in educational aspects of whistleblowing. One of the new initiatives is a mock whistleblowing experience running over one year for final-year medical students to equip future doctors and researchers with some experience in this difficult area.[26]

Legislation to protect whistleblowers is often scattered around different laws. In some countries, it is almost non-existent, too narrow, or severely deficient. In others, there are confusing differences where there are different state laws, such as in Australia. Even in the Nordic countries, which have had national research integrity bodies for many years now, whistleblower protection laws are only starting to be seriously implemented. In all of these legislations, there are serious deficiencies that still make it difficult to follow procedures and escape reprisals, which can be subtle and therefore impossible to prove. Certainly, current legislations do not encourage people to blow the whistle.[27] The four countries in which the previously described whistleblowing cases occurred are selected as examples.

US whistleblower protection laws

The USA has had whistleblower protection incorporated in several different laws for a number of years. One of these is the False Claims Act, which allows prosecution of those who knowingly submit, or cause another person or entity to submit, false claims for payment of government funds.[28] Under the False Claims Act's so-called 'qui tam' provision, any citizen with evidence of fraud against government contracts or programmes can sue, on behalf of the government, to recover the fraudulently acquired funds. As compensation, the whistleblower may be awarded a portion of the funds recovered, typically 15–25%. Such a suit remains under seal, which allows the protection of anonymity for the whistleblower, for at least 60 days, during which the Department of Justice can investigate and decide whether to join the action. This Act, however, only applies to substantial financial fraud, such as a fraudulent federal grant application.

The US Whistleblower Protection Act of 1989 applies to federal employees who make a disclosure on illegal or improper government activities.[29] Any information that the employee reasonably believes to violate laws, rules, or regulations, to be a gross waste of funds, gross mismanagement, or abuse of authority, or to be a significant and specific danger to public health and safety falls under protected disclosure. In contrast to many other laws, any disclosure channel is protected, including disclosure to media, without specifying a particular order of action. The US Office of Special Counsel, which was set up in 1979 with the main purpose of protecting whistleblowers in the federal employment sector, operates a confidential disclosure channel. An amendment, the Whistleblower Protection Enhancement Act of 2007, which would widen the protection to certain national security, government contractor, and science-based agency whistleblowers, was passed by the US House of Representatives in March 2007, and is awaiting vote in the Senate.[30] These examples are federal laws, however, and there are many different state laws.

None of these legislations stipulates how institutions should implement specific internal procedures for the protection of whistleblowers. Under the Public Health Service Act, each extramural entity that applies for a biomedical research or research-training grant must establish policies and procedures that provide for 'undertaking diligent efforts to protect the positions and reputations of those persons who, in good faith, make allegations'.[31] What these efforts should entail, however, is not made clear. In 1995, the ORI released guidelines for institutions on how to handle whistleblowing retaliation complaints,[31] and encouraged institutions to adhere to principles consistent with the Whistleblower Bill of Rights (Box 9.1) recommended by the Commission on Research Integrity.

UK whistleblower protection law

In the UK, the Public Interest Disclosure Act (PIDA) of 1998 was introduced, as is so often the case, after a number of public disasters, including the Clapham rail disaster in 1988, in which 35 people died and the subsequent investigation uncovered that workers had been concerned over safety of wirings systems but had not dared to speak out.[32] The PIDA aims to protect whistleblowers from victimization and dismissal

---

BOX 9.1   **Principles of the US Whistleblower Bill of Rights**[31]

1. Whistleblowers are free to disclose lawfully whatever information supports a reasonable belief of research misconduct as it is defined by the Public Health Service Act policy.
2. Institutions have a duty not to tolerate or engage in retaliation against good-faith whistleblowers.
3. Institutions have a duty to provide fair and objective procedures for examining and resolving complaints, disputes, and allegations of research misconduct.
4. Institutions have a duty to follow procedures that are not tainted by partially arising from personal or institutional conflict of interest or other sources of bias.
5. Institutions have a duty to elicit and evaluate fully and objectively information about concerns raised by whistleblowers.
6. Institutions have a duty to handle cases involving alleged research misconduct as expeditiously as possible without compromising responsible resolutions.
7. At the conclusion of proceedings, institutions have a responsibility to credit promptly, in public or private, as appropriate, those whose allegations are substantiated.

---

when they raise genuine concerns about a criminal act, a failure to comply with a legal obligation, a miscarriage of justice, a danger to health and safety, any damage to the environment, or an attempt to cover up any of these. It covers all employees in public, private, and voluntary sectors, but not unpaid workers or students. Whistleblowers are protected when they raise their concerns in good faith and follow specific rules (Box 9.2).

If a whistleblower is victimized after a protected disclosure, a claim can be made at an employment tribunal for compensation, and appeals can be made to the Court of Appeals. Confidentiality clauses in employment contracts that conflict with the PIDA are not legally binding. Beyond the work of organizations such as Public Concern at

---

BOX 9.2   **Disclosure routes protected under the UK Public Interest Disclosure Act (PIDA)**

Level 1:   Raise concerns internally.
Level 2:   If internal mechanisms fail or do not exist, use prescribed external routes, such as the Health and Safety Executive, the Inland Revenue, or the Audit Commission.
Level 3:   Make wider disclosures (including to the media) if the matter is exceptionally serious, there is reasonable fear of reprisals or cover-up, or internal mechanisms have not dealt properly with the concern.

Work,[33] there is little promotion or raising awareness of PIDA, and there is no monitoring or requirement to compile cases centrally. If cases are settled privately, they remain confidential. Although there is an indirect incentive to establish internal procedures, this is not a part of the legislation. Arguably, the prescriptive three-level approach may waste valuable time, and potentially allows for evidence to be destroyed.

Australian legislation

Australia has many laws that guide how disclosures in the public sector can be made, how they should be acted on, and how those who make disclosures should be protected. Since 1993, several Acts have come into force and some Bills have been proposed (Box 9.3). All eight states have different laws with various strengths and weaknesses, and none currently constitutes best practice. The New South Wales (NSW) Public Disclosures Act 1994, which would have applied to the whistleblowers in the Bruce Hall affair, protects public sector employees (who must have been employed at the time when the alleged misconduct occurred). Its scope is very narrow, and only information that shows corruption, maladministration, and substantial waste in public money falls under protected disclosure.[34] The routes of disclosure that are open are the Independent Commission Against Corruption, the NSW Ombudsman, and

---

BOX 9.3   **Australian whistleblower legislation**

Act or Bill	Jurisdiction
Whistleblower Protection Act 1993	South Australia
Whistleblower Protection Act 1994	Queensland
Protected Disclosures Act 1994	New South Wales
Public Interest Disclosure Act 1994	Australian Capital Territory
Public Service Act 1999, Section 16: 'Protection for whistleblowers'	Commonwealth
Public Interest Disclosure Bill 2001/2002 (Private Member's Bill)	Commonwealth
Whistleblower Protection Act 2001	Victoria
Public Interest Disclosures Act 2002	Tasmania
Public Interest Disclosures Act 2003	Western Australia
Public Interest Disclosure Bill 2005 (Government Bill)	Northern Territory
Public Interest Disclosure Bill 2006 (Government Bill)	Australian Capital Territory
Public Interest Disclosure Bill 2007 (Private Member's Bill)	Commonwealth

Auditor General; the public agency affected by the misconduct; and a Member of Parliament or a journalist (but only if disclosed to appropriate government authority as well). The disclosure must be substantially true if disclosed externally, and must be made voluntarily. Vexatious disclosures are not protected. There is no system of reporting disclosures, which makes evaluation and information on implementation almost impossible. As in the UK Act, there is no requirement for agencies to develop procedures for the protection of whistleblowers.

At the national level, Democrat Senator Andrew Murray tabled the third version of a Public Interest Disclosure Bill as a private member's Bill, which had its second hearing in the Australian Senate on 14 July 2007.[35]

A new whistleblower law in Norway

Norway, where Jon Sudbø's misconduct was discovered and where there were questions raised as to why no one in his department had come forward at an earlier stage, has only recently strengthened its whistleblowing protection by introducing amendments to its Working Environment Act at the end of 2006.[36] Under the amended Act, which came into force on 1 January 2007, and applies to both public and private sectors, all employees have a right to notify suspicions of misconduct in their organizations. The most important part is the notion that the procedure followed is justifiable and defensible – so-called defensible whistleblowing. Internal reporting or reporting to public authorities will automatically be regarded as justifiable. External notification should be made in good faith, and must be of public interest. The burden of proof in showing that a procedure was unjustified rests with the employer. Whereas it should be made in good faith, malicious reporting is still lawful as long as it is in the public interest. Under Norwegian law, institutions and organizations have specific obligations to establish whistleblowing procedures. In the case of reprisals, employees can take the case to the civil court. Despite this strengthened protection, Transparency International, a civil society organization campaigning against corruption, is concerned that, in practice, whistleblowers are not well protected and that the provision of justified or defensible whistleblowing is counterproductive.[37] Transparency International lists 19 countries with unsatisfactory whistleblower protection in the public sector (Box 9.4).[37]

BOX 9.4   **Status of public sector whistleblower protection laws in 34 countries**

Satisfactory: Austria, Canada, Estonia, Finland, Germany, Hungary, Japan, New Zealand, Poland, Slovak Republic, South Korea, Sweden, Switzerland, UK, USA

Unsatisfactory: Argentina, Australia, Belgium, Brazil, Bulgaria, Chile, Czech Republic, Denmark, France, Greece, Ireland, Italy,[a] Mexico, the Netherlands, Norway,[a] Portugal, Slovenia, Spain, Turkey

[a]A positive trend with improvements was reported in Italy and Norway.

Conclusions

The role of whistleblowers in maintaining research integrity remains an important one, and malicious whistleblowing is extremely uncommon. People who show the civil courage to speak up in unsatisfactory circumstances should be praised, not vilified. In an idealistic, completely open society with continuous discussions, whistleblowing should become redundant. However, human activity will never be without failings, and institutions and organizations are run by human beings. A well thought out and executed framework of legislation helps to protect whistleblowers, but the procedures at institutions are of crucial importance. National oversight and a national point of help and contact for whistleblowers should be instituted in all countries that take the integrity of their research output seriously.

References

1. World Medical Association International Code of Medical Ethics. www.wma.net/e/policy/c8.htm.
2. Rhodes R, Strain JJ. Whistleblowing in academic medicine. *J Med Ethics* 2004; **30**: 35–9.
3. Research Triangle Institute. *Consequences of Whistleblowing for the Whistleblower in Misconduct in Science Cases*. Washington, DC: Research Triangle Institute, 1995. ori.dhhs.gov/documents/consequences.pdf.
4. Near JP, Miceli MP. Effective whistle-blowing. *Acad Manage Rev* 1995; **20**: 679–708.
5. Van der Weyden M. Managing allegations of scientific misconduct and fraud: lessons from the 'Hall affair'. *Med J Aust* 2004; **180**: 149–51.
6. Scientific and financial misconduct [radio programme]. *The Science Show*, presented by Norman Swan. Australian Broadcasting Corporation Radio National, 13 April 2002. www.abc.net.au/rn/scienceshow/stories/2002/531406.htm.
7. The University of New South Wales. Council resolutions on Hall matter. 8 June 2004. www.unsw.edu.au/news/pad/articles/2004/jun/CouncilMNE.html.
8. What happens to the whistleblowers? [radio programme]. *The Science Show*, presented by Robyn Williams. Australian Broadcasting Corporation Radio National, 3 September 2005. www.abc.net.au/rn/science/ss/stories/s1451250.htm.
9. Australian Code for the Responsible Conduct of Research. Jointly issued by the National Health and Medical Research Council, the Australian Research Council, and Universities Australia. 2007. www.nhmrc.gov.au/publications/synopses/_files/r39.pdf.
10. Van der Weyden M. Preventing and processing research misconduct: a new Australian code for responsible research. *Med J Aust* 2006; **184**: 430–1.
11. Interlandi J. An unwelcome discovery. *New York Times* 22 October 2006. www.nytimes.com/2006/10/22/magazine/22sciencefraud.html.
12. Sudbø J, Lee JJ, Lippman SM et al. Non-steroidal anti-inflammatory drugs and the risk of oral cancer: a nested case-control study. *Lancet* 2005; **366**: 1359–66.

13. Report from the Investigation Commission appointed by Rikshospitalet–Radiumhospitalet MC and the University of Oslo, 18 January 2006, chaired by Anders Ekbom. Submitted 30 June 2006. radium.no/general/docs/ekbom/Report_Investigation_Commission.pdf.

14. Odling-Smee L, Giles J, Fuyuno I et al. Where are they now? *Nature* 2007; **445**: 244–5.

15. Washburn J. Rent-a-Researcher: did a British university sell out to Procter & Gamble? *Slate Magazine*. Washingtonpost.Newsweek Interactive 22 December 2005. www.slate.com/id/2133061.

16. Blumsohn A. Authorship, ghost-science, access to data and control of the pharmaceutical scientific literature: who stands behind the word? *Prof Ethics Rep* 2006; **19**: 1–4.

17. Blumsohn A, Barton IP, Chines A, Eastell R. Relationship of early changes in bone turnover to the reduction in vertebral fracture risk with risedronate – the HIP study. Presented at the 25th Annual Meeting of the American Society for Bone and Mineral Research, Minneapolis, MN, USA, 2003. www.asbmr.org/meeting/abstracts.cfm.

18. Baty P. Inaction fuels research row. *Times Higher Education Supplement* 29 April 2005. www.timeshighereducation.co.uk/story.asp?sectioncode=26&storycode=195664.

19. Baty P. Gag money rejected. *Times Higher Education Supplement* 16 December 2005. www.timeshighereducation.co.uk/story.asp?sectioncode=26&storycode=200366.

20. Blumsohn A. Scientific misconduct blog. www.scientific-misconduct.blogspot.com.

21. Thomson J, Baird PA, Downie J. *The Olivieri Report*. Toronto: James Lorimer and Co, 2001.

22. Australian Research Council Linkage Project. *Whistling While They Work: Enhancing the Theory and Practice of Internal Witness Management in Public Sector Organisations*. Socio-legal Research Centre, Griffith Law School. Draft report released 24 October 2007. www.griffith.edu.au/centre/slrc/whistleblowing/pdf/Whistleblowing_in_Aust_Public_Sector-Oct2007.pdf.

23. Rothschild J, Miethe TD. Whistle-blower disclosures and management retaliation: the battle to control information about organization corruption. *Work Occup* 1999; **26**: 107–28.

24. The Bristol Royal Infirmary Inquiry. *Learning from Bristol: The Report of the Public Inquiry into Children's Heart Surgery at the Bristol Royal Infirmary 1984–1985*. July 2001. http://www.bristol-inquiry.org.uk/final_report/report/index.htm.

25. The Shipman Inquiry. *Death Disguised*. 19 July 2002. www.the-shipman-inquiry.org.uk/fr_page.asp.

26. Faunce T, Bolsin S, Chan W-P. Supporting whistleblowers in academic medicine: training and respecting the courage of professional conscience. *J Med Ethics* 2004; **30**: 40–3.

27. De Maria W. Common law – common mistakes. The dismal failure of whistleblower laws in Australia, New Zealand, South Africa, Ireland and the United Kingdom. Presented to the International Whistleblower Conference, University of Indiana,

USA, 12–13 April 2002. www.uow.edu.au/arts/sts/bmartin/dissent/documents/DeMaria_laws.pdf.

28. Taxpayers Against Fraud Education Fund. The False Claims Act Legal Center. www.taf.org/whyfca.htm.

29. Whitaker LP. *Congressional Research Service Report for Congress. The Whistleblower Protection Act: An Overview*. March 2007. digitalcommons.ilr.cornell.edu/cgi/viewcontent.cgi?article=1031&context=crs.

30. H.R.985: Whistleblower Protection Enhancement Act of 2007. www.govtrack.us/congress/bill.xpd?bill=h110-985.

31. Office of Research Integrity, US Department of Health and Human Services. *Handling Misconduct – Whistleblowers.* ori.hhs.gov/misconduct/Guidelines_Whistleblower.shtml.

32. Hidden A. *Investigation into the Clapham Junction Railway Accident.* Presented to Parliament by the Secretary of State, November 1989. www.railwaysarchive.co.uk/documents/DoT_Hidden001.pdf.

33. Public Concern at Work. *PIDA News and Developments.* www.pcaw.co.uk/news/pidanews.html.

34. Drew K. *Whistleblowing and Corruption. An Initial and Comparative Review.* Public Services International Research Unit, University of Greenwich, London, January 2003. www.u4.no/document/literature/drew2002whistleblowing-and-corruption.pdf.

35. Murray A. Second reading speech. Public Interest Disclosures Bill, 2007. www.democrats.org.au/speeches/index.htm?speech_id=2203.

36. Seventh General Activity Report of GRECO (Groupe d'Etats contre la corruption/Group of States against corruption), March 2007. www.coe.int/t/dg1/Greco/documents/2007/Greco(2007)1_act.rep06_EN.pdf.

37. Transparency International. Progress Report 07. Enforcement of the OECD Convention on Combating Bribery of Foreign Public Officials. July 2007. www.transparency.de/fileadmin/pdfs/Themen/Internationales/TI_Progress_Report_18.7.07.pdf.

10 The role of the peer review process

Ana Marusic

Introduction

In the spring of 2007, the Council of Science Editors (CSE) made a survey of editorial practices in detecting research misconduct. The survey had a small response rate and was probably biased towards editors with interest or experience in publication misconduct, but it showed that editors relied mostly on peer reviewers to detect different forms of scientific misconduct or poor publication practices, such as duplicate publication, plagiarism, and image or data manipulation. The second most common answer to the question whether the journal made attempts at detecting misconduct was 'No'.

Can and should journals and the peer review process be responsible for detecting research misconduct? Most editors agree that peer review may not be good in detecting misconduct:

'Peer review will never be a perfect guard against fraud, inaccuracy, or originality ...'[1]

'The system is not designed to detect deliberate deception, for example, fabrication of the entire experiment, which only those on the spot can discover ...'[2]

'It would, however, be totally unrealistic to expect editors and the peer review process to be able to detect many of the potential forms of misbehaviour ...'[3]

Evidence indicates that reviewers are not good at spotting errors in manuscripts: a randomized study in the *BMJ* showed that reviewers correctly identified 2–3 out of 9 major errors deliberately introduced into a manuscript.[4] Yet it seems that both editors and authors have unwarranted expectations from the peer review process and researchers who volunteer for peer review. Just as the CSE poll showed that editors transfer many of their own duties to peer reviewers, authors also often presume that the peer review process gives a seal of approval not only to research originality but also to the research integrity of their work.[2]

There is obviously much confusion in the scientific community about the roles of individual stakeholders in scientific publications in promoting and protecting the integrity of the published work. They range from the recent statement that there is already too much regulation in science and that 'the last thing science, one of the most innovative and beneficial areas of public life, needs is more rules, laws and sanctions',[5] to calls for using criminalization and due process as the best way to address growing scientific misconduct.[6] This chapter will explore what journals and their editors can do to prevent, detect, and handle allegations of publication misconduct that may occur in their journals. Other chapters in this book deal in detail with preventing research misconduct (Chapter 6) and investigating allegations (Chapters 15 and 16), so this chapter will explore specific situations that arise in scientific journals and ways for journals to promote the integrity of the published record.

Preventing publication misconduct

It is always better to preserve health than to cure a disease – instead of 'treating' misconduct, it would be better if it could be prevented, so that a published article in a journal is a faithful representation of research performed by the authors. The best prevention of misconduct or misunderstandings about expectations from a journal, its editors, and its peer review and publication processes is to describe journal policies and procedures related to research integrity issues (Box 10.1).

BOX 10.1 **Basic editorial policies for ensuring the integrity of submitted and published articles suggested by the US Office of Research Integrity**

- Reporting suspect manuscripts
- Handling allegations of suspect manuscripts
- Request for signatures from all authors
- Submission of raw data
- Instructions to reviewers
- Literature corrections

Guidelines for authors and reviewers

Table 10.1 presents information on research integrity issues that are generally agreed to be necessary. This information should be in the journal guidelines for authors and reviewers, with an expectation that there are procedures in place that address the role of journals and their editors in research integrity issues. When authors and reviewers know exactly what is expected of them and what procedures are in place for addressing different aspects of their interaction with the journal, there is less chance of publication misconduct.

Just as in assessing the quality of care,[7] establishing *structure* (journals guidelines and declaration forms) and *processes* (manuscript submission; peer review; addressing

TABLE 10.1   Integrity issues in research, peer review, and editorial work that should be addressed in a journal's guidelines for authors and reviewers

Topic	Information in guidelines	Examples of unethical practices[a]
Authorship	• Definition of authorship/ contributorship • Types of authorship (individual, group) • Definition of unacceptable authorship practices • Order of authorship on the byline • Journal forms for authorship/ contributor declarations • Copyright terms and forms	Granting authorship to people who did not make a significant contribution Omitting researchers from the author byline Changing the number or order of authors without the consent of all authors Not involving all authors in reading and approving the manuscript before publication
Originality of work	• Definition of the originality of work • Declaration of previous presentation of work (meeting abstract, conference speech, presentation on the Internet)	Submitting the same work to more than one journal Publishing repetitive articles Using text and data from own prior articles without citation or publisher's permission Presenting work of others as own research Inappropriately publishing parts of the same study in more than one article Ignoring already-existing research
Competing interests	• Definition of competing interests for authors, reviewers, and editors • Forms for declaring competing interests • Procedure for handling manuscripts submitted by editors • Editors' competing interests: relations with publishers and owners • Editors' competing interests: commercial advertisements in the journal	Failing to disclose potential conflict of financial, personal, scientific, political, or other interest related to the submitted manuscript Publishing advertisements for a product next to an article dealing with the product Involvement of editors in decision and handling of their own manuscripts submitted to the journal

Topic	Information in guidelines	Examples of unethical practices[a]
Data presentation	• Study design • Use of adequate controls • Replication of experiments • Choice of statistical tests • Presentation of all data, including outliners and other unfavourable data • Special data presentation requirements (CONSORT, QUORUM, MOOSE, STARD) • Acceptable and unacceptable image manipulation • Interpretation of results	Misrepresenting the design of the study (a randomized controlled study instead of a study with systematic allocation of patients) Failing to disclose changes in protocols between replications of an experiment Failing to disclose the use of control from previous research Failing to disclose if experiments were repeated Favouring presentation of favourable data Choosing statistical tests that favour expected result Misrepresentation of personal communications quoted in the paper Creating imaginary data Deliberately misinterpreting presented results
Editorial policies	• Editorial policies and codes of practice accepted by the journal – from editorial organization or professional body/association: — trial registration — data sharing — data or material deposition — data accession numbers — acknowledgement of funding — ethics approval — patient consent	Not acknowledging funding for the study Not registering a clinical trial prior to patient recruitment Not stating the approval from ethics commission/institutional review board Failing to provide data for independent statistical analysis Not accepting free distribution of materials for non-commercial research Failing to submit data or materials to public repositories

Topic	Information in guidelines	Examples of unethical practices[a]
Peer review process and editorial decisions	• Description of the process (open, single- or double-blinded; posting on the Internet; policy for sending manuscripts for re-review) • Confidentiality of peer review and use of information from reviewed manuscripts • Suggestions for peer reviewers • Conflict of interest: authors rights for exclusion of peer reviewer(s) and editors	*For reviewers:* Failure to reject review of a manuscript because of conflict of interest Giving manuscript for review to others without informing the editor Failure to destroy the manuscript after review Providing information from reviewed manuscript to others Delaying review or writing unfavourable review to slow or prevent publication Presenting and submitting research from reviewed manuscript as own *For editors:* Publishing articles without any or proper peer review Publishing articles known to be erroneous or fraudulent Abusing privacy and confidentiality of the peer review process Using information from submitted manuscripts for own publications Making editorial decisions on the basis of factors outside of peer review and journal's policies Intentionally delaying publication of an article

Topic	Information in guidelines	Examples of unethical practices[a]
Allegations of publication misconduct	• Procedures in place for handling allegations	Ignoring allegations of misconduct
		Failing to keep evidence of misconduct
		Covering up evidence of misconduct
		Breaking confidentiality of inquiry
		Failing to disclose relevant conflict of interest
		Retaliating against persons filing an allegation

[a]The examples presented in this table are by no means comprehensive, but just illustrate possible breaches of research and publishing integrity.

competing interests for authors, reviewers and editors; editorial decisions; and handling appeals and allegations of misconduct) is needed to ensure that we can objectively assess the *outcomes* of research integrity practices. Unfortunately, evidence indicates that we may not have adequate structure for responsible publishing practices: analysis of instructions for authors in medical journals showed that there was great heterogeneity in the content and length of instructions among journals, that the instructions provided little advice on the scientific content, and that the advice provided was often contradictory among journals.[8]

Another problem with guidelines, especially when they are long documents in small print and with lots of legal language, is that they are difficult to read. Guidelines are useless if they exist but are not read. The current form of communication in the process of peer review and publishing is a questionnaire – a self-report of behaviour, which is burdened with a number of cognitive issues: understanding the question, recalling relevant behaviour, inferring and estimating the behaviour in question, mapping the answer to the response format, and 'editing' the answer for social desirability.[9] Research shows that, even during such a seemingly simple process as the declaration of authorship contributions:

- the cognitive task of mapping the answer to the response format of the contribution disclosure form influences the attribution of contributions and authorship[10,11]
- the authorship/contributorship declaration form has poor validity as a survey instrument[12]
- other psychological factors confound contribution disclosures as a tool to evaluate authorship of scientific articles.[12]

If journals want to ensure open, truthful, and reliable communication with authors as a prerequisite for the integrity of the published scientific record, then they should take into account the best available evidence not only from biomedical research, but also from other research fields related to communication in science.

Guidelines and codes of practice for editorial work

Journal editors should not demand transparency, responsible conduct, and honesty from journal authors and reviewers without disclosing their own responsibilities in ensuring the integrity of the published work. The profession of a journal editor is currently very different from other professions in biomedicine, where one has to pass official training, obtain a licence, and keep that licence by continuing education. Journal editors get their position usually without any formal education or training in scientific publishing, although they make very important decisions that not only are relevant to the academic careers of striving authors but also have direct effects on health practice. In many scholarly and academic journals, the editorial position is not a professional but rather a voluntary one, performed on top of the many professional obligations of a successful academic. Such editors are often not aware of accepted practices, and have no time for regular training in ethics issues.[13]

In the CSE survey of journal practices in ethics issues, half of the respondents identified informal resources for learning how to deal with issues of publication misconduct: journal staff, reviewers, editorial boards, legal departments, Web searches, journal articles, and, most often, colleagues. Only a small proportion of editors reported formal training in ethics. Half of the respondents looked to professional editorial organizations for guidance. Table 10.2 lists policies related to research and publica-

TABLE 10.2   Ethical guidelines and codes of conduct for biomedical journals proposed by international editorial organizations[a]

Editorial organization	Document
Council of Science Editors (CSE)	*White Paper on Promoting Integrity in Scientific Journal Publications* www.councilscienceeditors.org/editorial_policies/white_paper.cfm
European Association of Science Editors (EASE)	*Science Editors' Handbook – Ethical Issues* www.ease.org.uk/handbook/index.shtml
International Committee of Medical Journal Editors (ICMJE)	*Uniform Requirements for Manuscripts Submitted to Biomedical Journals: Writing and Editing for Biomedical Publication* www.icmje.org
World Association of Medical Editors (WAME)	*Policy Statement on the Responsibilities of Medical Editors* www.wame.org/resources/policies
Committee on Publication Ethics (COPE)	*Guidelines on Good Publication and the Code of Conduct* www.publicationethics.org.uk/guidelines

[a]The order of documents does not reflect their importance or recommendation to editors – editorial organizations are listed in order of their establishment, with the CSE established as the first editorial association 50 years ago.

tion integrity that have been formulated by different editorial organizations. Details of current policies are not addressed in this chapter, since they are subject to change as new issues and challenges emerge in research and publishing. The reader is directed to the websites of the various organizations (Table 10.2) for the latest updates and developments.

The policies, guidelines, and codes of practice formulated by editorial organizations are not prescriptive in nature, either for the members or for editors at large, but are suggestions for best practices. The notable exception to this is the Committee on Publication Ethics (COPE), which asks member journals to subscribe formally to the principles of the organization. Journals are expected to publish information on their membership and support of COPE principles, and may be subjected to the process for dealing with complaints against editors submitted to COPE.

Regardless of the organization to which they belong or to whose principles or policies they subscribe, it is important to make this clear to authors, reviewers, and readers. Journal editors should not only ensure the transparency of their own work and address their own responsibilities, but should also stay informed about developments and changes in editorial policies. Evidence shows that this is currently not the case. For example, the widely accepted and respected 'Uniform Requirements' of the International Committee of Medical Journal Editors (ICMJE)[14] has had at least five formal revisions and a number of editorial policy statements in its 25-year-plus history.[15] However, a recent study of the clarity of guidelines on authorship in medical journals showed that a third of the journals basing their authorship instructions on ICMJE policy cited an outdated version of the 'Uniform Requirements'.[16] Laxity in providing updated and clear guidelines is not limited only to authorship, but also includes standards in data presentation. A study of journal policies on data presentation from randomized controlled trials (the CONSORT requirements) showed that more than half of 167 high-impact medical journals cited an obsolete version of the 'Uniform Requirements', which endorses CONSORT.[17]

This evidence sends a clear message to the editors of biomedical journals – just as they expect their prospective authors to keep up with the newest practices of evidence-based medicine,[18] journal editors must show equal dedication to the best evidence and good practices in the profession of scientific publishing. Perhaps it is time to make the profession of journal editor more formalized, with official training and accreditation in place to ensure best editorial practices.

Detecting publication misconduct

The enterprise of scientific research is based on relatively poorly founded trust, and grant-awarding bodies fund research although there is no guarantee that it will be successful. The same is true for the communication of science: editors trust authors that a submitted paper is a truthful reflection of the research performed, they trust peer reviews to judge the science in a submitted paper fairly and honestly, and readers trust journals to select the best and most relevant research in the field.[13] Journals and their editors are not well positioned to detect deliberate deception, which is best visible to those at the place where research is actually performed.[2] However, because a journal article is probably the best documentation of the actions of a particular scientist that is visible to the scientific and general public,[19,20] scientific journals are often the first place where a breach of trust in science is discovered – many famous cases of blatant scientific fraud were discovered in this way in the past[2] and present, from Jan Hendrik Schön in physics, Woo Suk Hwang in stem cell research, and Jon Sudbø in oncology.[21]

Experience thus teaches that trust in not enough, and that the editors and their journals should follow the famous saying of the American journalist Damon Runyon: 'Trust but verify'. Editors should not run away from their responsibility to ensure the integrity of the published scientific record just because they are not direct observers of research. The scientific community expects them to do their best to verify the integrity of the work submitted to, reviewed by, and published in their journals. This does not mean that they have to consider all papers to be potentially fraudulent – errors in research occur more frequently and they can be corrected in the published record (Box 10.2).

BOX 10.2   **Scientific error versus scientific misconduct**

- *Scientific error* stems from a genuine mistake in the conduct of research or lack of knowledge and experience in good research and publication practices, such as in young researchers lacking guidance from their supervisors.
- *Scientific misconduct* is defined as falsification, fabrication, or plagiarism, as well as other practices that deviate from those accepted in all aspects of research – proposing, conducting, and publishing it.

After the retraction of two landmark articles about stem cell research in *Science* by Korean scientist Woo Suk Hwang and his collaborators, the Editor of *Science* asked a special external committee to evaluate how the papers were handled by the journal and if the procedures in place could be improved to protect the integrity of the published data and prevent deliberate deception.[22] One of the committee suggestions was that high-impact journals such as *Science* and *Nature* should give special scrutiny to submitted papers with potential risk and 'high visibility'. Journal editors criticized this decision and correctly argued that it is very difficult and actually discriminatory to mark some but not all papers as 'risky'.[23] Rather, all papers, in all journals, should be equally treated and receive the same standards of integrity verification.

With the development of electronic publishing and the enormous increase in the visibility of scientific research on the Internet, journals now have several tools at their disposal to discover unacceptable publication practices, such as repetitive publication and plagiarism, citation of retracted articles, and possible manipulation of numerical data or images in submitted papers.

Detecting repetitive and divided publication and plagiarized work

There are many terms that describe publication of the same research in more than one report: dual, duplicate, double, repetitive, fragmented, redundant, and 'salami' publication. They can be categorized in two major categories: repetitive and divided publications (Box 10.3).[24]

Repetitive publication is defined as 'appearance of the same information two, or more than two, times'.[24] A subset of repetitive publication is *partial repetitive publication*, where only a part of the information is repeated in a different context. *Divided* publication indicates division of the results from the same study into more than one article.

Repetitive publications constitute self-plagiarism. Plagiarism in general is defined as 'the appropriation of another person's ideas, processes, results, or words without giving appropriate credit'.[25] Although everybody agrees on the general definition (Table 10.3), the views on self-plagiarism are not uniform.[26] The World Association of Medical Editors (WAME) specifically addressed self-plagiarism in its *Publication Ethics Policies for Medical Journals*:[27]

> 'Self-plagiarism refers to the practice of an author using portions of their previous writings on the same topic in another of their publications, without specifically citing it formally in quotes. This practice is widespread and sometimes unintentional, as there are only so many ways to say the same thing on many occasions, particularly when writing the Methods section of an article. Although this usually violates the copyright that has been assigned to the publisher, there is no consensus as to whether this is a form of scientific misconduct, or how many of one's own words one can use before it is truly "plagiarism". Probably for this reason self-plagiarism is not regarded in the same light as plagiarism of the ideas and words of other individuals.'

BOX 10.3   Unethical publication practice: publishing the same information more than once[23]

Repetitive publication
This is publication of the same information in more than one article without appropriate declaration. Here, identity of information relates to scientific information in the article and not identity of words only.

Partial repetitive publication occurs when only a piece of information is republished in a different context, without identification of the original source.

Divided publication
This is publication of information from a single research study in more than one article. It is also called 'salami publication' or 'publication of least publishable items'.

Acceptable repetitive publication
Secondary publication is publication of the same information for different audiences, with clear acknowledgement of the first publication.

TABLE 10.3 Definitions of plagiarism by different editorial organizations

Editorial organization	Definition[a]
Council of Science Editors (CSE)	'Plagiarism is a form of piracy that involves the use of text or other items (figures, images, tables) without permission or acknowledgment of the source of these materials. Plagiarism generally involves the use of materials from others but can apply to researchers duplicating their own previous reports without acknowledging that they are doing so (sometimes called self-plagiarism or duplicate publication).'
European Association of Science Editors (EASE)	No definition available
International Committee of Medical Journal Editors (ICMJE)	No definition available
World Association of Medical Editors (WAME)	'Plagiarism is the use of others' published and unpublished ideas or words (or other intellectual property) without attribution or permission, and presenting them as new and original rather than derived from an existing source. The intent and effect of plagiarism is to mislead the reader as to the contributions of the plagiarizer. This applies whether the ideas or words are taken from abstracts, research grant applications, Institutional Review Board applications, or unpublished or published manuscripts in any publication format (print or electronic). 'Plagiarism is scientific misconduct and should be addressed as such.'
Committee on Publication Ethics (COPE)	'Plagiarism ranges from the unreferenced use of others' published or unpublished ideas, including research grant applications to submissions under "new" authorship of a complete paper, sometimes in a different language. 'It may occur at any stage of planning, research, writing, or publication: it applies to print and electronic versions.'

[a] Definitions are quoted from documents available at the websites listed in Table 10.2.

Self-plagiarism can have different forms (Box 10.4),[28] and journals would do best to address the current controversy about this form of publication by creating their own guidelines.

BOX 10.4   **Forms of self-plagiarism**[27]

Duplicate publication/presentation
This is the submission to a journal or conference of a paper that had previously been written for another journal or conference under a slightly different title.

Redundant publication
This is the reuse of some portion of previously published data in a new publication with no indication that the data have already been published.

Fragmented or piecemeal publication
This occurs when a complex study is broken down into two or more components, each of which is analysed and published as a separate paper.

Augmented publication
This occurs when a simpler study is made more complex by the addition of more observations or experimental conditions.

'Salami slicing'
This is the use of data from a large, complex study and dividing it to produce two or more papers.

Text recycling
This is the reuse of portions of previously published text in a new publication without reference to the original.

Repetitive and divided publications are not only unethical but also damaging when they occur in medicine and health care, because they give the impression of more clinical studies, when there actually was a single patient data set. Including repetitive articles in systematic review or meta-analysis gives biased evidence for health interventions. For example, in a case study of the impact of duplicate data on estimates of efficacy of a medication for postoperative emesis, 17% of full trial reports and 28% of patient data were found to be duplications, leading to 23% overestimation in the efficacy of the medication in question.[29]

In the past, a paper with repetitive research and outright plagiarism of others' research was most often detected by a good peer reviewer[24] – sometimes the actual author of the plagiarized work.[2] As such discoveries occur at the prepublication stage, the editor can contact the authors for clarification, and can either reject the manuscript or publish it if the reasons for repetitive or divided publications are acceptable. In both cases, the editor should use the opportunity to educate the authors about unethical publication practices by writing a detailed letter to them rather than using a standard journal letter form.

Already-published repetitive or plagiarized publications are usually discovered by journal readers. In cases of clinical trials, researchers performing a systematic review or meta-analysis notice the similarity between two or more studies and alert editors.[30]

Several electronic tools for systematic verification of the originality of work presented in a paper are available (Box 10.5). The simplest tool, albeit the least sensitive and specific, is a PubMed search including the name(s) of the author(s) and keywords. Such a search may retrieve publications with similar content and, in combination with the 'Related Articles' feature of PubMed, often reveals repetitive publications from the same author.[13] A more sensitive tool for searching PubMed is eTBLAST, free software that searches PubMed not for key words but for sections of text, and returns PubMed abstracts that are similar to text paragraphs entered into a search.[31] The disadvantage of this approach is that it detects text similarities only in abstracts in PubMed and not in the full texts of articles. Another freely available software is WCopyfind, which compares two texts and calculates the percentage of word strings, usually longer than 6 words.[31] There are several commercial plagiarism programs, which may be available to journals affiliated with academic institutions, as many universities use plagiarism software to detect and prevent plagiarism among students.

A prerequisite for effective plagiarism detection software is the existence of a database with information stored in an electronic format, either as a publicly available bibliographical database such as PubMed for abstracts or PubMed Central for full-text articles or as special databases from commercial vendors. This may not be suitable for scientific publishing for two reasons: if only abstracts are available, they may not accurately reflect the overlap of data in the whole article, whereas commercial plagiarism detection programs include different types of texts, mostly unrelated to scientific articles. Some plagiarism programs use crawlers to search the whole of the Internet,

---

BOX 10.5   **Electronic programs for detecting text similarities**

Freely available
eTBLAST – invention.swmed.edu/etblast/etblast.shtml
WCopyfind 2.6 – plagiarism.phys.virginia.edu/Wsoftwave.html

Commercial
EVE2 – www.canexus.com/eve/index.shtml
Glatt Plagiarism Services – plagiarism.com/
Turnitin – turnitin.com/static/home.html
iThenticate – www.ithenticate.com/

Special initiative in scientific publishing
CrossCheck – www.crossref.org/crosscheck.html

but they can access only those publications available for free. A service of CrossRef – CrossCheck, released in June 2007 – aims to create a database of published scientific content from publishers, which can then be searched with greater effectiveness. CrossRef currently collaborates with eight publishers – the Association of Computing Machinery (ACM), the BMJ Publishing Group, Elsevier, the International Union of Crystallography (IUCr), the Institute of Electrical and Electronics Engineers (IEEE), the *New England Journal of Medicine*, Taylor & Francis, and Wiley-Blackwell – in creating a database with relevant scientific and professional content. If a specific plagiarism detection service such as this could be incorporated into the electronic manuscript submission and review process, it would be a good tool to detect repetitive or plagiarized manuscripts at an early stage, before an article is published.

Some journals with relatively small numbers of submissions already routinely use on all submissions either a simple check against PubMed or another plagiarism detection program.[32] This is not feasible for large journals with thousands of submissions. However, as they accept only a small fraction of submitted manuscripts, verification of a paper accepted for publication should not be a problem.

When repetitive publications are found, it is advisable first to send authors a warning and request for explanation, rather than to make judgements on misconduct. Authors are often unaware that repetitive or divided publication of their own work is unethical and detrimental to the science and practice of medicine. In many small scientific communities, such as those in developing and newly emerging countries, where there is little research and few publications, the need to satisfy publication requirements for academic advancement leads to repetitive publications.[33,34] A good illustration of the magnitude of the problem is the case that we had in the *Croatian Medical Journal* with an author from a neighbouring small country in socio-economic transition. Routine checking of the abstract against PubMed revealed another publication with great similarity of both data and text. When we informed the author about the finding of a duplicate publication, he called us and asked in consternation, 'What did I do wrong? I did what my boss has been doing for the last 20 years! How do you otherwise expect anyone to get enough publications for academic advancement?' Cases like this carry two important messages: that authors do not read journal guidelines, because the originality of data was specifically addressed in our guidelines, and that journals cannot be just passive creators of rules but must be active educators in their community of authors, reviewers, and readers.

Detecting citations of retracted articles

When research has been found to be faulty, as a result of either an honest error or deliberate fraud, scientific literature has to be corrected. However, this is often not done: research into citation practices shows that, even when retractions are published in a journal and clearly marked in PubMed, they continue to be cited as a positive mention of the retracted research.[35] Some editors have called for active measures in preventing citation of fraudulent work, such as requiring authors to attest that they have checked their reference list for possible retractions.[36] In this respect, the 'Uniform Requirements' of the IMCJE changed in 2006 to require authors to check that none of the references in the paper cite retracted articles except in the context of referring to the retraction.[14]

PubMed has recently introduced an independent list of retracted articles, which is available under the 'Special Queries' option at the PubMed home page (Figure 10.1). This allows a search of all citations designated as retracted publications ('retracted publication [pt]'). A brief analysis of retracted articles at the time of writing this chapter shows that the first retraction in the PubMed appeared in a biochemistry journal in 1977. Since then, the number of retractions has steadily increased, with 25 retractions in 1970–79, 131 retractions in 1980–89, 309 retractions in 1990–99, and 378 retractions from 2000 to August 2007. In the last 7 years, the number of retractions per year of article publication ranged from 42 to 61 (median 56), compared with a range of 17–37 (median 32.5) in the 1990s. In medicine, a total of 41 clinical trials were retracted, including 7 meta-analyses and 25 randomized controlled trials.

Verifying accuracy of references

Journals usually trust that authors have done their best to ensure the integrity of cited references. This should not be the duty of the authors alone, and journals should take an active role to ensure not only that valid research is cited in published articles but also that it is cited correctly. Citation and quotation inaccuracies should be considered poor research practice, as they damage the credibility of a published scientific report. Research shows that the median prevalence of errors in citations is high – as much as 39%.[37] It seems that the availability of free electronic databases with bibliographical information that can be easily copied does not compensate for the sloppiness of authors, as a study of citation accuracy in gross anatomy articles showed no differences in errors for articles published before and after the earliest bibliographical entry in PubMed.[38]

In the past, journals proposed a number of solutions to the problem of citation accuracy, including submissions of a copy of the first page of every cited article, limitations on the number of references, and spot checks by editors or reviewers, but with little success (reviewed in Lukic et al[38]). Today, software solutions for reference management and online submission systems have the potential to eliminate the problem of inaccurate citations and quotations, but so far there is no evidence of improvement. Systematic review of the effectiveness of technical editing on the quality of research articles in biomedical journals has shown that only careful technical editing by editorial staff seems to be helpful.[37]

The accuracy of citations can be verified by special programs developed for manuscript management. For example, the eXtyles program checks references in a manuscript against PubMed, and retrieves possible errors in citations. Inera, the creator of eXtyles, is currently working with PubMed on a tool for retrieving retraction notices when reference lists contain retracted articles.

Detecting manipulation of images and numerical data

Although journals may be comfortable in accepting that part of their work should be the detection of publication misconduct, it can be argued that they can do little to

(a)

(b)

(c)

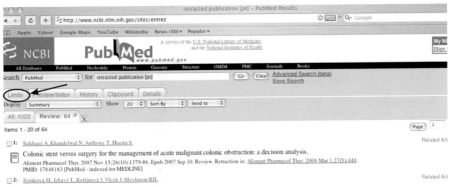

FIGURE 10.2   Searching for retracted publications in PubMed (source: National Library of Medicine, USA). (a) Step 1: select 'Special Queries' option at PubMed home page: www.ncbi.nlm.nih.gov/sites/entrez. (b) Step 2: select 'Retracted Publication': www.nlm. nih.gov/bsd/special_queries.html. (c) Step 3: specific papers can be found in the list of retracted publications by using the 'Limits' option.

detect possible falsification or fabrication of data.[2] This may have been the case in the past, especially for images, which were submitted as hard copy. Today, with the rapid development of digital imaging technology and the availability of cheap software that can be used to alter digital images, authors can manipulate images with greater ease – but journals also have more opportunities to detect such manipulations.

The *Journal of Cell Biology* and its managing editor Mike Rosner are pioneers in setting standards for presenting digital images in scientific articles.[39] The journal screens every image in all figures in accepted manuscripts to ensure that they have not been manipulated in a way that misrepresents the findings of an experiment; it takes about 30 minutes for a trained editor to evaluate a single manuscript. This time may be less for journals and manuscripts in which images are not the main way of presenting data. Journals can also use special electronic tools to verify the integrity of images, developed by the Office of Research Integrity (ORI) of the US Department of Health (Box 10.6).[40] These tools are small desktop applications that integrate into Adobe Photoshop, the most widely used software for image modification.

Although there is no simple detection software for problematic numerical data, available evidence shows that manipulation of numbers can often be spotted.[41] For example, the rightmost digits in measures are normally distributed.[41,42] When data are fabricated, the distribution of rightmost digits is almost never normal, because the human perception of randomness differs from mathematical randomness (for example, people faking numbers avoid repeating strings of the same digits, such as 1111 or 3333, because these do not 'look' random). For editors interested in possibilities for assessing numerical data, the ORI offers very useful tips for addressing suspicious numerical data.[43,44] Editors may rightfully be sceptical of their ability to detect such

---

BOX 10.6   **Forensic tools from the US Office of Research Integrity for detection of image manipulation**[40]

The site provides:

- **Forensic Droplets** – desktop applications for Adobe Photoshop that automatically examine features of a digital image

- **Forensic Actions** – sequences of steps in Adobe Photoshop that can be customized by the user to examine features of a digital image

The site also offers a number of sample images from past cases.

---

manipulation, but they can ensure that numerical data in papers are assessed by professionals. Some journals have a policy that all papers with numerical data undergo statistical review, and research in journals shows that statistical methods can be successfully used for the detection of data fabrication in clinical trials.[42] These findings and experiences of deliberate misrepresentation of data from clinical trials prompted some journals to require independent statistical analysis of specific studies.[45]

Handling allegations of publication misconduct

As other chapters in this book deal in detail with the investigation of allegations of research misconduct, only the role of editors in such investigations will be addressed here. The editor's role is specific and very important, because a journal is often the first place to receive allegations of scientific misconduct. As allegations can be made both during the prepublication process of peer review and after the publication of the article, we shall examine here the opportunities and actions available to editors if they receive an allegation of misconduct.

The editor's position in the investigation of research misconduct is a delicate one, because he or she does not have any legal power to initiate and perform the investigation. This is the task of bodies that are formally entitled to carry out such investigations.[25] Editors may be the first to discover misconduct and report it to the responsible body, but are often met with a frustrating lack of response[2,33,36] or even absence of any body to report to.[46,47] Disappointing outcomes or even open threats[13] will deter editors from processing allegations that they receive or from reporting misconduct that they detect. However, each allegation must be taken seriously, although one has to keep in mind that honest error on the part of an author does not mean scientific misconduct, which is defined as deliberate manipulation of research. In cases where collected evidence indicates reasonable doubt regarding the integrity of a publication, the editor should at least inform the author(s)' institution(s).

Whatever the final outcome, editors need to adopt a rational and open approach and to consider all parties involved in an allegation of misconduct. There are several good guides on handling allegations of misconduct,[25,48] but I find the 'Ethics

Flowcharts' from COPE[49] to provide the most practical guide for editors. COPE has created 16 algorithms for editorial action in allegations of misconduct, as well as for how COPE should handle allegations against the conduct of its member journals/editors (Box 10.7). The flowcharts address traditional forms of research misconduct, such as falsification, fabrication, and plagiarism, but also other unacceptable practices, such as the abuse of authorship and failure to declare conflict of interest. Contrary to the official definition of research misconduct in research in the USA, where authorship disputes are considered a personal dispute among researchers,[24] it can be argued that both the misuse of authorship and the failure to declare conflict of interest are forms of falsification or fabrication. Research integrity bodies in some countries include inappropriate authorship credits in the definition of misconduct.[48] Five out of 16 COPE ethical flowcharts deal with authorship issues, and COPE also provides guidance on signs that indicated authorship problems.

BOX 10.7   **COPE ethics flowcharts**[49]

1a. What to do when you suspect redundant (duplicate) publication in a submitted manuscript

1b. What to do when you suspect redundant (duplicate) publication in a published article

2a. What to do when you suspect plagiarism in a submitted manuscript

2b. What to do when you suspect plagiarism in a published article

2c. What to do if you suspect a reviewer has appropriated an author's ideas or data

3a. What to do when you suspect fabricated data in a submitted manuscript

3b. What to do when you suspect fabricated data in a published article

4a. Changes in authorship: the corresponding author requires the addition of an extra author before publication

4b. Changes in authorship: the corresponding author requests the removal of authors before publication

4c. Changes in authorship: there is a request for the addition of an extra author after publication

4d. Changes in authorship: there is a request for the removal of an author after publication

5. What to do if you suspect ghost, guest, or gift authorship

6. What to do if a reviewer suspects undisclosed conflict of interest (CoI) in a submitted manuscript

7. What to do if a reader suspects undisclosed conflict of interest (CoI) in a published article

8. What to do if you suspect an ethical problem with a submitted manuscript

9. How COPE handles complaints against editors

Allegations of misconduct before article publication

It is best that any problems or questions be resolved before publication. To effectively prevent publication misconduct and deter the publication of fraudulent data, it is very important and most helpful to the editor to have clear and publicly available journal policies and procedures for ensuring the integrity of journal publications. As outlined earlier in this chapter (see Table 10.1), policies and guidelines should address not only the responsibilities of authors and reviewers, but also those of the journal and its editors. A public statement such as that required by COPE is important not only for the 'protection' of the editors, but also for public trust in the transparency and honesty of editorial work.

Procedures for handling allegations of different types of misconduct at the prepublication stage are similar (Box 10.8): the editor should first collect evidence supporting an allegation, from the journal's files, from reviewers, or from both, then assess the quality of the evidence, and contact the author(s) for explanation. At this point, it is important that the editor have the backing of a clear and publicly available journal policy for alleged misbehaviour, as well as relevant disclosure forms signed by the authors or reviewers. If a satisfactory explanation is received from the author or reviewer, showing that an honest error took place or that the journal's instructions were not clear, the review process can be continued after appropriate correction. If the author's or reviewer's explanation is unsatisfactory or they admit guilt, the editor should write back, rejecting the submission and explaining the policy of the journal and what future behaviour is expected from them.

The editor should consider informing the relevant body or a person in the author(s)' institution(s) about their conduct. In such cases, it is fair to inform the author(s) of the actions taken. Of course, it is again advisable for the editor to be able to justify his or her actions by referring to already existing and publicly available journal policies and procedures. Equally important is that the person who raised the question of possible misconduct be kept informed about the actions taken.

BOX 10.8   **Handling allegations of misconduct in a journal**

- Treat each allegation seriously.
- Collect documentation from journal files, authors, reviewers, or readers.
- Contact authors for explanation.
- Keep a record of all communications with the persons involved.
- Keep all documents and communications confidential.
- Contact editors of other journals if necessary, keeping in mind the confidentiality of the process.
- Contact the persons or bodies responsible for research integrity at the author(s)' institution(s) if necessary.
- At the end of the allegation inquiry, inform all involved about the journal's final decision.
- Publish a correction in the literature when misconduct is confirmed.

It sometimes happens that there is no response, either from the author(s) or from the institution(s). In such a case, it is advisable to keep contacting the institution every few months, and, if there is continued failure to establish contact, to write to the authors and reject their paper, explaining the editorial actions and expectations for their future behaviour.

Journals differ in their ways of handling allegations of misconduct. Some journals have appointed a special research integrity editor[33] or a committee[50] with expertise in research ethics. This is definitely a better solution than dealing with allegations on a case-by-case basis. Having a defined structure (persons or groups) using a defined process to address allegations allows a uniform approach to all cases, as well as follow-up and analysis of experience over time.[33,50] The worst thing for a journal is to disregard allegations or reject articles with a standard rejection letter, because evidence shows that rejected articles get published in other journals.[2] Keeping documents and evidence of the journal's actions may be important and relevant for possible future formal investigation. Even in cases when editors do not receive any response, they will be sure that they did their best to protect the integrity of the scientific publication.

Allegations of misconduct after article publication

Allegations of misconduct *after* publication of an article are more common, because procedures in place in most journals are not intended to actively address misconduct.[2] The procedures for handling allegations do not differ greatly from those used in the prepublication process, but they differ in the outcome: if misconduct is confirmed in a published article, the journal has to publish a correction in the scientific literature (Box 10.9). The role and rights of journals and their editor in such cases are not clear, especially with regard to the question of who should retract the publication and when. In the past, retractions of the article had to be signed by all authors, after the investigation had been concluded in the authors' institution(s). In some countries, this is still the legal requirement for dealing with confirmed cases of misconduct. Over time, different practices have developed in different countries, and the procedures for retractions differ.[21,51,52]

Retraction can be requested by different stakeholders in the research and publication process – by the authors themselves, all or some of them, by the authors' institution or

---

BOX 10.9   **Correcting the literature – editor's checklist**[a]

- What is the nature of the correction request?
- Who makes the request?
- Who writes the correction?
- What verbiage should be used for the correction?
- When should the correction be published?

[a]*CSE's White Paper on Promoting Integrity in Scientific Journal Publications*, pp 62–70.[48]

legal representative, by laboratory directors, by the national body for research integrity, or by the editors or publishers. The most comprehensive definitions and types of literature corrections can be found in *CSE's White Paper on Promoting Integrity in Scientific Journal Publications*[48](Box 10.10).

Publishers differentiate between errata and corrigenda: an erratum is a correction of an error made during the publishing process in a journal, whereas a corrigendum corrects an error made by the authors.[3] Expressions of concern should be used with care, and only when there is definite evidence of misconduct; otherwise, this may become a legal issue and the journal may need to retract an expression of concern.[13]

There have been cases where articles have been physically removed from a journal, or replaced with a corrected version after the procedure of correction,[3] but most journals, publishers, and bibliographical databases have a policy that no published item should be removed from the scientific literature. For example, PubMed links the original article to the retraction notice and adds a statement and bibliographic information on retraction to the article retrieved in a search.

BOX 10.10   Correcting the literature – types of literature corrections[a]

Errata

Published changes or emendations to an earlier article, frequently referred to as corrections or corrigenda, are considered by the US National Library of Medicine (NLM) to be errata, regardless of the nature or origin of the error. The NLM does not differentiate between errors that originated in the publication process and errors of logic or methodology.

Retractions

Retractions identify a citation that was previously published and is now retracted through a formal issuance from the author, publisher, or other authorized agent. The NLM does not differentiate between articles that are retracted because of honest error and those that are retracted because of scientific misconduct or plagiarism. If the notification in the journal is labelled as a retraction or withdrawal, the NLM will index it as a retraction.

Expressions of concern

This indexing term was introduced by the ICMJE, and incorporated into the NLM system in 2004. It has been used on a few occasions. The expression of concern is a label used when an editor wishes to draw attention to possible problems but does not go so far as to retract or correct an article.

[a]*CSE's White Paper on Promoting Integrity in Scientific Journal Publications*, p 56.[48]

Conclusions

Evidence indicates that the scientific publishing community does not have adequate or consistent structure and processes to efficiently manage the 'quality of care' in research integrity and to be sure of an adequate outcome (Figure 10.2). The structure that exists for managing research integrity (guidelines, standards, policies, and performance statistics) is not consistent and reliable. What we do as journal editors ('process') also varies widely, and is rarely assessed. Finally, we do not know how to measure whether we have protected or even increased the integrity of published research ('outcomes'), because we lack continuous 'enrolment data' across journals and research disciplines, as well as longitudinal records and good measures of results from processes.

Editors cannot address these problems only in individual journals, but should do so at the level of the whole profession. Editors are not and cannot be the policing force of science,[53,54] and the problem of scientific misconduct cannot ultimately be solved by better peer review or more stringent editorial processes. This requires active and preventive work by all stakeholders in research, starting with the research and academic community itself.[54] As a part of this joint effort, journals and their editors are well positioned to detect publication misconduct, correct it in time, and promote responsible conduct of research and publication in their community.[13,55,56] They should think of themselves as captains of a good aircraft crew, who always first systematically check that it is safe to take off and fly with their passengers.

FIGURE 10.2   'Quality of care' in research integrity according to Donabedian's model of quality of health care as the relationship between service structures, processes, and outcomes.[7] The model posits causality among the three elements.

References

1. Godlee F. The ethics of peer review. In: Hudson Jones E, McLellan F, eds. *Ethical Issues in Biomedical Publishing*. Baltimore: The Johns Hopkins University Press, 2000: 59–84.

2. Rennie D. Misconduct and journal peer review. In: Godlee F, Jefferson T, eds. *Peer Review in Health Sciences*, 2nd edn. London: BMJ Books, 2003: 118–29.

3. Hames I. *Peer Review and Manuscript Management in Scientific Journals. Guidelines for Good Practice*. Oxford: Blackwell, 2007: 173–99.

4. Schroter S, Black N, Evans S et al. Effects of training on quality of peer review: randomised controlled trial. *BMJ* 2004; **328**: 673–7.

5. Horton R. The cloning fraud case is a scientific success story. *Guardian* 13 January 2006.

6. Sovacool BK. Using criminalization and due process to reduce scientific misconduct. *Am J Bioeth* 2005; **5**: W1–7.

7. Donabedian A. Quality assurance. Structure, process, outcome. *Nurs Stand* 1992; **7**(11 Suppl QA): 4–5.

8. Schriger DL, Arora S, Altman DG. The content of medical journal instruction for authors. *Ann Emerg Med* 2006; **48**: 743–9.

9. Schwarz N, Oyserman D. Asking questions about behaviour: cognition, communication, and questionnaire construction. *Am J Eval* 2001; **22**: 127–60.

10. Bates T, Anic A, Marusic M, Marusic A. Authorship criteria and disclosure of contributions – comparison of 3 general medical journals with different author contribution forms. *JAMA* 2004; **292**: 86–8.

11. Marusic A, Bates T, Anic A, Marusic M. How the structure of contribution disclosure statement affects validity of authorship: randomized study in a general medical journal. *Curr Med Res Opin* 2006; **22**: 1035–44.

12. Ilakovac V, Fister K, Marusic M, Marusic A. Reliability of disclosure forms of authors' contributions. *CMAJ* 2007; **176**: 41–6.

13. Marusic A, Katavic V, Marusic M. Role of editors and journals in detecting and preventing scientific misconduct: strengths, weaknesses, opportunities, and threats. *Med Law* 2007; **26**: 545–66.

14. International Committee of Medical Journal Editors. *Uniform Requirements for Manuscripts Submitted to Biomedical Journals: Writing and Editing for Biomedical Publication*. www.icmje.org.

15. Huth EJ, Case K. The URM: twenty-five years old. *Sci Editor* 2004; **27**: 17–21.

16. Wager E. Do medical journals provide clear and consistent guidelines on authorship? *MedGenMed* 2007; **9**: 16.

17. Altman DG. Endorsement of the CONSORT statement by high impact medical journals: survey of instructions for authors. *BMJ* 2005; **330**: 1056–7.

18. Strauss SE, Sackett DL. Using research findings in clinical practice. *BMJ* 1998; **317**: 339–42.

19. Claxton LD. Scientific authorship. Part 1. A window into scientific fraud? *Mutat Res* 2005; **589**: 17–30.

20. Claxton LD. Scientific authorship. Part 2. History, recurring issues, practices, and guidelines. *Mutat Res* 2005; **589**: 31–45.
21. Odling-Smee L, Giles J, Fuyuno I, Cyranoski D, Marris N. Where are they now? *Nature* 2007; **445**: 244–5.
22. Kennedy D. Responding to fraud. *Science* 2006; **314**: 1353. Supporting online material: Brauman J, Melton L, Miller L, Partridge L, Whitesides G. Committee report. www.sciencemag.org/cgi/data/314/5804/1353/DC1/1.
23. Rossner M. Hwang case review committee misses the mark. *J Cell Biol* 2007; **176**: 131–2.
24. Huth JE. Repetitive and divided publications. In: Hudson Jones E, McLellan F, eds. *Ethical Issues in Biomedical Publishing*. Baltimore: The Johns Hopkins University Press, 2000: 112–36.
25. Office of Research Integrity. *Managing Allegations of Scientific Misconduct: A Guidance Document for Editors*. Washington, DC: ORI, 2000. ori.dhhs.gov/documents/masm_2000.pdf.
26. World Association of Medical Editors. *WAME Listserve Discussion: Sanctioning an Author Who Has Plagiarized; What Is Self-Plagiarism?* www.wame.org/wame-listserve-discussions/sanctioning-an-author-who-has-plagiarized-what-is-self-plagiarism.
27. World Association of Medical Editors. *WAME Publication Ethics Policies for Medical Journals*. www.wame.org/resources/publication-ethics-policies-for-medical-journals#plagiarism.
28. Roig M. Plagiarism in the sciences: what do we really know? Presented at Mediterranean Editors and Translators' Meeting, Barcelona, 27–28 October 2006.
29. Tramer MR, Reynolds DJ, Moore RA, McQuay HJ. Impact of covert duplicate publications on meta-analysis: a case study. *BMJ* 1997; **315**: 635–40.
30. Chalmers I. Role of systematic reviews in detecting plagiarism: case of Asim Kurjak. *BMJ* 2006; **333**: 594–6.
31. Lewis J, Ossowski S, Hicks J, Errami M, Garner HR. Text similarity: an alternative way to search MEDLINE. *Bioinformatics* 2006; **22**: 2298–2304.
32. Bilic-Zulle L, Frkovic V, Turk T et al. Prevalence of plagiarism among medical students. *Croat Med J* 2005; **46**: 126–31.
33. Katavic V. Five-year report of *Croatian Medical Journal*'s Research Integrity Editor – policy, policing, or policing policy. *Croat Med J* 2006; **47**: 220–7.
34. Marusic A, Marusic M. Small scientific journals from small countries: breaking from a vicious circle of inadequacy. *Croat Med J* 1999; **40**: 508–14.
35. Budd JM, Sievert M, Schultz TR, Scoville C. Effects of article retraction on citation and practice in medicine. *Bull Med Libr Assoc* 1999; **87**: 437–43.
36. Sox H, Rennie D. Research misconduct, retraction, and cleansing the medical literature: lessons from the Poehlman case. *Ann Intern Med* 2006; **144**: 609–13.
37. Wager E, Middleton P. Technical editing of research reports in biomedical journals. *Cochrane Database Syst Rev* 2007; (2): MR000002.
38. Lukic IK, Lukic A, Gluncic V et al. Citation and quotation accuracy in three anatomy journals. *Clin Anat* 2004; **17**: 534–9.
39. Rossner M, Yamada KM. What's in a picture? The temptation of image manipulation. *J Cell Biol* 2004; **166**: 11–15.

40. Office of Research Integrity. *OSI Forensic Tools for Quick Examination of Scientific Images*. ori.dhhs.gov/tools/data_imaging.shtml.
41. Mosimann JE, Wiseman CV, Edelman RE. Data fabrication: can people generate random digits? *Account Res* 1995; **4**: 31–55.
42. Al-Marzouki S, Evans S, Marshall T, Roberts I. Are these data real? Statistical method for the detection of data fabrication in clinical trials. *BMJ* 2005; **331**: 267–70.
43. Office of Research Integrity. *Handling Misconduct – Technical Assistance. Statistical Forensics: One Digit Too Many!* ori.hhs.gov/misconduct/Tips_StatisticalForensics. shtml.
44. Office of Research Integrity. *Handling Misconduct – Technical Assistance. Statistical Forensics: Check Rightmost Digits for Uniform Distribution*. ori.hhs.gov/misconduct/ Tips_StatisticalForensics2.shtml.
45. Fontanorosa PB, Flanagin A, DeAngelis CD. Reporting conflict of interest, financial aspects of research, and role of sponsors in funded studies. *JAMA* 2005; **294**: 110–11.
46. White C. Suspected research fraud: difficulties of getting at the truth. *BMJ* 2005; **331**: 281–8.
47. Smith R. Investigating the previous studies of a fraudulent author. *BMJ* 2005; **331**: 288–91.
48. Council of Science Editors. *CSE's White Paper on Promoting Integrity in Scientific Journal Publications*. Reston, VA: CSE, 2006. www.councilscienceeditors.org/ editorial_policies/white_paper.cfm.
49. Graf C, Wager E, Bowman A, Fiack S, Scott-Lichter D, Robinson A. Best practice guidelines on publication ethics: a publisher's perspective. *Int J Clin Pract Suppl* 2007; **61**(Suppl 152): 1–26.
50. Wager E. Experiences of the *BMJ* Ethics Committee. *BMJ* 2004; **329**: 510–12.
51. Nylenna M, Andersen D, Dahlquist G et al. Handling of scientific dishonesty in the Nordic countries. National Committees on Scientific Dishonesty in the Nordic Countries. *Lancet* 1999; **354**: 57–61.
52. Puljak L. Croatia founded a national body for ethics in science. *Sci Eng Ethics* 2007; **13**: 191–3.
53. Brice J, Bligh J. Author misconduct: not just the editors' responsibility. *Med Educ* 2005; **39**: 83–9.
54. Marusic A, Marusic M. Killing the messenger: should scientific journals be responsible for policing scientific fraud? *Med J Aust* 2006; **184**: 596–7.
55. Gollogly L, Momen H. Ethical dilemmas in scientific publication: pitfalls and solutions for editors. *Rev Saude Publica* 2006; **40**(Spec No.): 24–9.
56. Laine C, Goodman SN, Griswold ME, Sox HC. Reproducible research: moving towards research the public can really trust. *Ann Intern Med* 2007; **146**: 450–3.

11 Can statistical analysis reveal research misconduct?

Stephen Evans

Introduction

The simple answer to the question posed in the title is 'yes'. This chapter will demonstrate not only that statistical analysis can reveal possible research misconduct, but also that, in some circumstances, it can provide such convincing evidence that misconduct has occurred that no corroboration is needed.

We first examine some characteristics of genuine data, together with the distortions introduced by alteration of original data or complete invention. Then we briefly discuss issues of misconduct that do not involve data manipulation. A number of published articles have discussed details of the potential use of statistical methods for detection of misconduct, and we summarize these. We describe how published examples of statistical analysis have been used to demonstrate the existence of misconduct. There is a tendency not to publish all of the instances where data manipulation has been detected using statistical analysis, possibly for legal reasons; consequently, these examples are limited in their scope. We then discuss what editors and journal reviewers might do to help with detection, and suggest an outline strategy for statisticians to check data for possible misconduct. Finally, we draw some overall conclusions.

This chapter concentrates mainly on the use of statistical analysis to detect fabrication and falsification of data. This latter form of misconduct clearly distorts research results and can have an impact on the public perception of research that is disproportionately large. However, the consensus of opinion – certainly among statisticians involved in clinical trials – is that fabrication and falsification are not the most common forms of misconduct that distort the research record.

There are areas of research misconduct in which statistical processes of analysis are largely irrelevant, but where statistical issues arise. Over-interpretation of results, selective reporting, and problems with subgroup analysis were identified in a Delphi survey by Al-Marzouki et al,[1] with considerable agreement among responders that they were both frequent and likely to distort results. These may have greater overall impact on the research record and decisions about treatments than outright fabrication or falsification. Each of the areas involving distortion is important in a statistical sense, but statistical analysis itself is not generally used to detect them.[2] The areas not involving outright fraud may often be detected by general peer review. The use of guidelines such as CONSORT[3] can help to ensure that the published literature is of high quality, including the appropriate use and interpretation of subgroups.

Characteristics of data

Genuine data

Genuine data are not necessarily perfect; real data often have accidental errors, and may in addition have patterns that can raise the suspicion of a naïve statistician. For example, genuine data may have measurements that have been made by some person recording the data using an instrument that requires some judgement to decide on the exact value, as opposed to data recorded directly from an instrument electronically without human intervention. When judgement is involved, psychology plays a role. *Digit preference* is the phenomenon by which particular numbers are preferred to be recorded or chosen, rather than a uniform distribution in which each number is equally likely to occur. This preference may be relatively universal in preferring 5 or 10, or it may be person-specific, some liking 3 or 7 as compared with 4 or 6. The element of judgement usually applies to the least significant digit in a number, though it may also apply to the penultimate digit. For example, in recording babies' weights using a metric scale, there may be a tendency to record the weight to the nearest 50 g or even 100 g. This phenomenon is not of itself misconduct or even accidental error – it is simply imprecision in recording. Such imprecision may be sensible, since recording, for example, birthweight to the nearest gram is neither necessary nor helpful. Another obvious example is the recording of blood pressures to the nearest 5 or 10 mmHg, as is often done in clinical practice. In research, some instruments may encourage the recording to the nearest 2 mmHg, but with modern digital measurement no digit preference should be expected, since the instrument will record to the nearest mmHg.

The phenomenon of digit preference may also be seen when converting between different measurement scales. If a scale is calibrated in inches but the research requires it to be given in centimetres, then digit preference may be seen because the measurements to the nearest inch appear to have particular values when written down in centimetres. This is illustrated in Figure 11.1, where entirely genuine measurements of height had probably been measured in some instances on a scale with inches but entered in the records in centimetres, so it can be seen that particular values occur much more frequently than others. In Figure 11.1, the values 157, 160, 163 and 165 cm, which correspond to 5 ft 2 in., 5 ft 3in., 5 ft 4 in., and 5 ft 5 in., tend to occur more frequently than the adjacent values in centimetres.

When data are examined as pairs of variables, for example relating weight and height, relationships will be seen between variables which are neither perfect nor totally random. There may also be outlying values which may be noted in two dimensions more easily than in one dimension. Such outlying values may be genuine, for example

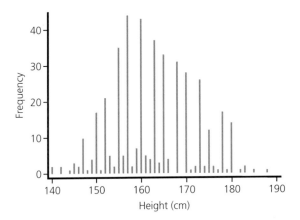

FIGURE 11.1 Frequency of particular values of height in a randomized trial.

the very tall person who also weighs very little, but they may also be recording errors. Statisticians are taught to check for possible errors in outlying values, since these may be influential in the analysis. There are statistical measures, such as Cook's distance, relating to the influence of particular observations, and in regression analysis it is good practice to check that these observations are not accidental errors. An introductory book on medical statistics, such as that by Kirkwood and Sterne,[4] should give further details of these aspects, under the heading of 'regression diagnostics'. One could argue that the common practice of quoting the minimum and maximum values in a set of data may not be sensible, since these are the two observations that are most likely to be subject to accidental error. At the same time, the careful reader may notice that these values are vulnerable to mistakes.

It is important for the applied medical statistician not only to be competent in statistics itself, but also to be familiar with the area of medical research, to enable checking of the data for accidental error. Such checking may, as a collateral effect, also indicate potential problems where misconduct might have occurred.

Altered data

For most situations where observations are altered, the motive is to obtain a particular result and usually to achieve statistical significance. Data are often altered to bring outlying observations into line with the rest. Outlying values increase the variance (standard deviation), making the prize of 'statistical significance' more difficult to obtain.

Data may also be altered to shift the mean in order to obtain a desired result. It is very difficult to detect a small proportion of altered observations, whether this was done to reduce variance or to change the mean, especially if the changes are small. One thing that can be noticed is the effect on bivariate or multivariate relationships. It is in these relationships, which will be distorted by changes in observations on one variable, that the potential exists for discovering evidence that the data have been falsified (altered).

In practice, it is most likely that a suspicion arises in relation to a set of data because the magnitude of an effect is unusual or implausible. This suspicion can alert analysts so that a comparison with original, perhaps handwritten, records or clinical notes can be done. Convincing evidence that falsification has occurred will have to come from such comparisons.

Invented data

Invented or fabricated data tend to be easier to spot than altered or falsified data. Once again, the key features of human psychology that lead to digit preference will mean that the features of invented data might be seen by examination of the last digits of values where no preference should be occurring. There have been a number of demonstrations that have shown that it is very difficult to invent data without a characteristic 'fingerprint', as it were, being left behind.[5,6] Invented data often have too little variability compared with genuine data, and the relationship between the different variables is very difficult to retain when data have been invented by hand.

Some people have suggested that statisticians should not reveal too much about the statistical characteristics of invented data and the methods that can be used to detect fabrication. The revelations might make it easier for a fraudster to circumvent the checks carried out using statistical methods. While this argument has some appeal, it is reasonable to suggest that science should still be an open process and that it is up to the ingenuity of statisticians to be ahead of the fabricators. We do not know whether fabricators have become more sophisticated in their invention of data.

Misconduct that does not involve fabrication or falsification

As was noted in the introduction, there is a great deal of misconduct that does not involve fabrication or falsification. It seems likely that these forms are more prevalent and have a more important impact on the totality of published research. Al-Marzouki et al[1] found 13 forms of misconduct for which there was majority agreement that they were both frequent and likely to distort the results. The selective reporting of particular time points or particular outcomes, and failure to report on adverse events, were among these 13 types of misconduct. Many investigators do not seem to be aware that these types of approach to presenting results are a form of misconduct. One way to minimize such problems is to have a pre-specified protocol and analysis plan. There has been a general move in recent years to have protocols, especially for clinical trials, published or at least submitted to the journal prior to or at the same time as the final paper describing the results. Gardner et al[7] carried out a survey of investigators, largely physicians, whose reports of trials were included in the *Cochrane Database of Systematic Reviews*. They noted that misrepresentation of the data and seriously misleading misinterpretations of the results were more frequent than fabrication or falsification, although still at a low rate. Ranstam et al[8] surveyed medical statisticians with a low (37%) response rate, but they reported, based on their experience, fairly high levels of knowledge of misconduct other than fabrication or falsification, as well as relatively high levels of the latter. It is possible that statisticians are more sensitive to this type of misconduct than are physicians. The rate measured 'per publication' is not high, but cumulative experience shows that, over a 10-year period, a high proportion of statisticians, perhaps even as high as 50%, will encounter some form of intentional misconduct, involving deliberate distortion. Much of the emphasis has been on clinical trials, but this survey suggested that epidemiology is at least as vulnerable, if not more so. The prepublication of protocols does not occur as frequently in epidemiology as in randomized trials, and this may explain the higher rate of this type of misconduct.

A further type of misconduct is failure to publish research at all, as noted by Chalmers.[9] This has an impact on systematic reviews, which are often taken as a strong form of evidence. Wager et al[10] produced guidelines for publishing by pharmaceutical companies, emphasizing the need not to suppress research.

Deliberate selection of inappropriate analysis methods to obtain a desired result

The use of inappropriate methods of analysis should be picked up by peer review. However, it may not be obvious whether this is deliberate or through ignorance. In their survey, Ranstam et al[8] found that misconduct of this type was 'moderately likely' and that it could well distort the results. There have been many surveys of whether statistical methods have been used appropriately, but sometimes this can be a matter of disagreement among experts. Cole et al[11] discussed the need to concentrate on errors that affect interpretation of the findings. Gore et al,[12] in a classic paper, surveyed misuse of methods, and, stemming from this work, various guidelines have attempted to minimize the use of wrong methods. Altman[13] has discussed more recent developments.

An interesting recent example of inappropriate presentation occurred in the first report of the VIGOR trial.[14] This used naproxen as the comparator for looking at the benefit of rofecoxib in terms of gastrointestinal effects. However, the authors reversed the comparator when reporting on coronary heart disease (CHD). This meant that a relative risk for CHD with rofecoxib of over 4 was reported as 0.2 – that is, as a benefit for naproxen. This was an incorrect presentation, even if it was believed (incorrectly as it has turned out) that the reason was a protective effect of naproxen. A very careful reading could detect this, but to many readers the impression given was that there was no concern about CHD for rofecoxib. The correct presentation was used in a subsequent publication by Mukherjee at al.[15] The *New England Journal of Medicine* editors published an 'Expression of concern' in respect of what they believed to be suppression of data in this trial,[16] although the original authors disputed this.[17] In this latter reference, the VIGOR trial authors quote the 'Expression of concern' by Curfman et al[16] using the correct comparator of naproxen to describe the excess of myocardial infarctions with rofecoxib. There is also a tendency, perhaps illustrated by the VIGOR report, to use the most powerful statistical methods (Cox model and cumulative risk in this case) to analyse data on benefit, but a less powerful method when it comes to harms (risk based on total events divided by total randomized, ignoring loss to follow-up). This type of approach can easily be noticed by good peer review.

Misuse of subgroups

Many statisticians believe not only that this area is misunderstood by clinicians, but also that abuse of subgroup analyses may be the most serious problem distorting results, especially of randomized trials. Wang et al[18] set out some useful guidelines, and a survey by Pocock et al[19] has shown that, even in major medical journals, the correct tests for interaction are not usually used. Subgroup results often appear in the abstract without the appropriate evidence based on interaction tests, which creates an overemphasis on subgroup findings.

All of these problems can lead to exaggerated estimates of treatment effects. Ioannidis and Trikalinos[20] have recently proposed a test for looking at published evidence on particular questions, including meta-analyses, which is able to detect whether there is evidence that a 'chase for statistical significance' is likely to have occurred. They show that there is evidence that such 'chases' have occurred, and they note that misconduct can result in an excess of statistically significant findings.

Methods of analysis that might reveal altered or invented data

In order for statistical analysis to reveal misconduct, a comparison must be made, either internally, within a data set, or with some external standard or set of data. In multicentre trials, it is possible to make comparisons between centres; if most centres are providing genuine data but there is fabrication or falsification in one or two centres, then this may be detectable. An alternative is to have good knowledge of what is expected in the results. This, however, relies on expert opinion unless a set of data is available with the same variables recorded in an equivalent setting.

Descriptive statistics – univariable

Good descriptions of the methods that may be used for univariate examination of the data have been given in several papers, for example that by Buyse et al.[21] As has been noted above, it is rarely the case that fabricated data lead to outlying values, so the philosophy of checking the data for accidental errors is different from the philosophy required for checking for misconduct. It has been stated that 'biostatistical methods can only point at problems: further investigations and hard evidence are needed to confirm fraud.'[21] We shall return to this issue later, but the methods suggested in that paper and its references are very useful in giving 'signals' of problems.

Examining means and medians and their differences is the first step. The reduced variability in fabricated data may also be an indicator, so the use of variances (or, equivalently, standard deviations) is vital. The shape of the distribution may also be important, so the statistical summary measures of skewness and kurtosis may also be helpful. Graphical summaries of the data have particular utility both in conventional checking and in checking for misconduct. It is always important to look at actual values rather than summary measures, so 'spike plots', as in Figure 11.1, or 'stem and leaf plots', as in Figure 11.2, can be helpful. These plots are like histograms on their sides, but they display the final digit of the data on an individual basis rather than indicating merely the total number of observations in a category. They can indicate whether

```
14* I 029
15* I 000222222222334555556677777777777777999
16* I 0000000000023333355555588888
17* I 0000233333355889
18* I 000
```

FIGURE 11.2 Stem and leaf plot for height in centimetres ($n = 87$). The first three heights are 140, 142, and 149; there are three values of 150, but nine values of 152.

particular values occur frequently – which cannot be seen in a histogram, where values are grouped. They can show whether digit preference is occurring. These plots provide similar information to a table of the last digits in showing digit preference, but they also reveal whether this digit preference is the same for the entire range of observations. Once again, it should be noted that digit preference itself is not an indicator of any misconduct.

Statistical computer programs will usually be able, as part of their descriptive statistics, to provide the skewness and kurtosis of observations. Many people are unaware of the utility of kurtosis, which shows, for a given standard deviation and mean, how close the data are to a normal distribution. Again, having data that are not normally distributed is not evidence of misconduct – but when data are expected to be normally distributed, this can be indicative of a possible problem. Invented data will typically have too little variability, but if an attempt has been made to add a few invented outlying observations at both low and high values in order to increase the variability, then the kurtosis will indicate this. For the data from which Figure 11.2 is a sample, the mean of 435 observations is about 162.6 and the standard deviation is about 9; the skewness is 0.18 and the kurtosis is 2.5. If a single observation with a value of 220 is added to the 435 observations, the mean is hardly changed; the standard deviation is also hardly changed, but the skewness becomes 0.6 and the kurtosis 5.1. There are statistical tests for non-normality of data, but these are designed for testing assumptions rather than detecting misconduct, though it is possible that they do have some utility in this latter field.

It is possible to use a chi-square test for digit preference that assumes a uniform distribution for the last digit. Application of this test to the height data shown in Figure 11.1 shows that the last digits are very far from a uniform distribution, with a highly significant result. As we have stressed, this is not itself showing any misconduct.

For each of the univariate methods, applied to each variable in a data set, it may be helpful to examine them not only by centre, but also, when a study continues for a long time with repeated measurements, over time.

Descriptive statistics for bivariate or multivariate data

The correlation coefficient or regression coefficients, i.e. slopes and intercepts, may be checked to look for either extremely high or extremely low values. They will usually be most useful when there are comparative results either from a series of centres or from other sets of data known to be genuine. Examination of an entire correlation matrix, and an equivalent graphic procedure known as a 'scatterplot matrix', can also be beneficial. In many instances, particular groups such as centres can be identified using different graphic symbols, which may help in identifying problems in particular groups or centres.

Various multivariate methods have also been suggested, including cluster analysis, star plots, and Chernoff faces. Both of the latter are graphical techniques displaying many variables simultaneously. They can be used either for single cases or for groups of cases such as centres where the mean or the variance could be used for display. Each of these can be used to reveal possible misconduct, but rarely can they show, unequivocally, that misconduct has definitely occurred.

There are various uses of the Mahalanobis distance, particularly to detect inliers in data. This involves examining many variables simultaneously, and can be useful for detecting invented values that are too close to a multivariate mean. This has been described in some detail in the equivalent chapter from the third edition of this book.[22]

Buyse et al[21] have suggested that, in some circumstances, Benford's law may be useful in detecting misconduct. It has proven to be useful in detecting financial fraud, but tends to be limited in medical research unless one is dealing with a very large number of variables, many of which must have values extending over several orders of magnitude. When the majority of data are for a limited number of variables (e.g. blood pressure), this law will not operate even for genuine data. The idea is that the first digits of all numbers in a large set of data do not show a uniform distribution, but 1 is the most common first digit (with about 30%), then 2, then 3, and so on, with 9 being the least frequent (5%). It is clear that, with systolic blood pressures, the first digit will usually be 1 and only occasionally 2, and virtually never between 3 and 6 (values in the 70s, 80s, and 90s are also possible). It is clear that many other types of variable are necessary to restore the pattern required by Benford's law. A problem, therefore, is that even genuine data may differ from the theoretical distribution suggested by Benford's law.

Inferential statistics

We have already alluded to the use of chi-square tests to make comparisons. This can employ a theoretical distribution, as with Benford's law for first digits or with a uniform distribution for last digits. This applies in circumstances where we expect genuine data to have no digit preference and so be close to the theoretical distribution. We can also use chi-square tests to see if data are 'too good' a fit to some distribution. This was used by Sir Ronald Fisher to suggest that Mendel's data were too good to be true. For more details, see the previous version of this chapter.[22]

We can compare means, variances, or distributions where there are good reasons to expect that two or more sets of data should be similar. It is clear that if the assumptions made are uncertain, then the strength of any inference drawn is weakened, perhaps to the point of precluding the use of tests of hypotheses. These may still be useful in terms of indicating a pattern that might justify a detailed investigation using non-statistical methods (see Chapter 16).

Baseline comparisons in randomized controlled trials

A particular situation where comparisons can be made and where the assumptions are strongly justified is comparing data at baseline from the different groups in a randomized trial. In usual statistical practice, it is not regarded as sensible to carry out significance tests comparing groups at baseline using several variables. The CONSORT guidelines, in the paper giving explanation and elaboration, suggest that this should not be done.[23] However, this argument makes the assumption that randomization actually occurred and that the data are genuine. Slattery (personal communication) has said that 'statistical measures of baseline imbalances in a pre-specified outcome measure have the same relationship to investigation of anomalies in randomization as measures of imbalance in final outcome have to assessment of treatment effect in a well-conducted trial.' He focuses particularly on the case where the outcome of the trial is a change from baseline in a particular variable (usually a continuous measure). It is important to realize that, even if randomization has not been subverted, some baseline differences in variables will be due to chance, and if a large number are tested, then about 5% will be statistically significant at $p < 0.05$, about 1% at $p < 0.01$, and so on. Extremely small p-values, either in the primary outcome variable or if they occur in a considerable number of other variables, are then good evidence that some form of misconduct has occurred. Examples where this has happened are given in the next section.

Even where digit preference is expected in genuine data, we can examine the distribution of first or last digits and make comparisons between randomized groups. They should be very similar distributions, and a chi-square test can be used to test for this similarity.

Descriptive statistics of changes

Many trials have repeated observations of the same factor at different times. The relationships between the observations made on different individuals at different times will be clear in real data. This makes convincing fabrication more difficult than faking data at a particular time point. Therefore, it is sensible to examine changes over time in continuous variables, analysing both the variance of the changes and the correlation between measurements at different times. It will be necessary to have experience in the field of study and/or similar datasets available for comparison.

Simple analysis of the pattern of changes can be indicative of a problem of misconduct, or at least of poor quality control. The statistical methods suggested for univariate data can be applied to the changes over time, and both graphical and statistical summaries can be useful.

Exaggerated effects and random noise

In much academic research, a particular outcome is desired – notably a result that is statistically significant. This requires a fraudster to manipulate data in particular ways.

Reduced variability in changes may be one way of achieving statistical significance. However, this means that the analyst who finds such reduced variability has an indication that fabrication or falsification has occurred.

As noted above, Ioannidis and Trikalinos[20] have suggested a new method for examining whether an excess of significant results occurs in some area of research. In contrast to an excess of significant results, there can be fewer significant results than expected. When there is a financial incentive for fabrication by investigators (particularly for pharmaceutical companies), invention of data may be motivated not by the desire to obtain a significant result, but by the fact that payment is for data as such rather than for a particular result. It has been said that this type of invention of data is unimportant since it simply introduces random noise. For example, Buyse et al[21] emphasize this point, correctly, in their discussion of the breast cancer trial where Roger Poisson altered data. However, in many situations, pharmaceutical company trials are carried out as non-inferiority or equivalence trials. In these circumstances, the generation of random noise can help to suggest that the two treatments under comparison are similar, when the truth may be that they have important differences; the object of the trial is then subverted because it is vital to detect these differences.

An important example is that of Dr Anne Kirkman Campbell, who was convicted of fraud in 2004 related to a non-inferiority trial. She was fined over $0.5M and ordered to reimburse the relevant company (Aventis) nearly $1M. In a warning letter to the company, the US Food and Drug Administration (FDA) said:[24]

> 'FDA's October 2002 routine data validation inspection of this investigator raised numerous concerns with her conduct of study 3014, including potential fabrication of study subjects, fabrication of study data, and enrollment of ineligible subjects. FDA investigated Dr. Kirkman Campbell and found that she falsified Case Report Forms (CRFs) that were submitted to the sponsor and falsified documentation to support the existence of a fictitious subject. Dr. Kirkman Campbell subsequently pled guilty to one count of mail fraud in connection with this fictitious subject and was sentenced to 57 months in federal prison.'

The extent of the fabrication is unclear, but the principle remains that invention of random data in such trials does distort the research record and can have grave public health consequences.

Much regulatory effort has been put into trial monitoring, examining the source documents – in some cases 100% of those documents. Relatively little energy has been put into statistical monitoring, which might enable source document examination to be done only on a sample basis. There seems to have been very little funding to carry out research into new methods for statistical monitoring, while large resources have been spent on other forms of monitoring that may not be as cost-effective.[25]

Examples

Most published examples of research misconduct do not give details of the statistical analysis carried out (if any was done) to detect the problem. Most statisticians who have been involved in investigations have chosen not to, or have been forbidden to, publish the methods. Involvement of individual statisticians in investigations is common, and the UK Panel for Research Integrity in Health and Biomedical Sciences has an eminent medical statistician, Professor Gordon Murray, on its board. They have not yet published any detailed examples of statistical analyses that have been carried out.

In the previous edition of this book,[22] some older examples were outlined – here we give some more recent ones.

Testing statistical methods using invented data

Taylor et al[26] used a set of data from a multicentre trial of a new drug for treatment of schizophrenia. Much of the data in the trial was based on rating scales rather than continuous measures. Taylor et al evaluated the application to these data of methods usually employed for continuous measures. It should be emphasized that there was no suspicion of any fraud in the original data. Taylor et al added deliberately invented data to see if the methods could detect such data. They did demonstrate that the Mahalanobis-type distance discussed above was a sensitive indicator for a single invented observation close to the multivariable mean. They employed elegant graphical procedures examining the entire correlation matrix for 18 questions from a psychiatric questionnaire. Again, they used their own manipulation of the data to illustrate that their method was capable of showing falsification graphically, and using a randomization test. This method also suggested that one of the genuine centres showed slightly abnormal patterns. Further investigation found that, though there was no evidence of fraud, there seemed to be some inconsistency between investigators. They suggested that these methods, intended to detect misconduct, could be used to focus training to ensure high-quality data collection, even where no misconduct had occurred.

O'Kelly[27] experimented with data on depression using a standard rating scale. As with the example from Taylor et al,[26] deliberately invented data were inserted into genuine data from a trial. The statistician was 'blinded' as to the nature, extent, and details of the fraudulent data, although he knew that fabricated observations had been included. Then he attempted to detect the false data.

The methods applied were not particularly sensitive or specific in detecting the invented data, but it should be noted that all of the data related to a single variable, measured on up to six occasions. It was noted that several centres had unusual patterns, but O'Kelly believed that these occurred because of poor data quality. What was required was training in recording of data. It is not clear whether there was a possibility that some previously undetected fraud had taken place.

Statistical methods used to detect actual misconduct

Al-Marzouki et al[28] describe the analysis of a set of data from what purported to be a randomized trial of a fruit and vegetable diet. These data were supplied to the *BMJ* for a paper that in the end they did not publish. Al-Marzouki et al concluded that 'the data from the diet trial were either fabricated or falsified and that the strength of the evidence is such that appropriate steps should be taken to deal with this matter'. The paper used statistical methods alone to draw these conclusions. An accompanying paper by White[29] described some of the processes that the *BMJ* went through in order to try to investigate the data more carefully.

The *Lancet* published an article on a trial that was possibly the same as that described by Al-Marzouki et al in the *BMJ*, but with extra data and the same lead author. The *Lancet* Editor subsequently published an 'Expression of concern' regarding that publication, and set out details of an investigation initiated by him.[30]

Al-Marzouki et al[28] used some simple techniques in their analysis of the data submitted to the *BMJ*. For comparative purposes, they also used similar data from a drug trial for which there were no reasons to suspect any misconduct. A key feature was making comparisons between the two randomized groups within the trial at baseline. Because this comparison is between groups (supposedly) formed by randomization, they must differ only by chance. Many of the simple comparisons of means or variances between the two randomized groups at baseline in the diet trial showed highly significant differences. Some very extreme results ($p = 10^{-130}$ for example) occurred. Making the same comparisons in the genuine drug trial of course found no such extreme results (although fewer variables were able to be studied in the genuine trial). Additionally, in the diet trial, not only was there considerable unexpected digit preference, but also the pattern of preference differed between the two randomized groups. It is very difficult indeed to imagine any mechanism by which a genuine trial could show this effect. In the drug trial, the only variable showing digit preference was height, but the pattern of these preferences was very similar in the randomized groups, as expected.

The key argument made by Al-Marzouki et al[28] was that, while differences in means might occur through subversion of the randomization, this would not lead to differences in variances or to differences in digit preference between randomized groups. If the data, although claimed to be recorded blind to the treatment allocation, had in fact been recorded by people who had different digit preferences, this would explain such a difference, but would not lead to notable differences in either means or variances. The conjunction of these three findings was regarded as convincing evidence of fabrication or falsification.

Although simple tests comparing the means and variances were used, the same effects could be seen using randomization tests. In such tests, no assumptions are made about data being normally distributed. The process carries out what are effectively a large series of randomizations using the supplied data, ignoring the grouping created by the original randomization. The results of calculating differences in means or variances or other statistics for several thousand randomizations are compared with the single result purporting to come from the original randomized trial. The single result is then compared with the results from the many randomizations, and is assessed as to whether it is more extreme than would be expected by chance.

Simple graphical display of the relation between height and weight at baseline also shows such dramatic differences between the treatment groups that it is clear that some form of misconduct has occurred. Figure 11.3 illustrates that, while the drug trial shows an expected pattern, the diet trial is entirely different in the two randomized

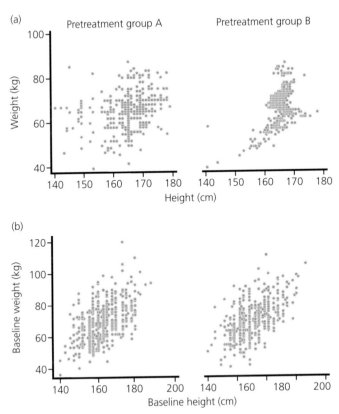

FIGURE 11.3 (a) Diet trial height versus weight at baseline in randomized groups. (b) Drug trial height versus weight at baseline in randomized groups.

groups. The pattern at baseline should be essentially identical for each randomized group in both trials. There has been no satisfactory suggestion to explain these findings, and the conclusion remains that fabrication or falsification occurred.

Sternberg and Roberts[31] have carried out a very interesting analysis of published papers on the effect of nutritional supplements on infection in the elderly. They noted problems related to inconsistencies between means and standard deviations, standard deviations that were too small, and too close agreement between studies. As it happens, the key author of these problematic studies had submitted work to the *BMJ* (as mentioned by Smith[32]).

What can editors and journals do?

In the previous version of this chapter,[22] it was noted that achieving convincing statistical evidence of fabrication or falsification usually requires the raw data from which the results in a paper have been derived. These are often difficult to obtain, and, unless they are supplied in a computer-readable form, considerable effort is required to enter them into a computer. Even if the data are available electronically, the analyses that might demonstrate misconduct are time-consuming, and most statisticians lack the training and experience to carry them out. Editors may not have access to such statisticians for routine review, and, even if they do, may not have funds to pay them.

There is no doubt that astute reviewers can check for consistency of data in tables and figures in submitted manuscripts. They may then become suspicious of results based solely on the manuscript. Inconsistencies may be a result of sloppy work, but may also indicate problems with integrity of the data. It is a cause for suspicion when significance tests only are quoted, without the key data required for their calculation. However, suspicion is not enough for evidence of misconduct, although it may be sufficient for a journal to reject the paper.

A definite problem is that, especially for specialist journals with part-time editors, the work involved in pursuing a case of possible misconduct is so great that the easy alternative of simply rejecting the paper is taken.

Richard Smith, a previous editor of the *BMJ*, has described some of the difficulties encountered where misconduct has been suspected.[32] Academic institutions in many instances do not wish to collaborate in investigating possible misconduct thoroughly.

Sternberg and Roberts[31] have given some fairly convincing evidence of misconduct, just based on published data, although it is an instance where several papers by the same author are available. It is more difficult when dealing with a single paper in isolation.

Conclusions

In Chapter 16, Barrett urges that allegations of misconduct be investigated properly and with due process. It is clear that in many instances statistical analysis routinely applied to data may be a way of detecting possible problems for which more intensive investigation may be required. It is relatively rare that statistical analysis alone can prove misconduct, but the diet trial case reported by Al Marzouki et al[28] demonstrates that it is possible, and the Sternberg and Roberts article[31] is also convincing. Gerber,[33] in discussing the epidemiological study by Sudbø that was retracted and the Hwang case, notes that authors must take responsibility themselves and that editors must be reassured that co-authors really have made the contributions required for authorship. He also comments on the need to obtain raw data, and says:

> 'Asking authors for primary data may be an unpleasant task for editors, if only because it is likely to raise the hackles of innocent contributors. However, if that is the price we have to pay to ensure that the Darsees, Hwangs and Sudbøs no longer find an outlet for their fraudulent work, so be it. But will these more stringent measures invariably reveal a cleverly manipulated fraud? No! A street-smart rogue will generally find a way to avoid detection, despite increasingly sophisticated methods of detecting fraudulent image manipulation.'

While Gerber, in relation to the Hwang case, emphasizes image manipulation, the same argument can be applied to data manipulation. Statistical methods may not always detect it, but these methods have not yet been tried routinely.

Following the European Clinical Trials Directive, expenditure on monitoring trials is large and possibly increasing. It is important to see whether the use of statistical methods such as those outlined here can be used in a cost-effective way to improve the process of trial monitoring, and to explore whether research might yield new methods that would be even more effective.

References

1. Al-Marzouki S, Roberts I, Marshall T, Evans S. The effect of scientific misconduct on the results of clinical trials: a Delphi survey. *Contemp Clin Trials* 2005; **26**: 331–7.
2. Assmann SF, Pocock SJ, Enos LE, Kaster LE. Subgroup analysis and other (mis)uses of baseline data in clinical trials. *Lancet* 2000; **355**: 1064–9.
3. Moher D, Schulz KF, Altman D; CONSORT Group (Consolidated Standards of Reporting Trials). The CONSORT statement: revised recommendations for improving the quality of reports of parallel-group randomized trials. *JAMA* 2001; **285**: 1987–91.
4. Kirkwood BR, Sterne JAC. *Essential Medical Statistics*, 2nd edn. Oxford: Blackwell Science, 2003.
5. Mosimann JE, Wiseman CV, Edelman RE. Data fabrication: can people generate random digits? *Account Res* 1995; **4**: 31–55.
6. Walter CF, Richards EP. Using data digits to identify fabricated data. *IEEE Eng Med Biol Mag* 2001; **20**: 96–100.
7. Gardner W, Lidz CW, Hartwig KC. Authors' reports about research integrity problems in clinical trials. *Contemp Clin Trials* 2005; **26**: 244–51.
8. Ranstam J, Buyse M, George S et al. Fraud in medical research: an international survey of biostatisticians. *Control Clin Trials* 2000; **21**: 415–27.
9. Chalmers I. Underreporting research is scientific misconduct. *JAMA* 1990; **263**: 1405–8.
10. Wager E, Field EA, Grossman L. Good publication practices for pharmaceutical companies: why we need another set of guidelines. *Curr Med Res Opin* 2003; **19**: 147–8.
11. Cole TJ, Altman D, Ashby D et al. BMJ statistical errors. *BMJ* 2004; **329**: 462.
12. Gore SM, Jones IG, Rytter EC. Misuse of statistical methods: critical assessment of articles in *BMJ* from January to March 1976. *BMJ* 1977; **1**(6053): 85–7.
13. Altman DG. Statistics in medical journals: some recent trends. *Stat Med* 2000; **19**: 3275–89.
14. Bombardier C, Laine L, Reicin A et al. Comparison of upper gastrointestinal toxicity of rofecoxib and naproxen in patients with rheumatoid arthritis. *N Engl J Med* 2000; **343**: 1520–8.
15. Mukherjee D, Nissen SE, Topol EJ. Risk of cardiovascular events associated with selective COX-2 inhibitors. *JAMA* 2001; **286**: 954–9.

16. Curfman GD, Morrissey S, Drazen JM. Expression of concern: Bombardier et al., 'Comparison of upper gastrointestinal toxicity of rofecoxib and naproxen in patients with rheumatoid arthritis,' *N Engl J Med* 2000; **343**: 1520–8. *N Engl J Med* 2005; **353**: 2813–14.

17. Bombardier C, Laine L, Burgos-Vargas R et al. Response to expression of concern regarding VIGOR study. *N Engl J Med* 2006; **354**: 1196–9.

18. Wang R, Lagakos SW, Ware JH et al. Statistics in medicine – reporting of subgroup analyses in clinical trials. *N Engl J Med* 2007; **357**: 2189–94.

19. Pocock SJ, Assmann SE, Enos LE, Kasten LE. Subgroup analysis, covariate adjustment and baseline comparisons in clinical trial reporting: current practice and problems. *Stat Med* 2002; **21**: 2917–30.

20. Ioannidis JP, Trikalinos TA. An exploratory test for an excess of significant findings. *Clin Trials* 2007; **4**: 245–53.

21. Buyse M, George SL, Evans S et al. The role of biostatistics in the prevention, detection and treatment of fraud in clinical trials. *Stat Med* 1999; **18**: 3435–51.

22. Evans S. Statistical aspects of the detection of fraud. In: Wells F, Lock S, Farthing M, eds. *Fraud and Misconduct in Medical Research*, 3rd edn. London: BMJ Books, 2001.

23. Altman DG, Schulz KF, Moher D et al; CONSORT GROUP (Consolidated Standards of Reporting Trials). The revised CONSORT statement for reporting randomized trials: explanation and elaboration. *Ann Intern Med* 2001; **134**: 663–94.

24. Food and Drug Administration. Warning letter to Aventis, 23 October 2007. www.fda.gov/cder/warn/2007/07-HFD-45-1002.pdf.

25. Liénard JL, Quinaux E, Fabre-Guillevin E et al. Impact of on-site initiation visits on patient recruitment and data quality in a randomized trial of adjuvant chemotherapy for breast cancer. *Clin Trials* 2006; **3**: 486–92.

26. Taylor RN, McEntegart DJ, Stillman EC. Statistical techniques to detect fraud and other data irregularities in clinical questionnaire data. *Drug Inf J* 2002; **36**: 115–25.

27. O'Kelly M. Using statistical techniques to detect fraud: a test case. *Pharm Stat* 2004; **3**: 237–46.

28. Al-Marzouki S, Evans S, Marshall T, Roberts I. Are these data real? Statistical methods for the detection of data fabrication in clinical trials. *BMJ* 2005; **331**: 267–70.

29. White C. Suspected research fraud: difficulties of getting at the truth. *BMJ* 2005; **331**: 281–8.

30. Horton R. Expression of concern: Indo-Mediterranean Diet Heart Study. *Lancet* 2005; **366**: 354–6.

31. Sternberg S, Roberts S. Nutritional supplements and infection in the elderly: why do the findings conflict? *Nutr J* 2006; **5**: 30.

32. Smith R. Investigating the previous studies of a fraudulent author. *BMJ* 2005; **331**: 288–91.

33. Gerber P. What can we learn from the Hwang and Sudbø affairs? *Med J Aust* 2006; **184**: 632–5.

12 The role of electronic tracking in monitoring data output in clinical trials

Erick Gaussens, Pierre-Henri Bertoye, and Jean-Marc Husson

Introduction

Information technologies (IT), and more specifically electronic tracking, are new partners in the detection or prevention of scientific misconduct, and have both strong and weak points. They cover any type of research – from initial concept to publication, from research and development (R&D) to marketing authorization, and during the life of a health product – and have been progressively introduced during the last 25 years.

Prevention and detection of fraud in clinical trials are issues where authorities, companies, contract research organizations (CROs), and other parties have a clear joint interest. Apart from the legal corpus that defines the boundaries between an acceptable practice and a questionable one, all stakeholders should converge toward a decrease in bad practices. The strategy should cover three aspects of health research:

- Good Clinical Practice (GCP) – protecting patients, facilitating good quality data, and preventing scientific misconduct. Standard operating procedures (SOPs) provide support for these different activities.
- Basic and continuous training.
- Clear, reliable, transparent information, with traceability concerning management and storage of data.

IT tools are essential in monitoring data output, but the question discussed in this chapter is whether they can prevent fraud and misconduct.

The real figures for 'fraud and misconduct' are not known in spite of the use of more and more sophisticated IT tools. It was recently claimed at a worldwide conference on research integrity that:[1]

> '... the fact that only 0.02% of the papers on PubMed is retracted seems to indicate that the impact of misconduct on science is slight.'

It was also pointed out, however, that there have been 300 inquiries per year in Germany (by the German Research Council) and 200 cases in the USA (by the National

Institutes of Health, NIH). And recent examples of scientific misconduct have been extensively publicized.[2,3]

The question of electronic tracking was not really addressed, with the exception of the need for:[1]

> '... the establishment of public digital repositories for primary research data with links to the published articles.'

As indicated at the same conference, research misconduct covers:[1]

> '... both the more limited view that focuses on plagiarism, fraud and fabrication (PFF) and the broader view that includes questionable research practices (QRP).'

'Publish or perish' is still a reality, and the pressure put on researchers and others working in different scientific fields, especially in the health industry, is well recognized. True figures are certainly higher than those that are known and published by authorities or journal editors, but a publication code is now available.[4]

This chapter will focus on the use of electronic tracking to detect and prevent scientific misconduct in the field of health products, mainly medicinal products. The European Union guidelines on pharmacovigilance[5] highlight data mining techniques for searching signals in pharmacovigilance databases, including Proportional Reporting Ratio (PRR), Bayesian, chi-square, log-likelihood, etc.

Inspection duties and powers within the information technologies (IT) environment

According to the International Conference on Harmonisation (ICH) guideline on GCP[6] and the European Directive 2001/20/EC,[7] *inspection* is the act by a regulatory authority of conducting an official review of documents, facilities, records, and any other resources that are deemed by the authorities to be related to the clinical trial and that may be located at the site of the trial, at the sponsor's or contract research organization's facilities, or at other establishments deemed appropriate by the regulatory authority. The ICH GCP guideline[7] defines *documentation* as all records, in any form (including, but not limited to, written, electronic, magnetic, and optical records, and scans, X-rays, and electrocardiograms) that describe or record the methods, conduct, or results of a trial, the factors affecting a trial, and the action taken.

In the European Union (EU), Directives 2001/20/EC[7] and 2005/28/EC[8] state that to verify compliance with provisions on good clinical practice and good manufacturing practice, Member States shall appoint inspectors to inspect the sites concerned in any clinical trial conducted, particularly the trial site or sites, the manufacturing site of any investigational medicinal product, any laboratory used for analyses in the clinical trial, and/or the sponsor's premises. They shall establish the legal and administrative framework within their GCP inspection operation, with definition of the powers of inspectors for entry to clinical trial sites and access to data.

In order to face the new challenges (see the following sections) arising in the electronic world, the GCP Inspectors Working Group, implemented by the European

Medicines Agency (EMEA), is developing a reflection paper on expectations for electronic source documents used in clinical trials, which endorses the set of 12 user requirements for source data published by the Clinical Data Interchange Standards Consortium (CDISC) in November 2006[9] (see below).

Electronic tracking and computerized systems in the clinical sphere: the context

It is nowadays clear (as shared by the EMEA GCP Inspection Working Group) that:

> 'Computers are being used increasingly in the conduct of clinical trials. This is already a well-established practice for data management, analysis and reporting at the sponsor or CRO site. Computers are also widely used in laboratories, and are an increasing feature of medical records. They are being used more and more for the capture of clinical data, at the study site, as an electronic case report form (eCRF), for patient diaries or other forms. These activities use a variety of software and hardware, and in particular several important categories of system – PC, LAN, WAN, laptop, email transmission, web-based systems, interactive voice response systems (digital phone enabled). The fundamental issues to be demonstrated remain common in many cases to both paper and electronic systems (e.g. traceability, change-control), though electronic systems present additional challenges in providing an adequate level of confidence in the data.'[10]

In the USA, a similar set of statements has been made in the Food and Drug Administration (FDA) *Guidance for Industry Computerized Systems Used in Clinical Investigations*:[11]

> 'There is an increasing use of computerized systems in clinical trials to generate and maintain source data and source documentation on each clinical trial subject. Such electronic source data and source documentation must meet the same fundamental elements of data quality (e.g. attributable, legible, contemporaneous, original, and accurate) that are expected of paper records and must comply with all applicable statutory and regulatory requirements.'

The impact of the electronic world on fraud and misconduct

We shall first describe three real cases of fraud and misconduct, linked with aspects of the electronic world. Then we shall progressively address various components, methods, and challenges of the IT world:

- What are the various computerized systems involved in trials and how do they interrelate functionally?
- How can we ensure the quality level required in each of these systems, in particular with regard to tracking correctness and reliability of data/information?
- How can we control and trace data/information when, as in the presented cases, systems are disseminated and a number of data flows circulate among them? (This

will give us an opportunity to introduce CDISC and other standardization initiatives such as eCTD.)

- How could we use advanced techniques, including data or text mining, to explore our data and document bases?

Within each of these topics, we take two approaches sequentially:

- the *IT biotope*: systems, methods, and guidelines
- the *fraud and misconduct viewpoint*: on the biotope itself, and on how to fertilize the biotope with suggestions coming from prevention and detection of fraud and misconduct in relation to our real cases.

Finally, we shall highlight the fact that, from an IT perspective, preventing fraud and misconduct could be supported by moving from information silos to an organized system. This move underlies a number of other initiatives, such as the eCTD Life Cycle,[12-14] a risk management plan for safety issues,[5] and the ICH Q 10 guidance,[15] which aims to 'develop a harmonized pharmaceutical quality system applicable across the lifecycle of the product emphasizing an integrated approach to quality risk management and science'.

Case reports

We present three case reports of questionable conduct discovered by the French Afssaps inspectorate:

Case report 1: documentation on intermediate analysis, before the database lock
In a multicentre clinical trial, the randomization list generation, selection and monitoring of centres, and data entry and data handling were subcontracted to a CRO. The clinical part of the trial lasted three years. The sponsor decided to change the primary efficacy endpoint two months before the database lock. The change to the primary endpoint was stated in the study report, Section 9.8: 'Changes in the conduct of the study or planned analysis'. The source of the new information that led to the change in end points was from two trials, and the decision regarding end-point revision was discussed with the regulatory authorities. The regulatory authorities accepted the modification, provided that the decision to revise the end points was not data-driven.

Section 11.4.2.3 of the study report, 'Interim analysis and data monitoring', stated that no interim efficacy analyses were performed during the trial. No information was provided in the report concerning any intermediate analysis.

Inspection pointed out the following:

- A blinded data set (an Excel document extracted from the SAS analysis data set) was sent by the CRO to the sponsor two months before the amendment relating to the change of the primary efficacy end point. This extracted database was sent by the sponsor to a second CRO, in charge of the analysis.
- The randomization list, generated by the CRO at the beginning of the study, was sent by the CRO to the bioanalytical department of the sponsor, by post, enclosing an e-copy and a hard copy, 12 months before the modification of the efficacy end

point and 10 months before the intermediate analysis. The sponsor replied that the randomization list was necessary to identify biological samples to be analysed, but was not used for the intermediate analysis.

In this context, the question was to know whether an unblinded interim analysis on the end point (or related data) had been carried out before taking the decision to change the primary end points, or whether the purpose of the intermediate analysis had been to oversee the quality of the trial with regard to the appropriateness of the design assumptions.

This case report demonstrates the importance of appropriate documentation of the trial:

- The description of any amendment to the protocol and in the analysis plan must be made clear.
- Documentation of any data transfers must also be made clear.
- Access to data must be protected.

Case report 2: bioanalytical part of a bioequivalence clinical trial[16]

This case describes the experience of an inspector with the bioanalytical part of a bioequivalence study; the method was high-performance liquid chromatography (HPLC) with UV spectrometric detection.

The documentation for each run of samples assayed showed that the chromatograms and the printout of the calibration parameters bore the signature of the technician responsible for performing the assays and the date of this signature. However, the chromatograms did not bear the date and time of signal acquisition, or the reference to the trial. The system did not have an audit trail, and the dates of analysis were recorded in a laboratory book. These dates could have been several days prior to signing by the technician.

The inspectors observed on numerous occasions that identical chromatograms were presented with different identifications. These identifications corresponded to different sampling times for the same subject or to different subjects, sometimes for different runs. It was therefore possible for the same chromatogram to appear with two to six different identifications. The plots of these chromatograms were visually superimposable, but the integration parameters were often modified, resulting in different baselines and therefore different results for the height and area of the tested product and internal standard peaks. Furthermore, the inspectors noted that identical chromatograms showing the same integration parameters (same baseline, and same position of the signal of the beginning and end of the peak) could include very different integration results (peak area).

The inspector also observed many inconsistencies between the peak area ratios calculated from the chromatograms of the calibration samples and the peak area ratios appearing on the printout of the calibration summary. According to the responsible people at the laboratory, it is highly likely that these chromatograms were subject to reintegration after they were printed out and that the modified chromatograms were used in order to determine the calibration parameters. The chromatograms shown to the inspectors and the laboratory book did not mention any reintegration or any rejection of the initial chromatogram.

This case report demonstrates the importance of appropriate documentation of the trial:

- Source electronic documents must be available rather than, or in addition to, printouts.
- All documents must be clearly identified.
- An audit trail must be provided, with all the assay-related events clearly recorded.

Case report 3: pharmacokinetic analysis of a bioequivalence clinical trial[16]
This case describes the experience of an inspector with the pharmacokinetic analysis of a bioequivalence study.

The European Note for Guidance on the investigation of bioavailability and bioequivalence states that AUC_{0-t} should be at least 80% of the AUC extrapolated to infinity in order to provide a reliable estimate of the extent of absorption. The CRO's SOP specified that 'if the value of extrapolation of AUC to infinity is >20% then revise the analysis'. The inspectors were told that, in this case, the number of points used to calculate the terminal half-life was increased step by step until an extrapolation of less than 20% was obtained. For some subjects, all time points from and including T_{max} were used for calculation of the terminal half-life. This resulted in the use for this calculation of values measured during the distribution phase and not in the terminal elimination phase, resulting in underestimation of the terminal half-life and thus of the extrapolated part of the AUC.

In addition, the extrapolation of the AUC was not calculated using the observed value for C_{last} (last measured concentration) but rather the computed value for the same time point, i.e. the concentration for that time point on the elimination line computed for the calculation of the terminal half-life. This method of calculation was not specified in the trial report. The extrapolation was more than 20% for 8 of the 24 subjects after administration of the test product and for 4 of the 24 subjects after administration of the reference product. The extrapolation reported in the trial report was less than 20% for all subjects for both products.

This case report demonstrates the importance of appropriate documentation of the trial and of appropriate reporting of the methods used.

The various computerized systems involved in clinical trials and their functional interactions

The IT biotope
From an IT viewpoint, the computerized systems found in clinical trials are of four types:

(1) systems to create, capture and transmit the data/information
(2) systems to store, organize, retrieve, and protect data ('databases') or documents

(3) systems to perform analysis, computations, presentation, etc., on these data and information

(4) classical systems, including PC, workstation or cooperative frameworks.

Figure 12.1 (a) and (b) looks at the different types of systems within different kinds of activity.

This collection of systems may be clustered into four functional domains:

1. **Trial data capture:**
    (i) The investigator will fill forms (paper, electronic, web-like, etc.) concerning the patient and the visit. Sometimes, the information filled in comes from databases (e.g. the personal database of the investigator or the hospital). It could be that some of this information comes from (and might be fed back to) private patient databases. In all cases, such private data storage, flows, and access shall be compliant with the EC Directive on personal data (95/46/EC).[17]

Electronic document management system:
* Where regulatory reports and dossier ... are managed (including CRF – for eCRF see below)
* Sometimes a single repository, sometimes several (e.g. per discipline)
* Sometimes also containing 'project documentation' (see 'File system' below)

File system or collaborative work systems (systems to help in sharing and drafting information):
* Where regulatory reports are sometimes authored (although the trend is to have this authoring in EDMS – see above)
* Sometimes containing project documentation, e.g. presentation explaining interrelations among trails, with bibliography, with other products, as well as planning a follow-up

Clinical database
* Where clinical data coming from the trials are managed as well the related queries (see below)
* Where blind/unblind/lock functions/procedures
* Where the reference data per trial (i.e. after data freeze) are uniquely kept
* This management is based on data structures derived in particular from the 'blank CRF', the brochure, the protocol, and the analysis plan
* Usually, this information is stored in the clinical database as well as in the EDMS
* Data, come from CRF or eCRF or from central laboratories
* eCRFs are stored in this DB or in a tightly coupled dedicated one
* Coupled with the randomization tool ⟶ Randomization and management of clinical drugs

Systems to control and follow-up each trial (visits, drug supply, CRF flows, etc.), mainly from a management view

Statistical analysis tool (often SAS)
* Where analysis plan is transformed into analysis functions/methods embedded in the trial design
* These functions/methods thus executed provide the statistical results tables
* SAS is often also used to extract data from the clinical database in particular to create the 'data sets' (see CDISC)

Other tools/methods to perform analysis based on the data in the clinical database and/or the laboratory database (see below)
* Pharmacokinetic/pharmacodynamic (PK/PD) analyses and/or specific methods (e.g. linked with a specific biomarker or a qualitative checklist)

FIGURE 12.1   (a) Computerized systems in the clinical sphere.

The database where the concentrations and any kind of measurement are stored:
- The storage structure is defined during the trial design phase
- As well as the ways to associate measurements with relevant patient data and the protocol
- Sometimes, data are only stored in file systems ⟶

The devices or systems used to capture the measured data (LIMS: laboratory information management systems)
- They could (should?) be interfaced with the laboratory database
- They could (should?) – in particular the LIMS – identify and track the samples used

The 'raw' data concerning a specific patient with no relation to any specific trial. **Privacy should be protected by encoding the patient's name if this data is to be used in the trial**

The PC, Apple Macintosh, etc. used by the investigator to perform his/her job
- Could be independent from any trial and linked with a personal database, a hospital one, etc.
- Could be dedicated to a specific (set of) trial(s)

Case report form: the paper form used to capture the data on each patient as defined in the protocol and the brochure

The electronic CRF allowing one to electronically capture, check and exchange data/queries with the clinical database

Data are transferred between all these systems. This could be through manual transfer (M) or through predesigned and encoded/validated electronic interfaces (E). **Even if electronic media such as Excel spreadsheets are used, if the transfer is not automated it has to be classified as M**

FIGURE 12.1 (b) Computerized systems in the clinical sphere.

(ii) In centralized laboratories, various devices will be used to create the databases (e.g. from samples associated with a patient or from information obtained from a scanner). Usually, these devices have internal databases to store, access, and retrieve these data. For some devices laboratory information management systems (LIMS) are used to capture all measurement-related information, including that created by the devices.

(iii) All this information must be appropriately transmitted and managed. This may be done manually by referring to a file system or, for example, an Excel spreadsheet, and then transmitted to the clinical trial coordination team. Alternatively, it can be done through electronic automated interfaces; in particular, parts of an eCRF could be dedicated for the purpose of data transmission.

2. **Trial data management:**

(i) Technical data (demographic data, patient characteristics, protocol structures, etc.) are received (manually or electronically), controlled, and organized, following predefined structures, into laboratory and clinical databases.

(ii) Usually, the clinical databases (coupled with eCRFs if there are any) also have functions to:
- engage in dialogue with any randomization system;

- trace queries made by the clinical trial coordination team regarding the investigators and any resulting changes;
- ensure that there are locking mechanisms in place (i.e. to prevent modification of data) as well as versioning mechanisms (to track successive changes in data sets);
- manage the lock on blinding/unblinding and any other changes.

(iii) Usually, a trial management system is used to associate the main technical information (visit days, investigator centre, etc.) with global trial management.

(iv) PV systems interact as well to analyse cases and if necessary to launch alarms that could be followed by unblinding any particular patient and provide a specific follow-up.

3. **Trial data analyses:**

(i) A variety of systems may be used, although SAS is often employed to extract data from the trial database.

(ii) The key point is that data are transferred, without modifying or erasing the source (manually or electronically) –and then what happens to them depends on what the analyst intends to do.

(iii) Data may be exchanged among various systems of analysis.

(iv) Sometimes, as, for example, in pharmacokinetics/pharmacodynamics (PK/PD), a reference database is used to harmonize and track such exchanges.

4. **Trial reporting and project management:**

(i) During a trial, the project team is following the ongoing trial and potentially making comparison with other trials, with bibliographical references, etc. These in turn could affect the ongoing study.

(ii) Usually, these discussions are documented and linked with decision minutes. They are often stored in a file system or exchanged within a collaborative framework. They can be extremely useful in understanding what actually happened during development.

(iii) In the end, everything ends up in an electronic document management system (EDMS), where reports are finalized and passed on to the competent authorities, partly as the development plan goes on, but largely through the submission of any variation and of the final dossier.

Figure 12.2 gives an overview of these functional clusters. As the figure shows, these clusters are also well linked by information flows:

Interaction 1:

- Data captured by the investigator as well as at laboratory sites are transferred to the trial data management team, and three situations might be encountered:
  - The transfer is *manual*: even if data are captured and organized in some electronic system (file system, spreadsheet, etc.) and transferred using electronic media, the trial data management team still manually insert the data into the appropriate database (labelled 'M data transfer' in Figure 12.2).
  - The transfer is *electronic* (labelled 'E data transfer'): there is no manual intervention in the transfer of data captured into the trial database; the most common example is the use of eCRFs.

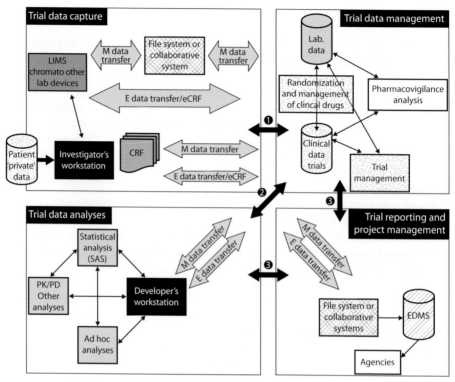

FIGURE 12.2 The four functional clusters.

- ○ A *mix* is common.
- Conversely, the trial data management team might query laboratory and investigator teams because, for instance, some data are obviously incorrect, absent, or badly labelled. Sometimes, to identify such a discrepancy, it is necessary to look not only at specific data (e.g. body weight) but also at a sequence of data (such as one incoherent measure among a sequence of transaminase levels), using some trial data analyses:
  - ○ These queries involve looking at trial data while the trial is still in progress.
  - ○ Depending on the data capture strategy, there may be more (eCRF) or less (M interfaces) information that is traceable.
  - ○ Whatever is traceable, the expected result is that some data initially captured (or absent) will be rectified, stamped as invalid, or filled in. The initial data should not be destroyed, even if eventually only final data will be considered.

Interaction 2:
- Data are extracted from the trial data management database in order to:
  - ○ perform analyses on the final frozen sets, which is the nominal case;
  - ○ perform intermediate analyses as identified within the trial protocol description passed on to the competent authorities and the research ethics committees;
  - ○ perform pharmacovigilance analyses, which could involve unblinding – this is also relevant to regulatory compliancy;

- o perform 'snapshot' analyses without unblinding, such as in the case of the adaptative protocol type of assays;
- o perform other kinds of snapshot analyses that were not necessarily expected and therefore not quoted before starting the trial – for instance, because a literature search questions the validity of a planned statistical cohort study.
- These extractions could be supported by electronic (E) or manual (M) transfers and therefore be more or less traceable. As stated earlier, more than one computerized system may be involved in the analyses, resulting in a variety of data transfers – once again E or M.
- Results of these analyses could then be:
  - o linked with queries (see 'Interaction 1');
  - o inserted into reports (see 'Interaction 3');
  - o used to modify the course of the trial and therefore the data – such situations are compliant if the rationale is described in the trial design as sent to the competent authorities and research ethics committees (RECs), including intermediate analyses and pharmacovigilance cases;
  - o used to assist in the investigation of unexpected/unforeseen situations (as in Case report 1 above).

In the two last cases, special attention must be paid to the traceability of the impact of the analyses, since it is not linked with data/information transfer but with *conceptual modification* (meaning some changes in the data, data structure, or methods that cannot be traced directly since they refer to human thinking outside the system) of the global data structure/values (see also 'Interaction 3').

Interaction 3:
- Regulatory reports include both data and results of analyses.
- Three kind of interfaces are most frequently implied:
  - o an E interface to include data sets (FDA; see also the section on CDISC);
  - o an M interface for all other cases (including storing scanned CRFs in an EDMS);
  - o sometimes electronic referencing of eCRFs contained in the clinical trial data management systems.
- Usually, the tools used cannot wholly prevent data/results being modified.
- The internal reports/slides linked with project management may also make use of data and results usually provided on a manual basis.

In the last case, *conceptual modification* may also come into play.

The fraud and misconduct viewpoint
There are three typical areas where fraud and misconduct could challenge/use the IT biotope:

1. *The reliability of data/information and of all tracked changes within each computerized system.*
   For example:
   - Is the 'blank' data structure predefined according to a clear methodology, and how are changes managed?
   - Is the insertion of data automated and /or controlled?

- Could data be modified or not, by whom, and when?
- Are methods of analysis predefined or adapted in an ad hoc fashion, and if ad hoc, how are they tracked?

This is the subject of the section below: 'How to track the correctness and reliability of the data within each of these systems: 21 CFR Part 11 and validation'. Case report 2 above shows clearly an example of all the above questions.

2. *The reliability of data/information flows and of all tracked changes between each computerized system and along Interactions 1–3:*
   - How do we ensure that data are not corrupted during exchange?
   - How do we ensure that the same data and data label apply in each system (the *standardization issue*)?
   - How do we follow these flows when systems are disseminated?

This is the subject of the section below: 'Systems are interrelated and disseminated: the needs for standards such as CDISC'. Case reports 1–3 above illustrate the difficulties in tracing information over multiple system interactions.

3. *Understanding of the existence, nature and impact of the conceptual modification mentioned in Interactions 2 and 3, as well as any potential investigation into databases held on the suspected PC.* For example:
   - This situation arises in cases where functional modifications are not directly traceable in the IT biotope, such that they need more contextual analyses and often global inspection of all data/information in the global trial/project environment (it is these that probably hide the most severe fraud and misconduct cases).
   - In the case of high suspicion but lack of evidence, the hard-disk or database deep investigation methods used by, for example, financial inspectors could also be used.

This is the subject of the section below: 'Some advanced approaches: how to explore databases and combinations of data and documents'. Case reports 1–3 above show that understanding a case implies the need also to confront data and data flows with associated documentation and bibliography.

In fact, all of these questions can be summarized in a two-part statement:

> *The IT biotope could help prevention and detection of fraud and misconduct if the computerized systems are not stuck in silos communicating through M interfaces, and if standardization of the data/information/documentation is encouraged.*

How to track the correctness and reliability of the data within each of these systems: 21 CFR Part 11 and validation

The IT biotope

In its *Guidance for Industry Computerized Systems Used in Clinical Investigations*, already quoted, the FDA states very clearly its objectives:[11]

'This document provides to sponsors, contract research organizations (CROs), data management centres, clinical investigators, and institutional review boards (IRBs), recommendations regarding the use of computerized systems in clinical investigations. The computerized system applies to records in electronic form that are used to create, modify, maintain, archive, retrieve, or transmit clinical data required to be maintained, or submitted to the FDA. Because the source data are necessary for the reconstruction and evaluation of the study to determine the safety and effectiveness of new human and animal drugs, and medical devices, this guidance is intended to assist in ensuring confidence in the reliability, quality, and integrity of electronic source data and source documentation (i.e., electronic records).

'This guidance supersedes the guidance of the same name dated April 1999; and supplements the guidance for industry on Part 11, Electronic Records; Electronic Signatures – Scope and Application and the Agency's international harmonization efforts, when applying these guidance to source data generated at clinical study sites.'

Its key features are recalled below.

Study protocols. Each specific study protocol should identify each step at which a computerized system will be used to create, modify, maintain, archive, retrieve, or transmit source data. The computerized systems should be designed:

(1) to satisfy the processes assigned to these systems for use in the specific study protocol (e.g. record data in metric units, blinding the study);
(2) to prevent errors in data creation, modification, maintenance, archiving, retrieval, or transmission (e.g. inadvertently unblinding a study).

Standard operating procedures. There should be specific procedures and controls in place when using computerized systems to create, modify, maintain, or transmit electronic records, including when collecting source data at clinical trial sites.

Source documentation and retention. When source data are transmitted from one system to another (e.g. from a personal digital assistant (PDA) to a sponsor's server), or entered directly into a remote computerized system (e.g. when data are entered into a remote server via a computer terminal located at the clinical site), or when an electrocardiogram, for example, at the clinical site is transmitted to the sponsor's computerized system, a copy of the data should be maintained at another location – typically at the clinical site, but possibly at some other designated site. Copies should be made contemporaneously with data entry, and should be preserved in an appropriate format (e.g. XML, PDF, or paper).

Internal security safeguards. These comprise the following:

- *Limited access with coding system.*

- *Audit trails*: it is important to keep track of all changes made to information in the electronic records that document activities related to the conduct of the trial (audit trails).
- *Date–time stamps*: controls should be established to ensure that the system's date and time are correct.

External security safeguards. In addition to internal safeguards built into a computerized system, external safeguards should be put in place to ensure that access to the computerized system and to the data is restricted to authorized personnel. A cumulative record should be maintained that indicates, for any point in time, the names of authorized personnel, their titles, and a description of their access privileges and codes.

Other system features. These comprise the following:

- *Direct entry of data.*
- *Retrieving data*: The computerized system should be designed in such a way that retrieved data regarding each individual subject in a study are attributable to that subject. Therefore, the information provided should fully describe and explain how source data were obtained and managed, and how electronic records were used to capture data.
- *IT system documentation*: For each study, documentation should identify what software and hardware will be used to create, modify, maintain, archive, retrieve, or transmit clinical data.
- *System controls*: When electronic formats are the only ones used to create and preserve electronic records, sufficient backup and recovery procedures should be designed to protect against data loss.
- *Change controls*: The integrity of the data and the integrity of the protocols should be maintained when making changes to the computerized system, such as software upgrades, including security and performance patches, equipment or component replacement, or new instrumentation.
- *Training of personnel* on the systems, their use, and the associated good practices.

All of the above features, if applied, allow all stages of a clinical trial to be addressed properly, including the reliability and tracking of data/information and of data/information flows within each computerized system and along the three global Interactions 1–3 above.

The fraud and misconduct viewpoint
If each computerized system involved in a clinical trial is set up and used as described in the above guidelines, then several fraud and misconduct actions can be prevented and tracked:

- All systems used should be known in advance, and their practices described.
- All actions on all data within each system must be able to be tracked and time-stamped throughout the audit trail, maintained by established practices and SOPs.

- Source data and documentation procedure should allow tracking of the origin of any data filed in the system.
- Protocol changes and their implementation must be able to be tracked.
- People allowed to intervene in the data should be recorded and their domain of actions defined.

However, it is essential that those managing the systems comply fully with all the terms of the guidance, which involves a cost in terms of proving that the systems are compliant (so-called 'validation').

It is essential that companies commit themselves to such an approach, adapting the requirements to their business models, size, and pragmatic change management: a sound computerized system is a trade-off between core electronic capabilities, efficient SOPs, and capacities to provide evidence of its use.

Systems are interrelated and disseminated: the need for standards such as CDISC

See the appendix to this chapter for more information.

The IT biotope

This subsection addresses the topic of reliability and change tracking of data/information flows between each computerized system and along the three global Interactions 1–3 mentioned above.

The IT biotope includes a number of different factors all interacting on the success of trials. Figure 12.3 shows this complexity. Additionally, it must be constantly remembered that data are continuously being disseminated using various systems as shown in Figures 12.1 and 12.2.

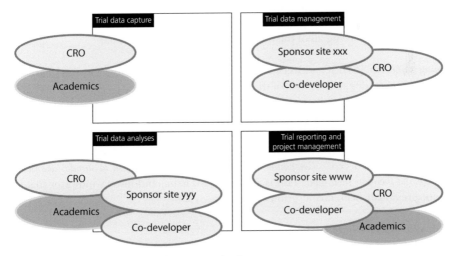

FIGURE 12.3   Dissemination of computerized systems.

In order to be able both to cover controlled exchanges among systems in various locations and to standardize the data and information located in different systems – a tangled mix of issues – the Clinical Data Interchange Standards Consortium (CDISC) initiative was born. The mission of CDISC is to develop and support global, platform-independent *data standards that enable information system interoperability* to improve medical research and related areas of health care. This mission has two aspects:

- laying down requirements for clinical electronic source records
- defining standards.

Requirements stated in the CDISC standard on electronic source records. Globally speaking, the CDISC reinforces 21 CFR Part 11 by stating 12 main principles, which are also shared and referred to by EU inspectors:

1. An instrument used to capture source data shall ensure that the data are captured as specified within the protocol.
2. Source data shall be accurate, legible, contemporaneous, original, attributable, complete, and consistent.
3. An audit trail shall be maintained as part of the source documents for the original creation and subsequent modification of all source data.
4. The storage of source documents shall provide for their ready retrieval.
5. The investigator shall maintain the original source document or a certified copy.
6. Source data shall only be modified with the knowledge or approval of the investigator.
7. Source documents and data shall be protected from destruction.
8. The source document shall allow for accurate copies to be made.
9. Source documents shall be protected against unauthorized access.
10. The sponsor shall not have exclusive control of a source document.
11. The location of source documents and the associated source data shall be clearly identified at all points within the capture process.
12. When source data are copied, the process used shall ensure that the copy is an exact copy preserving all of the data and metadata of the original.

Defining standards. CDISC addresses the four domains of activity described earlier. Figure 12.4 provides an overview of the CDISC models.

Eventually (and hopefully within a reasonable time frame), all clinical data will be standardized, as will be their exchange. However, there is a caveat. Unlike official standards such as ISO for quality control, such standardization is not so far covered by an external body. Any positive trend is curiously linked to the fact that more and more activities are outsourced.[18] *Companies will therefore increasingly need to standardize their exchange and therefore their data.* This is an important issue, and history indicates that it has not previously been taken seriously enough.

The fraud and misconduct viewpoint
The CDISC and dematerialization initiatives complement the 21 CFR Part 11 ones in order to improve the traceability and capacity for analysis of information flows and

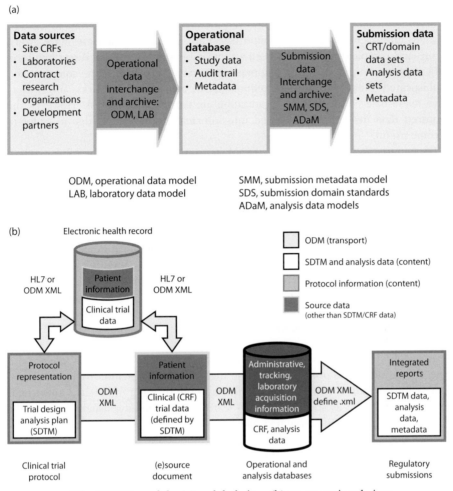

FIGURE 12.4   The CDISC models: (a) a global view; (b) an operational view.

storage. However, there is still some way to go before initiatives are followed up proactively by both pharmaceutical companies and regulatory agencies.

Some advanced approaches: how to explore databases and combinations of data and documents

The IT biotope
Some new technologies allow for searching databases or other documents:

- data mining
- text mining.

Data mining.[19-21] Traditionally, analysts have performed the task of extracting useful information from recorded data. However, the increasing volume of data in modern business and science calls for computer-based approaches. As databases have grown in size and complexity, there has been an inevitable shift away from direct hands-on data analysis toward indirect, automatic data analysis using more complex and sophisticated tools. The modern technologies of computers, networks, and sensors have made data collection and organization an almost effortless task. However, the captured data need to be converted into information and knowledge in order to become useful.

Data mining is the entire process of applying computer-based methodology, including new techniques for knowledge discovery, to data. It can be defined as non-trivial extraction of implicit, previously unknown, and potentially useful information from data. Data mining may also be defined as the process of extracting useful information from large data sets or databases.

Data mining is the principle of sorting through large amounts of data and picking out relevant information. It is usually employed by business intelligence organizations and financial analysts, but is increasingly also being used in the sciences to extract information from the enormous data sets generated by modern experimental and observational methods. The EU guidelines on pharmacovigilance[5] highlight data mining techniques for searching signals in pharmacovigilance databases, including PRR, Bayesian, chi-square, log-likelihood, etc.

Text mining.[22-24] This is sometimes alternatively referred to as *text data mining*, and refers generally to the process of deriving high-quality information from text. High-quality information is typically derived through the dividing of patterns and trends by approaches such as statistical pattern learning. Text mining usually involves the process of structuring the input text (usually parsing, along with the addition of some derived linguistic features and the removal of others, and subsequent insertion into a database), deriving patterns within the structured data, and finally evaluating and interpretating the output. 'High quality' in text mining usually refers to some combination of relevance, novelty, and interestingness. Typical text mining tasks include text categorization, text clustering, concept/entity extraction, production of granular taxonomies, sentiment analysis, document summarization, and entity relation modelling (i.e. learning relations between named entities).

Labour-intensive manual text mining approaches first surfaced in the mid-1980s, but technological advances have enabled the field to advance swiftly during the past decade. Text mining is an interdisciplinary field that draws on information retrieval, data mining, machine learning, statistics, and computational linguistics. As most information (>80%) is currently stored as text, text mining is believed to have a high potential commercial value. Increasing interest is being paid to multilingual data mining: the ability to gain information across languages and cluster similar items from different linguistic sources according to their meaning.

Text mining is used in several areas in the pharmaceutical and health industries, including business intelligence and support for discovery; it will probably also be used in the risk management field (e.g. for bibliographical searches).

These techniques used separately or in conjunction, allow for searching within both structured (data mining) and unstructured (text mining) information stored in clinical computerized systems, as well as in bibliographical bases (text mining) or, for example, laboratory device databases (data mining). However, these methods, to be efficient, need to be first guided by search goals and then be interpreted – they do not give all the answers, only hints.

The fraud and misconduct viewpoint

These methods could be extremely powerful if there is doubt about the integrity of data or reported information; this could be particularly valid for conceptual modification (see above):

- data mining to explore a particular database, including data 'erased' by someone but still somewhere in the system;
- text mining to cross-relate reports and informal documentation;
- text mining to find articles in the literature that relate to any doubts/hints concerning results, protocols, biomarkers, or statistical methods.

Conclusions

The situation today is not entirely clear. In spite of the use of sophisticated computerized silos, IT systems, and electronic tracking by authorities, companies, academic centres, and clinicians, many questions still exist concerning scientific fraud and misconduct. One of the most important issues arising in attempts to prevent this is the traceability of data from a concept or protocol to marketing authorization and publication. Data follow-up is currently often not transparent enough.

For clinical research in humans, basic questions such as bioethics, quality assurance, and GCP are in many cases not really endorsed. This leads to discovery by regulatory authorities, and more precisely by inspection teams, of possible cases of fraud and misconduct. The acronyms PFF (plagiarism, fraud, and fabrication) and QRP (questionable research practices) are for many reasons still fashionable.

Further publicity on fraud and misconduct would be welcome in order to educate scientists and prevent fraud. The recent cases of Hwang in South Korea and Sudbø in Norway are good examples of 'fabrication' of data, as scientific integrity has to be emphasized.

Better education and training on the question of scientific misconduct is the way to prevent it, and the development of such education and training should be tackled without further delay.

Glossary

Audit trail: for the purpose of this guidance, an *audit trail* is a process that captures details such as addition, deletion, or alteration of information in an electronic record without obliterating the original record. An audit trail facilitates the reconstruction of the course of such details relating to the electronic record.

Certified copy: a copy of original information that has been verified, as indicated by a dated signature, as an exact copy having all of the same attributes and information as the original.

Computerized system: this includes computer hardware, software, and associated documents (e.g. user manuals) that create, modify, maintain, archive, retrieve, or transmit in digital form information related to the conduct of a clinical trial.

Direct entry: recording data where an electronic record is the original means of capturing the data. Examples are the keying by an individual of original observations into a system, or automatic recording by the system of the output of a balance that measures a subject's body weight.

Electronic record: any combination of text, graphics, data, audio, pictorial, or other information representation in digital form that is created, modified, maintained, archived, retrieved, or distributed by a computer system.

Original data: for the purpose of this guidance, *original data* are those values that represent the first recording of study data. The FDA is allowing original documents and the original data recorded on those documents to be replaced by copies, provided that the copies are identical and have been verified as such.[25]

Source documents: original documents and records, including (but not limited to) hospital records; clinical and office charts; laboratory notes, memoranda; subjects' diaries or evaluation checklists; pharmacy dispensing records; recorded data from automated instruments; copies or transcriptions certified after verification as being accurate and complete; microfiches; photographic negatives; microfilm or magnetic media; X-rays; subject files; and records kept at the pharmacy, at the laboratories, and at medico-technical departments involved in a clinical trial.

Transmit: to transfer data within or among clinical study sites, CROs, data management centres, and sponsors, or to the FDA.

References

1. Tindemans P. An action-orientated summary of the First International Conference on Research Integrity, Lisbon 16–19 September 2007.

2. Kwang WS, Ryu YJ, Park JH et al. Evidence of a pluripotent embryonic stem cell line derived from a cloned blastocyst. *Science* 2004; **303**: 1669–74 [Retraction: 2006; **311**: 335].

3. Sudbø J, Lee JJ, Lippman SM et al. Non-steroidal anti-inflammatory drugs and the risk of oral cancer: a nested case–control study. *Lancet* 2005; **366**: 1359–66 [Retraction: 2006; **367**: 382. Comment: 2006; **367**: 196].

4. Committee on Publication Ethics (COPE). *A Code of Conduct for Editors of Biomedical Journals*. www.publicationethics.org.uk/guidelines/code.

5. European Union. *Rules Governing Medicinal Products in the European Union*, Volume 9A: *Guidelines on Pharmacovigilance for Medicinal Products for Human Use*. January 2007. ec.europa.eu/enterprise/pharmaceuticals/eudralex/vol-9/pdf/vol9A_2007-01.pdf.

6. International Conference on Harmonisation of Technical Requirements for Registration of Pharmaceuticals for Human Use. Guideline for Good Clinical Practice (ICH E6), April 1996. www.ich.org/cache/compo/276-254-1.html.

7. Directive 2001/20/EC of the European Parliament and of the Council of 4 April 2001, on the approximation of the laws, regulations and administrative provisions of the Member States relating to the implementation of good clinical practice in the conduct of clinical trials on medicinal products for human use. *Official Journal* L 121, 1 May 2001: 34–44.

8. Commission Directive 2005/28/EC of 8 April 2005, laying down principles and detailed guidelines for good clinical practice as regards investigational medicinal products for human use, as well as the requirements for authorisation of the manufacturing or importation of such products. *Official Journal* L 91, 9 April 2005: 13–19.

9. Clinical Data Interchange Standards Consortium (CDISC). *Leveraging the CDISC Standards to Facilitate the use of Electronic Source Data within Clinical Trials*, Version 1.0, 20 November 2006. cdisc.org/eSDI/eSDI.pdf.

10. GCP Inspectors Working Group: Reflection paper on expectations for electronic source documents used in clinical trials. EMEA public consultation 14 June 2007–31 April 2008.

11. Food and Drug Administration. *Guidance for Industry Computerized Systems Used in Clinical Investigations*. May 2007. www.fda.gov/cder/guidance/7359fnl.htm.

12. International Conference on Harmonisation of Technical Requirements for Registration of Pharmaceuticals for Human Use. *Electronic Common Technical Document (eCTD) Specification*, Version 3.2, 4 February 2004. estri.ich.org/ectd/eCTD_Specification_v3_2.pdf.

13. International Conference on Harmonisation of Technical Requirements for Registration of Pharmaceuticals for Human Use. *The eCTD Backbone File Specification for Study Tagging Files*, Version 2.6. estri.ich.org/STF/STFv2-6.doc.

14. European Union. *EU Module 1 Specification for eCTD*, Version 1.2.1, October 2006. ec.europa.eu/enterprise/pharmaceuticals/eudralex/vol-2/b/ectd_12-2006/eum1 spec.pdf.

15. European Medicines Agency. *ICH Topic Q 10: Pharmaceutical Quality System. Step 3: Note for Guidance on Pharmaceutical Quality Systems*. May 2007. www.emea.europa.eu/pdfs/human/ich/21473207en.pdf.

16. Le Blaye O. Inspection of bioequivalence trials: feedback from French inspections. Oral communication, DIA Euromeeting, Paris, March 2006.

17. Directive 95/46/EC of the European Parliament and of the Council of 24 October 1995 on the protection of individuals with regard to the processing of personal data and on the free movement of such data. *Official Journal* L 281, 23 November 1995: 31–50.

18. Aranha H, Wheelwright SM. Outsourcing: transition from business process outsourcing to knowledge process outsourcing. *BioPharm International* May 2007. biopharminternational.findpharma.com/biopharm/Article/Outsourcing-Transition-from-Business-Process-Outso/ArticleStandard/Article/detail/423191.

19. Cabena P, Hadjnian P, Stadler R et al. *Discovering Data Mining: From Concept to Implementation.* Upper Saddle River, NJ: Prentice-Hall, 1997.

20. Tan P-N, Steinbach M, Kumar V. *Introduction to Data Mining.* Upper Saddle River, NJ: Addison-Wesley, 2006.

21. Shmueli G, Patel NR, Bruce PC. *Data Mining for Business Intelligence: Concepts, Techniques, and Applications in Microsoft Office Excel with XLMiner.* New York: Wiley, 2006.

22. Feldman R, Sanger J. *The Text Mining Handbook: Advanced Approaches in Analyzing Unstructured Data.* Cambridge: Cambridge University Press, 2006.

23. Plantefol M. *Text Mining for Life Sciences: Pharmaceutical Business Case Study.* www. temis.com/fichiers/others/WP_TM_for_Life_Sciences_(light_version).pdf.

24. Ikonomaki M, Kotsiantis S, Tampakas V. Text classification using machine learning techniques. *WSEAS Trans Comput* 2005; **4**: 966–74.

25. Food and Drug Administration. *Compliance Policy Guide 7150.13.* www.cfsan.fda. gov/~pn/cpgpn6.html.

Appendix: CDISC references and links with HL7

The links with HL7 are shown in Figure 12.5. The entry point to CDISC references is www.cdisc.org/standards/, where all CDISC standards can be accessed, as shown on Figure 12.6.

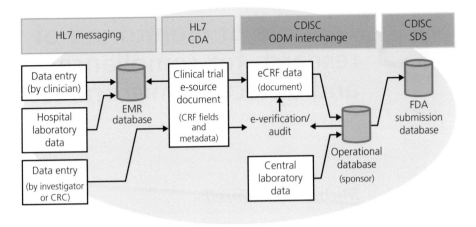

FIGURE 12.5   Links between HL7 and CDISC. *Source*: www.saic.com.

Standards in production	
Submission Data Standards Team	(SDTM IG V3.1.1) (SDTM V1.1) (SDTM IG v3.1) WebSDM edit checks for (SDTM 3.1.1)
Operational Data Modeling Team	(ODM V1.3) (ODM V1.2.1) See also (eSDI Document)
Analysis Dataset Model Team	(ADaM 2.0)
Laboratory Standards Team	(LAB)
Standard for Exchange of Non-clinical Data	(SEND V2.3)
Case Report Tabulation Data Definition Specification (define .xml)	(CRT-DDS V1.0)
Terminology	(Terminology)

Standards in development	
Submission Data Standards Team	SDTM IG V3.1.2 Draft SDTM V1.2 Draft Metadata Submission Guidelines. Appendix to the SDTM IG V3.1.1
Protocol Representation Group	(PRG)
Clinical Data Acquisition Standards Harmonization (CDASH)	(CDASH)

FIGURE 12.6   The CDISC standards.

13 The role of monitoring of research for compliance and detecting misconduct

Michael R Hamrell

Introduction

The task of monitoring of clinical studies is an expectation and requirement for the conduct of quality clinical trials, and places a responsibility on the sponsor of the study to ensure the quality of the data. The main purpose of monitoring a trial is to verify that the rights and welfare of the subjects have been protected; that the trial is conducted in compliance with the current protocol, Good Clinical Practice, and applicable local regulatory requirements; and that the data are collected and reported accurately and completely, and are verifiable in the source documents.[1,2] Failure to monitor adequately is often cited as a reason for poor execution of the study and for questionable or bad data, and can lead to misconduct.[3] The sponsor needs to ensure that the study is adequately monitored. Obviously, the nature, extent, and frequency of monitoring will be based on a number of factors, including the study design, the number of subjects, the therapeutic area, and end points, among other things. As a result, it is up to the sponsor to develop a monitoring plan for each study, based on these considerations.

One important consideration in clinical research today is the computerization of drug development. Advances in hardware and software technology have expanded information flow globally and allowed for the managing and processing of clinical data and information at very fast speeds.[4,5] Companies no longer develop drugs and products for a single market, but embark on multinational development programmes with large multicentre, multinational clinical trials being conducted. Along with this globalization of projects is the increased use of electronic technology to handle the communication and manage the data.[6,7] Much of the documentation and data that used to be handled and processed manually is now communicated electronically using the Internet and other electronic tools. The personal computer revolution, like no other technology change in recent times, has transformed the way in which we plan, work, and communicate regarding clinical trials. The computer has become essential for the organization and coordination and conduct of a clinical drug development programme.[8]

The standard that refers to the conduct of clinical trials is the concept of Good Clinical Practice (GCP). This describes the best business, scientific, and ethical standards for the conduct of a clinical trial. The elements of GCP have also been written and adopted by the International Conference on Harmonisation (ICH) in a consolidated document.[9] The ICH is a collaborative and cooperative effort by industry and regulatory authorities in the three major product development regions of the world – the USA, the EU, and Japan – to harmonize and coordinate the technical requirements for the development of new drugs and biologic products. It is from the expectations and requirements of this guideline that the focus moves to the assurance that a clinical study is conducted according to generally accepted practices for clinical research defined as GCP. The principles of GCP are based on regulations and laws developed in different countries and codified by law, as well as on guidelines and generally accepted practice. GCP also describes the methods and procedures used to ensure that the research is of the highest quality and that the data are reliable and valid. The design of a clinical study needs to include considerations for the conduct and validity of the study as well as the scientific principles. GCP begins in the design stage of the clinical study and continues through the planning and implementation of the study, and is followed by the conduct and management and reporting of the study results. In the USA, there are a set of regulations, described in the US Code of Federal Regulations (CFR), that provide the legal basis for GCP and the conduct of a clinical trial.[1] These regulations include the requirements for an institutional review board or ethics committee to oversee the research and the protection of the human subjects, the need for written documented informed consent, and the roles and responsibilities of the sponsor, the monitor, and the principal investigator.

In addition to the ICH Guidance on GCP, the US Food and Drug Administration (FDA) has issued other guidance related to monitoring.[10] In 1988, the FDA issued a guideline on the monitoring of clinical investigations.[11] Now 20 years old, this short document provides some basic principles and concepts for the role and responsibility of the study monitor. In 2007, the FDA issued a draft guidance document on the supervisory responsibility of investigators during the conduct of clinical trials.[12] Although it addresses the role of the principal investigator, the obligation of the sponsor through the monitor to ensure that these obligations are honoured is critical.

The FDA guideline for the monitoring of clinical investigations expects sponsors to establish written procedures for monitoring clinical investigations to ensure the quality of the study and to ensure that each person involved in the monitoring process carries out his or her duties. A single written monitoring procedure need not be developed for each clinical investigation. Rather, a standardized written procedure, sufficiently detailed to cover the general aspects of clinical investigations, may be used as a basic monitoring plan and supplemented by more specific or additional monitoring procedures tailored to the individual clinical investigation. The ICH Guideline (Sections 5.18.2(c) and 5.18.4)[9] also discusses monitoring and indicates that monitors should be thoroughly familiar with the investigational product, the protocol, the written informed consent form (and any other written information to be provided to subjects), the sponsor's standard operating procedures (SOPs), GCP, and the applicable regulatory requirements. The guideline (Section 5.18.5) also indicates that the monitor(s), in accordance with the sponsor's requirements, should ensure that the trial is conducted and documented properly.

It is clear from the regulations and guidelines that SOPs are expected to be in place to cover major functions within clinical research. However, many companies use both SOPs and operational guidelines (OGs) or work instructions (WI) to provide the written directions and procedures to the staff on the conduct of clinical research.[13]

In a typical FDA audit of a sponsor, the Inspector will often obtain a copy of the firm's SOP (for monitoring) and determine if it was followed (in accordance with the FDA's *Compliance Program Guidance Manual (CPGM 7348-810)*, Section III.A.2[14]). To the extent that the SOPs refer to an OG or other written instructions, it can be expected that a regulatory agency auditor (e.g. from the FDA) would directly ask to review these documents as well. Other OGs, study-specific monitoring guidelines, or written procedural documents would also be likely to be reviewed as part of the audit, since they constitute written instructions to the monitors on how to monitor the study. If there is a question about the instructions or training provided to staff to perform a particular function, operations and training manuals can also be requested and reviewed, if they exist *(CPGM 7348-810*, Section III.B.4[14]).

Trial design considerations

The design of the pivotal phase 3 studies in product development needs to meet the criteria for an adequate and well-controlled study. In order to satisfy this requirement, a study must involve a number of activities and proper planning. The plan for a clinical trial includes consideration of the key objective(s) of the study (disease-specific end points) and what variables to measure and in what population (primary disease patients, patients with refractory condition, etc.) in order to demonstrate safety and efficacy. Since these studies will form the definitive data set for assessing the safety and efficacy of a drug, consideration of data collection and monitoring practices to support the product's profile is essential. The development of the clinical protocol includes not only writing the protocol itself, but also creating all the other clinical documents essential to the conduct of the trial. This includes an informed consent document and the case report forms (CRFs). The clinical project group also needs to prepare the supporting documents to provide instructions and directions on the proper conduct of the study. These might include study procedure manuals; annotated CRFs; handling and processing instructions for samples; and dosing, treatment, or evaluation schemes to be used in the trial. The plan for a phase 3 study also involves the consideration of what data are needed in the specific target population to demonstrate safety and efficacy. Once these items have been identified, it is possible to begin to draft a clinical plan to address the end points. Once all of the key parameters of the study have been refined and agreed to by the team, a clinical monitoring plan can be developed. In order to generate a high-quality and reliable data set, there needs to be a plan for the monitoring and oversight of the study. Monitoring is essential for ensuring the compliance of the investigator and staff with the regulations and study procedures and for collecting high-quality, accurate data.[1,10]

Selection of investigators

One of the more important decisions a company has to make regarding the conduct of a clinical study is the identification and selection of suitable investigators. A sponsor is responsible for selecting investigators qualified by training and experience to conduct the investigation and for documenting this assurance. Before permitting an investigator to participate in an investigation, the sponsor must also obtain certain assurances from the investigator (Title 21 Code of Federal Regulations (21 CFR), Part 312.53(a)[15]). In the USA, these assurances regarding the conduct of the study and the specifics of where the study will be done are documented on FDA Form 1572, which is signed by the principal investigator or in an investigator agreement, and are accompanied by supporting documentation regarding the investigator's qualifications, such as a curriculum vitae (21 CFR 312.53(c)[15]).

Role of the monitor

The monitor (or clinical research associate (CRA), as he or she is often referred to in some regions) is one of the key persons involved in overseeing the conduct of studies and ensuring data quality. Monitoring itself is the process of overseeing a study to ensure patient safety, data quality, protocol compliance, and regulatory compliance. The monitor is also the 'eyes and ears' of the sponsor at the site. The clinical monitor is responsible for ensuring the completeness and accuracy of the subject's medical records, and ensuring that the regulatory documents are complete and up-to-date and that all the essential information required by the study is recorded on the CRFs. The major role of a regulatory agency review is evaluation of the data submitted in support of the marketing application. The data must be correct, be validated, and reflect the results and conclusions of the study so that the regulatory agency review can draw proper conclusions about them.[16]

As subjects complete the tests and procedures required by protocol at a particular visit, data and records are generated. They capture the subject's medical condition, treatments and progress. The FDA Investigational New Drug (IND) regulations require that the principal investigator maintain adequate and accurate records of each case as well as drug supply disposition (21 CFR 312.62(b)[15]). These records are called source documents. They are essential in documenting the existence of the subject and to substantiate the integrity of the study data. Once the data have been collected and recorded in source documents, they are transcribed or entered onto CRFs. The latter are data collection tools utilized by the sponsor for recording all protocol-required patient information to prove safety and efficacy. One of the monitor's main jobs is to verify the CRF entries against the medical records and other supporting documents and to verify that the data are correctly and accurately recorded on the CRFs. This is referred to as source data verification (SDV). The monitor also reviews the CRFs to ensure that they are complete, legible, internally consistent, and properly filled out. It is very important for an investigator to document all findings, observations, and interactions with a study subject. From a regulatory viewpoint, if something is not written down (or recorded electronically) it did not happen. The principal investigator needs to keep a thorough record (or 'audit trail') of a subject's status and all study procedures. This will ensure that another person such as a GCP auditor could 'recreate' the entire progression of the subject in the clinical trial many years down the road. A monitor also has the responsibility to represent the sponsor with the site staff and investigator, provide information about the study, gather information about progress at the site, and communicate issues and concerns.[10]

There are rare occasions when data are recorded directly onto the CRF, with no supporting source document. Although this practice is not recommended or endorsed, there are circumstances where it may be appropriate. The regulatory agencies have no policy against the use of a CRF page as a source (raw) document. There is no need to create a chart for the sole purpose of having another place to write something down. One needs to consider whether the data would be collected otherwise from the subject if they were not enrolled in a clinical trial. The other consideration from a GCP quality perspective is that, if there is a question about the integrity of the data, whether it can be substantiated or supported elsewhere. Values captured in this way may need additional supporting documentation to validate the integrity of the data. Any data to be recorded directly onto the CRF pages should be identified in the protocol (ICH Guideline, Section 6.4.9[9]), and any deviations from this practice should be noted as a protocol violation. How much monitoring is performed and the nature and extent of the review of records are typically covered by a detailed monitoring plan for the study. Although not required or specified by regulation, it is not uncommon in a phase 3 pivotal study for the sponsor to perform 100% source data verification.

Since sponsors use monitoring to verify the data collected and confirm regulatory compliance, one of the key questions is what should be done if there are deficiencies noted. The sponsor's SOPs should reflect the role of individuals in the review and evaluation of all monitoring reports, updates, CRFs, and other information received from a site. Regular feedback should also be provided to a site (in writing) regarding any deficiencies noted and action expected. Correction of any deficiencies or problems should be reviewed and checked at the next visit. The sponsor should also have steps in place to be taken to secure investigator compliance when issues arise. According to the FDA regulations, if a sponsor discovers that an investigator is not complying with the signed agreement (Form 1572), the general investigational plan, or the requirements specified by the sponsor, the sponsor needs to take positive, proactive steps to promptly secure compliance. If compliance cannot be obtained or is not satisfactory, the sponsor should discontinue shipments of the investigational drug to the investigator and end the investigator's participation in the trial (Box 13.1). The FDA also expects the sponsor to require the investigator to return the study drug and notify the FDA of the termination for noncompliance (21 CFR 312.56(b)).[15]

Detecting and dealing with non-compliance

Misconduct and fraud have occurred in all phases of clinical research, and include such things as enrolling unqualified subjects, backdating information, falsifying tests that were not performed, failing to report an adverse event, deviating from the pro-

---

BOX 13.1   FDA Regulation on Noncompliance – 21 CFR 312.56(b)[15]

A sponsor who discovers that an investigator is not complying with the signed agreement (1572), the general investigational plan, or the requirements in this part or other applicable parts, shall promptly either secure compliance or discontinue shipments of the investigational new drug to the investigator and end the investigator's participation in the investigation.

If the investigator's participation in the investigation is ended, the sponsor shall require that the investigator dispose of or return the investigational drug in accordance with the requirements and shall notify the FDA.

---

tocol, failing to get informed consent properly, covering up mistakes, and submitting false data for publication.

In an effort to be vigilant in the oversight of clinical trials, one needs to think about what kinds of clues might be seen to make one consider looking further at the conduct of the study:

- Is the investigator difficult to reach or communicate with? Are they working on many studies? Are they working within their specialty?
- When one examines the data collected, does the number of subjects appear to be realistic relative to the patient load and disease prevalence?
- When the data are reviewed, are they consistent with the rest of the study, and with scientific expectations and medical practice?
- Did the investigator report too many or too few adverse events or dropouts?
- Are the laboratory values consistent with the rest of the study population and study expectations?

All of these considerations may give rise to suspicions regarding misconduct. In addition, certain general findings may also raise suspicions about the study conduct and investigator's performance. When examining study data, it is also important to consider the plausibility or feasibility of the data collected. We often look for red flags when reviewing the data (Box 13.2). Are there too many (or too few) dropouts or serious adverse events (SAEs) or screen failures. It is important to look at the quality of the data collected as well. We should look for things such as numbers or values that seem to repeat, patterns that seem inconsistent (e.g. all values ending in zero, or an even number), exact days between visits, or exact number of pills used each month. While we strive for full compliance and quality data, people and medicine are not exact, and we should expect to find some variability.

Research misconduct

There are some rare circumstances where non-compliance can rise to the level of research misconduct. When monitoring a study, if one suspects misconduct, it is important to examine the data and evidence very carefully to determine whether there really

---

BOX 13.2 **Red flags for misconduct**

- No screen failures (or many)
- No dropouts or SAEs (or too many)
- Repetitive results (scales, blood pressure, etc.)
- Exact numbers (days between visits, pill counts, etc.)
- Missing source documents
- Dates of laboratory specimens do not match subject visit dates
- Inconsistent or clearly inaccurate data
- Results are 'too good to be true'
- Few SAEs or dropouts relative to other sites
- Laboratory values inconsistent with other studies or sites
- Complaints by subjects

---

is misconduct or whether the problem is related to poor execution or to lack of understanding of the protocol and study expectations or other variables. This could include not calibrating or improperly calibrating an instrument, not using the appropriate tool or instrument for the measurement, and not taking samples or assessments at the appropriate time, compared with not taking the measurement at all. When we look at different types of misconduct, it can be generally divided into three main categories. These include misconduct related to ignorance, laziness, or malicious intent.[17]

Misconduct from ignorance or being uninformed is usually based on a lack of understanding of the regulatory consequences of an action. The misconduct itself may be intentional, but the non-compliance is unintentional and not usually done to deliberately deceive. This would include things such as backdating the subject's signature on a consent form because the subject forgot to date the form, discarding source documents after transcription, and reporting transcribed data as original or 'recreating' source documents from CRFs.

Misconduct from laziness or sloppiness often results from non-compliance due to inattention to detail or lack of staff or proper supervision. Here, the misconduct may or may not be intentional, but the non-compliance is usually deliberate and repeated. This includes not obtaining consent from multiple subjects, rounding readings such as blood pressure or temperature to the nearest whole number, estimating a reading rather than actually measuring it, and careless transcription or recording of values.

In the most severe case, the misconduct is malicious or deliberate. This results from a direct action to deceive or mislead, and often includes outright falsification of data. The most serious violations might also include activities that put a subject's rights and welfare or their safety at risk, such as not obtaining consent or reporting adverse events. Deliberate or repeated non-compliance with regulations is considered misconduct, but may be not as severe as falsification of data. Falsification is the most serious violation in research. Falsification of data includes creating, altering, recording, or omitting data in such a way that the data do not represent what actually occurred.

This may include making up data, altering data obtained, or omitting data that were obtained and would otherwise be recorded.

Detecting fraud and misconduct

In order to detect fraud and misconduct, the monitoring of the study needs to be consistent, thorough, and vigilant. The monitor needs to constantly review all data and information derived during a clinical study for accuracy and ability to be verified (Box 13.3). Much time and effort will be spent reviewing and verifying records against the data collected. There should always be an original verifiable source document for all data. A monitor needs to be very detail-oriented and to focus on the quality of the data source, not just on whether a document exists. This means that they must be technically oriented and do more than just inventory the file, but also check names, dates, time sequence, and other parameters that establish that the data are real and accurate. Any inconsistencies should be questioned and pursued until a satisfactory explanation is obtained. In particular, the monitor should pay attention to any hints or direct suggestions of non-compliance. The messenger is often correct, and should not be dismissed without checking into the allegations.[17]

BOX 13.3 Detecting fraud

- 'Get technical' – read and evaluate X-rays, ECGs, laboratory results
- Do not just inventory the source document
- Question missing dates, times, blanks on CRFs, information
- Always pursue inconsistencies
- Do not 'shoot the messenger'

There can also be issues involving the principal investigator and their behaviour and attitude during a clinical trial and in their interactions with the monitor. Many of these issues can be addressed before the study starts, but they should be re-evaluated at regular intervals during the course of the study. Among things to consider are the following:

- How busy is the investigator?
- Are they working on many studies, are they seeing subjects within their specialty of medicine, do they seem to have an unrealistic number of subjects relative to study expectations?
- Are the data that they report consistent with the rest of the study data being obtained?

Even in a blinded study, definite trends can be noted regarding items such as laboratory values, and frequency of adverse events or end points reported (Box 13.4). Investigators themselves have reported that they are not always fully compliant with the regulations.[18]

BOX 13.4 **Investigator misconduct issues**

- Investigator working on many studies
- Investigator working outside specialty
- Unrealistic numbers of patients
- Data inconsistent with rest of study
- Agency not receiving SAE reports in a timely manner

Regardless of whether any deficiencies constitute fraud or just non-compliant performance, it is important to constantly remind the clinical investigator that they are responsible for the conduct of the study and are accountable for the results. This should include reminding them of their obligations in signing the investigator agreement. Regulatory agencies view this agreement as a contract between the investigator, the sponsor, and the government, and thus the obligation to follow the regulation is a legally binding agreement. A failure to respect this agreement can lead to serious consequences not only for the investigator but also for the sponsor and their resulting study data.

Use of computers

In clinical practice, it is common today to use computers for a number of aspects of a clinical trial that used to be performed manually or using paper forms. We use computers to transmit clinical laboratory results directly from the laboratory to the investigator, and to the sponsor during clinical trials.[6,7] Sponsors also use computers for remote electronic CRF data entry systems or contract with contract research organizations (CROs) for clinical data entry, analysis, and reporting. When the electronic records/electronic signature rule was finalized, the FDA reiterated that the same documentation expectations and requirements for records and access as defined in the IND regulations still applied, regardless of whether or not the records were created and/or maintained on paper or electronically.[19] Although it was not explicitly stated until recently, the FDA has for many years considered computer systems used in drug development, regardless of where and how they are used, also to be subject to regulatory requirements, audit, and inspection.[20]

The computer is a valuable and powerful tool for data collection and processing, but it can also create tools for the verification and checking of data. Electronic CRFs can be programmed not to accept inappropriate values, to do range checking (e.g. one cannot have a temperature of 98 °C!), and to verify the logic of data entered (e.g. a male cannot be pregnant!) before it is even entered into the database. This can greatly enhance the ability of the monitor to check and verify data. On the other hand, computers can create new challenges for data integrity. Using software programs that do not feature an audit trail or keep track of changes can facilitate someone who is intent on misconduct.

Preventing misconduct

Sponsors can take a number of proactive steps to minimize the chance for misconduct to occur. They should avoid placing needless requirements or unreasonable demands on the site during the study. Constantly changing the protocol, procedures, and forms makes it difficult for the site to complete things accurately. If changes do need to be made, they should be performed in a planned timely manner. Making a major change to a protocol or documentation practice and then demanding that a site implement it immediately may not be possible, and can lead to frustration and other problems for the site. The monitor should pay close attention to complaints and concerns expressed by the site personnel. If they express frustration or problems with one's process, this could be an indication that they might consider cutting corners. In the USA in recent years, it has sometimes been the practice of companies to offer bonuses or monetary incentives to a site to enrol 'three more subjects this month' or 'complete all outstanding queries by Friday'. Such financial inducements can sometimes be too tempting to people, and can lead to misconduct.

Dealing with misconduct

There are several major actions that can be taken in dealing with potential misconduct in clinical research. These include taking appropriate steps to prevent its occurrence by identifying and minimizing the risk, being vigilant in monitoring for signs of any misconduct, and promptly investigating and reporting any misconduct activity to the sponsor and regulatory agencies, as required.

Prevention of fraud and misconduct is the best way to deal with compliance issues in clinical research. When evaluating and monitoring a site, it should be ensured that all the study staff have the necessary resources and support needed to accomplish their tasks. This includes training in what constitutes misconduct and falsification. There are a number of helpful hints for detecting and preventing misconduct. First, the monitoring process needs to be more than a physical inventory of documents, records, and visits. One needs to have the technical ability to read and evaluate X-rays, ECGs and laboratory results. This is not to suggest a scientific evaluation, but rather a thorough cross-check of dates and visits according to the correct time, subject ID, etc., and it includes raising questions about missing dates or times or blanks on CRFs and pursuing inconsistencies. Generally, if it doesn't look right, it probably isn't. It is important for monitors and research staff not to be intimidated. In other words, one should not be afraid to confront an investigator or member of staff with inconsistent or confusing information and see what the response is. Most importantly, one should never discount the source of the information. Monitors are the front-line personnel for the sponsor at the site, and if they raise a question about integrity or data quality, it should be thoroughly investigated. If potential non-compliance or misconduct is detected, one should trust the monitor and put the burden of proof on the clinical investigator or the staff. All allegations of misconduct need to be investigated and addressed. This can be facilitated by cultivating whistleblowers, establishing rapport with study staff, being approachable and available, listening to their grievances, and observing working conditions. All complaints should be assumed to be credible until demonstrated to the contrary after thorough evaluation and supervisory review.

Future prospects

So, how do we prevent fraud and misconduct going forward? All staff who participate in a research project need to be trained and informed on what misconduct is and how to detect it. The staff need to be aware of some of the warning signs of problems as well. There is also an increased risk of misconduct when there are increased pressures such as academic advancement, financial reward, and time constraints. All research staff need to be educated on how to be sensitive to a perceived increased risk of misconduct, and to be trained on how to minimize those risks. Training should address how to document data appropriately, and should include all levels of staff. Training programmes should also cover the consequences of misconduct – for the individual, as well as for the study. Detection of some kinds of problems, such as an unqualified staff member or an employee under increased stress, can also be addressed early, so that the practices can be corrected and the potential for misconduct avoided.

One of the more important steps is general training and education on the principles of good clinical practice and clinical research. Henry Beecher, who wrote about the problem of research misconduct in the USA in 1966, stated that 'the more reliable safeguard (for protecting research participants) [is] the presence of an intelligent, informed, conscientious, compassionate, responsible investigator'.[21] In 2000, the US Public Health Service published a Research Misconduct Policy. This required, among other things, that all research staff within the intramural or extramural programmes funded by the Agency complete a course on the Responsible Conduct of Research (RCR).[22] Originally suspended and then revised and reinstated, the implementation of the training was made the responsibility of institutions. This was based on recommendations that suggested that 'instruction in the standards and ethics of research is essential to the proper education of scientists'.[23] Numerous programmes now exist to offer certification for monitors, coordinators and principal investigators. Several professional associations in the USA and Europe, as well as a number of universities, now offer programmes on GCP and research conduct. It is now possible to obtain a master's or other university degree in clinical research or regulatory affairs.[24] Although training does not guarantee quality, it helps to ensure that all individuals understand the rules about and the consequences of misconduct.

References

1. Horowitz AM. Good clinical practices. In: Simmons R, ed. *Multi-Company Multi-Country Clinical Trials*. Chicago: InterPharm Press, 1993: 123–52.
2. Spilker B. Monitoring a clinical trial. *Guide to Clinical Trials*. New York: Raven Press, 1991: 430–8.
3. LePay D. GCP at FDA: metrics, guidances, initiatives and strategies. Presented at DIA EuroMeeting, March 2007.

4. Hamrell MR. Good clinical practice and computer validation. *GCP J* 1999; **6**(3): 14–17.

5. McFadden E. Computer systems for data management and data entry. *Management of Data in Clinical Trials*, 2nd edn. New York: Wiley, 2007: 56–75.

6. Hamrell MR. The use of computers in multinational drug development. *Regul Affs J* 1993; **5**: 569–76.

7. Hamrell MR. Computerization in multinational drug development. In: Simmons R, ed. *Multi-Company Multi-Country Clinical Trials*. Chicago: InterPharm Press, 1993: 201–18.

8. Spilker B. Use of meetings, documents and computers to assist in planning and managing drug studies. *Guide to Planning and Managing Multiple Clinical Studies*. New York: Raven Press, 1991: 251–75.

9. International Conference on Harmonisation of Technical Requirements for Registration of Pharmaceuticals for Human Use. Guideline for Good Clinical Practice (ICH E6), April 1996. www.fda.gov/cder/guidance/959fnl.pdf.

10. Woodin KE, Schneider JC. Regulations and GCPs. *The CRA's Guide to Monitoring Clinical Research*. Boston: Thomson Centrewatch, 2003: 47–53.

11. Food and Drug Administration. *Guideline for the Monitoring of Clinical Investigations*. FDA, 1988. www.fda.gov/ora/compliance_ref/bimo/clinguid.html.

12. Food and Drug Administration. *Draft Guidance for Industry: Protecting the Rights, Safety, and Welfare of Study Subjects - Supervisory Responsibilities of Investigators*. FDA, May 2007. www.fda.gov/OHRMS/DOCKETS/98fr/07d-0173-gdl0001.pdf.

13. Hamrell MR, Wagman BR. Standard Operating Procedures in clinical research: A beginner's guide. *Qual Assur J* 2001; 5: 93–7.

14. Food and Drug Administration. *Compliance Program Guidance Manual (CPGM 7348-810). Sponsors, Contract Research Organizations and Monitors*. FDA, February 2001. www.fda.gov/ora/compliance_ref/bimo/7348_810/default.htm.

15. Subpart D – Responsibilities of Sponsors and Investigators. *Investigational New Drug Regulations*. Part 312.53(2), Title 21, Code of Federal Regulations. www.accessdata. fda.gov/scripts/cdrh/cfdocs/cfCFR/CFRSearch.cfm.

16. Piantadosi S. Misconduct and fraud in clinical research. *Clinical Trials: A Methodologic Perspective*. New York: Wiley, 1997: 539–63.

17. Woollen S. Misconduct in research – innocent ignorance or malicious malfeasance? Presentation by Stan Woollen, FDA 2003. www.fda.gov/oc/gcp/slideshows/2003/gcp2003.ppt.

18. Martinson B, Anderson M, de Vries R. Scientists behaving badly. *Nature* 2005: **435**: 737–8.

19. Food and Drug Administration. 21 CFR Part 11: Electronic Records; Electronic Signatures; Final Rule. *Fed Regist* 1997; **62**: 13429.

20. Food and Drug Administration. *Guidance for Industry: Computerized Systems Used in Clinical Investigations*. FDA, May 2007. www.fda.gov/OHRMS/DOCKETS/98fr/04d-0440-gdl0002.pdf.

21. Beecher H. Ethics and clinical research. *N Engl J Med* 1966; **274**: 1354–60.

22. Office of Research Integrity. *Responsible Conduct of Research (RCR) Education*. ori. dhhs.gov/policies/RCR_Policy.shtml.
23. Federal Research Misconduct Policy. *Fed Regist* 2000: **65**: 76260–4.
24. Woodin KE, Schneider JC. Job descriptions and academic programs. *The CRA's Guide to Monitoring Clinical Research*. Boston: Thomson Centrewatch, 2003: 268–75.

14 The role of routine enhanced audit

Nicky Dodsworth

Introduction

With the introduction of the first European Good Clinical Practice (GCP) Directive (91/507/EEC) more than 15 years ago, sponsors have been responsible for introducing a system of quality assurance (QA) and audits. The number and quality of audits have increased significantly within the last few years, especially following other important publications such as the ICH GCP Guidelines 1996,[1] the Data Protection Directive (95/46/EC),[2] the Clinical Trials Directive (2001/20/EC),[3] and the GCP Directive (2005/28/EC).[4]

Monitoring processes at the study site must be adequate to detect possible fraud and misconduct. The monitor is the person who regularly interfaces with the site, and therefore should be the first person to detect a possible problem. Sometimes, however, the people who work closely with the possible fraudster may be too close to notice, or too concerned about their position, to raise the alarm. The monitor may become complacent over time. Fraud or misconduct can be found during a random, routine audit, but usually suspicions have already been raised by the monitor to the QA team. It is therefore the role of the auditor to collect the evidence and present this to the operational staff within their organization, any external parties concerned, and, most importantly, to the site staff.

It is important that audit policies be established to ensure that issues that are identified, or potential issues that may arise at a particular site be highlighted to the QA department and that plans be instigated immediately to investigate whether there is a possibility of some type of misconduct. QA departments need to be established with suitably qualified and experienced auditors to ensure the proper conduct of audits. Audit policies usually cover high-risk programmes and high-risk compounds. Auditors need to ensure they are conducting effective audits in order that they can detect possible fraud or misconduct, rather than finding the same observations again and again.

This chapter discusses the role of the auditor during random, planned audits and how they can maximize their effectiveness in detection and analysis of possible fraud or misconduct at an investigator site.

Auditor qualities and skills

The auditor is a key member of the team in assessing the trustworthiness of scientific and medical researchers, which is essential to ensure that public confidence in clinical research is maintained.

It is not a requirement of an auditor to be 'liked', but a friendly approach is usually well received by those being audited. Intimidating questioning techniques are not effective or necessary. Auditors need to be diplomatic and persuasive at times. They must be able to audit firmly but fairly. Detection of fraud or misconduct is a sensitive issue and highly emotive. The motive for fraud may be laziness, professional recognition, or financial gain. Fraud may take many forms, including piracy, altered or ignored data, or complete or partial fabrication of data or plagiarism. In order to be effective in their work, auditors should therefore be trained to detect any type of fraud or misconduct, but this may not have happened.

Auditors are usually fully conversant in GCP and relevant regulatory standards. Training auditors on skills and basic knowledge to perform an audit is a common process. They must have the necessary knowledge, which includes local laws and regulations, GCP, the Declaration of Helsinki, data protection, standard operating procedures (SOPs), and clinical and pharmaceutical knowledge. One of the problems for auditors is that GCP is constantly evolving, and they need to be constantly aware of changing requirements and new trends.

Auditors are likely not to have had specific training on how to detect fraud, and very little understanding of legal implications. It is not being suggested here that auditors need to be fully conversant with legal issues, but some training in this area can only be considered helpful. An auditor must be aware of the potential for fraud and misconduct, although cases of fraud are rare. The auditor needs to be able to distinguish between error and honest differences of opinion on the one hand and concealment on the other. Irregular data needs to be challenged – and this is not an easy task for an auditor. Auditors have to to rely on their instincts and experience, as well as their technical abilities.

Many auditors are not conversant with ISO 19011, the international standard on how to conduct audits – typically less than 10% of those asked.[5] This is really surprising, as ISO is the gold standard for defining how auditors plan, prepare, perform, report, and follow up on audits. Many auditors are less comfortable in the planning, reporting, and follow-up stage. Therefore, they need to ensure that they have comprehensive training in all aspects of auditing. Site audits can be viewed as repetitive, but auditors need to be trained and to have the required skills to do more than just follow SOPs and checklists. Generally, auditing skills improve with time as auditors become more adept at finding problems.

Auditors are usually very dedicated people and understand fully the significance of their role within an organization. It is vital that an auditor can manage the audit process, and this is usually relatively easily achieved. However, it is more difficult to manage the behaviour of those who are audited. Interpersonal skills need to be considered as much as technical elements – auditors must be able to present their findings to those who do not wish to listen. Often, those that are audited are not positive about an audit, but they must understand that the process is not aimed at them personally and that everything must be kept on a professional level. The case is slightly different for fraud or misconduct, because here the integrity of the individual is in question; however, the auditor must maintain a similar approach.

At present, auditors do not work to any ethical code of practice. If an auditor were to be deficient in their conduct, this would call into question the professional competence of all auditors. Trust, confidence, and credibility must be reflected in the service provided by an auditor. Perhaps, a code of conduct for auditors will need to be established in the future.[6]

Audit planning

All audits require excellent planning. This is based on information provided to identify the exact scope of the audit. As with all audits, the procedures and resources are usually carefully defined in SOPs. Most site audits follow sponsor SOPs, and there is little room for deviation. Site audit plans can easily be drawn up without too much thought and planning if the SOPs are well written. If site audits were to follow a systems-based approach, then a great deal more thought would be required, and this would undoubtedly add value to the site audit.

It may be useful to briefly outline the systems-based approach to auditing before going any further. This is the latest trend in auditing, and does provide a more meaningful outcome. Systems audits are usually more complex, and can take several weeks to complete. Systems-type audits may reduce the need to conduct study-specific audits. This can be seen by many as a reduction in costs and a possible saving in resources. European inspections are now following a systems-based approach. Each system is reviewed, and information on how the system is operating is obtained by reviewing study-specific information. Study-specific information provides an example of how a particular system is working. Site audits are therefore usually study-specific, and there is less variation in the content and approach to the audit. Both types of audit have their place, and can be used within a balanced audit schedule to complement one another.

One or more objectives are generally established for a study audit based on the importance of the trial with regard to submission to a regulatory authority, the number of subjects in the study, the type and complexity of the protocol, any problems identified during monitoring or during previous audits, or the level of risk to the trial subjects. Another significant part of audit planning is to specify the goals of the audit: goals can be defined to include early detection and correction of problems occurring at the site, compliance with regulatory requirements, data protection and ethics, confirmation of the conduct of monitoring, and so on.

The result of good planning is to develop a well-written audit plan to ensure that the audit scope, the standards used to measure performance, and the logistical aspects of the audit are fully detailed. Box 14.1 gives an outline of the audit scope for a site audit. The audit plan additionally defines the location of the audit(s). The choice of a site for a routine audit is usually based on one or more of the following factors: highest recruitment, staff new to clinical research, abnormal numbers of adverse events (high or low), and issues noted at monitoring and geographical location.

BOX 14.1   **Outline of audit scope for a site audit**

This should include:

- Review of essential documents (ICH GCP, Section 8)[1]
- Roles and responsibilities of site staff, including interviews and review of CVs and training records
- Acceptability of site facilities and equipment
- Completeness and accuracy of the CRF against the source data
- Confirmation of drug accountability and compliance

The sampling level, which is the standard method for routine audits, must also be defined in the audit plan. This assists the auditor in making an accurate estimation of the required time to conduct the audit at the site. Most routine audits are successfully conducted by two auditors at a site for two days. During this time, it is likely that only eight case report forms (CRFs) may be reviewed fully against the source data, but this will of course depend on both the size and complexity of the study and the associated CRF.

The timescale on which the audit is to be conducted also needs to be considered. Ideally, at least two weeks' notification is provided for routine audit. The audit plan finally defines the audit reporting process. It outlines when the results will be disseminated to the auditees and other responsible parties.

Once the plan has been drafted by the auditor, it is important that it be reviewed by operational staff. They provide useful information and guide the auditor in their plans. The final decision on the site for the audit, however, must rest with the auditor. Communication is important, and good communication at this stage does lead to a more positive audit process. Notification by the QA department that an audit is being planned is not welcomed by everyone, and the auditor plays a key role in diplomacy at this stage.

Audit preparation

Preparation, preparation, and yet more preparation is vital. As with most things in life, if one is well prepared for a task, then the actual delivery will go much more smoothly. Auditors do need to be prepared for all eventualities. They need to spend an adequate amount of time gathering information about the study from both internal and external sources. The amount of information gathered before a site audit can vary – an example is provided in Box 14.2.

The auditor's next task is to review these documents and gain an understanding of the study and the processes, and to become familiar with what has been happening at the site. Issues noted in monitoring visit reports provide a useful insight for the auditor. Review of these documents also shows any conflicts in them; for example, the monitoring guidelines and the protocol are not always in harmony. Gaps and conflicts need to be noted by the auditor, and these will then need to be followed up with the operational team in-house and at the study site.

Many auditors like to work with standardized checklists. GCP auditors, however, while considering how they can improve the value of the audit, may use the basic checklist, but should adapt this for each audit. For example, while reviewing the protocol, it is recommended to review the interfaces between groups/departments. This is often an area that can cause an error to occur. These study-specific interfaces can then be added to the basic checklist. Also, when using a standard checklist, all the information necessary to find deficiencies may not be apparent. By reporting on all areas of non-compliance generally, an opportunity may be missed to identify and make the auditees aware of the problem areas and best practices. Therefore, the value of the audit may not be maximized. The auditor must probe more deeply to get beyond superficial facts and identify root causes.

Auditing practice also tends to mirror the latest regulatory inspection trends. For example, a current trend is the regulators' view that sponsors and monitors need to improve their methods of training of investigators and site personnel. Training is often limited to the study initiation meeting and/or investigator meeting, but it should be continuous throughout the study. As a result, auditors must spend more time reviewing CVs and training records to ensure that this is happening.

BOX 14.2   **Documents required before a site audit**

The following documents may be required (as applicable) in final approved versions:

- Protocol and any amendments
- Blank CRF/eCRF
- Patient informed consent form (English and other languages)
- Patient documents, e.g. diary cards, questionnaires
- Site evaluation, initiation, and monitoring visit reports
- Monitoring guidelines
- Relevant SOPs
- In-house files
- Previous audit reports

Audit conduct

Much has been written about the conduct of site audits. A particularly concise summary has been prepared by the Association of the British Pharmaceutical industry (ABPI) and the British Association of Research Quality Assurance (BARQA).[7] As previously noted, most site audits involve two auditors. Both should be taking notes during the interviews and reviews, but only one should take the lead in writing up the report. Audits performed soon after a clinical trial starts to recruit provide the most benefit, as any actions can be implemented and problems corrected.

The commonly understood purpose of site audits is to check to see that the protocol and applicable regulations are being followed. Site audits are especially effective in ensuring the quality of the clinical procedures performed – usually by people who are not under the direct control of the sponsor. Audits should be conducted in sufficient depth to understand the activities that have been conducted at the site. Procedures must be sufficiently robust to enable any allegations of fraud or misconduct to be substantiated or refuted. Audits conducted on the same study at different sites in different geographical locations can provide an insight into audit trends. Many studies conducted are multicentre and multinational, and it is common to have similar issues identified. It will also be easier to detect possible fraud or misconduct, as the auditors will already have established the more common types of findings for a particular study.

Following the opening meeting, the auditor typically interviews selected personnel from the study site. It is important that these personnel be present and can devote sufficient time to the auditor for this process to be effective. If site staff need to be elsewhere and cannot give the required time, the auditor may assume that they are similarly short of time to conduct the clinical study. During this interview process, information about the site staff's responsibilities and the training that they have received will be gathered.

Throughout the audit, the auditor will require periods to review documents related to the study. The documents required include:

- all the essential documents as defined by ICH GCP[1]
- SOPs (if present at the site)
- CVs and training records (if not part of the study file)
- calibration and maintenance records for any equipment used during the trial
- investigational medicinal product delivery and accountability records (if stored separately in a pharmacy).

Most of the audit process at the study site will be spent on review of the source data against the CRFs. This can be approached in different ways by the auditor. Sometimes, a sampling approach is taken; sometimes, a 100% review is performed. A 100% review is almost always conducted on patient informed consent forms, whereas a sample of subjects is usually chosen for source data verification. The choice of the patients/CRFs depends on several factors. Usually, CRFs and source data are taken from the beginning of the study, the middle, and the most recently completed data – from this review, an improvement can usually be seen and any teething problems in

CRF completion should be overcome. Subjects are also usually chosen for review if they have had a serious adverse event during the study or have violated the protocol. It is important that auditors review a sufficiently large sample to ensure that they are confident that practices at the site are going well; the selection of only two or three subjects does not adequately represent the validity of the data. It is important for the sample size to be large enough that the findings can be extrapolated across all enrolled subjects and, when added to information from three or four sites, across a whole study.

Throughout the process, the auditor will be reviewing the accuracy and validity of the information provided in the CRF, diary card, questionnaires, etc., against the information provided in the source data.

The timing of the consent process relating to study procedures being conducted is always carefully evaluated. Many consent forms do not allow for the recording of a consent time, and this is often missing from the source data. For many protocols, this process is often a requirement but is not necessarily defined.

During the audit process, deficiencies will be noted by the auditor. These need to be categorized. This process will highlight which issues are isolated ones and which are more systematic failures. As mentioned above, auditors should concentrate on the various audit interfaces as well as on the more standard audit processes. One typical audit interface at a site audit would be the interaction between the study nurse and the laboratory staff: questions relating to this area typically include how samples arrive at the laboratory, how the laboratory is notified that the patient is on a clinical trial and which tests need to be performed, and how abnormal results are notified. As can be seen, this one interface raises many questions.

As with all audits, the evidence gathered during the audit must be balanced and objective. In the case of possible fraud or misconduct, it is particularly important to substantiate the observations made and to fully explore possible reasons for these errors. It is unlikely that the auditor can have a 'second shot' at trying to secure any evidence should the need arise.

Just before the audit close-out meeting, the auditor usually requests a short time to evaluate the issues, and this will depend on the findings. This time is invaluable in defining the severity and implications of the findings. The close-out meeting should not be just a list of what has been found, but a detailed summary of the findings and their impact on the study at the site. Evidence must be carefully presented to the site staff, and any non-compliance defined against ICH GCP,[1] local laws, or the protocol. The close-out meeting may also be a time to clarify any issues. This should be performed before the findings are presented.

The close-out meeting is also an important time for the site staff to be able to give any feedback and take part in the discussions. The team that started the audit should be available at the end. Presentation of findings and the reactions of the site staff need to be handled carefully, especially if issues arise relating to possible fraud or misconduct. The 'people skills' of the auditor come into force at this time. Nobody likes to be told that they have made a mistake, whether intentional or not, so the presentation of findings needs to be handled sensitively. However, for most findings, once they have been presented and the relevant GCP or protocol violation referenced, most auditees find they have little to say in their defence. In particularly difficult audits relating to fraud or misconduct, the situation is different, staff may be withdrawn or very defensive, and in some cases one can only agree to differ in one's opinions.

The audit report

This is an essential phase in the audit process and should be written as soon as possible after the audit, while it is still in the auditor's mind. The audit report is a presentation of all the results of the audit, and must be consistent with the audit objectives and accurately reflect the findings and conclusions of the audit. The content of the report is crucial, as it presents the findings of the audit and their level of significance. Audit reports typically have limited circulation, to minimize any possible misinterpretations that may affect the auditees. Only staff who are adequately informed to judge the report in the context in which it was written should be copied in on the full report. In most cases, the report will begin with a summary; this is usually intended for senior management and those with less time to read the key findings and recommendations.

The auditor's writing style needs to be clear and unambiguous. The use of acronyms and abbreviations must be kept to a minimum to avoid any confusion. Active language is far more arresting than passive. As with general rules on writing, one needs to consider one's audience. The structure of the report can vary between organizations. Some reports are wordier and are longer, others take a tabular approach, and some combine both styles. Whatever the approach, evidence must be presented carefully and the observations linked to the relevant guidelines/laws that may have been violated.

The report should provide an outline of the site setting, which most of the readers will not have visited, and a photograph can be useful.

The audit report should be addressing systematic problems, and not be simply a list of unlinked mistakes. It is important for the auditor to be able to identify problems, but they must be aware of the 'bigger picture' – that is, an understanding of how these findings all fit together and why the errors have occurred. It is also to be questioned why these errors were not found during routine QC by the monitor, and the question of fraud or misconduct may also need to be raised. In some cases, 'best practice' is presented. This can be useful as a recommendation, but may easily be dismissed by the audience. Box 14.3 outlines an example of how an audit finding can be presented.

When audit findings are reported, they may be graded to show their level of importance. Grading is usually similar to that of the regulators – for example, critical, major, and other/minor/recommendations. Audit reports also suggest improvement and advice on how to correct actions and how to respond to audit findings. All recommendations should be achievable and practical. Most findings from a site audit will be addressed by the monitor, but some may need input from other groups, such as data management. Recommendations should also be able to be closed so it is clear when recommendations have been completed.

The summary of findings/observations/actions often found at the end of a report is its most important component. This is the section that, after the initial summary, is most likely to be read by senior management. There must be a summary as to whether

---

BOX 14.3   Example of how an audit finding can be presented

Audit finding:	An investigator has not been reviewing laboratory reports. No information on clinical significance has been reported, although several values were out of the normal range
Interface:	Investigator/study nurse/laboratory
Root cause:	On further questioning during the audit, it was found that the study nurse had been filing the laboratory reports before the investigator reviewed them
Recommendation by QA:	As soon as the laboratory reports are received by the study nurse, they must be forwarded immediately to the investigator. Laboratory reports must be reviewed, and the clinical significance of the results documented and action taken, if required, by the investigator. The investigator must sign and date the laboratory report to show the timely review
Auditee's response:	This is where space is left for the responses

---

the site's performance is good or bad, compliant or non-compliant, and, if it is below standard, what needs to be done.

In some cases, auditor involvement may cease with the release of the audit report. This is what routinely happened in the past. The audit report is the end of one process, but the beginning of another. A more modern approach is to follow up with measurement and improvement where other in-house staff or other groups within the QA team may be involved. In some organizations, the auditor will still be very active in supporting the corrective action process (making sure that the error does not happen again) and the preventative action (preventing other errors before they can occur). There are advantages to both systems, but this additional step is now seen as the real value of the audit.

A brief explanation of the CAPA (corrective and preventative action) process may be useful here. The CAPA system identifies, assesses, evaluates, implements, and monitors solutions to address actual or potential non-compliances. Some organizations apply CAPA to systems other than QA (e.g. customer complaints). Without the identification of the root cause of an audit finding, this system cannot be successful. The corrective and/or preventative actions are then identified and timelines agreed. After the CAPA has been implemented, QA verifies, and then finally the CAPA can be closed. The CAPA system and associated introduction of key performance indicators are really seen to enhance an organization's quality culture, performance, and compliance.[8]

Audit follow-up

Audits will only be effective with successful and timely follow-up. The follow-up process must be well structured and controlled. It is the auditor who generally defines responsible persons to decide on, initiate, and implement any necessary corrective actions and preventative measures. The auditor determines the adequacy and timeliness of the actions taken on the reported findings, although, as mentioned above, this may be delegated to another in-house auditor. An assessment of the effectiveness and the benefits from these measures also needs to be undertaken with respect to continual improvements.

Within the industry, it is often recommended to follow up the audit report with a presentation to some of the auditees. The interaction is not intended to 'point the finger' at the faults of the auditee, but rather to give management and the groups concerned the opportunity to ask for more information than would be routinely covered in the audit report.

It is often found that ownership of findings can help those that need to respond to the audit report to understand what needs to be done to correct any deficiencies and, most importantly, what they can do in future to ensure that these issues do not happen again. This approach works best with systematic inconsistencies rather than one-off cases that are out of the auditees' hands. Of course, with site audits, investigational site staff are not directly involved in this debriefing. However, monitors are involved, and when they next go back to their various sites to discuss findings and corrective actions, this is far easier, as the monitors will fully understand what their role is in the follow-up process.

Findings related to possible fraud and misconduct will be classified at least as major, but more likely as critical. These types of findings need to be followed up until conclusion and evidence must be produced to show that all request actions have taken place. If any activities are not followed up and there are further repercussions, then a repeat audit may be requested. The adequacy of the follow-up in such cases may be out of the hands of the auditor or with limited auditor involvement. With these types of findings, input from senior management and regulatory and legal specialists is generally required.

As part of audit follow-up, corrective actions must be included to determine the root cause. For example, if one patient at a site had not signed a patient informed consent form before study procedures were conducted, we would want to establish why this had happened and to prevent it from happening again. The root cause may have been quite simple and easily explained – for example, the investigator was on holiday, and a more junior member of the team, who had not been adequately trained, was involved with the patient's care and treatment. This leads us to question whether the site had been adequately trained on the protocol and their responsibilities, and whether they understood GCP.

Another key to a successful audit is to categorize findings according to whether they are isolated incidents or more systematic errors. The example above appears to have involved just one patient at a site. The error made, if only made in isolation, does show misconduct, but it can be assumed that this was unintentional. Isolated incidents such as this, although regrettable and significant, can be remedied simply, and repercussions are limited. A series of significant audit findings at a site are far more worrying.

ISO 19011[9] defines the standards for the measurement and improvement of issues following audit, and this is not covered by GCP. It is hardly surprising that many auditors find the follow-up stage fairly daunting.

Finally, at the end of the audit process, audit certificates are issued for site audits. Their aim is not to state compliance with GCP, but rather to provide a neutral statement that informs that an audit has taken place.

Conclusions

Today's GCP environment is continually changing, new regulations are being introduced, protocols are being amended, disease states are changing, and there is continual evolution of information being produced during the trial relating to the investigational medicinal product being tested. With all this to take into account, it is no wonder that investigators or site staff think that they can commit fraud or misconduct and get away with it. They think that it will be lost in the vast amount of information being produced.

It is vital for the pharmaceutical industry to ensure that their QA programmes cover as much of the group's clinical trial work as possible. Site audits should not be replaced by systems audits, as they provide invaluable information that can mainly be identified by the auditor who visits the site. There are other detection mechanisms – for example, fraud may become evident when statistical analysis is performed or when peer review of an article is conducted. This is late-stage detection, and it is far better to detect fraud early in a study during a site audit so that something positive can be done about it and the study may be retrievable, as more patients can be recruited at another site, for example.

One of the auditor's roles is to detect and confirm fraud. Auditors play a pivotal role in this process. With many audit findings, auditors do find it difficult to define whether mistakes have been made in innocence or intentionally. Sometimes, it is difficult to differentiate between serious and less serious offences. There are many 'grey' areas in GCP auditing. Training of site staff or other operational staff is often cited as an issue, and is becoming more significant in the eyes of regulators, but for fraud and misconduct this is not often the case. Auditors must be provided with the necessary training and have the key skills to detect, report, and possibly follow up these sensitive issues.

Once fraud or misconduct has been detected by the auditor, it is important that established standards be in place to deal with this appropriately. Detection of fraud or misconduct by the auditor is just one of the steps; without follow-up, detection has very limited use. Institutions and research sites should have established their own guidelines on how they deal with misconduct and fraud. In England in 2004, the NHS issued an R&D Good Practice Guidance document that clearly outlines to NHS Trusts guidance policies for research misconduct and fraud.[10] Auditors do not currently review financial aspects of a trial, and issues relating to financial wrongdoing are not currently audited in Europe, but perhaps in the future auditors should review this aspect as well. This will, of course, mean further training and perhaps additional divisions within existing QA groups.

Attempts to deal with fraud are, to date, inadequate, and more needs to be done in the future.[11] At a meeting of the Royal College of Physicians in November 2001, it was agreed that a national body was required in the UK to educate, audit, detect, and deal with research fraud. The UK panel for Research Integrity in Health and Biomedical Sciences and the UK Research Integrity Office (UKRIO) were finally established in March 2006, but with no statutory basis, so it remains to be seen how effective they will be. In many countries, there is still no mechanism in place at all to deal with these allegations. Such a development would surely be welcomed by the QA community internationally, as they are becoming increasingly impatient with what they perceive as a lack of follow-up when problems are detected at trial sites. Fraudulent activity will only continue unless practices are put in place to deter would-be fraudsters.

References

1. International Conference on Harmonisation of Technical Requirements for Registration of Pharmaceuticals for Human Use. Guideline for Good Clinical Practice (ICH E6), April 1996. www.ich.org.
2. Directive 95/46/EC of the European Parliament and of the Council of 24 October 1995 on the protection of individuals with regard to the processing of personal data and on the free movement of such data. *Official Journal* L 281, 23 November 1995: 31–50.
3. Directive 2001/20/EC of the European Parliament and of the Council of 4 April 2001, on the approximation of the laws, regulations and administrative provisions of the Member States relating to the implementation of good clinical practice in the conduct of clinical trials on medicinal products for human use. *Official Journal* L 121, 1 May 2001: 34–44.
4. Commission Directive 2005/28/EC of 8 April 2005, laying down principles and detailed guidelines for good clinical practice as regards investigational medicinal products for human use, as well as the requirements for authorisation of the manufacturing or importation of such products. *Official Journal* L 91, 9 April 2005: 13–19.
5. Waddell A. Audit training. *Quasar* 2006; **97**: 20–1.
6. Priya B. Is it time for a code of conduct for auditors? *GCP J* 2007; **14**: 10–11.
7. The Association of the British Pharmaceutical Industry in conjunction with the British Association of Research Quality Assurance. *Guidelines on the Conduct of Investigator Site Audits*. 1994. www.abpi.org.uk.
8. Patel H. Introduction to CAPA. *Quasar* 2006; **95**: 8–9.
9. BS EN ISO 19011: 2002 Guidelines for Quality and Environmental Management Systems Auditing.
10. NHS R&D Forum Good Practice Guidance. *R&D Forum Advice for NHS Trusts: Research Misconduct and Fraud*. July 2004. www.rdforums.nhs.uk.
11. Wilmshurst P. Fraud in research. *Clin Med* 2002; **2**: 159–60.

SECTION 5

INVESTIGATION OF RESEARCH MISCONDUCT

15 Handling whistleblowers: Bane and boon

C Kristina Gunsalus and Drummond Rennie

Introduction

The US Commission on Research Integrity[1] held 15 public meetings all over the USA, and heard testimony from many scores of witnesses: researchers, accused scientists, whistleblowers, administrators, politicians, patients, and members of the general public. On one particular morning, we heard a series of young female scientists. Each had blown the whistle on a colleague whom she suspected of research misconduct. Each had stuck to her guns through a long-drawn-out and bitter process. Each had endured ostracism and retaliation. For each, the event had effectively ended her career as a scientist. Yet each was entirely vindicated by formal investigation.

In this chapter, we examine why such a sorry state of affairs should result when such people, the whistleblowers, should be one of our most valued resources, and we suggest ways to put things right.

What are whistleblowers and why should anyone care?

Whistleblowers: a definition

A whistleblower is a person who calls attention to wrongdoing, usually from within an organization. The term is broad, covering everyone from the one-time anonymous caller all the way to one who pursues charges doggedly over a number of years and across jurisdictions. Whistleblowers may be correct or mistaken; our usage here is of the broadest sort, meant to encompass all those from a person first raising charges to one whose charges have been validated. The Glazers, in their classic book *The Whistleblowers: Exposing Corruption in Government and Industry*, define whistleblowers as 'employees who publicly disclose unethical or illegal practices in the workplace'.[2] Whistleblowers serve as an irreplaceable quality-control mechanism, and history shows that we ignore them at our peril, as the vast proportion of cases of scientific misconduct are revealed only by the courageous action of whistleblowers, often taken at great personal cost. Science often operates at an intimate level. A colleague can, as happened in the notorious Darsee case (described by Kohn,[3] p. 85), see a scientist put several different dates on an electrocardiograph strip as it runs during a short experiment on a dog's heart. No one outside the laboratory could ever have detected that the falsification had taken place. So insiders are the only ones who *can* report many problems, being on the spot with access to necessary information. In this respect, their actions make them – or should make them – an invaluable boon to their employers and society.

The reality is more complicated. Even vindicated whistleblowers have found their careers seriously damaged, if not irreparably destroyed: instead of being honoured, they are frequently seen as the bane of their employing organizations. This boon–bane paradox is understandable once a few important characteristics of workplaces, whistleblowers, and human nature are explored.

Challenges in discovering and responding to wrongdoing

One of the most difficult problems in any organization is how to discover and respond to wrongdoing and allegations of wrongdoing. In any setting, people misunderstand each other, work at cross-purposes, and disagree about how to achieve mutual objectives. Where people work together, there will inevitably be some quantity of conflict, disagreement, and even wrongdoing. This reality is already complex and challenging before adding the layers of complexity that accrue when the differences or misunderstandings involve reports of transgressions.

Handling whistleblowers should be understood as a larger matter than simply responding when a report of misconduct arises. An effective response to whistleblowing requires fundamentally good habits of management, sensible internal checks and balances, and effective systems for determining facts when problems arise. It requires understanding that, although problems that surface through official processes (internal investigations or audits, etc.) present their own challenges, those processes are part of the administrative structure of the university. As such, their findings seem easier for organizations to deal with effectively than those stemming from unsolicited reports of misconduct lodged by insiders who come forward voluntarily, in a self-appointed way, and who may be far from dispassionate about the charges.

Finally – and most difficult for those who wish to ensure the integrity of work done in their environments – responding effectively and accurately to whistleblowers means constructing systems that take into account the reality that reports of problems rarely surface placidly, and may be presented by someone who is stressed, emotional, unpleasant, unreasonable, or angry – and still correct about a matter that goes to the heart of the work done by the organization. Moreover, the circumstances of complaining about a colleague's behaviour are so fraught, so dangerous, and so often complicated by personal ties that even reasonable individuals may seem unreasonable or unbalanced. While large-scale clinical trials of drugs in patients require audit, this is exceedingly expensive, and the scientific enterprise would grind to a halt if forced to submit to such daily scrutiny.[4] So the facts remain that only co-workers are in a position to observe and report research misconduct and that it is very costly in personal terms.

'Good-faith' whistleblowing
Our discussion will focus on the problems surrounding responses to good-faith whistleblowing, or reports that are made in reasonable belief that the complaint is true. Most

definitions of 'good faith' require that the person reporting the misconduct must do so with reasonable care and with the belief that the charges are true (Box 15.1). Where an allegation is filed maliciously – in the knowledge that the allegation is false, or in reckless disregard for its truth or falsity – different considerations come into play. Although there is often a period of time in which the central truths are not known, the steps for responding to an allegation are fundamentally the same through the completion of the fact-finding, so the original processes should all be the same. The only time

---

BOX 15.1   **Whistleblowing definitions**

Whistleblowing

The Glazers, in their classic book *The Whistleblowers: Exposing Corruption in Government and Industry*, define whistleblowers as 'employees who publicly disclose unethical or illegal practices in the workplace'. They reference the six-part requirement for justifiable acts of whistleblowing developed by Norman Bowie, a writer on business ethics:[2]

'(1) that the act of whistleblowing stem from appropriate moral motives of preventing unnecessary harm to others; (2) that the whistleblower use all available internal procedures for rectifying the problematic behavior before public disclosure, although special circumstances may preclude this; (3) that the whistleblower have "evidence that would persuade a reasonable person"; (4) that the whistleblower perceive serious danger that can result from the violation; (5) that the whistleblower act in accordance with his or her responsibilities for "avoiding and/or exposing moral violations"; (6) that the whistleblower's action have some reasonable chance of success.'

Whistleblowing

According to the *Oxford English Dictionary*, whistleblowing is:[30]

'(d) to blow the whistle on (a person or thing): to bring an activity to a sharp conclusion, as if by the blast of a whistle; now usu. by informing on (a person) or exposing (an irregularity or crime).

'**whistle-blower** chiefly U.S., one who "blows the whistle" on a person or activity (Used in this sense for the first time by PG Wodehouse, 1934, in "Right Ho, Jeeves.").'

Good-faith whistleblowing

According to the US Office of Research Integrity:[24]

'"**Good faith allegation**" means an allegation of scientific misconduct made with a belief in the truth of the allegation which a reasonable person in the whistleblower's position could hold based upon the facts. An allegation is not in good faith if made with reckless disregard for or willful ignorance of facts that would disprove the allegation.'

Continued ➤

BOX 15.1   *(continued)*

Good-faith allegation

According to the UK Medical Research Council:[31]

'Good faith allegation means an allegation of scientific misconduct made by a complainant who honestly believes that scientific misconduct may have occurred. A complainant who recklessly disregards evidence that disproves an allegation has not made the allegation in good faith.'

Abuse of privilege

According to the Office of Research Integrity:[28]

'Although an allegation of scientific misconduct might otherwise be privileged, the whistleblower may be liable for defamation if he abuses the privilege. Abuse of the privilege may occur in several ways:

- the whistleblower knows that the defamatory matter is false (or he has reckless disregard for the truth);
- the defamatory matter is disclosed for some purpose other than that for which the privilege is given;
- the disclosure is made to a person not reasonably believed to be necessary for accomplishment of the privilege's purpose; or
- the allegation includes defamatory matter not reasonably believed to be necessary to accomplish the privilege's purpose.

'These various abuses may be described collectively as "bad faith" or "malice".

'ORI believes that an allegation which is not made in good faith or which violates the confidentiality of the accused should not be protected. For example, a whistleblower might abuse the privilege by making an allegation he knows to be false or by disclosing misconduct to unauthorized persons such as the media. Such bad faith disclosures constitute abuse of the conditional privilege and would not be protected against defamation actions.

'Though bad faith whistleblowers may forfeit the conditional privilege, case law clearly instructs that the conditional privilege carries with it a presumption of good faith. In other words, the burden of showing bad faith falls on the plaintiff who brings suit for defamation.

'Good faith whistleblowers are not obliged to (nor should) conduct exhaustive investigations before bringing serious problems to attention; examples of bad faith: hearing gossip from an unreliable source known to hate the person about whom the report is made and rushing off to file an anonymous written complaint.'

---

at which the handling of a malicious whistleblower differs is *after* the determination of falsity of the charges and disposition of the matter.

However, being wrong about charges does not necessarily make them maliciously motivated: as will be seen, many – perhaps most – charges are mistaken. Thus, being proven wrong is a necessary, but not sufficient, component of being found to be a malicious whistleblower. To be found to be malicious, a charge must have been known to be without merit, or have been brought with utter carelessness for its accuracy.

Even if meanly motivated, a verified charge is not a malicious charge. To make the situation even more complicated, if a set of charges is verified as true, the motives of the whistleblower, however mean-spirited or spiteful, are by definition not malicious charges. Allegations brought by a whistleblower that are substantiated cannot be viewed as malicious however much antipathy the whistleblower might have felt for the wrongdoer or however happy the outcome makes the whistleblower. The importance of this distinction becomes clear when exploring how frequently allegations are rooted in conflict or discord within a workplace.

The whistleblower

Whistleblowers are difficult and can appear 'flaky'. It is not only the complex personal relationships and organizational setting surrounding allegations of scientific misconduct that make evaluation of the good faith of whistleblowers difficult: the actions of the whistleblowers themselves often muddy the waters.

First, whistleblowing is nerve-racking for a variety of reasons – not least because complainers as a class provoke uncomfortable emotions. As a rule, people in organizations dislike and are wary of those who present evidence of problems that cause complications and headaches for administrators and can make others look bad. Indeed, across cultures, we did not like children who carried tales, and we do not like people who do the same as adults. Daily life inside the organization can quickly become difficult and uncomfortable for a whistleblower. Whistleblowers routinely report feelings of anxiety,

---

BOX 15.2 Effects of whistleblowing

Studies on whistleblowers reveal time and again that whistleblowing is a perilous activity. A representative comment is: 'Not only do most whistleblowers get fired, but they rarely get their jobs back. Most never work in the field again ... of the several dozen whistleblowers I have talked with, most lost their houses. Many lost their families. It doesn't happen all at once, but whistleblowers' cases drag on for years, putting a tremendous strain on families. Most whistleblowers will suffer from depression and alcoholism' (Alford,[5] p. 19).

Excerpts from *Consequences of Whistleblowing for the Whistleblower in Misconduct in Science Cases*[33]

'Another study published in the same year (U.S. Merit Systems Protection Board, 1993), although focused on a much broader range of misconduct by government employees than just scientific misconduct, went well beyond perceptions of the propensity to report and feelings of vulnerability. It collected information from over 13,000 government employees to examine the extent of exposure to misconduct, the extent to which those exposed reported the misconduct, the reasons why some did not report, and what happened to those who did. Key findings from this study included the following:

Continued ➤

BOX 15.2   (*continued*)

- Eighteen percent of those surveyed reported personal awareness of misconduct;
- Half of those who knew of misconduct had reported it (up from 30% in a 1983 survey);
- Of those who did not report the misconduct, 60% believed that reporting it would have no impact and 33% did not report because they feared retaliation;
- Thirty-seven percent of those who reported the misconduct reported subsequent threats or retaliation; and
- Nearly half of all those who reported threats or retaliation believed that they experienced each of the following: shunning by coworkers or managers (49%); verbal harassment or intimidation (47%); and poor performance appraisals (47%).

Other studies have focused on those who have reported retaliation (GAO, 1993). However, we know of no study that has specifically investigated whistleblowers in cases of scientific misconduct. This study is ground-breaking in that regard.'

'The survey shows that institutional officials, as a group, are involved in almost all (88%) of the cases that experienced the most serious negative outcomes, while only about a quarter of the accused (24%) and fewer colleagues (18%) and professional societies (6%) are reported to be responsible for such outcomes.'

'**Case outcome.** Complainants whose allegations were partially but not fully confirmed were the most likely (79%) to experience negative consequences. Those whose allegations were totally unsupported were next most likely (74%) to report adverse consequences followed by those whose allegations were fully supported (68%).'

'Not a single whistleblower reported that their whistleblowing had a positive impact on their careers.'

'More than two-thirds of all whistleblowers reported experiencing at least one negative outcome as a direct result of their whistleblowing. Conversely, nearly one-third did not experience any adverse consequences of blowing the whistle.

- **Whistleblowers most likely to have experienced an adverse outcome** of their whistleblowing included:
  - lower ranking faculty and students/fellows in basic science departments;
  - those who alleged misconduct by their colleagues.

- **Whistleblowers least likely to have experienced an adverse outcome** of their whistleblowing included:
  - academics in clinical departments;
  - workers in non-academic settings (particularly government workers);
  - those with senior administrative positions in their institutions;
  - those who allege misconduct by individuals at a different institution.

BOX 15.2   *(continued)*

- **Blowing the whistle was most likely to have adverse outcomes** in situations in which:
  - fabrication of data was alleged;
  - the case received some publicity;
  - the allegations were made to a senior administrative official or misconduct official of the institution or to the funding agency;
  - the allegations were made both within and outside the institution;
  - the allegations were made to many different types of individuals;
  - the allegations were subjected to an investigation.

In general, these findings suggest that *whistleblowers are most at risk of adverse outcomes in high profile cases in the basic sciences, especially when those cases gain notoriety outside the institution and the complainant is a lower ranking faculty member or student.* Institutional officials and funding agencies appear to put the interests of their organization above those of the whistleblower. While this may well seem appropriate to such officials and agencies, because more than 70% of cases result in no findings of misconduct (according to ORI records), this pattern definitely suggests a failure in mechanisms to protect vulnerable whistleblowers from retaliation.'

'The seeds of nearly every negative action taken against a whistleblower are sown during the active phase of the investigation. Very few whistleblowers suffer adverse consequences exclusively in the period after the case is closed.

The most serious negative consequences – loss of position, loss of research resources or opportunity, and denial of advancement – simply do not happen without substantial involvement and direction by institutional officials. Lesser negative outcomes – hassles, pressures, and delays – also frequently come from institutional officials but are equally as likely to come from the accused. These findings suggest that *for whistleblowers to suffer the most serious negative outcomes, institutional officials must play a significant role in dealing with their cases.* [emphasis in original] The accused can also cause problems for whistleblowers but generally *the consequences attributed to the accused tend to be more widespread but less severe than those attributed to institutional officials.'* [emphasis in original]

---

apprehension and vulnerability, as well as experiencing mistreatment, threats and retaliation against them for their reports (Boxes 15.2 and 15.3).

Forms of retaliation can be social, such as shunning, or more active, including verbal harassment, intimidation, poor performance appraisals, and dismissal.[5] For example, the whistleblower in one extensively investigated and litigated case, Nancy Olivieri, suffered massive retaliation of every sort, up to and including loss of her job, until her vindication and court-ordered restoration. The acts of retaliation included anonymous hate mail to Olivieri's supporters, which was revealed, ultimately, to be from her own senior colleague and co-investigator, Gideon Koren. This came out when his DNA was

---

BOX 15.3   **Effects on the whistleblower: the case of Eric Poehlman, 2006**

A classic case of a whistleblower who suffered, despite ultimate vindication, is that of Walter DeNino. Working in the laboratory of the prominent researcher Eric Poehlman at the University of Vermont in the late 1990s, DeNino was unable to reconcile data, and called the irregularities to attention after intensive internal efforts to seek corrections. Although others in the laboratory had similar concerns, only DeNino, one of the most junior researchers, spoke up. For his troubles, he was ostracized, discredited, and threatened with lawsuits and the loss of his job. Through what *Nature* called 'an arduous and sometimes ugly investigation process', DeNino's character was smeared. Poehlman charged that the data had been fabricated by DeNino himself and that DeNino was raising questions out of homophobia and jealousy.[34] Ultimately, DeNino resorted to hiring his own attorney to protect his name and rights. The report of the university's panel investigating the charges against Poehlman detailed many instances that 'display Dr Poehlman's contempt not just for the truth, but for this Panel, the University, and his profession'.[35] And yet DeNino was described as one of the 'lucky' ones:[36] '[a]s a whistleblower, he was very cautious in making an allegation and he was well-protected by the policies and actions of the University of Vermont'. (Apparently, this means that he did not lose his job – instead, only being threatened with its loss.) During the six years after he first raised his concerns until Poehlman was sentenced to prison, DeNino was under a cloud while Poehlman pursued an aggressive defence. In the words of his attorney Philip Michael, 'A lot of whistle-blowers are retired. For Walter, this is something that will follow him for the rest of his life.'[36,37]

   Poehlman's case is one of the few that has been criminally prosecuted in the USA, with prison time, fines levied for fraudulent use of federal research funds, and the requirement that 10 scientific papers be retracted (an intensive effort to assess the validity of his other 200 published articles is underway).[37] Even though many others had private questions about Poehlman's work, none were willing to come forward until after the 24-year-old DeNino had gone to the authorities. A tenured professor working in the same laboratory space has told a reporter that his early advice to DeNino was 'first, understand that no matter how you proceed, everyone loses. Your career will be ruined because no one is going to protect you. The university will come out bad and Eric's reputation will be destroyed.' Yet this was an egregious case warranting criminal prosecution.[38]

---

identified on the envelopes as part of extensive forensic analysis that Olivieri and her supporters initiated and paid for.[6]

   Robert Sprague, a tenured professor who revealed the presence of fabricated data in publications affecting treatment with psychotropic medications of an extremely vulnerable population (mentally retarded individuals, often institutionalized), found himself the subject of an investigation before his documentation about the misconduct of another was examined. During the time of his wife's terminal illness, Sprague was obliged to defend himself as well as his motives for speaking up. He says of the experience of whistleblowing: 'the analogy to a disaster is not accidental, but deliberate. Many whistleblowers never recover from their experiences, especially if their family ties are not strong.'[7]

Most organizations, including research universities, institutes, and hospitals, value a dispassionate professional effect: we judge this to be more 'objective' and 'scientific'. While, as members of these organizations, we can appreciate enthusiasm and even passion, we inculcate a detached and unemotional style of delivery when discussing results. This supports the myth of research as impersonal, unbiased, and impartial. The process of deciding to file a complaint about the veracity of work can be so threatening that by the time a person has summoned the courage to convey the information in some fashion (whether by seeking advice from someone who feels obliged to pass the information along or by invoking a more formal official procedure to report concerns), the strain of going against the grain of the organizational culture by 'complaining' is likely to have extracted a toll. Those who fall under the general umbrella of whistleblowing – calling attention to something that is not right in their larger group environment – are likely to be stressed, and may experience severe psychological distress. In turn, this translates into behaviour that can be emotional and erratic. This, of course, undermines the credibility of the whistleblower, extends their isolation, and exacerbates the toll of whistleblowing, in a continuing vicious cycle.

Dislike breeds mistrust. It takes a long time for people who like and respect each other to come to the point where they conclude that serious things are amiss: those who like each other search for alternative explanations and work together to try to resolve problems. However, if communications or relationships are not good among group members, it becomes far easier to believe ill of others, not ask the right questions, or, if these are asked, not to get, or really hear and appreciate, suitable answers. Social psychologists term this the 'sinister attribution bias': once relationships fray, it is far easier to attribute malice to the actions of those you do not like than to those you do.[8] The combination of low status in an organization with lack of access to information, communication, and good will or trust among group members easily leads to misunderstandings and conflict. In turn, we then start labelling others and concluding things about their character.

Attribution theorists find that there are two stages to concluding that the conduct of others arises from their dispositions rather than the circumstances in which they find themselves: first, we consider whether the action was intentional. If we conclude that it was intentional ('she went in and filed the report when she didn't have to'), and the result on us is strongly positive or negative, we are more likely to conclude that the outcome is the result of the person's disposition.[9]

To give an example, when Margot O'Toole raised questions about the work of Thereza Imanishi-Kari, the points she made about problems with the quality of the work were all validated – eventually. Yet, even today, more than 20 years later, the prevailing understanding in the scientific community is that she was a jealous, obsessive failure. In a review of a book on the 'Baltimore Case' by the science historian Daniel Kevles, one of us (CKG) wrote:[10]

'Kevles starts by describing Margot O'Toole, the young post-doctoral fellow who questioned the accuracy of a paper of which Baltimore was a coauthor. Kevles reports that she was "virtually bred to confront trouble." Even more, "Civil rights protests and demonstrations against the Vietnam War had flourished during her undergraduate years, likely encouraging her familial propensity for dissent." The sources for the paragraph containing the latter statement include notes of a telephone conversation in 1993 between two people neither of whom is O'Toole or anyone in her family. In contrast, Kevles learns from direct interviews with Baltimore that his family's "left-leaning" heritage and his exposure to the McCarthy hearings as a high-school student undergirds his principled objections to Congressional inquiries into questioned science.

'Thereza Imanishi-Kari, O'Toole's supervisor and a coauthor with Baltimore of the paper in question, is described as "vivacious, competent, quick on her feet and formidably smart." On the next page, we learn that she "broke the laboratory rules against smoking and neglected to meet M.I.T.'s requirements for getting ahead." Whereas Imanishi-Kari merely "neglected to meet" standards for getting ahead, what O'Toole "seemed at heart to crave was recognition as an insightful scientific critic and, more important, legitimation as a practicing scientist who was not incompetent because she could not get Bet-1 to work".'

The bias Kevles demonstrated is starkly revealed in this comparison. This sort of bias is exactly what we all must guard against.

Sometimes the whistleblower digs in. While many give up in the face of these daunting barriers, those who persist tend to dig in, out of some combination of principle, stubbornness, commitment, and personality. This persistence can make the stress even worse, and has the side effect of making the whistleblower appear vindictive and self-righteous, further undercutting his or her credibility, likeability, and the probability of gaining a fair hearing in the institution. The whistleblowing experience often dominates the life of an individual caught up in it, becoming the primary focus and driving motivation. The more insistent such a person becomes, the more those made uncomfortable by the strength of emotion and inconvenience of the allegations push them away.

Sometimes the whistleblower is being disciplined, which further clouds the issue. People who seek to expose wrongdoing are often the subject of disciplinary action, so it is difficult to discern whether there is, in fact, a serious problem or simply a person attempting to divert attention from his or her own deficiencies. Charges often arise from the disgruntled, and the charges can be both correct and at the same time deeply rooted in the same shortcomings that led to the discipline in the first place. The charges can just as easily be mistaken or confused, and there is hardly anyone as exasperatingly stubborn as the person with a cause; either way – right or wrong – this is not an easy individual with whom to interact. Since it is natural for us to prefer the prickly and obsessed to be wrong, our capacity to assess the charges can be strongly affected by assimilation biases that give greater weight to information that supports preferred conclusions.[11]

It is small wonder that these people, who are disrupting organizational life often in an overly emotional manner, come to be disliked and may not be heard in a dispassionate or open-minded manner. This effect is only exacerbated when the person against whom their charges are filed is well-liked, very powerful, or both, and who therefore finds it easy to get others to accept his derogatory characterizations of his accuser. Because reputations in institutions are built through a combination of direct experience and word of mouth, it is simple – and commonplace – for the better known and senior person to skew the perception of a less-known or junior person. If the 'answer' is known before the facts are collected and reviewed ('she's just jealous or trying to divert attention from her own failures', etc.), determinations rooted in fact may become well-nigh impossible to achieve.

Complexity and messiness are endemic in these situations. Numerous intertwined issues make things even worse for those who must resolve the allegations. Charges are followed by counter-charges, often filed on a number of fronts. It is not unusual for a whistleblower to allege wrongdoing not only with handling of data or authorship credit, but also of misuse of grant funds, regulatory violations (e.g. treatment of animal subjects or hazardous substances), or violation of intellectual property requirements (Box 15.4).

BOX 15.4 **The Berge case**

Pamela Berge was a PhD student in nutritional sciences at Cornell University who collaborated with researchers at University of Alabama–Birmingham (UAB). She did her thesis research on cytomegalovirus (CMV), a common infectious cause of birth defects, as a possible cause of low birthweight. UAB had built up an important database on maternal and congenital CMV, and researchers there extended access to Berge, including a stint in residence at UAB as a visiting graduate student. After receipt of her degree, Berge attempted to publish papers on her findings, but her manuscripts were repeatedly rejected.

At a meeting of the Society of Epidemiological Research in 1990, Berge attended a presentation of research by another graduate student working with the group. Concluding that her own work had been plagiarized, Berge filed charges with UAB. Two investigations found her allegations to be baseless. Berge then secured copies of UAB grant applications through the Freedom of Information Act and, rather than going to the Office of Research Integrity of the federal government, next filed a federal lawsuit alleging extensive wrongdoing by UAB in its annual progress reports filed with the National Institutes of Health, including 'submerging' her work and countenancing plagiarism of it by a graduate student. The basis for her lawsuit is an old, Civil War-era statute known as the 'Lincoln Law' after the president who advocated for it. The law is designed to reward those who helped

---

Continued ➤

BOX 15.4   *(continued)*

bring miscreants to justice by reporting (blowing the whistle, as it were) those profiteering in supplying to the government, originally those selling defective items to the Union Army.

After a 10-day jury trial, a decision was rendered in Berge's favour, the jury effectively agreeing that she had been robbed, and awarding $1.65 million in damages, of which $489 000 was to go directly to Berge plus an additional $215 000 in punitive damages.

UAB appealed. While this process had been unfolding, the Office of Inspector General of the federal agency heard of the lawsuit that Berge had filed, and conducted a separate investigation, to assess whether the office should be prosecuting the matter as a federal crime. That investigation reported 'no evidence' of criminal violations in either grant applications or progress reports. It went on to say that many of Berge's assumptions behind her allegations were 'in error or exaggerations of the truth'. However, this report never made its way into evidence at the federal trial on Berge's charges.

When the UAB appeal came up, the earlier court judgment was entirely reversed. In its decision, the appeals court rejected all of her claims, saying that 'once the surface is scratched, there is nothing to Berge's claim except her complaint that Fowler [the other graduate student] did not give Berge's work the notice she felt it deserved'. The court went on to say, 'we also decide that no responsible jury could conclude that a multi-million dollar grant, continually renewed over a period of more than a decade, undertaken by three internationally-respected scientists engaged, in part, in the collection of the world's leading database on CMV, would be reduced or eliminated due to UAB's lack of expertise in an area that could only be bolstered by the work of an unknown graduate student in nutritional sciences – work that when reviewed by independent scientists at peer-reviewed journals was determined to be "scarcely comprehensible … extremely difficult to read and even more difficult to evaluate … and so cavalier in its design and conduct as to induce great skepticism in any findings reported from it." The hubris of any graduate student to think that such grants depend on the results of her work is beyond belief.'[37]

This should be no surprise, because it makes sense on two levels. First, those who commit research misconduct have frequently been found to be guilty of financial or other improprieties; the evidence is that a person who cuts corners in one arena (say, recording data points) is more likely to be taking shortcuts in another as well. A clear example of this is Mark Spector, who fabricated research results; by the time the magnitude of his scientific fraud was fully revealed, other unsavoury aspects of his conduct had also come to light: he did not hold the undergraduate degree he claimed, he was engaged in passing bad cheques, etc. As described by Kohn[3] (pp. 208–10):

'After the forgery had been exposed, Spector's credentials were checked. It was found that, as a student in Cincinnati, he had been sentenced to a suspended prison term for forging his employer's signature on two cheques made out to himself. Another investigation revealed that a paper Spector had published with C. Douglas Winget was also under suspicion of having been fabricated by Spector …When the wrongdoing of Spector became evident, Winget tried in vain to replicate this exciting experiment. This was thus another footprint in Spector's falsification trail.'

Second, once relationships have frayed and a sinister attribution bias kicks in, it is easy to see wrong at every turn.

The sheer complexity of such a situation is dismaying to those in the hierarchy who simply see a total mess that could be avoided (they hope) if they simply 'kill the messenger' by casting out the troublemaker who is raising these undesirable points in an apparently unseemly fashion.

Whistleblowers are frequently wrong. Furthermore, would-be whistleblowers are frequently – in fact, usually – mistaken. In most organizations, the vast majority of complaints filed are not substantiated upon investigation. That is, complaints arise because of misunderstandings, personality conflicts, incomplete information, and the like. Because most allegations are not substantiated or are disproven, it increases the difficulty of the true whistleblower who is correctly raising a concern, as the expectation among those to whom he complains is that he has simply got things wrong.

One of us (CKG) was personally responsible for receiving allegations of misconduct for a period of almost eight years on the campus of a major US research university with more than 30 000 students. From records of four years of that time (1989–93), annually somewhere between 80 and 90 concerns about the integrity of research were brought to the central campus office responsible for receiving such complaints. As background, the USA uses a two-part system for reviewing allegations of misconduct: for those charges that rise to the level of the definition of misconduct (as opposed to disputes, misunderstandings, and items not covered by the policies on misconduct), first an 'inquiry' is conducted as a form of triage. This is supposed to be a structured, although relatively quick, review of the charges. Those that demonstrate sufficient grounds then move on to a more legalistic and formal procedure known as an 'investigation'.

Of the questions and concerns handled in that four-year period, only 14 of the 80–90 contacts for assistance led to 'cases' processed under the university's academic integrity policy. The majority were inquiries that ended the matter there. Three of the proceedings were full-fledged formal investigations, each preceded by an inquiry. In that time, there was one official finding of research misconduct. Put another way, of the problems brought to attention annually, three to five were judged as sufficiently serious or credible to require inquiries under the procedures generally adopted in the USA following federal guidelines, and of those, one investigation resulted every other year. Only one of the investigations resulted in a finding of research misconduct according to the prevailing legal definition.

At the same time, in the cases that did not result in a finding of misconduct, most featured recommendations that aspects of the conduct of the questioned researchers were found lacking in expected professionalism in research or mentoring. Such shortcomings in conduct were addressed through other mechanisms than sanctions for research misconduct, such as retraining in good practice, increased oversight, or restrictions of privileges.

Although these numbers are not formal, they seem to agree with other numbers that are reported in an informal fashion, as well as with the information in the USA of cases overseen by the federal research-funding agencies. For example, in the same period of time as covered by the informal Gunsalus numbers, the National Science Foundation reported 222 cases, of which 10 resulted in federal investigations and 30 were investigated by the home institutions of the researchers, and there were eight investigations that both federal and institutional officials investigated. In that time, four cases resulted in formal findings of misconduct. The Office of Research Integrity (ORI) (using a different metric for reporting) reported receiving 'around 200' allegations per year, of which 30 became formal investigations each year, while at the same time, about 20–30 cases were 'closed' (apparently, the cases closed could be from the same or previous years). In any given year, in that era, ORI reported that it closed 50% of its cases with findings of misconduct. Since that time, they have revamped their procedures, and numbers are now kept more precisely. The volume of concerns and complaints seems to be rising in the wake of continued publicity about research misconduct and greater awareness of reporting mechanisms. ORI, for example, reported its highest caseload ever in 2006.[12,13]

The fact that complainants are frequently wrong makes sense. It is often difficult, especially for someone at the bottom of a hierarchy, to have access to full information about a given situation. Imagine a junior scientist lodging a complaint about having been denied credit for his or her work on a project. Frequently, that person will be intimately familiar with his or her own labours, but have no clue about the work of others in the group, the history of the project (which may be lengthy), its funding arrangements, or the efforts of collaborators in other locations. It is easy to over-appreciate the role that one has played oneself and to downplay the work of others.

How big is the problem? Unfortunately, we do not know how common such acts or persons are. In spite of a number of ingenious proposals over the years for assessing the true incidence of serious acts of research misconduct, the scientific community has vigorously resisted such scientific efforts, even though they were proposed solely to establish prevalence rates of gross misconduct, and were specifically designed to be brief cross-sectional studies, and *not* to be a way of policing science on any continuing basis.[14,15] We are left instead with a series of surveys asking questions such as whether an individual is 'aware' of a range of various research misdeeds. Most of these surveys take no account of multiple reports of the same act, nor do they use precise or even common definitions of what constitutes research misconduct. Because of that, we have difficulty placing any reliance on them. Nonetheless, for the sake of completeness, we note that the range of misdeeds that they report range from under 2% for six of the top 10 'misbehaviours' (although, in that survey, 33% of respondents said they had engaged in at least one of the top 10 misbehaviours during the previous three years) to between 44% and 50% of respondents having personal knowledge of two or more types of misconduct.[16,17]

A growing problem. The number of complaints arising from interaction problems will always be larger than the number of validated cases of research misconduct. Most cases that become formal reviews of conduct will involve significant animosity among the parties by the time they require investigation, so the need for rigour in assessing allegations and professional conduct is intense. It is impossible to know how many of the complaints that come forward have substance to them and are yet not properly reviewed. Similarly, we cannot know how many complaints never come forward because of the known costs of whistleblowing. What we do know is that few significant cases of research misconduct have ever been discovered *except* through the actions of whistleblowers.

At the most serious end of the spectrum, whistleblowers have brought to light clinical findings that have affected treatment protocols nationwide based on fictitious patients (Breuning) or enrolled patients in trials when the patients did not fit the protocols.[18,19] Numerous cases (Darsee, Long, Slutsky, and Poehlman) would have distorted the research record, the continuing progress of science, and ultimately the treatment of patients. Fabricated or falsified data that make their way into print lead to a misuse of resources, energy, and the hopes of investigators in fruitless attempts to replicate and build upon that work (see Kohn,[3] p. 104). Plagiarism deprives the rightful authors of credit for their work, and advances frauds at the expense of others. These are effects from which the community of scholars deserves and needs to be shielded. Whistleblowers are the ones who make that possible. That they are difficult to deal with and often wrong does not change this calculus.

As we have said, people who are prepared to blow the whistle when they identify misconduct, and are prepared to fight the subsequent battle, tend to have prickly personalities – made more prickly by the reaction that their whistleblowing provokes. On the organizational side, and making things worse, it is rare for institutions to have the expertise to provide a rigorous, credible investigation, as running a structured, analytical review process that meets all legal and scientific standards in a quarrel about scientific data is hugely demanding. In our experience, this is not often achieved – and this in a country with decades of experience with an official, national policy that must be followed to sustain a finding of research misconduct. A 1998 study by the ORI documents the challenge:[20]

> 'ORI conducted a content analysis of 21 inquiry reports that were not submitted to the Office of Research Integrity because an investigation was not recommended and ORI had not previously requested the report. ... This study demonstrated that more than half of the institutional inquiry reports that were not submitted to ORI were significantly deficient. Fifty-seven percent of the reports did not contain the information required to establish PHS jurisdiction. Thirty-three percent contained information on no more than four of the nine criteria used to determine whether an investigation was warranted and another 28 percent were marginal, covering only five criteria. Seventy-one percent provided information on only three or fewer criteria for determining compliance with the regulation. And finally, 57 percent of the reports did not contain the detailed information required to justify the decision that an investigation is unwarranted.'

Kay Fields, a senior scientist in the Division of Investigative Oversight at the US Office of Research Integrity (ORI), confirms that recent years have seen little improvement. She comments that 'only very rarely do we receive a report from an institution, as required by Federal policy, that is sufficiently complete to assess on the first round whether the finding arrived at by the institution can be sustained. Typically, we must request additional information, and sometimes additional investigation, to develop a conclusion about the sustainability of the finding'.[21] This state of affairs can be understood when reflecting upon how infrequently individual universities are called upon to conduct the most serious investigations, how often administrative staff members turn over, and the brevity of the half-life of organizational memory. Alan Price, former Director of the Division of Investigative Oversight at the US Office of Research Integrity, now a private consultant, comments that 'most of the Research Integrity Officers at research institutions that we worked with and/or trained in the 1990s have retired or moved on from their positions, leaving a generation of RIOs to be educated in what ORI wants and needs in investigation reports, admission statements, and documentation'.[22]

We are left having to rely on whistleblowers, so we must change our attitudes. The scientific community will not allow research into the incidence of scientific misconduct, and daily audit to flag serious misconduct is ponderous and would raise all sorts of practical and social issues. At the same time, much clinical research is not replicated. Journal peer review, which starts with the assumption that authors are doing their best to tell the truth, is well-nigh useless as a way of revealing misconduct, because the editors and reviewers are not in the authors' laboratory. So, we are left with whistleblowers to alert us to serious problems. Unfortunately, when problems arise, the procedural path forward for such individuals is often not clear, and their reception is often hostile. The irony of our instinctive responses is that we resist this knowledge, even when knowing about problems is clearly in our best interests, both inside the research organization where the problem arises and for the larger research community that depends upon the veracity of reports for continued forward progress. It should be obvious that we must change our attitudes and responses to whistleblowers if we are to move ahead.

Practical advice for responding to whistleblowers

Policies and people

Responding effectively, professionally, and responsibly in the face of the myriad challenges presented by a whistleblower boils down to a realistic set of policies implemented by sensible people. Part of such a response to whistleblowers requires that we understand conceptually the problems discussed above and be prepared to counteract the natural impulses that can lead us and our research institutions astray. The central point that we must understand, accept, and make part of all our actions is that, at several critical junctures, our intuitive response will be the wrong one.

Provide clear guidance: policies, procedures, protections, and resources

The organizational dynamics that we have already mentioned vastly complicate the effective receipt and processing of reports from whistleblowers. Not only do all these elements muddle and blunt a strong institutional response, but the underlying conflict that often leads to allegations being lodged in the first place is also likely to be a confounding factor. Many people, already distrusting a story from a dislikeable complainant, will recoil from the unpleasantness of it all and hope to avoid it.

In addition to all this, there are the problems that occur when the institution's policies are not clear or helpful, and do not take account of the barriers that the institutional structure can present to those who wish to bring potential wrongdoing to light. For example, most working scientists are unlikely to know what policy applies to their particular concerns, or where to report them.

Devise institutional responses understanding the concerns of the whistleblower

For the organization wanting to ensure the integrity of research done under its auspices, it pays to consider these situations from both sides. The person with low power in the institution, and whose future is often at the mercy of his or her supervisor(s), faces a difficult and challenging path. At the same time, especially if the matter is a fundamental one of ethics, members of the institution may feel a strong obligation to address it. Indeed, institutional policies may require reporting of serious concerns. It should be borne in mind that research suggests that employees go to external authorities 'only once they come to believe that internal channels are closed to them, that the organization is not moral, and that senior management is inert or complicit in the wrongdoing'.[23]

When developing institutional policies, it is helpful to imagine that you are a junior scientist who begins to have concerns about data in the laboratory in which you work. What should you do? How do you chart a reasonable professional course? Where do you get advice? Who can help you make a reasonable cost-benefit analysis for each course of action? Each of these questions should have clear and available answers, and resources to assist in sorting out a solid, professional approach.

Make policies and help easy to find

There should be a website and brochures or other documents that explain the institution's policies on misconduct, including definitions of what is considered against the rules, how to report misconduct, what protections are provided against retaliation, and other related matters (Box 15.5). Resource people – those who can advise and guide anyone with concerns – should be clearly identified and should be readily accessible. It does little good to provide an office to advise those with concerns if the office is not staffed or is not open. Not only must the policies be clear and accessible, but they should also be provided to each person who raises a concern, so each knows fully his or her options.

BOX 15.5   **Useful institutional policies**

- Research misconduct (definitions and procedures)
- Responsible professional conduct (see sample below)
- Support resources for employees (see UCSF plan)
- Non-retaliation for bringing information to light (see sample definitions)
- Workplace violence (information for employees on what to do in the event that they feel threatened by physical violence)

Sample policy on non-retaliation: University of California San Francisco, excerpt on policy[40]

'*Reporting allegations of suspected improper governmental activities* – Any person may report allegations of suspected improper governmental activities. Allegations of suspected improper governmental activities may also be reported anonymously. Further details on the role, rights, and responsibilities of the Whistleblower can be found in Section IV A of this policy.

A. **Making reports** – The University recommends that any reports by persons who are not University employees be made to UCSF's Whistleblower Coordinator (see Section IV A). Normally, a report by a University employee of allegations of a suspected improper governmental activity should be made to the reporting employee's immediate supervisor or other appropriate administrator within the operating unit. However, in the interest of confidentiality when there is a potential conflict of interest or for other reasons, such report may be made to the Whistleblower Coordinator or another University manager who may reasonably be expected to review the alleged improper governmental activity on behalf of the University. All University employees, and especially academic or staff employees in management roles, should be aware of and alert to any communications that may constitute reports of allegations of suspected improper governmental activity and be prepared to refer such reports to the Whistleblower Coordinator.

B. **Retaliation protection** – The rights and protections of University employees and applicants for employment when making protected disclosures are covered by the Policy for Protection of Whistleblowers from Retaliation and Guidelines for Reviewing Retaliation Complaints.[41] Below is a summary of the local implementation:

Filing complaints – UCSF is committed to protecting employees and applicants for employment from interference with making a protected disclosure, or retaliation for having made a protected disclosure, or for having refused an illegal order as defined in this policy. A retaliation complaint (grievance plus sworn statement) may be filed under an applicable grievance or complaint resolution procedure, or with the Whistleblower Coordinator, or with the employee's supervisor. Employees who elect to file a grievance unaccompanied by a sworn statement made under penalty of perjury that its contents are true or

BOX 15.5 *(continued)*

are believed to be true are not covered by the retaliation provisions of the California Whistleblower Protection Act. The complainant must file the complaint within 12 months and must sufficiently detail facts to support the allegation.

Whistleblower Coordinator – The Whistleblower Coordinator accepts and reviews all retaliation complaints and administers local processes related to investigation and resolution of retaliation complaints. Where appropriate, the Whistleblower Coordinator refers matters to existing grievance procedures and reviews conclusions and remedies for cases heard through existing grievance procedures. The Whistleblower Coordinator may also refer a complaint to a designated Retaliation Complaint Officer for fact-finding where a grievance process is not appropriate. In such cases, the Whistleblower Coordinator receives and acts on fact-finding reports submitted by retaliation complaint investigations.

Retaliation Complaint Officers – Under the direction of the Whistleblower Coordinator, designated Retaliation Complaint Officers (RCOs) ensure a competent investigation is conducted on the allegation of retaliation or interference. The RCO works with the Whistleblower Coordinator to ensure the following:

- existing grievance procedures, where applicable, allow for adequate investigation and report of RCO findings on the allegations; or,
- hearing officers or arbitrators, where applicable, adequately cover the allegations; or
- a competent and timely fact-finding is conducted on allegations that are not appropriately handled by existing grievance processes. The RCO shall present findings of fact to the Whistleblower Coordinator within 120 days unless an extension is granted by the Coordinator.

The designated RCOs for UCSF are:

- Campus Human Resources Director for staff employees on campus;
- Assistant Director for Human Resources for staff employees in the Medical Center;
- Director of Faculty Relations for academic employees, including faculty;
- Director of Student Relations for students.

C. State Auditor – Reports of allegations of suspected improper governmental activities may be made to the State Auditor. Under the law, the State Auditor is prohibited from disclosing the identity of a whistleblower unless he or she obtains the whistleblower's permission to do so, or when the disclosure is to a law enforcement agency that is conducting a criminal investigation.'

Continued ➤

BOX 15.5   *(continued)*

Sample policy on responsible professional conduct: University of Illinois at Urbana–Champaign policies on academic integrity[42]

'The University of Illinois is dedicated to learning and research and hence is committed to truth and accuracy. Integrity and intellectual honesty in scholarship and scientific investigation are, therefore, of paramount importance. It is the responsibility of the faculty and staff to maintain high ethical standards of professional integrity.

Responsible professional conduct: guidelines for teaching, research, and service
The Faculty Senate has endorsed the following set of guidelines for the campus.

Members of the University of Illinois at Urbana–Champaign campus community are expected to adhere to the highest standards of professional conduct in carrying out their teaching, research, service, and other professional responsibilities. Such conduct is subject to norms and ethical codes that vary somewhat among disciplines, as well as to differing individual perceptions and interpretations; but certain general ethical guidelines reflecting the commitment of the campus to these standards are applicable to all faculty, staff and graduate assistants on the Urbana–Champaign campus.

Some types of conduct, expressly forbidden by University rules and regulations (see, e.g., University of Illinois Policy and Procedures on Academic Integrity in Research and Publication, Policy and Procedures for Addressing Discrimination and Harassment, and University of Illinois Policy on Conflicts of Interest and Commitment) may have severe consequences. Others, not formally proscribed, are nonetheless properly included among the matters to which campus standards of professional conduct apply. Some are addressed in the formalized codes of ethics some disciplines have adopted or are reflected in prevailing practices in various disciplines. Where the University's standards surpass such other norms, it is the University's standards to which members of the campus community are expected to adhere.

The following guidelines relate to activities involved in fulfilling instructional responsibilities, in acquiring and using data in the course of conducting research, in authoring scholarly publications, and in interacting professionally with other individuals on this campus and elsewhere. No set of guidelines can cover all of the kinds of cases to which professional ethical considerations apply. Moreover, the interpretation of specific guidelines in actual situations may be uncertain, and the assessment of complex situations to which a number of different standards and other important considerations apply may be difficult. Those who find themselves faced with such further problems in these areas of academic life should seek the advice and counsel of campus and professional colleagues and appropriate administrators who may be able to offer advice or suggest actions to mitigate the problem.

BOX 15.5   *(continued)*

Instructional responsibilities
Members of academic units have a fundamental obligation to respect the dignity of all students and to foster their intellectual growth and development.

(a) Faculty members should explain at the beginning of each course the grading criteria to be used and the requirements for successful completion of the coursework. Such criteria and requirements should be clear and should be applied consistently and fairly.

(b) Faculty members should ensure that students are provided feedback and guidance to facilitate their academic progress.

(c) Faculty members should acknowledge sources of and observe copyright for materials prepared for course distribution.

(d) In any student–faculty collaboration, the intellectual contributions of the student should be fully and appropriately acknowledged.

Handling of data
Individuals conducting research are obligated to record and preserve data in a manner that accurately reflects the work done, and that allows appropriate scrutiny and evaluation of those data.

(a) Falsification of data, fabrication of data, and unacknowledged appropriation of the data of others are unethical; they are also violations of the University's academic integrity policy.

(b) Data (including source materials) should be retained for an appropriate length of time after publication so that they are available for inspection by collaborators or, when appropriate, by other qualified individuals.

(c) Data should never be withheld from collaborators except for purposes integral to the project.

(d) Individuals conducting research should consider carefully all results, including those that do not fit research expectations.

Authorship, attribution of credit, and other publication practices
Authors should conform to formally promulgated and/or generally observed standards and practices for authorship and attribution of credit in their disciplines.

(a) Plagiarism is unethical and is a violation of the University's academic integrity policy.

(b) Authorship should be accorded to those who contribute both actively and meaningfully to a study.

(c) Authors (including co-authors) have responsibility for their publications and should respond in an appropriate forum to legitimate inquiries about their data, methods, or interpretations.

Continued ➤

BOX 15.5 *(continued)*

(d) Authors should adhere to the standards and requirements of journals to which they submit manuscripts, particularly with respect to simultaneous submissions and originality of research.

(e) Authors should acknowledge funding sources that support their research.

(f) Authors should publish only those findings that result from careful consideration of the materials under study and, when appropriate, replication or verification of the study.

(g) Authors should present in publications of experimental research sufficient information about methodology to permit others to repeat or extend the work.

Professional conduct

Members of the University community must honor contractual obligations in teaching, research, public service, and other professional responsibilities. They should further conduct themselves in a professional and collegial manner in all dealings with each other.

(a) Members of academic units should provide an environment for professional development of all staff.

(b) Individuals assessing the work of others should base their assessments on appropriate professional criteria. Due to the inherent conflicts of interest, no individual should initiate or participate in institutional or educational decisions involving a direct benefit or penalty to a person with whom that individual has or has had a sexual relationship.

(c) Members of academic units should seek collegial resolution of professional disputes.

(d) Individuals engaged in teaching, research, or public service should respect and abide by legitimate and reasonable requests for confidentiality.

(e) Individuals conducting research have an obligation to follow procedures that assure the ethical treatment of human subjects and animals, as well as applicable regulations.

(f) Individuals engaged in research and teaching should understand and comply with pertinent regulations for health and safety in the workplace; should see to it that students and collaborators in learning or research projects understand and comply with these regulations; and should work to minimize risks to health and safety in the learning or research environment.

(g) Individuals conducting research should spend research monies in ways consistent with the goals stated in contract documents.

(h) Individuals conducting research and/or the officials of their administrative units have an obligation to keep clear records of expenditures and to make these records available to appropriate parties.'

BOX 15.6   **Resources for whistleblowers**

The UK Research Integrity Office (UKRIO)

Part of the Programme of Work for UKRIO is to provide 'help-line and guidance for those involved in allegations and concerns over the conduct of research in health and biomedical sciences'.

From its website:[43]

'The Office is available to provide guidance to those who wish to raise concerns or seek advice on any aspect relating to the conduct of research. The Office will receive requests for guidance on the Office Helpline or in Emails, fax or written format. On receiving requests for guidance the Office will fulfil an impartial advisory role, ensuring that the most appropriate advice and guidance is made available from the Office Team or through the Register of Advisers.'

Public Concern at Work[44]

Public Concern at Work (PCaW) is an independent authority on public interest whistleblowing. It was established as a charity in 1993 following a series of scandals and disasters. PCaW has played a leading role in putting whistleblowing on the governance agenda and in influencing the content of legislation both in the UK and abroad.

PCaW promotes compliance with the law and good practice in organizations across all sectors. In practical terms, it focuses on the responsibility of workers to raise concerns about malpractice and on the accountability of those in charge to investigate and remedy such issues. It does this by:

- offering free advice to people who are concerned about danger or malpractice in the workplace but who are unsure whether or how to raise the matter;
- providing compliance toolkits, training, and consultancy on accountability in organizations and on self-regulatory and regulatory cultures;
- influencing public policy through research and educational activities.

The Government Accountability Project (GAP), USA[45]

GAP's mission is to protect the public interest by promoting government and corporate accountability through advancing occupational free speech and ethical conduct, litigating whistleblower cases, publicizing whistleblower concerns, and developing policy and legal reforms of whistleblower laws. GAP was founded in 1977 as a non-profit, public-interest organization. Its national office has been in Washington, DC since the institution's inception (a Seattle office was opened in 1992).

GAP's major programme initiatives focus on both government and corporate accountability related to nuclear oversight, food and drug safety, worker health and safety, international reform, and national security. It develops whistleblower laws and policy reform both domestically and internationally. GAP also conducts

Continued ➤

BOX 15.6 *(continued)*

an accredited legal clinic for law students, and offers a year-round internship programme for undergraduates and law students.

'How to blow the whistle and still have a career afterwards'
This is the title of an article by CK Gunsalus[46] that is specifically directed at those in the scientific community concerned about research misconduct. It can be provided to whistleblowers as a useful resource.

Whistleblower's Bill of Rights
In late 1995, the Commission on Research Integrity of the US Public Health Service drew up a list of the rights and responsibilities of whistleblowers (in their 'Whistleblower's Bill of Rights'). They proposed that retaliation against a whistleblower be defined as a form of misconduct, and that institutions had a duty to protect whistleblowers by giving them relief against reprisals and by holding those who retaliate accountable. Institutions should give whistleblowers, who often have special expertise, the opportunity to comment on relevant information during the process. The process must be timely, whistleblowers must assist it, and, at its conclusion, institutions have a responsibility to credit whistleblowers whose allegations are substantiated. At the same time, the whistleblower must allow the process an opportunity to function, while maintaining confidentiality, and must understand the consequences for those they accuse, and be prepared to correct their own errors.

Responsible Whistleblowing: A Whistleblower's Bill of Rights[1]
   (a) **Communication:** Whistleblowers are free to disclose lawfully whatever information supports a reasonable belief of research misconduct as it is defined by PHS policy. An individual or institution that retaliates against any person making protected disclosures engages in prohibited obstruction of investigations of research misconduct as defined by the Commission on Research Integrity. Whistleblowers must respect the confidentiality of sensitive information and give legitimate institutional structures an opportunity to function. Should a whistleblower elect to make a lawful disclosure that violates institutional rules of confidentiality, the institution may thereafter legitimately limit the whistleblower's access to further information about the case.
   (b) **Protection from retaliation:** Institutions have a duty not to tolerate or engage in retaliation against good-faith whistleblowers. This duty includes providing appropriate and timely relief to ameliorate the consequences of actual or threatened reprisals, and holding accountable those who retaliate. Whistleblowers and other witnesses to possible research misconduct have a responsibility to raise their concerns honorably and with foundation.
   (c) **Fair procedures:** Institutions have a duty to provide fair and objective procedures for examining and resolving complaints, disputes, and allega-

BOX 15.6   *(continued)*

tions of research misconduct. In cases of alleged retaliation that are not resolved through institutional intervention, whistleblowers should have an opportunity to defend themselves in a proceeding where they can present witnesses and confront those they charge with retaliation against them, except when they violate rules of confidentiality. Whistleblowers have a responsibility to participate honorably in such procedures by respecting the serious consequences for those they accuse of misconduct, and by using the same standards to correct their own errors that they apply to others.

(d) **Procedures free from partiality:** Institutions have a duty to follow procedures that are not tainted by partiality arising from personal or institutional conflict of interest or other sources of bias. Whistleblowers have a responsibility to act within legitimate institutional channels when raising concerns about the integrity of research. They have the right to raise objections concerning the possible partiality of those selected to review their concerns without incurring retaliation.

(e) **Information:** Institutions have a duty to elicit and evaluate fully and objectively information about concerns raised by whistleblowers. Whistleblowers may have unique knowledge needed to evaluate thoroughly responses from those whose actions are questioned. Consequently, a competent investigation may involve giving whistleblowers one or more opportunities to comment on the accuracy and completeness of information relevant to their concerns, except when they violate rules of confidentiality.

(f) **Timely processes:** Institutions have a duty to handle cases involving alleged research misconduct as expeditiously as is possible without compromising responsible resolutions. When cases drag on for years, the issue becomes the dispute rather than its resolution. Whistleblowers have a responsibility to facilitate expeditious resolution of cases by good faith participation in misconduct procedures.

(g) **Vindication:** At the conclusion of proceedings, institutions have a responsibility to credit promptly – in public and/or in private as appropriate – those whose allegations are substantiated.

It is in the research institution's best interest to learn of problems early when they are most amenable to intervention and correction. This is best for the whistleblowers as well. Beyond the institution's own policies, there are resources available for whistleblowers that include step-by-step ways to think about the process; organizations should be familiar with such resources, and provide links to them (Box 15.6).

Provide choices for reporting

It is essential to provide an array of choices to the would-be whistleblower: if there is only one place to lodge a complaint, and that place is with the very person about whom the whistleblower has a concern, that will squelch the report at the beginning – or send it to outside venues such as reporters, external investigators, funding agencies, or politicians. None of these avenues are truly in the best interests of the organization or the whistleblower, so the most fundamental guideline is to provide an array of entry points for those with concerns to raise and explore their concerns. This means that not only should an employee always be able to go to a designated office (e.g. a research integrity office) to report a concern, but also it should be possible for that person to go to an ombudsman, a student advice office, the department head or dean, and so forth. Each of these offices will need training and support for how to recognize a research integrity problem, as well as instructions on what to do when one arises. In the best practice, coordination among all the possible points of entry occurs on an ongoing basis, so that one-time training does not attenuate over time.

Do not make reporting a duty

Some organizations have policies that impose a duty (often described as an ethical duty) to report wrongdoing. While this is fine in theory, in practice this is useless advice and will only lead to disdain for the rules. However desirable it would be to think that we live in a world where all problems can and must be reported, this is not realistic. Given the severe consequences that whistleblowers face in reality (remember: people do not like 'tattletales'), sometimes it is simply not realistic to raise the concern. The broader the consequences of the wrongdoing, of course, the more compelling the need for reporting becomes – and the more potentially severe are the consequences. One study found that whistleblowers reporting on systemic organizational corruption or major activity (i.e. misconduct that involves over $100 000 in losses and that is occurring frequently) are the most likely to experience organizational reprisals.[21]

If a whistleblower discovers a fraud in a clinical trial affecting the treatment of patients, the ethical imperative to report is high – and so may be the potential costs of the action. On the other hand, if a summer research intern or early master's programme student discovers minor fudging of data by a powerful superior – and especially if the organization is not well organized to receive and process complaints efficiently – common sense and survival skills might suggest simply leaving the laboratory as quickly as possible.

Do not promise confidentiality to a whistleblower when you might not be able to honour the promise

Some members of an organization, by virtue of their duties, will have an obligation to report once they become aware of possible malfeasance. For example, the person who signs as being responsible for a research grant is obligated to pursue evidence of misuse of funds or harm to subjects of research. The officer of the university responsible for compliance with grant or safety regulations has a similar reporting responsibility. Thus, there is an inbuilt collision between the obligation to pursue information about possibly serious wrongdoing and wanting to promise a confidential haven to a person in distress who is seeking advice. No unequivocal assurance of confidentiality made to a whistleblower can be honoured when information emerges in its midst about a potential violation that must be investigated. Every person who serves as an entry point for complaints should be thoroughly trained about these constraints.

Take steps to prevent retaliation against the whistleblower

In the most serious cases, retaliation against whistleblowers is often taken by the very institutional officials responsible for the overall environment.[24,25] All individuals involved – and especially the accused – must be cautioned early and frequently not to take any adverse actions against the person bringing charges. All individuals affected by the allegations (accused, witnesses, and officials) should be cautioned explicitly to avoid even the appearance of retaliation in word or action. (For example, an impermissible remark would be 'We're all having to go to these ridiculous meetings because Marjory here is so thick that she cannot interpret the data' – which could be as harmful as slashing the tyres of the whistleblower or suspending him from work.) If disciplinary action is under way at the time the charges are made, the university should have a procedure for suspending, or at the very least reviewing, the discipline while the charges are examined, and should consider arresting any discharge or other steps. This will require not only legal advice, but also some common sense.

The whistleblower should be able to bring a companion to meetings, much as the seriously ill are often advised to bring a companion to medical visits: having along a person who is more impartial can assist in hearing what is said more clearly and remembering it better. The whistleblower is likely to be under severe stress, and may neither hear nor remember very clearly. These situations carry a high cognitive load, and whatever can be done to lower the stress and increase the likelihood of measured responses should be done.

The whistleblower and his or her companion should also be cautioned to maintain a professional demeanour and should be clearly reminded of the rules during an investigation: it is best, for example, for the whistleblower (and advocates) to avoid contact as much as is feasible with the accused or witnesses in the investigation. This both reduces friction and any suggestion of attempting to tamper with the investigation. If the witnesses are all in the same laboratory, they and the accused should be cautioned not to discuss the investigation and should be given guidance about how, realistically, to do that. If animosity is running high, it may be wise to devise some creative strategy to separate people, and to consult with individuals trained in conflict resolution about how to manage relations to maximum positive effect. If there is a politic way to advise the whistleblower about the difficult dynamic of the situation, that should also be done. One of the books on the trials of whistleblowers starts with the quote, 'I've learned two things from being a whistleblower. When you go out in public, do not cry and do not talk like your hair is on fire. If you do, no one will listen. It makes them uncomfortable' (Alford,[5] p. ix). This is an important truth about the emotional environment of misconduct allegations – and the more the whistleblower understands this and can behave accordingly, the better things will go for all, and especially for the whistleblower. Of course, at the same time, the accused must be cautioned to avoid vindictive conduct and to steer clear of investigators outside the formal process, and should be as balanced as possible, too.

The whistleblower should be assigned one point of contact for information on the process of reviewing the allegations, to whom any additional evidence or information can be provided, and who can assist should any perceived acts of retaliation occur. This should be a person who can be both neutral, and will be perceived as such by the whistleblower, and also someone possessing sufficient authority to intervene in the event that retaliatory actions are taken. (Similar steps should be taken for the accused, but this chapter is not about those precautions.) Continuing efforts to keep the whistleblower informed as to the state of the review, for example weekly or so, can assist the whistleblower in maintaining a professional equilibrium.[26] All steps that can signal to the whistleblower that a measured, even-handed review is under way will bring a payoff in increased trust, and likelihood of complying with the process, and will reduce the personal toll.

Assign responsibilities carefully

The person selected for receiving, assessing, and investigating complaints must be selected as much for character traits as for professional credentials. Not only must the person assigned these responsibilities be reputable and have credibility among the researchers who will be interacting with the office (whether as witnesses, panel members, administrators, complainants, or respondents to allegations), but he or she must also have a personality that is sufficiently robust not to wilt in the face of conflict and unpleasantness. He or she must have the ability to put aside other duties to devote sufficient time when a significant investigation requires it. Many research organizations have foundered in their responses to allegations when they have responded slowly and the investigation has dragged on past reason. A diligent administrator who is nonetheless slow to respond will compound the difficult situations that allegations of wrongdoing can present: the stressed whistleblower will become more and more distraught as time passes and will become more likely to take steps to get others involved.

The person managing the process should be advised to take some time to acquaint himself or herself with the research literature on conflict resolution and managing anger in conflict situations, as this can be most helpful in recognizing patterns of reaction and constructive responses to them (see Allred,[9] pp. 238–40).

Devise systems for separating personalities from facts. Train those responsible for conducting and presiding over investigations

Experience in dealing with the problems of misconduct investigations, buttressed by research in social psychology and conflict resolution, demonstrates that many problems can be avoided, or at least minimized, through awareness of the cognitive biases that infect human interactions and of the places where misconduct investigations tend to go awry. This includes acknowledging the difficulties in being impartial in assessing facts when allegations are brought, and the difficulty of protecting from retaliation those who have brought allegations.

In the USA, a series of programmes, starting with ad hoc seminars hosted by the American Association for the Advancement of Science, the Association of American

Medical Colleges, federal agencies, and other higher education associations provided early training for institutional officials. Over time, the federal agencies responsible for overseeing integrity in federally funded research have begun providing such programmes. Given turnover in administrative positions and the natural attrition of knowledge in the gaps between cases at any given institution, periodic training and reminders for those responsible for these procedures should be built into any system that may need to respond to whistleblowers.

What are the right questions to ask?

Asking the wrong questions almost always yields the wrong answers. When allegations of misconduct have been received, the correct question to ask is, 'How can we correctly assess the validity of these allegations in a way that will stand the test of time?' The question is *not*, 'How do we make this go away?' or 'How do we protect [fill in the blank here] from adverse repercussions of the allegation?' or 'What is the fastest way to conclude this mess?'

Two critical questions to ask frequently during the process are, 'What if this is true?' and 'What evidence would resolve these questions?'

Assess allegations consistently and even-handedly. Have a set of standards for assessing allegations

Ultimately, a review of allegations of misconduct must be rigorous: each judgement must rest on demonstrated and documented facts, not instincts or preferences. As reports of investigations are developed, the institution should build in a review process, much as scientists seek peer review of their work to validate it. An objective observer reviewing a draft report, for example, can often see holes, oversights, and other problems that the author(s) of a report might not see, having been too closely engaged in the work.

Protect against conflicts of interest

It is inevitable that members of the same institution, especially long-standing members, will have impressions about each other, as well as alliances and grudges. While those who know the setting and the research are best able to assess allegations, it is important to screen potential reviewers of allegations to protect to the maximum possible extent against conflicts of interest. Anyone who has been a direct collaborator of the accused or the whistleblower/accuser has a conflict of interest, and should not serve on a panel or as a reviewer of the allegations. Anyone with strong personal alliances or animosities should be avoided. (One of us (CKG), very early in her career, naively proposed that a scientist of Turkish national origin should serve on a panel reviewing allegations against a scientist originally from Greece. This was rectified before the investigation began, but in the interim, it was perceived as an attempt to predetermine the outcome of the investigation.) Similarly, anyone who has previously reviewed the charges and formed conclusions should be avoided: the goal is to achieve an objective, rigorous review of the facts. Taking shortcuts may well lead to a longer process if the original result is questioned and then must be redone.[27]

Seek professional support for investigations

A credible review of allegations of wrongdoing requires professional experience and expertise. Not only are there intuitive responses that are wrong at key points in investigations,[28] but there is much evidence that assessing truthfulness is extraordinarily difficult. Ekman's research, for example, demonstrates that even experienced law enforcement officers are no better than 50–50 at assessing credibility.[29] Moreover, advanced training in a technical field does not necessarily qualify an individual to conduct interviews or to assemble legally unassailable conclusions that may well affect the professional careers and reputations of those involved in investigative procedures. A bit of humility would help even the most brilliant academic tackle this new investigative field, with its own standards and protocols.

In many organizations, the people who have the inclination, training, and professional expertise to conduct a credible investigation are found in human resources or legal departments, in security divisions that do serious investigations into criminal activities, and in specialized law firms. These are individuals who encounter disgruntled employees with regularity. At base, a whistleblower is a disillusioned and disgruntled employee, whether from principle ('this is not right'), personal grudge, or some combination.

Whether the research organization 'grows its own' expertise through training already-trusted staff or secures consulting advice from others experienced in internal investigations, when the time comes for a formal investigation, it is critical to understand the need for professional expertise and to seek it out. The research organization must ensure that its decisions are credible, will withstand scrutiny (from funding agencies or the press), and will stand the tests of time.

Carpe data

One of the most important and overlooked steps is to secure original versions of all research data about which serious questions are being raised. In some situations, this is not of critical concern: in allegations of plagiarism, for example, original copies of manuscripts are rarely necessary to determine whether words or ideas have been used without proper attribution. On the other hand, it is often not possible to make a definitive determination of falsification or fabrication of research data without access to the original, primary data.

Conclusions

Even though whistleblowers are often wrong or misinformed, and can be annoying, they risk their careers to bring to light potential problems with the integrity of research. They must be respected not least because, in the context of research misconduct, they are the best (and often the only) mechanism for quality assurance that we have.

References

1. Commission on Research Integrity. *Integrity and Misconduct in Research: Report of the Commission on Research Integrity.* Washington, DC: US Department of Health and Human Services, Public Health Service, 1995.

2. Glazer MP, Glazer PM. *The Whistle-Blowers: Exposing Corruption in Government and Industry.* New York: Basic Books, 1989: 4.

3. Kohn A. *False Prophets. Fraud and Error in Science and Medicine.* Oxford: Basil Blackwell, 1986.

4. Rennie D. Editors and auditors. *JAMA* 1989; **261**: 2543–5.

5. Alford C. *Whistleblowers: Broken Lives and Organizational Power.* Ithaca, NY: Cornell University Press, 2001.

6. Thompson J, Baird P, Downie J. *The Olivieri Report: The Complete Text of the Report of the Independent Inquiry Commissioned by the Canadian Association of University Teachers.* Toronto: Lorimer, 2001.

7. Sprague RL. The voice of experience. *Sci Eng Ethics* 1998; **4**: 33–44.

8. Ross L. The intuitive psychologist and his shortcomings: distortions in the attribution process. In: Berkowitz L, ed. *Advances in Experimental Social Psychology,* Vol 10. New York: Academic Press, 1977: 173–200.

9. Allred K. Anger and retaliation in conflict: the role of attribution. In: Deutsch M, Coleman PT, eds. *The Handbook of Conflict Resolution: Theory and Practice.* San Francisco, CA: Jossey Bass, 2000: 236–55.

10. Gunsalus CK. Book review: *The Baltimore Case: A Trial of Politics, Science, and Character,* by Daniel J Kevles. *N Engl J Med* 1999; **340**: 242.

11. Chaiken S, Gruenfeld D, Judd C. Persuasion in negotiation and conflict situations. In: Deutsch M, Coleman PT, eds. *The Handbook of Conflict Resolution: Theory and Practice.* San Francisco, CA: Jossey Bass, 2000: 144–65.

12. Office of Research Integrity. *Debarments imposed on six respondants in 2005: Cases Forwarded to 2006 Highest in More than Decade.* Rockville, MD: Office of Research Integrity, US Department of Health and Human Services, 2006: 2. ori.dhhs.gov/documents/newsletters/vol14_no2.pdf.

13. Rhoades L; Office of Research Integrity. *ORI Closed Investigations into Misconduct Allegations Involving Research Supported by the Public Health Service: 1994–2003.* Rockville, MD: Office of Research Integrity, US Department of Health and Human Services, 2004. ori.dhhs.gov/publications/documents/Investigations1994–2003-2.pdf.

14. Rennie D. The editor: mark, dupe, patsy, accessory, weasel, and flatfoot. Presented at Conference on Ethics and Policy in Scientific Publication, National Academy of Sciences, Washington, DC, October 1988. In: *Ethics and Policy in Scientific Publication.* Bethesda, MD: Council of Biology Editors, 1990.

15. Rennie D. Proposals concerning the role of journals in preventing fraud and responding to allegations of fraud. Presented at AAAS–ABA National Conference of Lawyers and Scientists Project on Scientific Fraud and Misconduct. Report on Workshop Number Three. National Academy of Science and Engineering. Irvine, CA, 17–18 February 1989.

16. Martinson B, Anderson M, deVries R. Scientists behaving badly. *Nature* 2005; **435**: 737–8.

17. Swazey J, Anderson M, Louis KS. Ethical problems in academic research: a survey of doctoral candidates and faculty raises important questions about the ethical environment of graduate education and research. *Am Sci* 1993; **81**: 542–53.

18. Rennie D. Breast cancer: how to mishandle misconduct. *JAMA* 1994; **271**: 1205–7.

19. Office of Research Integrity. *Research Specialist Sentenced to Federal Prison for Almost Six Years.* Rockville, MD: US Department of Health and Human Services, 2006: 2. ori.dhhs.gov/documents/newsletter/vol14_no2.pdf.

20. Office of Research Integrity. *Study of Inquiry Reports Not Submitted to ORI.* Washington, DC: Office of Public Health and Science, US Department of Health and Human Services, July 1998. ori.dhhs.gov/documents/inquiry_not_submitted_ori. pdf.

21. CKG personal communication, November 2007.

22. CKG personal communication, Alan Price, Price Research Integrity Consultant Experts, Lago Vista, Texas, February 2008.

23. Rothschild J, Miethe TD. Whistle-blower disclosures and management retaliation. *Work Occup* 1999; **26**: 107–28.

24. Office of Research Integrity. *Consequences of Whistleblowing for the Whistleblower in Misconduct in Science Cases.* Rockville, MD: US Department of Health and Human Services, 1995. ori.dhhs.gov/documents/consequences.pdf.

25. Dyer C. Whistleblower who was excluded from work for five years wins apology. *BMJ* 2008; **336**: 63.

26. Gunsalus CK. Preventing the need for whistleblowing: practical advice for university administrators. *Sci Eng Ethics* 1998; **4**: 75–94.

27. Reich E. Purdue dogged by misconduct claims. *Nature* 2007; **447**: 238.

28. Gunsalus CK. Institutional structure to ensure research integrity. *Acad Med* 1993; **68**: S33–8.

29. Ekman P. *Telling Lies: Clues to Deceit in the Marketplace, Politics, and Marriage.* New York: Norton, 2001.

30. 'whistle', *n. The Oxford English Dictionary*, 2nd edn. Oxford: Oxford University Press, 1989.

31. Medical Research Council. *Medical Research Council Policy and Procedure for Inquiring into Allegations of Scientific Misconduct.* Statement by the Medical Research Council, London, 1997.

32. Office of Research Integrity. *Handling Misconduct – Whistleblowers: Protection for Whistleblowers.* December 1993. ori.hhs.gov/misconduct/Whistleblower_Privilege. shtml.

33. Research Triangle Institute. *Consequences of Whistleblowing for the Whistleblower in Misconduct in Science Cases. Final Report. Commissioned by the Office of Research Integrity.* Washington, DC: US Government Printing Office, 1995. ori.dhhs.gov/ documents/consequences.pdf.

34. Powell K. Misconduct mayhem. *Nature* 2006; **441**: 122–3.

35. *University of Vermont Investigation Report, in the Matter of Eric T. Poehlman, Ph.D. (Dated April 4, 2001).* Burlington, VT: University of Vermont, College of Medicine, 2001: 1–39.

36. Interlandi J. An unwelcome discovery. *New York Times Magazine* 22 October 2006.

37. Sox HC, Rennie D. Research misconduct, retraction and cleansing the medical literature: lessons from the Poehlman case. *Ann Intern Med* 2006; **144**: 609–13.

38. Dalton R. Obesity expert owns up to million-dollar crime. *Nature* 2005; **434**: 424.

39. Synopsis of published decision by the US Court of Appeals, for the Fourth Circuit, No. 95-2811, decided January 22, 1997.

40. University of California, San Francisco. *150-23 Reporting Improper Governmental Activities and Protection against Retaliation ('Whistleblowing').* policies.ucsf.edu/150/15023.htm.

41. University of California Whistleblower Policies. ucwhistleblower.ucop.edu/policy.html.

42. University of Illinois at Urbana Champaign. *Academic Staff Handbook, 2008.* www.ahr.uiuc.edu/ahrhandbook/chap5/default.htm.

43. The UK Panel for Research Integrity in Health and Biomedical Sciences (UKRIO). *Helpline and guidance for those involved in allegations, and concerns over the conduct of research in health and biomedical sciences.* London: The UK Research Integrity Office, 2008. www.ukrio.org.uk/sites/ukrio2/the_programme_of_work/helpline_and_guidance.cfm.

44. Public Concern at Work (PCaW). www.pcaw.co.uk.

45. Government Accountability Project (GAP). www.whistleblower.org/template/index.cfm.

46. Gunsalus CK. How to blow the whistle and still have a career afterwards. *Sci Eng Ethics* 1998; **4**: 51–64. poynter.indiana.edu/see-ckg1.pdf.

16 Conduct of an inquiry into alleged misconduct

Jane Barrett

Introduction

Allegations of alleged research fraud or misconduct can come from many sources, but, worryingly, often they are unearthed by chance. The role of whistleblowers is discussed fully in Chapter 9; their contribution to the detection of misconduct must not be underestimated. Perhaps the most common source of allegations of misconduct is the pharmaceutical industry, monitors and auditors visiting investigator sites being the people with the greatest opportunity to detect the possibility of fraud or misconduct. The majority of companies have robust procedures in place to govern the handling of such concerns. Within academia and hospitals, too, there is a growing awareness of the need for defined methods to deal with such serious allegations, and in many countries there are now bodies to provide guidance and steerage in cases of concern (Chapter 17).

Whatever the source of information on alleged fraud and misconduct, inquiries into those allegations must be conducted properly and thoroughly. If corners are cut, or if set procedures are not followed, vital information can be lost, the guilty are given an opportunity to cover their tracks, the careers of others may be put at risk, and, most importantly of all, patients' lives and well-being are potentially put at risk. It is the risk to patients that drives most of us involved in inquiries into fraud and misconduct. There have been all too many cases of patients being given treatments that they did not need, put into studies for which they did not meet the entry criteria or for which they had contraindications, or subjected to new treatments without the many assessments that would have ensured their safety. At least one valuable medicine has been withdrawn from the market due to fraud (Debendox was withdrawn from the market after William McBride published a paper falsely claiming teratogenicity in animals[1,2]), and it is impossible to know how many drugs have been licensed on submissions containing some amount of fraudulent data, even if that amount was small. Patient safety must always be the driving force behind attempts to investigate and eradicate research misconduct and fraud.

The introduction throughout Europe of the Clinical Trials Directive[3] means that the conduct of clinical trials involving medicinal products must, by law, be in accordance with Good Clinical Practice (GCP). It further means that anybody making any false declaration in a submission to an ethics committee or in an application to carry out a clinical trial is guilty of a criminal offence. Strangely, it does not mean that someone fabricating data is automatically similarly guilty.

Allegations of fraud or misconduct

Allegations of fraud or misconduct can be made by anyone involved with biomedical research, including patients, co-workers, other academics, or a sponsor. While the accusations or concerns may take differing forms, their receipt and subsequent handling must be harmonized, following carefully laid-out procedures to ensure fairness and parity for all involved. It is essential that all those employed by a pharmaceutical company or in health care or academia be fully trained in that organization's standard operating procedures (SOPs) for the reporting and investigating of allegations of research fraud and misconduct. A good SOP makes a statement to would-be fraudulent investigators that such behaviour will be actively sought and firmly handled if suspected. It gives a framework and protection for those who have concerns that fraud or misconduct has occurred. It allows for a standardized and impartial investigation, and, if necessary, an appropriate punishment. Guidelines for the production of these SOPs have been published, for example by the UK Department of Health.[4] The key elements of such SOPs are included in Table 16.1.

Most non-industry SOPs detail the possible sanctions available to deal with those found to have been involved in fraud or misconduct. These include

- letter of reprimand
- supervisory monitoring of future research
- withdrawing approval for the research
- barring the researcher from further research in the organization or from applying for further funding
- reporting researchers to their professional bodies and ethics committees
- suspension/dismissal
- requesting withdrawal or correction of published or pending papers.

The problem with many of these sanctions is that they do nothing to prevent the researcher moving to another hospital or university, in the same country or abroad, and starting again. Indeed, there is a strong chance that the lessons learned from being caught once will enable him or her to avoid detection in the future.

Who should handle allegations?

One matter of concern is that very few SOPs outside the pharmaceutical industry, and a worrying number of them within it, dictate that allegations of research fraud or misconduct should be made to two individuals simultaneously. The reason for reporting to more than one person is to avoid the possibility of collusion – yet the chances of this being a reality within the health service and academia would seem to be theoretically much higher than collusion between industry and researcher. Within National Health Service Trusts in the UK, for instance, the vast majority of SOPs on fraud and

TABLE 16.1 Key elements of standard operating procedures (SOPs) for dealing with allegations of research fraud

Element	Explanation	Comment
Definitions of fraud and misconduct	As defined by Wellcome Trust, UK Medical Research Council, health authorities, etc.	Widest possible descriptions should include falsification, fabrication, plagiarism, and piracy
Expectations and warnings	Those making allegations will put their name to them, although confidentiality will be maintained. If allegations are found to be vexatious, disciplinary action may be taken	Necessary to avoid petty or anonymous reporting
Descriptions of policies	Whistleblower protection and other elements	Provides legal protection
Roles and responsibilities	Named job titles for those receiving allegations, those investigating, and those supporting	See comment below on who should handle allegations
Purpose	To give a framework to those who feel that they need to make allegations and those who wish to declare their own breach of GCP	Important to allow 'self-reporting'
Process and investigation	Allegations in writing, to specified people, appointment of appropriate people to investigate. 'Appropriate people' are decided on a case-by-case basis	Often treated lightly, yet perhaps the most important element
Outcome of the above	Decision to take matter further, possible disciplinary action	Sanctions are listed above
Appeal	For example if allegations are thought to be malicious	Panel includes parties not involved with hearing of allegation
Documentation	Comprehensive notes of all stages, handled in accordance with data protection legislation	Must track details of process

misconduct state that the Director of Research and Development is the only person to be told of allegations. This strategy is risky. The chair of the relevant research ethics committee or independent review board might be an appropriate second person. Within industry, the most usual persons designated to receive allegations of alleged fraud and misconduct are the medical director and the head of quality assurance.

Pitfalls in handling allegations of research misconduct

There are two major pitfalls that can occur during the handling of such allegations. The first is that the person reporting a concern is not afforded the protection that the law allows. Whistleblowers are almost always protected under public disclosure laws (e.g. the Public Interest Disclosure Act 1998 in the UK[5]) if they raise honest concerns about suspected misconduct in their workplace. They must be shown to be acting in good faith, must have reasonable grounds to suspect that there has been misconduct or fraud, and must have followed the documented procedures for their company or institution. If the person (or persons) to whom they report their concerns does not treat them with confidentiality, and the allegations and their perpetrator become widespread knowledge, there may well be personal repercussions against the whistleblower. This topic is covered in detail in Chapter 15.

The second major pitfall is that if the handling of the allegation does not follow due process, maintaining absolute confidentiality, then those specifically involved with the perpetration of the fraud or misconduct may come to hear of the suspicions. This would allow them the time and opportunity to destroy evidence such as forged signatures on consent forms, to create previously missing data such as patient diary cards, or to modify patient records to make it seem that an ineligible (or even fictitious) patient actually did have the condition under investigation in the study. If the fraud were very serious, knowledge that it was soon to be unearthed would give the perpetrator a chance to move away or even leave the country. There have actually been cases of suicide or sudden unexplained death when researchers suspected of serious misconduct believed they were about to be caught out.

Best practice

It is unacceptable now for any organization involved in biomedical research not to have robust and straightforward SOPs. An alarming number of those reviewed for this chapter, however, were vague and unhelpful on the actual steps to be taken. The use of such words as 'appropriate' and 'adequate' are common, but very few could actually be worked through in real life without hesitation or challenge. It is impossible to produce a template for best practice that would cover all places in which research could be undertaken, as there are major differences between how the process would flow in hospital medicine versus the pharmaceutical industry, for example, but it is possible to agree on key points to meet the classification of best practice in every situation:

1. **Fraud and misconduct must be defined.** It is helpful to say what it is not, as well as what it is, so, for example, there might be:
   (i) a published definition that many have agreed on already, including falsification, fabrication, plagiarism, and piracy

   (ii) a statement that misconduct can be deliberate (e.g. intentional fraud), reckless, or negligent

   (iii) some examples: fabrication of laboratory data, forging ethics committee approval, failure to obtain appropriate consent, gift authorship, etc.

(iv) what it is not: honest error, differences in opinion (sloppiness and careless-ness are often quoted as not being misconduct – but sometimes can be);

2. **A statement that suspected fraud and misconduct will be taken seriously and fully investigated.**

3. **The need for the reporter of suspected fraud or misconduct to report under his or her own name.** The SOP must state that confidentiality must be preserved, but it is not best practice to allow anonymous accusations.

4. **A statement that malicious or unfounded accusations** may trigger disciplinary processes.

5. **A statement that those reporting concerns about possible fraud or misconduct will be protected under law** if they follow certain steps laid down in the SOP.

6. **The job titles of more than one person**, ideally based in more than one depart-ment, to whom such allegations should be made, with the guidance that any two of them should be notified at the same time.

7. **Clear descriptions as to who will follow up such allegations.** Specific job titles should be given – or, at the very least, the name of a group of people should be given, such as the quality assurance department in a pharmaceutical company, avoiding such phrases as 'appropriate persons'.

8. **The process that these named people will follow should be described** – for example that a 'for cause' audit will be performed, or that the research and devel-opment department of a hospital will perform a full assessment of the work done so far. While it is difficult to make a statement that would work equally well for clinical and industrial settings, it is relatively straightforward to write one for an individual setting.

9. **Outcome and sanctions should be described**. One outcome is that no misconduct was found. In such a case, there may still have been deep concerns raised during the assessment of the allegation, such that the body investigating may wish to consider bringing in outside expertise to assess the matter further. Whatever the outcome, it must be made known to those involved, including the person making the allegations, and the person against whom they were made. This step is often omitted. The sanctions are rather particular to the organization involved, but they do need to be defined in a best-practice SOP. Within the pharmaceutical industry, such sanctions are usually covered under human resources (HR) processes and SOPs.

10. **The appeal process must be described**, as must the job titles of those from whom the appeals panel might be drawn. It should be made clear how many of those named by job title earlier in the SOP will be part of the panel. The fact that the panel's decision will be final should be made clear.

Is there a case to be answered?

At some point in the investigation of possible fraud or misconduct, a decision must be taken as to whether or not there is a case to be answered. Unfortunately, no SOP can make this decision, but it should define the elements to consider that make it more or less likely that fraud or misconduct has taken place.

The input of those managing the study data can be most helpful in making this decision. The data from the suspected site can be plotted and compared with data from the study as a whole. As a rule of thumb, fabricated data vary less widely than data obtained from real subjects. For example, the haemoglobin in the study population as a whole may vary between 11 and 18 g/dL, but an investigator inventing study data may only enter values between 13 and 16 g/dL – a range fitting into his or her definition of 'normal'. Similarly, the use of rescue analgesia at the site under investigation may show anomalies if looked at separately from the rest of the study; perhaps the amount taken by patients randomized to receive active medication does not differ from those supposedly taking placebo, or it differs widely from the amount taken by patients at other sites.

Adverse events, particularly serious unexpected adverse events, will also be less common – or even absent – if the patients do not exist or are not really in the study. Reporting of serious adverse events requires many additional forms to be filled in, and possibly direct contact from the sponsor company, so would call unwanted focused attention on a fraudulent investigator. Similarly, the data monitoring group could assess whether the patient withdrawal rate differed at the suspected site when compared with the study as a whole. If the study grant provides for payment to be made per patient visit, most money will be made if all patients complete all visits, so a patient withdrawing early, in addition to triggering serious adverse event reporting forms, will also mean less payment.

The expert opinion of statisticians can be useful in deciding whether or not fraud or misconduct may have taken place. Manipulation of data can be used to show larger differences between groups than really exist, to reduce the variability of results, or to invent extra data.[6] A statistician may be able to show that all patients worst affected by the disease under investigation had received active medication at one site, while those least affected had received placebo. He or she may also show statistically significant improvement on the study drug at one site, whereas analysis of the other sites added together without a suspect site may not.

GCP requires that unused medication and containers be returned by patients at the end of a study, and leftover medication counted or weighed as appropriate. If drug containers are all unblemished at the end of a study, exactly the correct amount of medication has been used, or tubes of ointment have all been squeezed in the same way, it almost guarantees that they have not actually been given to patients. In real life, patients do not follow study protocols in similar ways.

Forgery of essential documents can be proven by specialists in the field. For example, ethical review of clinical research is vital to protect the rights of patients, but because it takes time to obtain independent ethics committee or institutional review board approval, an investigator may start a study pretending that it has been applied for and obtained. With scanners and modern copying equipment, it is relatively easy to produce a letter capable of passing a casual inspection and seeming to give ethical approval to start a study. Thus, effectively patients at that site are denied the protection given by impartial review of the protocol.

If any doubt exists as to whether or not fraud or misconduct exists, external expertise should be sought. It is not acceptable to hide behind friendship or reputation, or to fail to respond to suspicion. Fear of repercussion on a pharmaceutical company and attendant loss of prescriptions does not justify turning a blind eye to possible fraud, nor does fear that it might not be possible to prove a case. Vigilance and reactive investigation are vital. Experienced external investigators have the ability to review data, assess concerns, and produce a rating of the likelihood of fraud or misconduct having taken place, with a detailed plan of suggested further action, all without the suspect site being aware of the process.

Table 16.2 contains elements that point towards or away from the likelihood of wrongdoing.

The fame of the suspected investigator should never be seen as persuasive against fraud or misconduct being likely, nor should his or her likeability. Neither of these is a bar to confirmation that extensive fraud has been carried on over several years, as many cases have shown.[7]

The responsibility for deciding whether or not to pursue the allegations lies with the person or persons so identified in the organization's SOP, and it is also for them to decide whether or not, or when, to inform the person or persons against whom the allegations were made. This last decision in particular must not be taken without input

TABLE 16.2 Is there a case to be answered?

More likely that fraud/misconduct exists	Less likely that fraud/misconduct exists
• Immaculate case record forms • Difficulty arranging meetings • Differences from other sites in multicentre study or compared with previous studies (patient numbers, dropout rates) • Odd days/hours worked if automatic date and time stamps used • Dates for assessments not corresponding to working days • Too many studies being conducted for site staff availability • Uniformity of supposed patient-generated materials (consent form signatures, diary cards) • Unlikely number of patients with target condition • Inability of site to find documents when asked, but these are produced later • Evidence that staff member has been asked to lie or has been threatened	• Different pens used at different times • Openness to inspection • Plausibility of elements in research project (patient numbers, treatment outcome) • Study documentation 'looks real' (e.g. patient documentation may have extraneous marks) • Site staff involved with other research in addition • Different styles of marking diary cards, errors, incomplete data recording • Patient demographics match the expected • On-site master files in good order • Wrong amount of medication left when returned by patients (patients do not follow rules!)

from the relevant organization's legal department, because, handled badly, it could result in charges of defamation being brought against those making the allegation and those investigating it. If there is any suggestion that the person bringing the allegation has been threatened, great care must be exercised, and the possibility of involving the police should be considered very seriously.

Investigations

Any investigation of allegations of research fraud or misconduct must be conducted in such a way as to protect both the person making the allegations and the person against whom they are made. If the allegations are not substantiated, or are found to be untrue, there must be a process in place to remove all details from personal files and restore any damage done to reputations.

In many countries, there are national bodies involved in the investigation of research fraud and misconduct that can advise and support the relevant institutions; these are covered in more detail in Chapter 17. But it is still the responsibility of the institutions or companies to whom allegations of fraud or misconduct have been made to carry out a full investigation and to take action against those found to have acted dishonestly. The national bodies in some countries, such as the USA and France, can themselves take direct action. For example, the US Office for Human Research Protections (OHRP) can order the closure of institutions, as can the Food and Drug Administration (FDA), which can also circulate the names of the wrongdoers on their 'Black List', and the Office of Research Integrity (ORI) can also recommend federal funding be withdrawn.

In the UK, the General Medical Council (GMC) is the most prominent body involved in the investigation of research fraud and misconduct, although they cannot act until a formal complaint is made, and they have no authority to deal with non-medical research personnel. The GMC stated clearly in the early 1990s that their Fitness to Practise Panel would treat proven clinical research fraud very seriously. Since that time, the doctors accused of research fraud, reported to the GMC, and found guilty of serious professional misconduct, have, in the majority of cases, had their licences to practise medicine withdrawn either permanently or for a period of time, and some have had limitations placed on their future research activity.

The GMC, in common with many of the other national bodies involved in this area, have made it clear that doctors who do not report allegations or evidence of scientific fraud and misconduct to the appropriate body may find themselves facing sanctions. Nurses, midwives, and other health-care workers are also similarly responsible to their governing bodies for their behaviour. In recent studies, more than 40% of researchers surveyed stated that they were aware of research misconduct but had not reported it,[8] and those working in an academic medical setting stated that a typical research coordinator would probably do nothing if he or she became aware that a principal investigator or research staff member was involved in an incident of misconduct.[9] A fifth of those surveyed had first-hand experience of actual research misconduct in the past year, but only a quarter of them said that they would report it to the appropriate authorities.

There are criminal sanctions that can be brought against fraudulent researchers. These are seldom pursued in Europe, but criminal charges have been brought in cases of research fraud in other countries – in South Korea (Hwang Woo-Suk) and the USA (Eric Poehlman), for example. In most countries, there is no law specifically relating to fraud – criminal prosecutions need to draw elements from laws relating to deception, theft, offences against the person, and forgery and counterfeiting. The police and judiciary invariably find it difficult to understand the intricacies of research fraud, and, as the amount of money involved is usually relatively small by their standards, they might not be particularly motivated to follow a case through.

Several countries, of which the UK and Germany are examples, have a process to bring together two or more pharmaceutical companies with suspicions about the same doctor to enable a joint case to be made. Contact is made with the industry's trade associations in strict confidence, and introductions are effected between the different companies. A company must have a clear concern about an investigator to enter this process, but the joint action can be very helpful if neither company has sufficient evidence to bring a case but the combined information is compelling. Sadly, there are no sanctions if a company refuses to cooperate or investigate.

In a health-care or academic setting, once an allegation of fraud or misconduct has been made, the following steps may be instituted:

1. The research and development (R&D) director would initiate a preliminary investigation. To allow for the possibility that the R&D director may potentially be implicated in the allegation, another person must be specified in the SOP to take that role.
2. If indicated, a 'for cause' audit should be conducted by the group responsible for research governance (called by different names in different countries).
3. If research misconduct or fraud is still suspected, the R&D director should inform the suspected researcher's manager, and seek advice from HR and other relevant departments such as finance and legal. Liaison with third parties such as the research sponsor, research ethics committee, and others should be considered.
4. If appropriate, a full investigation should be implemented. The investigational team might – perhaps should – include someone with expertise in the field under investigation, someone from HR, and a representative from the university if relevant. It is important that the team should not be directly involved in the research project, and it may be appropriate to use an entirely external investigational team.
5. If research misconduct or fraud is confirmed, the relevant sanctions should be imposed, which may include reporting the researcher to the relevant professional body.
6. The person who reported suspicions or allegations and the researcher should both be informed of the outcome of the investigation, and their rights of appeal stated. If the investigation reveals that the accusations have not been made in good faith or were frankly malicious, disciplinary action against the person who instigated the investigation should be brought, in accordance with the organization's disciplinary policy.

Within pharmaceutical companies, the process is very similar:

1. The relevant line manager and the quality assurance (QA) manager would evaluate the report, and be responsible for taking follow-up action, performing an audit, and presenting findings to senior management.
2. A designated senior executive in the company would be responsible for agreeing and coordinating appropriate action with all the relevant departments (e.g. the need for external investigation) and informing the relevant authorities.
3. The head of regulatory affairs would be responsible for reporting any confirmed case of fraud/misconduct to appropriate regulatory agencies if deemed appropriate by the team charged with the investigation.

In a pharmaceutical company document, there should be a clause on the need to avoid subjecting the company to accusations of defamation, and a statement to the effect that misconduct or fraud performed or knowingly assisted by any member of staff would be regarded as gross misconduct and relevant disciplinary action would be taken. There should also be a statement to the effect that any data confirmed as being fraudulent will be excluded from any study analysis, that confirmed cases of fraud will be notified to the appropriate regulatory authorities, and that if any investigators, researchers, or contract research organizations (CROs) are found guilty of misconduct or fraud, all studies with which they have been involved will be reviewed.

The role of an independent investigator

At present, relatively few countries have an official mechanism in place for the investigation of suspected research fraud and misconduct. It was for this reason that MedicoLegal Investigations Ltd (MLI) was established in the UK in the mid-1990s, as a private independent agency supported financially by the pharmaceutical industry to detect, investigate, and, if indicated, prepare a case for prosecution of those suspected of research fraud or misconduct. The combined skills of widely experienced professional detectives and pharmaceutical physicians are used, making it less likely that the pitfalls discussed earlier, such as those involved with the misconduct becoming aware of the suspicions, will be encountered.

When an independent investigator is called in by a pharmaceutical company or other research unit, the process begins with a careful study of the allegations or suspicious circumstances. Witnesses and those reporting the suspicions are interviewed, documents are examined, and recommendations for a course of action are made. If a 'for cause' audit has not been carried out, the independent investigator may participate in one – or at least brief the auditors to look for specific items. A company involved purely in the assessment and investigation of research fraud will also be able to use their knowledge of forensic science laboratories and how best to work with them. They also understand how best to handle whistleblowers and how to establish that the allegations stem from correct motivation. It should be more than possible to conduct discreet enquiries, establish whether or not a problem exists, and conclude matters without any whistleblower being identified, or indeed the prime suspect even being aware that he or she is under investigation, should no credible evidence be found to justify a full investigation.

The benefits of using specialist investigation services in this area are that they fully understand the delicate nature of fraud and misconduct, the issues relating to preservation of evidence such that it can be used in disciplinary hearings or court cases, and the management of whistleblowers. Also, they are impartial and truly independent of the pharmaceutical company, university, or hospital.

There have been concerns in the past about the investigation and possible prosecution of those suspected of research fraud or misconduct, but the vast majority of researchers in every field are good, honest, and dedicated. They are being failed if those who commit fraud can evade justice. If evidence is properly processed, more evidence will become available, and whistleblowers can be confident that they will be treated fairly and independently. If suspected fraud is handled by the inexperienced, however, it is possible that those committing fraud will escape punishment due to errors of conduct resulting from such inexperience.

Often information can only be obtained from research patients in person, but of course pharmaceutical companies do not have details beyond initials, dates of birth, and gender of patients who are claimed to be participants in clinical trials. Company monitors have access to source documents, and as part of their routine monitoring check the names on patient consent forms against hospital or general practice notes, and check the contents of those notes, but neither consent forms nor source documents can leave the investigator's site, and any document identifying a patient further, such as a laboratory test, must be anonymized before it is sent to the company for data entry. So sponsors rely heavily on the integrity of the site investigators that patients really exist. When – and only when – there are good reasons to doubt the existence of patients in a study, an external investigator will attempt to make contact with the patients alleged to be in the study. The sponsor company is prevented from doing this by data protection legislation, and indeed informed consent forms normally state that patient details will at all times be kept secret from the pharmaceutical company funding the study. However, investigators independent of sponsor companies can (under carefully controlled circumstances) speak to patients directly once they have consented to cooperate.

In the UK, health-care authorities and trusts hold computer records of all patients falling under their care, and MLI has obtained permission from the data protection authorities to ask those who hold the records to forward a specially written letter to the patients identified from a study.[10] At this stage, the patients' names and addresses are not made known to MLI, and the letters sent to the patients by this route are carefully worded, referring to the fact that some research in which they may have been included is being reviewed. There is no mention of any suspected wrongdoing. The patients are given a reply-paid envelope and asked to give their details if they are happy to be contacted to talk further. The response rate is very high, especially if children have been involved in the research, but, worryingly often, the first question that they ask when seen is, 'What research?'

Written statements are taken from patients if strong suspicion or evidence of misconduct emerges from preliminary investigations. They are always told that they may be called to give evidence in a judicial hearing at a later date, but are never told bad news and are left alone. It is important that they be kept updated at regular intervals so that at all times they know if they will be called on in the future, and they are encouraged to make contact with the independent investigators at any time to share concerns.

All evidence gathered, including patient statements (with written consent), is passed to the sponsor company. If the investigation shows that no wrongdoing actually took place, or that it is at best unlikely that it did, the matter is laid to rest. If, however, there is evidence of deliberate fraud or significant recklessness or dishonesty, the case will be taken further by the company, perhaps with further help from the independent investigators.

If solid evidence of fraud or misconduct is found at a site, the research ethics review committee that gave permission for the study is asked for details of all studies approved for that site in the previous five years. The relevance of this is that, in all but one case so far investigated by MLI, there have been found to be earlier studies also containing fraudulent data. The medical directors of other pharmaceutical companies identified from this list are informed of the findings so far, and are helped to choose whether to carry out a 'for cause' audit or use independent help to investigate whether or not there was misconduct on their study or studies. The final option – to do nothing and to ignore the evidence – is fortunately very rarely exercised.

When a compelling dossier of evidence has been collected, the independent investigators help the company or companies to refer the researcher, and sometimes other members of staff at the research site, to the relevant bodies for disciplinary action. There is growing determination on the part of such bodies to stamp out research misconduct, as shown by part of the statement by the Professional Conduct Committee of the GMC at the end of the disciplinary hearing for Dr Geoffrey Fairhurst, found guilty of serious professional misconduct and removed from the register of doctors in 1996. It said the following:

> 'Trust lies at the heart of the practice of medicine. Patients must be able to trust doctors with their lives and wellbeing ... Medical research must always be conducted with scrupulous honesty and integrity.'

Because of the constant pressure in the pharmaceutical industry to achieve rapid development and approval of new drugs, there will always be the risk of conflict of interest between speed of development and patient safety, and investigations of suspicions of fraud and misconduct relate directly to patient safety. As independent investigators, MLI have seen several instances where, to save money, only one auditor performed a 'for cause' audit at sites where misconduct was suspected. This is dangerous for two reasons: first because lack of corroboration of findings can weaken later proceedings, particularly if evidence has subsequently been destroyed, and, second, because it lays the lone auditor open to malicious accusations when reports of malpractice are made later.

Conclusions

When a biomedical researcher is found guilty of fraud, it is devastating not only for them and their families, but also for their co-researchers and their patients. When doctors lose the licence to practise medicine, their reputation and their lives may be ruined. But it is critically important to investigate all allegations of research fraud and misconduct. Fraud strikes at the very basis of duty of care, integrity, and ethics. In the past, fellow researchers in health care and academia have sometimes chosen to ignore it, and pharmaceutical companies have tacitly condoned it by not investigating fully and bringing necessary prosecutions.

It is important that all companies and institutions involved in any way with biomedical research take responsibility for their employees, but researchers too must be held accountable for intentional misconduct and fraud. Medical research remains vulnerable if it lacks an effective mechanism to detect and pursue fraud. To pretend that fraud does not exist and to have no mechanism for it to be reported and investigated is to condone it. To take no action when fraud is suspected or when blatant evidence is seen is not acceptable.

SOPs provide a framework to report and follow up suspicions of fraud and misconduct, but they are useful only if they are regularly reviewed and updated, and if everyone concerned has been trained to use them correctly, and does so. Their presence alone neither provides a safeguard against fraud nor makes all investigations of fraud guaranteed free of unpleasantness. What SOPs can do is to give an approved and defined mechanism to those who suspect wrongdoing, and a well-thought-out plan of how to proceed to those receiving the allegation.

There must be a widespread and unequivocal acceptance that failure to act on suspicions of fraud is itself serious misconduct, with clear and unambiguous statements in all areas of research that research misconduct will not be tolerated and will be punished if found. There must be robust and well-established procedures to allow the reporting and handling of concerns, such that individual bias cannot be allowed to influence matters. And, finally, there must be an acceptance of the application of the same rules, no matter who sponsors research, whether it be industry or academia.

The vast majority of researchers are honest and would never so much as contemplate misconduct or fraud. However, to pretend that clinical research fraud and misconduct do not exist is to allow bad medicine, bad science, and, above all, abuse of patients. Only by detailed procedures, carefully and consistently carried out, can we eradicate fraud.

References

1. McBride WG, Vardy PH, French J. Effects of scopolamine hydrobromide on the development of the chick and rabbit embryo. *Aust J Biol Sci* 1982; **35**: 173–8.
2. Humphrey GF. Scientific fraud: the McBride case – judgment. *Med Sci Law* 1994; **34**: 299–306.
3. Directive 2001/20/EC of the European Parliament and of the Council of 4 April 2001, on the approximation of the laws, regulations and administrative provisions

of the Member States relating to the implementation of good clinical practice in the conduct of clinical trials on medicinal products for human use. *Official Journal* L 121, 1 May 2001: 34–44.

4. Department of Health. *Research Governance Framework for Health and Social Care*, 2nd edn. London: Department of Health, April 2005.

5. Public Interest Disclosure Act. 1998.

6. Evan S. Statistical aspects of the detection of fraud. In Lock S, Wells F, Farthing M, eds. *Fraud and Misconduct in Medical Research*, 3rd edn. London: BMJ books, 2001: 186–204.

7. Barrett J. Fraud and misconduct in clinical research. In *Principles and Practice of Pharmaceutical Medicine*, 2nd edn. Edwards LD, Fletcher AJ, Fox AW, Stonier PD, eds. London: John Wiley and Sons Ltd, 2007: 631–41.

8. Sheehan JG. Fraud, conflict of interest, and other enforcement issues in clinical research. *Clev Clin J Med* 2007. **74**: S63–7.

9. Pryor ER, Habermann B, Broome ME. Scientific misconduct from the perspective of research coordinators: a national survey. *J Med Eth* 2007; **33**: 365–9.

10. Jay P. Research fraud/misconduct: a glance at the human side. In Lock S, Wells F, Farthing M, eds. *Fraud and Misconduct in Medical Research*, 3rd edn. London: BMJ books, 2001: 216–21.

SECTION 6

THE WAY FORWARD

17 The role of national advisory bodies

Michael Farthing

Introduction

Public confidence in the veracity of research across science, social science, arts, and humanities is totally dependent on the personal integrity of those involved in all aspects of the research and publication process. Investigators, research students, research sponsors, authors, peer reviewers, and journal editors must operate within an ethical framework that is transparent and has principles that are understood and accepted by all of the stakeholders in the research community. This is currently known as responsible conduct of research (RCR), of which there are a number of scholarly descriptions in the published literature.[1]

Many organizations have produced detailed accounts of these principles and have published guidance as to how they should be embedded into everyday practice (Box 17.1). Despite the broad acceptance of these principles, research misconduct has been reported from many countries around the world, including the UK and other European countries, the USA, Australia, and a number of countries in South-East Asia.[2-7] This misconduct has involved scientists, academic and hospital clinicians, general practitioners, and both research students and principal investigators, many of whom in recent years have had international reputations. Perhaps even more surprising is the flurry of high-profile cases that have involved some of the elite scientific journals such as *Nature* and *Science*, resulting in a multiple retractions. Many will, however, not be surprised by these events, as the peer review process was never set up to detect fraudulent work, although astute reviewers have been able from time to time to raise the possibility of research misconduct and bring it to the notice of a journal editor. Research misconduct is not limited to biomedicine. During the past five years, there have been a number of cases in other disciplines that have reached the press, including physics,[8] nano-electronics,[9] and ecology.[10]

There seems to be little doubt, however, that during the last 10–15 years there has been an increased awareness of research misconduct and the need for research institutions to establish a value system that places RCR very high in the minds of researchers. In addition, there has been a drive for the development and implementation of codes of conduct that make it absolutely clear what is expected from an investigator.[11-19] Indeed, there are many published codes of best practice developed by universities

BOX 17.1   **National advisory bodies and other relevant agencies**

National advisory bodies

Denmark	fi.dk/site/english
France	www2.cnrs.fr/en/8.htm
Finland	www.tenk.fi/ENG/function.htm
Germany	www.dfg.de/en/index.html
Netherlands	www.knaw.nl/english/index.html
Norway	www.forskningsradet.no/en/Home
Sweden	www.vr.se
UK	www.ukrio.org.uk
USA	ori.dhhs.gov

Other relevant agencies

European Science Foundation	www.esf.org
Committee on Publication Ethics (COPE)	www.publicationethics.org.uk

and other research-intensive organizations, funding agencies, and national and other independent bodies committed to ensuring high standards in the conduct of research. There is evidence, however, that many either do not read or do not act on these guidance documents, and the success in incorporating their content into institutional values systems seems to be limited. Despite these laudable interventions, it is quite clear that research fraud and other misdemeanours, including breaches in good publication practice, continue to occur and may indeed be increasing in frequency. Certainly, in recent years, the reporting of major cases of misconduct seems to occur in the scientific and daily press with depressing regularity. So why are current safeguards against research misconduct at an institutional level apparently failing? What are the flaws in the current system? And what steps have been taken at a national level to try to improve on the situation?

Flaws in the current system

If there was a simple solution to the instillation of the broad principles of RCR and the prevention and detection of research misconduct, it would certainly have been found and implemented by now. It is clearly a complex multifaceted process without a single cause, and thus there is no simple, single remedy. A variety of factors, however, have been put forward as possible contributors, including failure to embed high-level RCR values across the research community; the increasingly competitive research environment (particularly in some of the sciences); inadequate supervision of younger researchers, poor monitoring, and audit of research; and a lack of widely applicable techniques to detect misconduct. I would suggest that, while there is a sense that detection of research fraud is difficult and that, as far as research misconduct is concerned, 'crime does appear to pay', it will be a challenge to make major inroads into the current position.

Failure to instil the values of RCR

Failure to instil the values of RCR has to be the priority for all institutions engaged in the research business. Saying it is one thing – implementation is quite another. The process should begin as early as possible in an individual's educational experience, and certainly before embarking on research training. The new researcher should be required to read the host institution's guidance documents and 'sign off' that he or she has fully understood the standards of conduct that the institution expects from its researchers. Supervisors should continually reinforce the need to adhere to the highest standards of responsible research and publication conduct, and should provide both support and oversight to ensure that this really is a reality in day-to-day practice. It has been argued that this principle of honesty in all academic activity needs to be implanted in schools and continued throughout university education, even for individuals who do not ultimately pursue a career in research.

The competitive environment

There is a concern that the rapid growth of research in bioscience and medicine and the sometimes 'unhealthy' competitiveness between researchers to be first in making a major breakthrough in a 'hot' area places researchers at risk of committing misconduct. This pressure may be heightened if there is potential for commercialization. Coercion from research supervisors may also, in some instances, encourage a young researcher to commit research misconduct. 'Encouragement' may be subtle in the form of giving a co-worker a target to produce an abstract of original work to comply with a submission deadline for a major scientific meeting. An excessively short deadline might, if the work was not sufficiently well advanced, lead to an individual taking a 'shortcut'. Difficulty in obtaining research funding, even by large, prestigious research groups, has led to principal investigators taking 'shortcuts' during the preparation of new research grant applications, such as by the inclusion of fabricated data to support the application.

Supervision

It has been suggested that when research groups grow in size, supervision of individual researchers can be compromised. In addition, some very senior investigators of large research groups find that they are spending increasingly greater periods of time outside the laboratory because of external commitments. This may result in reduced contact time with research students and co-workers, and has the potential to facilitate the dissociation of primary research outputs from subsequent data analyses. This could open the way to data manipulation and/or fabrication. In the Schon case, for example, investigators were unable to find or gain access to laboratory notebooks that would have underpinned the subsequently discredited published work. Regular scrutiny of primary research outputs by supervisors or co-workers would help to minimize such 'leaps of faith'.

Monitoring and audit

It has always seemed strange to me that, for many years, the business community, universities, and other public and private institutions have accepted totally the need for financial audit on an annual basis and regular audits of governance processes. There will usually be a line in the budget to cover the costs of these activities. In the UK, universities and other degree-awarding bodies also undergo a regular audit of teaching by the Quality Assurance Agency every four or five years to ensure that the highest standards are maintained. None of these regulatory exercises are optional.

However, in the UK, there is no equivalent process to quality-assure research conducted in the same institutions. In the major research-intensive universities, research costs often account for the largest expenditure component in the annual accounts, but are not subject to any routine internal or external audit. The Research Assessment Exercise (RAE), which occurs every five or six years and has been running in the UK since 1986, looks primarily at input (grant funding) and output (quality of publications), but is not set up to evaluate the veracity of published research or to quality-assure internal processes of research governance. Its main purpose has been to increase selectivity in the allocation of the central funding of research infrastructure, with the result of refocusing resources on the elite, most research-intensive universities. Papers published in top journals such as *Nature* and *Science* will be very helpful to an institution in improving its ranking in the peer group league table (and support the case for increased research funding), even if they are subsequently retracted in the months or years after the RAE!

It is not true to say, however, that audit does not exist in the research community. The majority of major clinical trials (certainly those sponsored by the pharmaceutical industry) are subject to the principles and processes of Good Clinical Practice (GCP) and are regularly audited throughout the conduct of the study. Some institutions also attempt to ensure research quality on a prospective basis, although, as far as I am aware, this has not been widely adopted and does not appear in the majority of guidance documents. When proposed, it has usually been rejected on the basis that it is too difficult and too expensive, and would put yet another burden on the shoulders of researchers who are already complaining about the escalating bureaucracy that now engulfs the research community. I do not think that HM Revenue and Customs in the UK would be too impressed by those arguments with respect to financial matters!

Problems with detection

Most accept that the peer review process was designed to assess research quality and to improve the final publication through an iterative process – not primarily to detect research misconduct. Indeed, it might be argued that the process has failed totally to identify many (if not most) of the recently discovered high-profile cases. It has been suggested, however, that the peer review process lacks robustness and that competition between high-ranking journals to get the most influential papers may sometimes inadvertently facilitate the publication of fraudulent research.[20]

Although traditionally peer review has been conducted through a screen of anonymity, increasingly in biomedicine, physical sciences and mathematics, and other disciplines, the process is progressively becoming more transparent such that for some journals 'open peer review' (in which the identity of all parties is revealed) is becoming the norm. Will this make misconduct easier to or more likely that it will be detected by a reviewer or an editor? Sadly, I doubt it. I believe that we will continue to be largely dependent on the whistleblower to reveal concerns about research practice, such that further steps can be taken to establish whether these concerns have a sound basis and a full inquiry is warranted. There is an ongoing need, however, to ensure that research organizations have processes in place to enable whistleblowers to express their concerns in a safe and protective environment. It should no longer be necessary or acceptable for an individual to have to leave an institution before feeling comfortable about expressing concerns about the conduct of a colleague.

The way forward

It has been clear to me for the past 10 years that internal, institutional self-regulation is and will continue to be inadequate for dealing with the rogue elements who discredit the research environment for the majority of honest investigators in the research community. Most research-intensive institutions will sign up to guidance that promotes RCR and have processes to deal with breaches of that conduct, but few are proactive in the routine monitoring and audit that are necessary to ensure prospectively that the work that emanates from them has a veracity in which the international community can place its trust. There is also still evidence that some institutions are reluctant to carry robust inquiries into allegations of research misconduct and to impose disciplinary actions on the perpetrators of this misconduct. Might it help, therefore, to involve a third party, a 'watchdog', to ensure that institutional processes are fully utilized?

Is involvement of a third party a deterrent?

From the foregoing discussion, it might be concluded that, despite the dissemination of comprehensive guidance and other education and training initiatives, there has been no dramatic decline in the reporting of misconduct cases. Many countries have created national bodies to advise on and in some instances to investigate allegations of research misconduct. Presumably, they have considered that a supra-institutional influence could be helpful in ensuring consistency of guidance on processes to manage misconduct, at the same time acting as a third party to provide external advisers to join the local team conducting the inquiries.

The international response to the establishment of national bodies

A growing number of countries have set up national bodies to deal with research misconduct, some of which have been functioning for more than 15 years. In general, all of these bodies were set up following one or more politically embarrassing, serious cases of research misconduct in the respective country. The list in Box 17.2 is not intended to be exhaustive, but aims to be illustrative of the diversity of approaches that a variety of countries in Europe and North America have taken to address the handling of misconduct at a national level.

BOX 17.2   **A brief history of the evolution of national bodies to advise on research misconduct**

1989	USA	Office of Scientific Integrity
1992	USA	Office of Research Integrity
1991	Finland	National Advisory Board on Research Ethics
1992	Denmark	Danish Committee on Scientific Dishonesty
1994	Norway	National Committee for the Evaluation of Research Dishonesty in Healthcare Research
1997	Sweden	Committee for Research Ethics
1999	Germany	German Research Foundation
1999	France	INSERM Office of Scientific Integrity
2005	Netherlands	National Committee on Scientific Integrity
2006	UK	UK Panel for Research Integrity in Health and Biomedical Sciences

---

The USA established the Office of Scientific Integrity (OSI) in 1989,[21] probably prompted by a series of more than 20 high-profile cases over the preceding decade. In 1992, this became the Office of Research Integrity (ORI), which now deals with all cases of research misconduct that arise from publicly funded research in the USA. The ORI deals with about 100 new cases each year. It does not normally undertake the investigation of cases (this is left to the employee's institution), but oversees the process, provides external advisers, and holds a central database of referrals and outcomes. The ORI has a comprehensive website (see Box 17.1) that includes all of its policy documents and annual reports, including a detailed account of cases that have been reported to the ORI in each year.

Finland founded its National Advisory Board on Research Ethics in 1991.[22] The Board is subordinate to the Department of Education. In 1998 it issued guidelines for the prevention, handling, and investigation of misconduct and fraud in scientific research, which are applicable to both private and public research institutions. The Board does not conduct investigations, but is informed of all inquiries and investigations and receives a final report from the investigating institution. The Board considers appeals on the outcome of inquiries. The number of cases considered by the Board increased steadily during the 1990s, with a total of 47 cases reported by 2000. In 2006, the Board was asked to give an opinion on four cases of alleged misconduct, none of which were subsequently upheld.

In 1992, the Danish Committee on Scientific Dishonesty was established.[22] In 1997, this developed further into three separate committees to deal with research in (a) natural sciences, agricultural, and veterinary science; (b) health and medical science; and (c) social science and the humanities. The committees have jurisdiction over researchers employed by public institutions and those who have had academic training. The committees have a joint chairperson to ensure uniformity across the fields of research, and are supported by a secretariat from the Danish Research Agency. The chair is a high court judge and the committees are directly responsible for investigating allegations of research misconduct. The committees publish an annual report that includes anonymized accounts of the cases considered and their outcomes. From 1992 to 1998, the committees received 45 allegations of research misconduct, of which 25 were investigated. The committee continue to consider about 7–12 cases each year.

The Norwegian National Committee for the Evaluation of Dishonesty in Health Research was established in 1994,[22] influenced strongly by the Danish experience. Although initially researchers resisted the establishment of this committee, a national survey confirmed that 40% of principal investigators in Norway considered that fraud in health care was a problem. Like the Danish committee, this committee investigated allegations of research misconduct on behalf of employers. Between 1994 and 2000, 11 cases were investigated. The committee also had a role in promoting good practice. However, for several years, the committee has ceased to function, but the Norwegian Research Council has called for its reinstatement. The Norwegian Minister for Education and Research is currently considering setting up a committee that covers all specialist areas along the same line as the Danish committees.

Sweden established a national committee for research ethics in 1997. In 1999, a parliamentary commission made wide-ranging recommendations in a report on good practice in research designed to increase public oversight of research systems, including setting up a national commission to deal with allegations of research misconduct. The Swedish committee conducts investigations at the request of universities and colleges along the lines of the Danish model.

Following the Hermann and Brach scandal in Germany in 1999, in which suspicions were raised about 47 published papers (sometimes called 'the fall of German science'), the German Science Research Council (DFG) formulated its 'rules of good scientific practice' and set up an independent committee of scientific research ombudsmen to consult on scientific 'failure'. The DFG acts as an advisory and mediating body on behalf of any person who is affected by scientific 'failure'. Although investigations are carried out at an institutional level, receipt of public funding from the DFG is conditional upon adoption of its mediating and ombudsman functions.

The French research agency INSERM created the Office of Scientific Integrity (Délégation à la l'Intégrité Scientifique) in 1999. This oversees the investigation of allegations of scientific misconduct involving INSERM personnel, but does not have a wider jurisdiction over other public sector institutions engaged in research. In 1999 and 2000, 43 cases of alleged research misconduct were considered. France does not have a national body with the responsibility to investigate or advise on allegations of research misconduct. The Committee for Scientific Ethics (COMET: Comité d'Ethique pour les Sciences), however, is an advisory body with respect to developing national guidance on research misconduct, but is precluded from involvement in individual cases.

A pan-European perspective

The European Science Foundation (ESF) has published a policy document on good scientific practice in research and scholarship in which it draws on the best experience in Europe (see the ESF website in Box 17.1). The ESF supports the concept of independent national bodies, but feels that it is necessary to work towards a pan-European approach to handling research misconduct.

The UK response

In the UK during the last 10 years, there has been an evolving debate as to whether we are doing enough to prevent, detect, and investigate research and publication misconduct. In 1997, a group of editors founded the Committee for Publication Ethics (COPE). Its main function was to provide a forum for debate of ethical issues in biomedical publishing and to provide advice to editors on cases in which there were concerns about possible research and publication misconduct. In 1999, COPE published its guidelines on good publication practice, which it continues to update regularly.

In 1999, a joint consensus conference on misconduct in biomedical research took place in Edinburgh. The panel's major conclusion was that a national panel should be established, with public representation, to provide advice and assistance on request. The report went on to suggest that the national panel might (a) develop and promote models of good practice for local implementation; (b) provide assistance with the investigation of alleged research misconduct; and (c) collect, collate, and publish information on incidents of research misconduct.

Progress in establishing this body was slow, but finally the project was taken forward jointly by Universities UK (representing the higher education sector) and the Department of Health. The UK Panel for Health and Biomedical Research Integrity was launched in April 2006, and is working along the lines proposed by the Consensus Conference in 1999. The panel has funding for a three-year period in the first instance, with support from the Department of Health, the Higher Education Funding Council, the Medical Research Council, the Biotechnology and Biological Sciences Research Council, the Wellcome Trust, and the Association of the British Pharmaceutical Industry.

Professor Sir Ian Kennedy chairs the board that oversees the project during its first three years. The project director and support staff have been appointed and have set up the UK Research Integrity Office (UKRIO) within the Universities UK administrative offices. The Board has developed a code of good practice that includes an approach to the investigation of misconduct allegations applicable to universities, NHS organizations, research institutes, and industry. The UK Panel is also providing an independent guidance service for whistleblowers through a telephone helpline.

The Panel is assembling a register of advisers who will support its programmes to promote research integrity in the UK and be trained to act as external advisers on research misconduct inquiries. UKRIO will develop and maintain a web-based resource to support the UK research community.

The project will be reviewed during its third year, and a recommendation will be made regarding possible models for future financial support of the initiative.

A global perspective

Research, particularly scientific research, is increasingly a global exercise. This is well exemplified by the 'big experiments' that are now the norm in the physics world, often involving many investigators from a large number of countries. In medicine and biomedicine, the authorship lists of multicentre studies continue to grow in length, and often cross several continents. The research governance of such studies presents a major challenge to the lead investigators and to the study sponsors and funders. If research misconduct is suspected in these situations, it can be extremely difficult to perform an adequate investigation, since individual parties may have concerns about sharing information across continents because of fears of breaching confidentiality and subsequent litigation. There is a need to accept that research is now well established as part of the globalization agenda, and appropriate measures must therefore be in place to ensure a high degree of cooperation between national and international bodies when research misconduct crosses continents.

Future challenges

There are still many unanswered questions. Will the UK Panel be able to effectively influence the biomedical research community in the UK and reduce the frequency of research misconduct? The Panel will carry out an annual survey of research misconduct allegations and the outcome of inquires in the UK, and thereby monitor any changes taking place at a national level. However, it will be difficult in the first few years to separate attainment bias from any true changes in incidence. The Panel will also attempt to influence the research culture by promoting good practice and encouraging employers to get tough on their employees who are found to be in breach of practice guidelines. It is hoped that the regular use of independent experts on misconduct inquiry panels will encourage a spirit of openness and transparency that has not always been apparent. The temptation to 'bury' a report that has found evidence of serious research misconduct will hopefully be an event of the past.

Will additional measures be required to dissuade investigators from committing research fraud, such as enhanced approaches to monitoring research quality or even regular research audit? It seems bizarre to me that monitoring and audit of UK research spending, which is currently approaching £3 billion, remain patchy and usually rudimentary. Is this a sustainable position for the future? I suspect that it is not. The software to detect plagiarism is becoming increasingly available to journal editors and research funders, and may in the future be used routinely to check the veracity of a research paper or grant application. Considerable progress has been made in the evaluation of statistical techniques to detect data sets that have not been generated in a biological system. It seems likely that a combination of these approaches will be used before publication to increase confidence in a paper, particularly when concerns have been raised during the peer review process.

Will it be necessary to make a change in the law to make research fraud a serious offence like financial fraud? This has not been seriously considered in the UK, but Norway is currently looking at the possibility following the retraction of a paper in the *Lancet* authored by the Norwegian cancer expert Dr Jon Sudbø.[23] Hwang and colleagues are apparently going to be prosecuted in the South Korean courts.[24] It has been argued that, unlike financial fraud, research fraud is a victimless crime. However, a patient harmed by a drug that came to market through a fraudulent clinical trial might see it differently. Similarly, funding agencies, particularly government-funded bodies, have responsibilities to ensure that the funds that they disperse are used appropriately and not for improper purposes such as fraudulent research.

References

1. Steneck NH. *Office of Research Integrity Introduction to the Responsible Conduct of Research.* ori.hhs.gov/publications/ori_intro_text.shtml.
2. Lock S. Research misconduct: a résumé of recent events. In: Lock S, Wells F, eds. *Fraud and Misconduct in Medical Research*, 2nd edn. London: BMJ Books, 1996: 14–39.
3. Lock S. Research misconduct 1974–1990: an imperfect history. In: Lock S, Wells F, Farthing M, eds. *Fraud and Misconduct in Biomedical Research*, 3rd edn. London: BMJ Books, 2001: 51–63.
4. Cyranoski D. Your cheatin' heart. *Nat Med* 2006; **12**: 490.
5. Normile D. South Korea picks up the pieces. *Science* 2006; **312**: 1298–9.
6. Normile D. Panel discredits findings of Tokyo University team. *Science* 2006; **311**: 595.
7. Marshall E. Scandals shake Chinese science. *Science* 2006; **312**: 1464–5.
8. Giles J. Plagiarism in Cambridge physics lab prompts calls for guidelines. *Nature* 2004; **427**: 3.
9. Broomfield G. Time to write up? *Nature* 2002; **418**: 120–1.
10. Abbott A. Prolific ecologist vows to fight Danish misconduct verdict. *Nature* 2004; **427**: 381.
11. Working Party. *Fraud and Misconduct in Medical Research. Causes, Investigation and Prevention.* London: Royal College of Physicians, 1991.
12. Medical Research Council. *Policy and Procedure for Inquiring into Allegations of Scientific Misconduct.* London: MRC Ethics Series, 1997.
13. Medical Research Council. *MRC Guidelines for Good Clinical Practice in Clinical Trials.* London: MRC Clinical Trials Series, 1998.
14. General Medical Council. *Research: The Role and Responsibility of Doctors.* www.gmc-uk.org/guidance/current/library/research.asp.
15. Committee for Publication Ethics (COPE). *Guidelines on Good Publication Practice.* www.publicationethics.org.uk/guidelines.
16. Public Health Laboratory Service. *Scientific Misconduct. Procedures for Raising and Inquiring into Allegations.* London: PHLS, 1997.
17. Steneck NH. Fostering integrity in research. *Sci Eng Ethics* 2006; **12**: 53–74.
18. BBSRC, DEFRA, FSA and NERC. *Joint Code of Practice for Research.* 2003. www.defra.gov.uk/science/documents/QACoP_v8.pdf.

19. *Australian Code for the Responsible Conduct of Research*. 2006. www.nhmrc.gov.au/ publications/synopses/r39syn.htm.

20. Adam D, Knight J. Publish, and be damned ... *Nature* 2002; **419**: 772–6.

21. Rennie D, Gunsalus CK. Regulations on scientific misconduct: lessons from the US experience. In: Lock S, Wells F, Farthing M, eds. *Fraud and Misconduct in Biomedical Research*, 3rd edn. London: BMJ Books, 2001: 13–31.

22. Nylenna M, Andersen D, Dahlquist G et al. Handling of scientific dishonesty in the Nordic countries. *Lancet* 1999; **354**: 57–61.

23. Horton R. Retraction: Non-steroidal anti-inflammatory drugs and the risk of oral cancer: a nested case-controlled study. *Lancet* 2006; **367**: 382.

24. Basu P. Focus on fraud. *Nat Med* 2006; **12**: 490–4.

Index

Note to index: 'case' after a name denotes a misconduct case

Spector case 238–9
Sudbo case 29, 76–7, 125
Wilson case 79
research regulations, noncompliance 39
responsible conduct of research (RCR) 277
failure to instil the values of RCR 279
retaliation protection, institutional policies
244
retracted articles/publications
detecting citations 148–51, 156
PubMed search 150–1, 156
risk:benefit ratios in trials, misinformation 9
rumour-mongering 6

S
salami publication technique 8, 146
sanctions 264, 267
Science, on integrity verification 143
science ethics, funding for scholarship,
teaching and research 40
scientific data
analysis
definition 46
selection of inappropriate methods (to
obtain desired result) 165–6
see also statistical analysis
characteristics of genuine data 161–3
characteristics of invented/altered data
163–4
data mining 194
digit preference 162
direct entry, defined 196
malicious sequestration 31
manipulation 51–2, 149–50, 265
misconduct not involving fabrication or
falsification 164–6
multiple fabrications 31–2
presentation
examples of unethical practices 138
information in journal guidelines 138
quality 100
scientific dialogue model 37
scientific error, vs scientific misconduct 36,
143
Sedgwick case 74
self-plagiarism 145–6
self-regulation, inadequacy 281
Sheffield University UK 126
Siddiqui case 74

significance tests, multiple 7
sinister attribution bias 235
slovenliness 8
social transfer of values 10
source data verification (SDV) 203
source documents, defined 196
Spain, bullfighters 44–5
Spector case 238–9
spike plots 167
sponsor companies, inspections 101
Sprague, Robert 234
standard operating procedures (SOPs) 201–2
allegations of fraud/misconduct made to
two individuals simultaneously 261
allow 'self-reporting' 262
appeals panel 264
best practice 263–4
guidelines for production 261
job roles and responsibilities 262
key elements for dealing with allegations of
research fraud 262
outcome and sanctions described 264
process and investigation 262
review and updating 272
standard of proof (civil proceedings) 39
statistical analysis 161–76
baseline comparisons in randomized
controlled trials 169
Benford's law 168
chase for statistical significance 166
correlation/regression coefficients 167–8
descriptive statistics
bivariate or multivariate data 167–8
changes/fabrication 169
univariable 166–7
difficulty of detection of research
misconduct 173–4
digit preference 167
dishonest use 7
exaggerated effects and random noise
169–70
examples of detection of research
misconduct 170–5
excess/fewer significant results 170
inappropriate methods (to obtain desired
result) 165
inferential statistics 168–9
kurtosis 167
Mahalanobis distance 168, 171